2008/1781

2nd of the Trilogy

KT-238-709

CRAFTING

Slot

£3.00

c662

Willie Gavin, Crofter Man

Willie Gavin, Crofter Man

A Portrait of a Vanished Lifestyle

DAVID KERR CAMERON

BIRLINN

This edition first published in 2008 by
Birlinn Limited
West Newington House
10 Newington Road
Edinburgh
EH9 1QS

www.birlinn.co.uk

First published in 1980 by Victor Gollancz Ltd

Copyright © the Estate of David Kerr Cameron 1984
Introduction copyright © Jack Webster 2008

All rights reserved. No part of this publication may be reproduced,
stored or transmitted in any form without the express written
permission of the publisher.

ISBN13: 978 1 84158 709 7
ISBN10: 1 84158 709 5

British Library Cataloguing-in-Publication Data
A catalogue record for this book is available from the British Library

Typeset by Hewer Text (UK) Ltd, Edinburgh
Printed and bound by CPI Cox & Wyman, Reading, RG1 8EX

Author's Note

This is a portrait of crofting life in the bare and sometimes bitter landscape of Scotland's North-East Lowlands. It is, closely reconstructed, the life of one crofter man in particular and, beyond that, the wider story of a croft and its people. Their time is past and done with now but their days were typical of the crofting experience in that old countryside. It is a record assembled mainly from a family's folk memory and to avoid any undue embarrassment I have blurred Willie Gavin's real identity. To his folk, who gave so freely of their memories, I am deeply indebted.

Acknowledgements

For permission to quote and reproduce copyright material the author wishes to thank the following: Margaret, Marchioness of Aberdeen; the Bailies of Bennachie and Routledge and Kegan Paul.

Among those who so kindly helped to locate and identify photographs which reflect the life and work of the old landscape, he wishes particularly to thank the following: Gavin Sprott of the National Museum of Antiquities of Scotland; Ian Hardie and Tam Forsyth of *Aberdeen Journals*; Douglas M. Spence of D.C. Thomson; and *The Scots Magazine* for permitting the use of material from the Robert M. Adam collection.

Contents

Introduction

Having published *The Ballad and the Plough* at the relatively late age of fifty in 1978, David Kerr Cameron gave notice of a significant new talent on the Scottish literary scene. This book was the story of the old farmtouns – big farming units that dominated the Scottish agricultural landscape from the mid 1800s till the Second World War. They were the basis of a whole way of life, employing large numbers of men and women, whose children populated parish schools before they themselves took their place in the cycle of rural life. They survived in an atmosphere of hard work, camaraderie and dry, good humour that produced a rich texture of life, even if the material reward for their efforts was no more than a pittance. The way of life was petering out in David Kerr Cameron's childhood of the 1930s, but not before the boy had gathered enough of its essence to produce this masterpiece.

Two years after the publication of *The Ballad and the Plough*, and encouraged by its success, he produced his second book, *Willie Gavin, Crofter Man*, a work which celebrates a way of life far removed from that of the big *fermtouns*. Another integral component of the Scottish rural scene, the crofter was at least his own boss, though his work was no less hard or more financially rewarding because of that.

David Kerr Cameron observed rural life from the heart of Aberdeenshire, where his paternal grandfather was grieve (the Scots word for a farm overseer) to Lord Aberdeen at his Haddo

House estate. His own father was a typical horseman of the day, employed on the old farmtouns, moving if necessary from one to another at the term-times of May and November, or staying for as long as he and the farmer were in agreement.

Cameron was born in March 1928 and went to school at the villages of Tarves and Pitmedden, leaving at fourteen to become a milk-boy at Cairnbrogie farm. (As an interesting aside – and in view of his later literary success – these farms were next door to the Gight estate, family home of a boy called George Gordon who achieved fame under the name of Lord Byron.) Young Cameron was of the generation that just missed conscription during the Second World War but was nevertheless in time for the compulsory National Service that claimed most able-bodied youth in the post-war years. Returning from service with the RAF, he became an agricultural engineer. But he had written a good essay at school and never forgot his headmaster's nod towards a career in journalism. It was advice he clearly took to heart. Whilst standing in for the agricultural editor during my early days on the *Aberdeen Press and Journal*, I recalled the occasional freelance contribution landing on my desk from a totally unknown David Kerr Cameron. It was clear the man could write. As a minor journalist myself at the time, I didn't realise I was making judgments on the work of one who was not only more mature in years but was on the first rung of a ladder that would take him to prominence as one of the best Scottish writers of the twentieth century.

He quietly entered the world of journalism with the *Kirriemuir Herald* before joining the staff of the *Press and Journal* as a sub-editor and then heading south to a similar post on the *Daily Telegraph* in Fleet Street, where he spent the rest of his career and emerged as a writer of real substance. It has long been the inclination of many a newspaper sub-editor to turn towards writing, believing they can surely do better than some of the over-blown prima donnas whose mediocre efforts they are obliged to knock into shape before inflicting them on an unsuspecting public, and it was maybe this feeling that spurred David Kerr Cameron to write the books that merit him a place in the world of Scottish letters.

Willie Gavin was a real-life figure, disguised along with others for the sake of family members and friends. In fact, as Cameron later told me quite openly, he was writing about his own maternal grandfather, Willie Porter, a crofter from the North-East who was a truly authentic representative of his breed in all his inherited dour devotion to the land. To the outsider it may make little sense to enslave yourself to such a life of unremitting hardship and drudgery, but to the Willie Gavins of this world there was no choice: it was all in the blood, deep in the marrow of the bone. They accepted a bond with the land that would never be broken and never be questioned.

Some crofters would divide their time between the land and another job to improve their chances of financial survival. In Willie's case, that other job alone could have kept him afloat, even brought him prosperity, for he was a stone-mason of uncommon skill and ingenuity. But that was not enough to satisfy the proper balance of this man's life.

Whereas soil that was thin or stony was of no interest to the owners of the farmtouns, this was precisely the kind of terrain the crofters would try to make fertile. Kerr Cameron paints a beautifully lyrical picture of how the crofter took on this thankless task, 'stitching the quilt of the landscape' in the tucks and folds of the countryside where 'small fields fought for a foothold with the whins and the broom, forever in danger of losing ground as they supported their inmates in that special thraldom of hope that distils slowly to the acuteness of despair'. What a beautiful and sensitive observation of the crofter's work.

It was a way of life that would draw to a close, coinciding movingly with Willie Gavin's own passing. The crofters' land-scape was indeed an ancient one; their ways and qualities were those of a vanished world.

When Willie was seventy-five and in failing health he knew it was time for his tenancy to end, a realization which turned him quiet and withdrawn. Before his last 'hairst' (harvest) he was hoeing his turnips, and one day, Grannie Gavin went to cry him in when he didn't come home for dinner. She found him sprawled between the drills. They brought him home in his barrow, not yet dead but near enough. Whatever the circum-stances of his end, Willie Gavin had lived like most of his breed – with a rare dignity, strange and beautiful.

Jack Webster
March 2008

I

The Old Crofter Man

Willie Gavin inherited two things from his father: his new tile hat and the old Gavin croft. The one he wore long to funerals after that fashion had turned to the bowler; the other was a heartbreak to him, all of his days. Yet he would not leave it; the croft was in his blood, gripping him like a fever. He had been born into the dark recess of its box-bed and it had beckoned him from the cradle. He was never able to see past its old thatched dwelling and the rickle of its old *biggings*, or to lift his gaze beyond the immediate horizon of its small bare fields.

If ever a man should have sold his inheritance, it was Willie Gavin; and it is difficult now to know what possessed him, and drew him into the life. A love for the land perhaps, and its possession; a hunger certainly for that strong identity and continuity of family and race that passes down in an ancestral landscape – a hunger no less in the bare Lowlands of Scotland's North-East than in the wilder glens of the West, with their memory of the brutal Clearances. Whatever it was, in Willie Gavin it ran deep, and like most of his kind, and for most of his life, he ran in the double harness that was the curse of the old crofting existence: working away by day and coming home to do his croft work by night, often enough by the light of the wintry stars. The bitter irony of it was: he had no need to. Other men might take on crofts, with their ceaseless work and their treadmill slavery, to keep themselves and their families out of the chill charity of the parish poorhouse; Willie Gavin was a craftsman and a good one at that, a master stonemason in that now-distant time when biggings for both man and beast had been accorded the dignity of stone, and sometimes the grandeur of granite, and when the glint and sparkle of mica in the landscape had drawn the eye constantly to the old builders' skill. In that time before the fraudulence of the composition block and the instant obscenity of asbestos scarred the countryside, men like Willie Gavin had built their own memorials in the old stone biggings that would long outlast them and the sons who came after them. His skill in his prime, folk said, was proverbial and even now, in that bleak landscape that lies between the blue mound of the Grampians and the growl of the grey North Sea there are old men who will stop in the bygoing to take a look at the simple harmony of an old farmtoun or the plain lines of a stark grey kirk among the trees and say quietly: 'Willie Gavin biggit it' – meaning not that his was the hand that chiselled its every stone but that his was the eye that gave it dour grace.

The tribute might have pleased the crofter man well enough had he heard it, for certainly, had he been minded to, he might have set himself up in a fine, stone-built house on the edge of the little quarrytoun that had taught him his trade. There he could have put past a winter of ease after the hard-building of summer. And had he, like so many of the old North-East masoning men, been tempted to the States for a season or two of work, there was no telling: he might have become a rich man with a trowel in his hand. It would have been a wonder, people said, for the folk over there to see the ease with which his eye could take the pure lineaments of the stone out of the grey granite lump. And surely there had been folk who would have been pleased to see the back of him for a while for other reasons, for all his life Willie Gavin had that awkward, unbending kind of integrity that made other folk uncomfortable. As a masoning boss he drove hard – punctilious about time-keeping, strict on the avoidance of oaths (even when the chisel slipped), demanding at times the kind of workmanship that was beyond the lesser-gifted. He was never an easy man to please, or to work with.

But it was the croft, not the masoning trade, that was his life: he cared little about the stone he could so easily master, much more for the soil he never could conquer. Folk said whiles that he cared more for his bit *grun*, his land, than he did for his wife and bairns and maybe he did; rotting fences would have to be replaced supposing they should all of them starve, which they often damned nearly did. He would have been a poor crofter man had it been otherwise. All the same, his creed was iron-clad and he was as hard on himself as he was on everyone else: however sharp the hunger in his belly he would clean and oil his spade, or sharpen his scythe and set it away against the next day's work, before he stepped indoors for his own supper. For all that, his family found it difficult to forgive him. And the old croft betrayed him.

It took its toll slowly, consuming him, honing him with work, morning and night, year after year. By the time he came to put away his mason's white moleskins for the serviceable cords in a landsman's brown that would take him through his years of retirement, it had begun to drain him. That was the way of it with the old crofter men. His measured stride as he stepped round his biggings or through his small cornyard (tightening a thatch-rope here and there) after a bad night of storm or high wind, would falter a little now and then, and as the challenge of harvest or the rush of spring work drew on you could see him begin to gird himself mentally for the onslaught.

But his obsession with his small fields remained undimmed. And though his ladder legs had forsaken him, he still built his few ricks of *hairst* with his own hands. Now and then folk would tryst him away, putting the occasional job of masoning his way, mindful of the careful workman he still was. The old crofter man took the work, glad of the *siller* it would bring in, repointing the school playground wall maybe, or repairing the kirkyard dyke, and for a day or two the old magic would return as he handled simple stones with his old arrogance and the speed of the trowel awakened a memory of the man he had been. But maybe it all mattered little to him by then, for who was there to see him? Just the school bairns let out for their playtime, or the ghosts of earlier Gavins long into the kirkyard and finally at peace. Long before the end of the afternoon he would be away home, mindful of the load of turnips he had still to barrow into the byre or the hay he might turn in the swath before the night air came down.

Always his fields drew him home, and his small hairsts, hard won though they were, were a delight to him; they put a lightness, a jauntiness almost, into his step as he took down the croft close in the morning to get his scythe, sharpened and waiting, and strode into the standing corn. For Willie Gavin that was a moment of fulfilment, of consummation, and maybe you had to be a crofter man yourself to understand it. By then, the young fresh-faced mason man of the proud farmsteads and the stark kirks had himself grown gaunt: frail and grizzled, his tall sinewy frame stooped in the shoulders from the careless un-concern of too many wettings and damp clothes and the rheumatic rewards they could bring. The heavy Kitchener that had been the manly adornment of his youth had for long seemed too heavy a burden on that austere face, and the skin had begun slowly to waxen and tighten over the cheekbones. Willie Gavin had come to look what he was: the old, archetypal crofter figure.

Near the end of his days, and as the clouds of war loomed dark over the countryside, his smallholding and his few beasts became his entire life and he was never happy away from them, not even in his Sabbath pew. He would be anxious to be home, in case a *stirk* should sicken. Twice a year, though, he would willingly put on his best tweeds, his Sabbath patent boots and his bicycle clips and set off with the other crofter men for the estate office, his half-year's rent in the frayed wallet he kept closed with one of Grannie Gavin's old black-elastic garters. There, with the tenants of the farmtouns (some of them men of substance), the croft men would be given a bottle of ale, a token of the laird's esteem (or maybe to stifle complaint) as their siller was counted into his safe and entered upon the grand page of his ledger. That ale was like fine wine on Willie Gavin's lips, a sacrament almost as potent as the Communion he took regularly in his own plain kirk. That day, that conclave of farming men, gave him status as a holder of land. It gave him identity. Maybe that was important to Willie Gavin and to the old crofter men like him. It is difficult to say now, for they were a different breed entirely; and they spoke seldom of the hopes that drove them.

Folk said that Willie Gavin was a dour man and likely he was, for he had never had the facile gift for friendship and, God knows, he never had but little to smile about. His plight was the same as that of the other croft men: the silver that came in from one year's harvest was already bespoken for next year's seed. It was always so. Far away, in Edinburgh and London, there were kindly pinstriped men who worried about Willie Gavin and his kind. Masters of the careful form and the unshakeable statistic, they looked at the old crofting landscape with genuine concern, shaking their heads on the homeward trains and calling its way of life a finely balanced economy. Theirs was a flight of the wildest fantasy. Its reality was a stark subsistence, often at its lowest ebb.

A Patch of the Lonely Moor

The crofts came down in the generations like a good watch or a tinker's curse, sifting the men and imposing their own kind of suffering on their women; they preserved a close patriarchal society. They stood all round that cold countryside, singly and in the colonies that emerged and endured, though more sparsely, into the 1930s, anachronistic memorials to men with impossible dreams. They sat everywhere on the fringe of the good farming ground, in everybody's way, though nobody would have given you a thank-you for their sour bit parcels of land or their damp dwellings. They stitched the quilt of the landscape where the farmtouns lost interest, where the soil was thin or stony and, often enough, practically non-existent – on the edge of the moor, the side of the moss, the steep brae-face of the hillside where even the sure-footed Clydesdale was hard put to it to stand its ground and the plough came up from its down-furrow on its side, its draught beyond the power of any beast. It was a compromise that avoided the reproach of outright defeat, though it made for a poor, protracted agriculture.

But that had mattered little to the crofter men, for they existed always beyond the uttermost pale of respectable farming, their quaint ways at times almost an endorsement of the events that had placed them there. Gathered on the bare hillside, in the tucks and folds of the countryside, their small fields fought for a foothold with the whins and the broom, forever in danger of losing ground as they supported their inmates in that special thraldom of hope that distils slowly to the acuteness of despair. It was no wonder whiles if their folk went quietly mad with a strange lucidity of mind that knew itself to be at odds with the landscape. Yet they would not quit, though neighbour and laird were against them, for where else could they go? They faced both whiles for the land they had so hardily won, whether from the moor or the hill; blessed the rushes that sprouted as the ready material of thatch for their few ricks of harvest while knowing the warning they gave: they were there by nature's tolerance.

The crofts had been there for as long as most folk could mind, going back to that time of the land improvers and their harsh inexorable rule of change, when their first biggings had been little better than beggarly hovels. In that maelstrom the crofts had taken the poor ground and it is likely that their early tenants, those men and women who carved them from the hill and the moor, were often those shaken loose from the multi-tenanted farmtouns of the ancient landscape – the folk left sadly without affiliation as the new single-unit farmtouns of an improved agriculture rose over the ruins of their old dwellings and the time-hallowed pattern of their run-rigs.

Sometimes, it is true, the great farming improvements of the late 1700s and early 1800s were the work of lairds of integrity, men with a sense of compassion. But they, too, were caught in the fever of change as they geared their estates to the new high farming that would keep agriculture (and food production) apace with the Industrial Revolution. Just as surely, they marked out the ground, laying the good acres together to form their new farmtouns, thrusting the sub-tenants of the old communities overnight – and at best – into the role of hired hands and the indignity, twice yearly, of the feeing fair. It would have been surprising if hardy men had not chosen, at times, to secede from that new order.

Often the crofts hugged the roadside as though they were afraid to leave it; sometimes they sat away at the back of the hills on the lonesome end of some stony track. Occasionally, even the track would peter out so that a man leaving the old holding in a hurry would put his bike on his back and strike over the fields for the nearest known road. A postman, to find some of them, would have to know the parish from childhood. Not that it mattered greatly: few of the croft folk took such a thing as a posted newspaper, weekly or daily, and most dwelt blissfully incommunicado and innocent of the world's affairs. And even when someone wrote them a letter (which was seldom), by the time it reached them the delay had smothered that immediacy which is the vital spark of communication. Only the seed catalogues were perused with any semblance of urgency and these at least were kept for a month or two – an indication of their importance – before being carefully quartered for the privy nail. Packmen, though, called upon these lonely outposts, stumbling on them almost by accident as they crested a hill. Their very isolation, where no merchant called, in some cleft of the land where the silence was immortal, made them venues of fast trade, though doubtless their voracious, peat-reeked occupants scared the hell out of the packman. There were other places still, so far from the beaten paths of civilisation that they were as lost to the Word of God as to the Post Office. The track had long defeated the minister's bike. Their strange inhabitants dwelt there in the peace of all eternity and even the tinkers avoided them.

Of that rage for improvement, the birth of crofting was maybe the greatest betrayal of all; it deluded men, then trampled on their dreams. Folk took on crofts for the independence they thought they gave and doomed themselves to long disappointment. They believed they were perhaps putting a tentative first foot on the farming ladder and found instead that their position was untenably ambiguous in that new countryside and in a restructured society: they were neither masters nor hired men.

Sometimes the croft's appeal lay in the deep-seated desire for a house that would be a home, settled and secure, in that new farming landscape of the tied house and the wandering cottar; the occupants found soon enough that the laird was sometimes as hard to please, and always to pay.

For all his sad past, the crofter was (and remains) a charismatic figure, a romantic one even. He stands in the grey gloam of history indistinguishable at times from the ancient cottar, a man whose alternative lifestyle still sheds its deep attraction for wearied city folk. He has begotten his own mythology. The poor cottar stands nowhere so richly robed in legend. Yet it was the crofter who was the new man on the landscape. We can speak of him safely only after the days of Improvement and the betrayal of the Clearances. Always he is a lonely figure.

Climate and temperament, as well as terrain, distanced men of Willie Gavin's kind from their crofting contemporaries of the West. One, with the sad Gaelic of his song, lived in the kind of pastoral tradition that Moses himself might not have found unfamiliar; Willie Gavin's world was rooted in the arable pattern of the bare eastern seaboard with its harder lifestyle and its hardier men. The Gael's holding was (and still is) the main form of settlement; in the East the crofter man's was the least-regarded. Willie Gavin's neighbours were not the lonely and sometimes beautiful hills; they were the fields of his farmtoun neighbours where the ceaseless winter ploughs drew unending furrows and the spring harrows raised that vapour of dust that betokens good husbandry. Round him the ritual of work went on like an obsession, giving rest to neither man nor beast.

Unlike his Highland counterpart, Willie Gavin was a member of no community of crofts but a man on his own. Neighbourliness might bring a fellow crofter along the road to feed and milk his beasts should a close relative be so inconsiderate as to die away from his own folk. And the visit of the threshing mill might take one crofter man to the place of his neighbour with his barn fork under his arm. But there it ended; the Lowlands crofter man was concerned with no common pasture; no souming (that system of grazing calculation that balanced the crofting ecology of the old Highlands); no summer removal to the high shieling that took the women and girls out of the western crofting community for most of the summer. His primary implement was not the archaic foot-wielded *caschrom* (hallowed by history and somehow binding its user to the primordial past) but the iron plough, horse-drawn. His acres were his own and he engaged in no lottery of the run-rigs. If they were brothers at all under the skin – and even in the 1930s Willie Gavin still clung to a Hebridean *croman* to hoe between his turnip rows – there would have been little that they recognised in each other's crofting. The one, whatever his present hardship, bathed still at times in that aura of tragedy and romance that was the legacy of the Clearances. Living beyond that legend, Willie Gavin, crofter man, was an even lonelier figure, one of contempt when his crofting failed and he could not feed his wife and children. It was only the emblem of the sickle and the Free Kirk's psalms that united them. And maybe something else: the central place the croft took in each of their lives. In 1883 – the year that the Gavin croft, coming near to the end of its first-recorded lease, was drawn in plan and carefully measured by the laird's surveyor – the Napier Commission, after a century of evictions in the Gaelic kingdom, was conducting its now-famous inquiry into crofting and the disintegration of a society. It would define the crofter man, and pin him to the landscape like a dead butterfly to the wall, as 'a small tenant of land with or without a lease, who finds in the cultivation of his holding a material proportion of his occupation, earnings and sustenance, and who pays rent directly to the proprietor'. As a definition it has rarely been bettered.

Despite the late emergence of the crofter class, however, 'croft' had long been an honourable word in the language, feeding its long roots from an Anglo-Saxon past, enshrined in the litigious Latin of ancient charters and holy feus from at least as far back as the twelfth century. It has described the plots of bishops and saints (and sometimes of the Devil), bestowals on poets as well as the habitations of humbler men, giving the irony of its grand past to the patch on the inhospitable moor, its grace to the holy glebe. It is a vague and unlimiting term, irritatingly unquantitative. A croft could be as big as you cared to call it, so small as to be unworthy of the name (which many of them were). In the North-East Lowlands, where the cautious outlook ensures a landscape not given to extremes, there might be the occasional oddity that ran to all of twenty-five acres, though most (outside the early crofter villages) fell between seven and fifteen. That, though, was on the estates in the prime farming areas; up-country where the heather encroached harder on the corn, they might be as small as three acres, divided into half-acre plots. At that, the least a man could hope for was a steady and fairly lucrative secondary occupation to keep him from the edge of starvation. Or failing that, charitable neighbours.

For all its hardships and its heartbreak, the spread of crofting continued in the North-East Lowlands well beyond the high tide of farmtoun improvement – indeed, for some time after the farmtouns had hit their peak of prosperity. Even into the 1880s there were hopeful men still breaking in ground from the moor and the hillside. Much of the early crofting settlement was planned, well intentioned if not always successful; some of it, at first, was quietly behind the laird's back though it would not be long before he came to hear of it. Some of it, especially in that indeterminate time of pause while the landscape shrugged off the past, was contrived to bend the old countryside to the new, even to stimulate some form of local light industry, a visionary concept that owed more to the dreams of the planner than the hard realities of the northern landscape. It was in some ways a step into the past, for those intermediate crofting settlements were neither recognisably crofting nor acceptably new villages. They returned to an idea centuries old and one from which even the capital Edinburgh itself had grown when it could no longer huddle on its famous Rock: allotments of land, running down either side of a broad main street, on which the burgher kept his cow and his stock, with a back lane out to the common grazing of the burgh moor. Most were founded on a belief in the wrong industry at the wrong time.

Kincardine's Luthermuir, that old weaver toun, dates from 1771 and was more successful than most. Local landowners laid out the ground as feu crofts and the township's first *clay biggings* were raised by the croft villagers themselves when they were not taking in their secondary income at the handloom or bringing the adjoining moor under cultivation. Their enterprise brought the start of the coarse-linen and Osnaburghs boom to the Mearns and neighbouring Angus.

There were subtler schemes. On Speyside at Rothes, already a settlement of sorts, the Earl of Seafield in 1776 gave leases of thirty-eight years on holdings or 'tenements' of an eighth of an acre for ten shillings (50p) a year. The further two acres, optionally available though, were without the security of the lease, and if the earl was looking for some kind of wholly industrial development he died a disappointed man. It never materialised.

Some of the little lairds' touns were novel in their approach. Some twenty years earlier, the first Earl of Fife, who as Lord Braco, MP for Banffshire, had astonished the House with his piquant advice to 'give our own fish guts to our own sea maws' (thus betraying his fishing concerns), laid out the new town of Newmill in Strathisla. Each settler would have five or six acres, but in scattered lots. In the main street of the town, each crofter (to anticipate the use of the term) had a quarter of an acre of land for his *clay hoose* and biggings. The dwellings were single-storey thatched but-and-bens, and each barn would have two doors to create the through-draught so desirable for threshing by flail or for *sheelin'* the grain. The accompanying land for cultivation, however, would be in three strips, each numbered, so that every crofter would have an inbye strip, a 'middle strip' and one at some distance − a more sophisticated version, when you come down to it, of the old run-rig with all its interminable squabbles and lack of cohesion. It would be easy enough to scoff at the plan but in all probability the countryside was not yet ready for more radical change. There was a further concession, typical of all such townships: each settler would have the right to cut peats on the moor behind the village. There were a hundred feus, and so fascinating is the whole idea that it seems sad to have to report its failure. But that, alas, was the case. Few of the new town's original 330 inhabitants were the weavers for whom the planners had hoped.

There was an even more charitable instance of new settlement by the same landed line, that briefly linked east with west. In the 1830s the fourth earl allotted another hundred plots, this time of ten acres each, on the Hills of Fisherie − at the centre of the region of experimental crofter villages. They were for the dispossessed of the Highlands, victims of the Clearances. Though their folk had to break in the hill from the heather, that was better than being part of some laird's grandiose scheme. Most of the old crofter men must have preferred it, for it was where their dreams began: with a patch of the hill or the lonely moor.

3

The Crofter Folk

The croft folk were sometimes less than welcome in genteel society and often unacceptable among their tenant neighbours of the farmtouns. Their antecedents might be questionable and, besides, they were guilty at times of not knowing when to defer to their betters. Their standing, indeed, in the subtle structure of country society was little better than that of the cottars who were usually their nearest neighbours and who married happily into croft families without feeling either that they were going up or going down in the world. There was just this one difference: the crofter's domicile was more permanent.

There was reason enough, if little excuse, for being uncivil about the crofter folk's past. Some, to be sure, would have come down in their generations from that time when men refashioned the landscape; that had left its sad debris, people without hope or a place on the land who might have drifted to the cities of a growing industrial age but had chosen instead to become the wanderers of the road: little better than tinkers many of them, hawking their respective trades round the countryside, taking the track between one farmtoun and the next, the road from one new village community to its neighbour to mend a berrypan here, sell a besom there. It is likely that some of these folk were the first occupants of the early scattered crofts, for there came always a time in a man's life when he had to forsake the road. He would put down his pack on a bit of the moor where fortune had taken him and start a new life – and sometimes a dynasty. If you were come of crofter folk it did not pay you to have a long memory, for sooner or later it would tell you something you had no wish to hear.

But not all the first squatters were folk of the road (though it is fairly certain that neither were they the cream of society) and the pattern of settlement and the kind of situation it created may also have had something to do with the lingering suspicions about the croft folk's past. Not infrequently, where the settlement was unplanned, there grew up enclaves of crofter men and their families. One such colony arose, in the early 1800s, on the flanks of Bennachie, that most modest of North-East mountains, and its story demonstrates not only their determination as frontiersmen but the kind of action that brought them legally to heel. It leaves its own taint of unsympathetic lairdship. Their historian was the Rev. N.L.A. Campbell: his account is reprinted in that fascinating portrait of the Lowlands landmark, *The Book of Bennachie*:

> In the colony there was no trouble about title deeds. As a man's family increased it was an easy matter to increase the number of rooms, and the even greater problem of building a new house for a new settler presented little difficulty. The materials were to hand in plenty and the story is told how once the neighbours completed a house for a new settler in a single day and celebrated the event by a supper that same evening in the newly erected home.

The Rev. Campbell goes on to give a picture that was probably true of other early crofting communities, far from the centres of local administration and their more sober inhabitants: '[they] were a law unto themselves. They had their private supply of whisky which paid no duty and as to other forms of private property, well, some of them had their own ideas – and these ideas rather vague concerning thine and mine . . .'

There seems no reason to doubt the minister or to seek further reason for the retribution such free-wheeling behaviour brought on them. Such lawless freedom was unthinkable for poor squatters, and the local lairds could be relied on to make sure it did not last. In 1859, by legally encompassing the commonty, the no-man's-land on which the crofter families had settled, they acquired a crofting community, ready-made. That year, writes the Rev. Campbell, allowing himself the merest hint of irony, 'John Esson signed a lease waiving all claim to compensation and agreeing to pay £2 10s a year for the privilege of using the house his own hands had built and tilling the fields, five and a half acres, which by the sweat of his brow he had fenced and trenched from the hill.'

By such means, through law or persuasion, were the early croft settlers given their status on the laird's rent-roll and a place, officially, on his land.

Whatever its shortcomings, theirs was a society knit by obligation and kinship (both the need of poor men) and as frequently rent by vendetta; where the lustre of forebears could be worn like a badge or a family misdemeanour tell against you unto the third and fourth generations, making plain at times a conspicuous lack of preferment. There was despotism, nepotism, and all kinds of favour (if a man did not look to his own, who would?). The ties were at once subtle and powerful; commitment at times painfully enduring.

There was this you could say for the croft folk, it grew out of their social isolation: they were a kittle crew, sensitive to every nuance of slight. If you were a friend, well and good (though that did not always save you); if you were not, their wrath could be scarifying and you might as well leave the parish. Persistent worshippers though many of them were, they could at times be damnably poor forgivers.

So what type of people were they, the later croft folk, settled in their sometimes insular communities? They were first the people whose smallholding had long gone with their trade and sat near the road: the blacksmith, the *souter* (the shoemaker), the tailor, the saddler – a whole motley of men whose commercial interest made sure their croft work was always behindhand and who grew schizoid and sometimes demented from balancing the urgency of one against the irreconcilable demands of the other. Because he was kept busy mending other men's reapers, the smith's hairst was always late. Besides these men, the succourers of any community, there were the men who, even late into the 1920s, still found their work at the great farmtouns of the Clydesdale era: bailies (stockmen) and orra men, horsemen and even grieves, those bailiffs of the big touns whose belief in hard work made them excellent candidates. There were the men who broke horses and brave men who travelled stallions round the countryside to the terror of all other road-users, their salacious beasts a constant reminder of the force that made the world go round, that fertility on which a dour countryside was founded. There were roadmen crofters who took time off every hairst (it was part of their agreement) to take a farmtoun *fee*, letting their wives shear their own few acres with the *heuk*; estate workers, masons and ditchers and dykers, foresters and carpenters (all those who did not have to dance close attendance), who kept the laird's domain by day and their own by night; postmen whose double life could delay the mail; and men now and then without other visible means of support and who were supposed to have siller in the bank. There were others, of course, who lived perilously between the poles of freedom and starvation, who had no regular, supplementary role and took casual work where and when they could find it. They might get seasonal jobs, the womenfolk, if they lived not too far from the coast, when the fish-curers came canvassing round the country communities for herring-gutters. And a croft man, if he had a cart and a beast fit enough to pull it, might get contract carting, taking the fish from

the boats to the curing yards from July to September. When the
herring boom was at its height folk thronged to the little North-
East ports from deep in the country, eager for the siller they
could take home to help their poor, subsistence economy. Some
of them were hard cases, unwilling to call any man master. They
might be short of this world's gear but they were never short of
an opinion whether or not it was asked for. Some were too
awkward for their own good or anybody else's. Yet all shared the
crofter's classic dilemma: their bit of ground could not keep
them, yet it needed them most when they were needed elsewhere.

One of the North-East's most notable antiquarians and farmers, Willie Cook, a man who believed the past of that countryside should not be forgotten, at ninety recorded his early
memories of the crofter folk whose smallholdings ringed his
father's farmtoun. His reminiscences, like the Rev. Campbell's in
The Book of Bennachie, paint the portrait of a folk whose kindliness
combined with some oddity of character and a determination not
to pay duty on good whisky:

> I knew many of the crofters of Auchleven. Three acres they
> rented, half an acre to the shift. As I grew older, and able to
> drive a pair of horses, I would be sent down to plough the
> crofts. The kindly crofter wives would bring me tea and
> jammy pieces. They were in the habit of putting a handful of
> cloves in the tea-caddy, and the tea tasted very clovy.
> Naturally there were some great characters, whose rough
> corners had not been polished off in a day when travel was
> slow and dear. One I remember was Lang Ross, a great tall
> streik of a man, who had been grieve at Overton of Premnay,
> and had the knack of breaking in the vicious young horses.
> When a lad he was fee'd at Overhall, where the best barley
> grew. He used to tell me about setting off with the foreman

about four in the morning with two carts loaded with bags of barley. Their destination was the Cabrach, where the Highlanders had gathered from their crofts on their shelts. The barley bags were opened and the grain poured into the panniers, a bushel or two to each pony. Premnay barley properly malted and Cabrach water from the still, blended well together. Today in the little glens, from which folk have long vanished, they tell me you can still find the odd ruined stills, where no gauger came.

It was, and is, a lament for a lost landscape.

There were only two things the old croft folk had in plenty: bairns who ran the hills bare-footed all summer long, and dogs, and it wasn't easy to know which were the worst, except that you could threaten the child when its father's back was safely turned. Crofters' dogs though were deaf to all entreaty; they saw all goodwill as a character weakness. They lolled with panting tongues by every croft gable all through the North-East Lowlands, awaiting the unwary cyclist or, latterly, the renegade car, for there was this you could say for croft dogs: they were not lacking in courage. They did not discriminate. Male or female, master or servant, it was all the same to them; they were as readily inflamed by the glimpse of an ankle in a lisle stocking as the sight of clerical cashmere demarcated by the minister's bicycle clips. The trick, when you knew it, was to pedal like the wind as you came up to some roadside croft and then, as you drew level, tuck your feet up (on the front-wheel forks), trusting to the momentum to carry you beyond the old dog's interest – or into the sight of his master working in some roadside field. He might see your plight (if you were a friend) and cry the beast to heel. Still and all, it was the kind of thing that could unbalance a stately matron and up-end her into the ditch. And again, the tactic could work only where

the slope was with you. In the face of a gradient there was
little you could do – except to keep pedalling, lifting your feet
off the pedals only fractionally ahead of Old Spot's teeth and
(preferably) with the kind of precision timing that brought the
pedal up sharply under his salivating jaws. An old dog could
learn something from that; in time you could get his respect
and then you were somebody in the parish. He might *gurr*
savagely and show you his teeth but your passing would be
unmolested. Saddest of all though was the plight of the bairn
on the school road: there was little he could do but sue for
friendship.

The need to get along with the rest of the world was
something a croft child had quickly to learn, for his was never a
promising start in life and the future was generally heavily
circumscribed. Indeed, it could be easily predicted: it was into
the rough world of the farmtouns as a fee'd horseman; in some
instances, into an apprenticeship with a local tradesman; sometimes into the police force in the southern industrial cities; into
the ministry (with a background that made it easy to believe in
the Devil); exceptionally, into an academic world that took
him away from the life completely and often from all sympathy
with it.

Such then was the old landscape of the crofting men: it made
them hard where it did not break them entirely; even so, it
sometimes twisted them, in time intolerably, and soured them of
life. Its folk were poor, without two sixpences, most of them, to
rub together, and sometimes as shorn in spirit. Most went to the
kirkyard leaving little behind them.

Willie Gavin's immediate neighbours, their crofts lying to
either side of his own, were McPhee and McCaskill, unremark-
able men whose destinies were as delicately poised and whose
whole future, like his own, could be cast into jeopardy by a year
of persistent rain and the bad hairst that followed it. The names of

their holdings – Bogside, Whinfield and Hillbrae – were a reminder not only of the terrible lack of imagination in the Doric soul but of its propensity for facing dreadful truths squarely and at whatever the cost. Their emphasis on location, so typical of that hard landscape, was also a reminder of their fringe location and a warning to every mail-order clerk against the advisability of sending anything on credit to such an address. In some cases, perhaps, the crofter holdings had been christened before their folk ever put a plough-point into the ground; but they had not been disappointed. As the years would prove, their beliefs had been well founded.

The men were not so much friends as bondsmen in a common predicament. Lang Andra McCaskill did work for the estate and was therefore suspect, for there was no telling what a man who was always falling in with the factor might let slip about a neighbour's affairs and there is no doubt that Lang Andra lost friends because of it. Besides which, there was the suspicion, quite unfounded, that he was sometimes looked on favourably when the rents had to rise. And he *was* known to be ambitious for a bit more ground and kept his crofting affairs very much to himself. For all that, he was not a bad man, willing enough to put in an appearance at the threshing mill and as pleased to have a day's work in return.

The McCaskills left nobody in doubt that they were superior kind of folk who were not able to call everybody their equal. Mistress McCaskill was come of farmtoun stock, a farmer's daughter. Modest though her father's toun was, she had been unwilling to leave it for the come-down of crofting life and Lang Andra, it was said, had a sore job getting her. They had superior bairns too, who made a success of life and were hardly out of the school before they were away to the city or to fine jobs in the south. And the McCaskills, seeing nothing for them at home, had not hindered them.

McPhee, on the other hand, was no threat to anybody and was always referred to (even by the croft children) as Puir Angus, in that homely kind of benediction that at once enlightened those with understanding of the speak to Angus's misfortune in life without in any way offending him (which would have been unforgivable). For the truth of it was that Angus was a bit simple-minded, apt indeed to forget where he was going before he was halfway there whether it was the inn or the kirk, though generally he was more often to be found in the one than the other.

'Poor stock,' folk said, sympathetic about the way the drink had taken hold of him, and wondering where in hell he got the siller to pay for it anyway. As a second livelihood Puir Angus did some shepherding; there was, after all, little damage you could do to a sheep short of hitting it over the head with an iron bar. His croft, Bogside, was always behindhand: he lost his hay whiles through reluctance to put his hand to the scythe and his stirks never looked healthy enough to go anywhere near to a market, let alone attract the eye of the farmers who came looking for beasts to fatten for the mart. Even his hairsts were saved only in the nick of time by a son who hung up his grocer's apron in Arbroath and came north to labour under the September sun. He did it for his mother's sake, folk said, and sure enough, she was a dominating figure who treated Puir Angus badly but somehow managed to steer him from one staggering year to the next – and always to the estate office on rent days. Yet she had three children by him, a son and two daughters, all of them as sharp as thistles. You would wonder, folk said, how he had managed it. But that was just the rough speak of the croft folk. Willie Gavin would not have liked it, for he never made fun of his crofting neighbour. Late on a summer evening when his own croft work was done for the night, he might take a walk along the road to give Puir Angus a help with his hay or with his *stooking* for an hour before bedtime. Puir Angus would be grateful for that, a different man, sober and sensible and almost overcome by the gesture.

'God, but it is fine to have friends,' he would say, in his own way as lonely a man.

4

The Testimony of a Tombstone

Grace was the first of the Gavins, born into the 1800s before they were barely begun. We know little of her now, though if her son inherited her looks, she may have been a handsome woman with features finer than the common clay of her class in that far landscape. But the documentation of her days is brief: only the words of a weathered headstone in a country kirkyard erected in homage by her son John in his middle years and some time after her death – the one single and determined act of a man who took little in his own life seriously and whose action in this speaks loudly of his love for his mother. In the Scots manner of such things, it duly records his own passing.

It is a simple stone without the ostentatious decoration of its Victorian time; a slab rounded on top to bear the ravages of the northern rains and the years and gently lichened. It stands near the dyke at the lower end of the kirkyard as though, after all, the crofting Gavins had been admitted only to the fringe of the respectable dead; its position and the hanging lie of the grassy ground long made family burials difficult in all but the driest weather. It is here that the Gavin story begins, and it is here that it ends. The old stone, a little indistinctly now, makes the one bold statement about Grace's existence; it says simply:

Erected by
John Gavin, Whinfield Croft,
In memory of His Mother,

Grace Connolly, who died
Feb. 20th, 1868 . . .

It goes on to record the croft tree of the Gavins and the women who married into them, the inhabitants of the croft house up from the burnside; the tireless folk who ceaselessly worked the small fields belonging to it. At the end of their hard-working years they had been brought to lie where the manse trees overhung the wall, to fill the family lair and have their names in turn chiselled into its cold granite and maybe (in the case of later arrivals) embellished with gilt, their splendour in death almost greater than anything they had achieved in life.

There is no mention of a husband to Grace Connolly. Not on the stone; neither in the family's long memory. The past is silent on her relationships with men and with the one in particular who passed down the Gavin name; we do not know whether Grace Connolly was taken in marriage or in a moment of biblical adultery. But the lack of a proclaimed progenitor for her crofting dynasty is no proof that her union was unblessed. Nor is the absence of the Gavin name a condemnation for then, as now, in that northern countryside death returned the withered old woman to the bloom of her girlhood, to lie through eternity in the innocence of her maiden name.

Yet his lack is lamentable, an inconvenience perhaps, in a landscape where many families suffer similar affliction, more than an embarrassment, for it is in the kirkyard that a countryside seeks the roll of its past and it would have been fine (and seemly) if he had been able to put in an appearance. There is a persistent rumour, no more, of a seaman who could not leave the sea for a land-locked life; who sailed away and never came home. It is not possible now to say whether he existed other than as a romantic figment to cover family discomfiture in a straiter age; what is sure is that the Gavin croft did indeed lie only ten miles from the

sea and but a little way off the Cadger's Road that led directly
from it.

The association must have been brief, however it ended. For
that there is some supporting evidence, threads at least that lead
to that conclusion: John Gavin was an only son and never spoke
of sisters, though he was born in a countryside where large
families were the rule when Grace was only twenty-nine and
with many more child-bearing years ahead of her. And fond
though he had been of his mother, as an old man John Gavin was
never heard to mention his father.

The truth of it all was something that only Grace Connolly
knew, and alone by the dyke in her quiet grave she raised no
scandals. And folk taking a turn round the kirkyard before going
in to the Sabbath morning sermon, if they noted the lack of a
male founder for the Gavins' line, would be kind to her.
'Maybe,' they would say one to another, 'she lookit for the
hats owre lang – and let all the bonnets gang bye.' Silent Grace
would remain, a mystery in life to all later Gavins.

Yet if the facts of her personal destiny are few it is not difficult,
even now, to fill out the pattern of her days or to clothe the stark
record of her existence from the folk memory of the region; or to
set that against the grander tapestry of history. When she was
born, Burns, Scotland's national poet, was only nine years dead,
his name not nearly so resounding as it would yet become, and
Waterloo was still twelve years away. It was a violent landscape,
disease-ridden still, stalked at times by the kind of grinding want
that would leave country folk, after a bad hairst, gaunt and
hollow-eyed. Blind beggars wandered the old baulks and the
drove roads tethered to the lean and slavering dogs that would
wile a path for them by the lochside and through the bog; bands
of vagrants, fearsome in their tatters, roamed unwashed to the
terror of the lonely farmtouns, where their demands could be
resisted only at the risk of grievous injury. The years that

followed Waterloo would swell their numbers as men made redundant by the prospect of an enduring peace joined the ranks to wander from hamlet to hamlet. Often enough the new vagrants had vivid memories of the battle; the Duke of Wellington was a hero in the land, and in the ballads they sometimes sang. Some of them were Irish and they travelled their women with them. For all we know, Grace, with her Irish name, may have been one of them.

It was a landscape not yet tamed and largely unfenced, its fame as the future cradle of fine bulls and pedigree livestock as yet undreamed of. It was a countryside barely entered upon the maelstrom of farming improvement. In 1805, shortly after Grace's birth, there came home from Harrow and Cambridge – and more immediately from the grandeur of the Levant – the gilded youth who would transform much of that bare North-East Lowlands landscape. His inheritance was the Big House by the river – and a prospect so drear and forbidding that his first impulse was to remount and spur his horse back the way they had come. His second was quickly to sell it. It was a chill January day when the man who would soon be a statesman of note (and one day, prime minister) came home to the estate he had not seen since the days of childhood. What he saw was a house empty and long neglected, spectral in the winter-grey light. Fuel was stacked haphazardly round it, sheds filled with logs leaned against it, and from it ran its one brief avenue – all the way down to the peat moss. It was all but a ruin and unlike many a similar laird's dwelling it lacked even the quality of kindliness. All about him, as he entered upon lairdship, lay a harsh, barren landscape, one without the softening outline of trees, lacking dykes, hedges and fences, one in which his tenantry, at best, lived in two-roomed hovels and struggled to maintain themselves from subsistence farming on sour and stony ground.

Slowly the landscape would be reworked, the new single-unit farmtouns rise at the centre of their walled fields. And from the young laird's policy of improvement there would spring, too, many of the croft holdings that would come on to his rent roll (935 by 1870), some of them where the plough had never reigned before, some on the fringe of what would one day be rich farming land, a few perhaps where some squatter had already scratched out a plot and a bare existence. Somehow, from somewhere, Grace Connolly became a statistic in that turmoil of change and (with her consort, if he existed) began to break in the ground along the burnside.

It is speculation, though not unlikely, that they were squatters at first, tethering their milk cow on the burn bank and clearing a patch of the boggy ground to grow poor-quality oats or bere (barley). Their harvest would be won with that abiding emblem of commissars and crofter men, the sickle, and would be easily gathered – a hairst that even at the best of times hardly sufficed to keep them beyond the reproach of other folks' charity and in a bad year reduced them to shameless beggary. Driven by need after a bad year, the young croft woman would have gone *thigging* round the countryside: begging the seed corn that would sow next season's harvest from the better-off farmtouns. A fine-looking woman, she may have had little trouble getting a small sackful of seed, and more keeping herself out of the farmer's hands, always supposing she had a mind to. In those bitter years the grain was for the folk and the beasts would want, the horses being put on a starvation diet and worked lightly through the winter in the hope that they would survive it. With hardly a cart in the parish the corn had gone to the miller in a bag strapped to the pony's back with *rushen* cords, the lime and dung for the fields, the peat from the moss, panniered to where it was needed on the poor beast's back, though like the women of her time Grace would have carried the seed corn to the spring fields and the sowing hopper in a small sack on her head. If she had time at all to herself, maybe in the long winter evenings, she filled it with her factory *shank*, knitting stockings for a manufacturer by the light of the *puirman* (the rustic bog-fir candelabrum of the old countryside) for the siller it would bring in, lighting her short clay pipe with an ember of peat, like many another croft wife, before she sat down. If men came her way, after John Gavin's father, we cannot know of it; but if the merry, sociable son took the mother's temperament she may well have given a man a bed whiles, and succoured him in the bygoing.

If the portrait of Grace Connolly's past lacks hard confirmation, it cannot be far from the truth, for the folk who knew her son never heard him speak of territorial connection elsewhere – not even the grandson who was the constant companion of his old age. Besides that, there was the fact, accepted through the countryside, that the Gavins had always been crofter folk and in Whinfield for as long as anybody could mind. It is with the mid 1860s and the knowledge of John Gavin's connection with the farmtoun on the hill beyond the burn that all speculation finally ends. Grace's son, by then, was in his mid-thirties, a dapperly good-looking man, and the events of that time are etched firmly in his family's folk history.

Like many of the later crofter men, John Gavin was a ploughman, a horseman, at the farmtoun on the hill, walking winterlong behind the plough with a break now and then to cart turnips home from the frost-rimed fields to the beasts in the byre; his favourite grandson never heard him speak of any other employment. One dull afternoon in the fall of the year when the hairst was well past he stabled his pair early to marry Rachel Annand, one of four sisters of the same parish, all of them with the kind of face far stronger on character than in beauty. Only a short time before, one of them had wed the master of John's farmtoun and with her sister so comfortably ensconced in the master's bed it is just possible that Rachel inadvertently succumbed to the wiles of the jovial little man ten years older. The countryside would long remember their union, for in the pithy recollection of its folk memory: 'The ane marriet the fairmer and the tither the fee'd man.' They also said the lass had maybe not had the best of the bargain.

In the circumstances of the time the event was almost certainly celebrated in the farmtoun's barn, and the lavish preparation for such an occasion has been delightfully recorded by Helen Beaton in her book *At the Back o' Bennachie*, much of which is in the old Doric of its region:

There were many and great preparations at the bride's home before the wedding day and if it was a farm the barn was swept clean from roof to threshold. Tables were then placed in the middle of the floor; and planks of wood, resting on two bushels of oats or barley, acted as supports, thus providing strong seats for the guests.

The preparations for the wedding feast also constituted a large item. Large junks of beef were boiled or roasted in very large pots or ovens, which were hung over a fire of sticks and peat, the fire being usually built against a dykeside or other suitable place. When the beef was roasted for large parties or weddings, peat was piled on the top of the oven lid, and puddings were fired under an old tray or sheet iron in the same manner. To baste the beef and ascertain if the pudding was firing properly was usually hot and trying work for the cook.

Fowls were sent in large numbers to the bride, and as the fowls were not so large as they are now, it was not unusual for a man to eat a whole fowl! There were boiled puddings, and milk puddings with currants in them, and these, owing to their thickness, required a knife to cut them before a spoon could serve them out. At a wedding feast, knives, spoons and forks, and several other things, were turned out of drawer or press, where they rarely saw the light of day, except for such high occasions, and at Yule and Fastern's E'en.

After the guests had eaten a *rimrax* of substantial food, large bowls of strong toddy were handed round, and after such rounds it was not uncommon for a number of the male guests to be found under the table.

The feast itself, however, was far from being the end of it. Mrs Beaton again:

> Fan they hae done wi' eatin' o't,
> Fan they hae done wi' drinkin' o't,
> For dancing they gae tae the green,
> An' ablins, to the beatin' o't.
> He dances best that dances fast
> An' loups at ilka reesin' o't
> An' claps his hands frae hough tae hough,
> An' furls aboot the feezins o't.

Lamentably, Mrs Beaton reports, 'The end of a wedding was frequently more boisterous than seemly.' If there was a man who would have enjoyed such a day it was the convivial bridegroom; his new brother-in-law, they say, was less than pleased with the sudden degree of kinship.

Willie Gavin was the couple's first-born and his mother (in the way of mothers) favoured him. The sisters who followed him, resentful of that and of the endless croft chores, and maybe of being forced as children to carry squealing pigs on their backs to the market in the kirktoun, took away from the life or anything approaching it as fast as their feet and presentable suitors could carry them. Certainly, they did better for themselves than the young weaver's lass that their brother would bring into the croft, but what is interesting now is the strides a young crofter lass could make in society when she put her mind to it. One wed a fruit traveller who shortly came to rest in his own shop in Aberdeen's fishing community and did as well with the hard liquor which he was also licensed to sell as ever he did with his groceries. Another took on a policeman of that same city, a man of such impeccable character and integrity that retirement took him into the role of bank messenger and also man-of-mystery, for he spent most of his life riding the rails in a locked compartment and surrounded by siller between that northern city and the money houses of London. With his croft lass he ended his days in a fine granite house in the doucely residential fringe of the city. The third and youngest stayed at home for a time till finally, with fine judgement, she married a mere farm-toun strapper whose career immediately took flight as the chauffeur of the first car in the parish.

Folk said old John Gavin's daughters had all done well for themselves and they did. In one generation they severed all connection with the old croft way of life and rose into the lower ranks of the middle classes; they sent their own children to good schools and if they returned whiles to the croft in the 1920s and '30s, it was in the motor cars they all ran and on a journey that was more a measure of the distance they had gone in life than any genuine pilgrimage. Their brother was pleased enough to wel-come them; he took their smart-suited men round his small croft fields on a Sunday afternoon with the same good grace he would have shown to any young farmtoun lad. But he was never sorry to see them go. He shut their car doors behind them without regrets. And he never envied them.

It was a family divided also by other tensions. Old John, when he had given up his ploughman's work in later years, had gone reluctantly out to his fields or the byre, driven by his wife. It was she who directed the croft work (and did much of it) and after her man's death she would give young Willie the same benefit of her advice, and was critical even of the wife he had brought home and not above hinting that had he tried harder he might have done better. Her son though had little need of her direction for he was a different kind of man from his father, a different man entirely, and their conflicting natures had long been a source of dissension. Old John, for example, was careless of his roadside fences – the only ones he had – so that his son, home at the weekend from his masoning work, would chide him over the broken paling wire or the rotting fenceposts that threatened to collapse at any moment and give the livestock their freedom.

'Ye'll need to mend the paling, man,' the son would remonstrate, cross in his soul at such dereliction, contemptuous even and quite unable to understand the man who could allow it. 'Gin ye dinna get it seen to, the beasts will be out onto the road.'

'Maybe, maybe . . .' Old John was always a man to admit his faults freely (even some he didn't have, so amiable was he). 'But where the devil would they gang tae, anyway, supposing they were free the morn? The girss is nae better ben at Bogside.'

There was an irony in their exchanges for they would precipitate a pattern that divided the mason man from his own sons: the bickering between his father and grandfather stirred a deep resentment in the grandson who would become the companion of Old John's later years and who inherited much of his sociable nature. Many years later he would recall the conflict that had separated the Gavin generations:

My grandfather and I got along exceptionally well. My own father, however, was rather critical of my grandfather on many occasions. He would take issue with him about such and such a piece of fencing that needed attention – that would be toppling down. Or it might be something else that might be needing attending to. He was quite critical of my grandfather in many, many cases and I was rather resentful of him for that particular reason.

The voice now, like many another from the old crofting landscape, is transatlantic. It was a wound that never healed.

There is something else we know about the Gavins and that too with certainty: they lived long. The weathered tombstone in that quiet kirkyard that records their crofting years bears its bald testimony to that. Grace, the first of them, was sixty-five when she died. She had lived to see her first grandchild take his first faltering steps and maybe she had marked the dour set of him and known that life would not be easy on him. The son who had loved her so, and erected a stone to her memory, poor ploughman-crofter though he was, lived to be eighty-one; the wife who had steered him so relentlessly between one day and the next, to be eighty-six. Willie Gavin himself died in his seventies tired out with work, but the up-country weaver's lass he had brought into the family, for all the hardship of her life, survived to the age of ninety-six. All the Gavins now are out of the crofting life or anything remotely like it. They were a dour breed mainly, not to be meddled with, respected rather than widely loved – folk, it was sometimes said, with a good conceit of themselves and more independent by far than they had any right to be.

5

The Croft Biggings

Willie Gavin loved the old landscape: all the days of his masoning life he travelled its roads, first on foot, later on, when they became common, by bicycle. Pratt's *Buchan*, his favourite reading, gave the history of every ruin and farmtoun and castle of its region; it lay with the family Bible, unlocking the past of that far countryside. He loved its seasons, its sorrows and its several rejoicings: the sweet scent of clover hanging over the evening fields, the blaze of broom on the hill as it gathered the last of the sunlight, the ease of autumn in the soul as well as the melancholy of the winter parks lying still and bare. It was his landscape and he sought no other.

The old croft of his folk and his boyhood stood at the centre of that awareness, the thing that focused his life. It was strung with its near neighbours by the roadside, its sour ground stretching down to the burn. Beyond that the good farmland rose, gently at first, and then into the fine swell of the brae that set Laverockhill's fields up to the sun. The big farmtoun – where the young ploughman John Gavin had once driven a Clydesdale pair – sat smug with prosperity, its low sandstone steading and well-slated roofs claiming the ridge for their own, aloof from the croft ground below. Behind it lay the old castle, ruined and lichened now, a flawed jewel amid the farmtoun fields but like an old brooch on a bosom, gathering the green shawl of the countryside to it still. Past it on the ridge ran the old road to the sea, a dry highway in that time before drainage had let traveller and tink alike into the shelter of the howe and along by the burn-side. Away to the left it passed the door of the old milltoun, a farmstead now with steep, hill-hung fields, where once they had reaped the wind to mill the shorn corn and fill the girnals of the parish. But that day was gone, bye and done with now, the old millstones, if they had survived at all, long into the hidden heart of some dyke where the farming improver had thrust them, for they had not been strong on memorials, the folk of that old landscape. It was a lonely place, now that folk no longer brought their grain to it, up and away from the world; dreich among the huddled firs that ringed it, bent and wind-twisted – arthritic crones that walked the gloam skyline and gave the old place its aura of foreboding. Neither grocer nor baker's van could reach it and its folk, understandably, had a diminishing circle of friends. By it now and then, on the old road, came only the weird and travelling folk at one with its haunted past.

On the other side of Laverockhill the old road on its way to the sea came down the rump of the hill where it eased out to the flatlands and the well-worked fields of more modest one-, two- and three-pair farmtouns where the tenor of life was taken slow-footed at the Clydesdale's pace – a strange dour world uneventful except for the occasional outbreak of murder; a world in which a sophisticated man might have felt himself menaced by the guttural speak of unshaven faces when all they were offering was the awkwardness of friendship.

From its lonely height the old road watched the path of its usurper: a beige, stone-metalled ribbon that ran through a landscape so bare it had difficulty finding obstacles to put in its progress. Along it went the same kind of folk, better-dressed now, more of them maybe with a place to call home. It carried still the scholar to his imprisonment, the cottar to his new farmtoun fee, servant maids to secret embraces, the bad case of fever and folk with diphtheria; it carried the bride to her bedding and the shaven corpse of the man who had never in his life worn anything but a five-day beard and known nothing but the sweet breath of the parks to the long rest of eternity. On that day at least they would clear the roads for him and keep the turnip carts about the farm steading till his funeral had gone past.

It was a road, even at the turn of the century, hardly adequate for the job it had taken on; only the early cyclists of the era could meet without confrontation and with anything wider came a need for prolonged negotiation. A heavy run of traffic or the slow progress of the traction engine shifting its threshing mill on from one place to the next could put the work of the farmtouns back half a day. But slow though its commerce was, it was the only road the croft folk had to carry them out into the world, and as time wore on more and more of them would take it and never look back.

Like its near neighbours the Gavin croft turned the grey stone of its barn gable to the passing traffic and sandwiched its dwelling house between that and the byre. The cowshed took the low end of the long-house bigging and that too was traditional, looking back to a past when it had been necessary to ensure that the cow-*strang* ran the way of the *midden* at its gable rather than into the circle of its folk as they sat round their fire. Across from the house, beyond the croft close that led down from the road, the kitchen garden was guarded by a stone wall that baffled both bairn and wandering beast, its three other sides enclosed by tall beech hedges and the windowless wall of the milkhouse where the dark was undisturbed between one milking and the next. Behind that again was the old crofter's turnip shed and toolshed; it was here that Willie Gavin housed his trestles and planks, all the tools of his masoning trade as well as his barrow, his croft implements and the bicycle that would carry him from home whenever he had need of it. At the bottom of the croft close, forming the base of the 'U' layout and shutting the steading off

from a view of its fields, was the old stable bigging that now
housed the calves and, abutting it, the hens' *cruive*.

The cornyard, with room for a half-dozen small crofter's ricks,
lay behind the barn and its engine house, where the crofter man's
Ruston oil engine lurked in the gloom, a monster of unpredictable behaviour that frightened all but the brave. In autumn,
when his hairst was in, his stackyard was the pride of the old
crofter's heart; it was here that he would be found whiles leaning
into a stack as he took a late-evening smoke, with a look on his
face that was the nearest he ever came to contentment. It was
here, too, that a bairn or croft man would come to make the
short calls of nature in that old landscape – so naturally that a man
might walk away from you as you talked, round the corner of a
cornrick, and reappear a moment later buttoning his flies without
ever having interrupted the flow of the conversation. (In any
case, it would have been unmanly to go anywhere else to *pish*;
the nearest dykeside or gable or roadside would also do duty by
day, the chamber pot – only in extremis – by night.)

Screening the cornyard and much of the croft steading from
the road was a scraggy line of elderberry trees (the *bourtrees* of that
old countryside) and a single red rowan. Good godly folk though
the Gavins had always been, they had kept the mountain ash
there to ward off evil and even if Willie Gavin no longer believed
in the witches nor the power of the glamourie they could cast on
his beasts, he would tweak its branches in the bygoing and,
bending down to the bairn with him, whisper urgently:

> Rowan tree and reid threid
> Keep the witches frae their speed.

Maybe it had been planted in Old John Gavin's day or even in his
grandmother's, for once there had been a time when the rowan
tree was a talisman that grew at every croft gable; when, to

protect the beasts, a cross of *rodden* twigs was placed above the byre door. Long ago that had been, when superstition had gripped the poor crofter folk and a still-born calf or a cow going unexpectedly dry was a disaster; glad enough the old folk had been of their enchantments, the things that had made them at times bow less to God and more to the Devil.

The bourtrees and the rowan brought back the past, so that you would wonder whiles what kind of folk had they been; and what kind of dwelling had they *biggit* there, those folk who had first tilled that land? A squalid hovel, like as not, created from what the countryside yielded. Made of turf perhaps, one-roomed certainly, with the cow brought in to one end of it when the days of the year drew in. For folk whom life or the laird might suddenly move on there would be little incentive to build for permanence and it is likely their poor dwellings differed little from those of the century before, witheringly described, in *The Social Life of Scotland in the Eighteenth Century* by Henry Grey Graham:

The hovels of one room were built of stones and turf without mortar, the holes in the wall stuffed with straw or heather or moss to keep out the blasts; the fire, usually in the middle of the house floor, in despair of finding an exit by the smoke-clotted roof, filled the room with malodorous clouds. The cattle at night were tethered at one end of the room while the family lay at the other on heather on the floor. The light came from an opening at either gable which whenever the wind blew in was stuffed with brackens or an old bonnet to keep out the sleet and the blast. The roofs were so low in northern districts that the inmates could not stand upright but sat on stones or three-legged stools that served for chairs, and the huts were entered by doors so low and narrow that to gain an entrance one required almost to creep. Their thatching was of ferns or heather, for the straw was all needed for the cattle.

But in time the Gavins, with the laird's help or maybe without it, had raised a better dwelling on that spot by the side of the track, a house that took the basic shape that would carry down to the 1900s, and in the case of some of the old crofts, up to World War II. It was a layout as familiar in the West, where it would endure even longer, sitting easily on the land and drawing all the materials for its construction from it: the single-storey but-and-ben with a between-ends *closet* formed by the box-beds the folk shut themselves into at night; the walls built of rubble stone and mortared with clay and faced inside and out perhaps with lime mortar. They were but little different, if at all, from the crude dwellings of the farmtoun tenantry a short time before and much the same kind of humble abode in which Burns himself had once, humorously, admitted:

> There lonely by the ingle cheek
> I sat and ey'd the spewing reek
> That filled with hoast-provoking smeek
> The auld clay biggin'.
> An' heard the restless rattons squeak
> Abune the riggin'.

The shell of such a bigging about the mid 1800s would have been no more than £30 and maybe as little as £20, and the innovation by that time of the *hinging lum* (the hanging chimney) did much to ameliorate the smoky conditions that had so demonstrably irritated a poet's lungs. The hinging lum was a wooden canopy over the fireplace, tapering upwards, and extending into the room. Besides that, the fireplace would have an ash-well that needed clearing out only once every three weeks and if the swee had not as yet become a familiar and convenient fitment to swing pots and kettles on and off the fire, there was at least the *rantle-tree*, a crossbar of iron set into either side of the chimney to take the links and pot crook. Floors were earthen – as they would be in some cases right up to the 1930s – the roofs, in the North-East, straw-and-clay thatched, as were those of the abutting barn and byre. *Strae an' clay* thatching would also last long in the North-East Lowlands, a muddy, mucky process that involved running the clay between the oat or barley straw to bind it. Even after the Whinfield croft had been roofed with red tiles underneath, its tenant John Gavin yearly brought the thatching that covered them up to scratch. His grandson, his labourer in the early years of this century, remembers the work: 'I used to help my grandfather in rethatching the croft house. He would have all his thatch ready beforehand as well as the mortar. It was mostly mud, and it was used to keep the thatch in place.'

If their folk and their dogs sometimes gave the old crofts a bad name, their poor tumbledown biggings did as little to enhance it. In constant need of repair, there were times when they were kept together as much by clever improvisation – a patch here, a prop there – as by the agency of good mortar or the concern of the estate whose interest, in any case, would have to be solicited and which (understandably) would often have preferred to raze the old biggings and consolidate their acres with those of a neighbouring holding where the tenant was having better luck in keeping his steading together. It is possible that John Gavin was an exasperating tenant. More than likely, since his lackadaisical negligence even upset his own son. Or, born forty years before the Education Act took the youngsters of that spare countryside into the schoolroom on a regular basis, it may have been that he was incapable of putting his complaints onto paper. It is possible, even, that he could write nothing more than his name. But he had borne long and patiently the steady seep of rain into his byre (and perhaps come to the belief that such neglect was a crofter man's lot) when he stepped into the cowshed with his nine-year-old grandson one morning early this century. Nearly eighty years after, the small boy who had stood that day with his grandfather in the cowshed would recall the incident – and with it, perhaps, the moment when the power of literacy began to change the old crofter–laird relationship and the balance, for once, swung the crofter's way:

> In my early years some of the outbuildings of my grandfather's croft were getting into quite a dilapidated condition – in fact the cow byre was not even leak-proof. So I said to my grandfather one day 'Why don't you make an appeal to the estate factor for a new byre? This building isn't fit to keep stock in! The beasts are getting soaked . . . Maybe it isn't harming them much, but it's a situation that shouldn't exist.'

Old John that day had swithered, uncertain of his ground, unsure what to say to a youngster who did not know how it was between a man and his laird: What could he do? he asked finally with resignation. 'Let me write to the factor, Granda, and tell him. It might make him sit up!' Reluctantly the old croft man had agreed. And his grandson remembers:

> So I sat down and wrote a letter. I was regarded at school as having a pretty good command of the English vocabulary. So I wrote the factor a nice letter. I cited the grim shape the cow byre was in, and made an appeal. I don't know now whether I signed the letter in my grandfather's name or not – they would certainly know he had never written it. He couldn't. At least, I never recall him writing at all.
>
> Anyway, I wrote this letter and not many days after we had a visit from the factor, who came to see the byre for himself

and inspect its condition. And he thought it was in quite a pitiful state and sanctioned approval of a brand new byre, which was then erected and made my grandfather very happy.

I did the same thing with the barn and that was replaced. It was the factor who made the decision, granting a request for a new outbuilding or home. The estate architect then drew up the design – the specifications and dimensions and so on – which was to be adhered to.

But if Old John Gavin had been pleased with his new croft biggings, the son who was to follow him was less so. When he came home from burying his father in the kirktoun's cemetery, cold though the November day was, he had taken a walk round the old croft house and its steading. Neither by then spoke well of the old tenant, and as his mason's eye picked out the points long overdue for attention, the plans were already milling in his mind. Yet even Willie Gavin, with all his fluency in calculations, his skill in reading plans and his considerable standing (by then) in the community, felt a countryman's hesitation in writing to the laird. His son, Old John's companion and confidant, remembers:

I recollect, some years after that, after my grandfather had passed on, that my father, who was a master mason, realised that during the winter months particularly the building trade was adversely affected – you know, by extreme frost or the severity of the weather. Or the road conditions would be such that they would find it hard to get to work, to a job they might be on ten miles away and the only means of getting there by bicycle.

So my father thought he would like to take over the old croft himself, on his own. He went to see the factor and of course was granted permission to do this – to get the croft. But the dwelling house by this time, like the rest of the buildings,

had got to the stage where it had seen better days. So my
father asked me would I write a letter to the factor *again*, this
time making an appeal for a new dwelling house!

This I did and it was subsequently granted. My father, being
a mason, erected the building himself. . . . Did all the stone
work, that is.

The traditional but-and-ben bigging that Willie Gavin walked
round when he came home from his father's funeral – and in
whose equally traditional box-bed he had raised his first cry in
the world – he would transform into a two-storey stone-and-
lime house the equal of any of its kind on that stark landscape. He
would do it single-handed. Within weeks, as soon as he had the
estate architect's plans in his hands, he shifted his family into the
croft barn and set their box-beds in there after them. Then he
started to tear down the old croft house in which he had been
born, stone by stone.

The house he built was a bit dour and forbidding (like the man
himself, folk would say) but it was a fine croft house for all that
with its blue-slated roof and its garrets, dormer-windowed,
looking out over the garden to the countryside beyond. Inside,
the closet was extended and walled off to the ceiling; a wooden
porch was built on at the door where his mother had once grown
scarlet runner beans, a glassy vestibule that was neither inside nor
out but which thwarted the wind that blew constantly at the old
woman's back as she sat by the fire. If he had not been a mason
man, folk would have said he was getting above himself. In time
he would rebuild barn and byre to the same standard, discarding
the old *clay thacking* for the maintenance-free convenience of
corrugated sheet-iron, though he would refrain from painting it
the violent red that so many of the croft men favoured (maybe to
give their biggings the 'warmth' that the old red tiles once had
bestowed). His two-stalled byre in which his milk cows and his

fattening stirks stood two to a stall (and chained to the *traviss*) was given new built-in troughs (*trochs*) for the turnips, hayracks (*hakes*) for the beasts' straw and was new-laid with the causey stones that would bring its modernity into line with that of the grand farmtouns. Both biggings were lit by skylights let into the slant of the roof, the barn additionally by a small window in its gable, where an outside stone stair led up to the small corn loft he had created in its rafters – a novelty, like the little barn-mill he would install, about any holding of its size. For all that though, he stuck by the old tradition in setting its two doors facing each other from opposite walls, something unchanged from the days of the flail; their through-draught had helped to winnow the grain. And when his father's old *shelt* had no longer need of it, he would rebuild the old thatched stable as his calf-house.

The croft though had two further structures that dominated the lives of its hard-working folk: the water pump and the privy. The first stood by the hens' *ree*, the latter (with irreproachable logic) across from the midden by the old stable's gable. The pump, the trunk of a majestic larch bored and sunk into the ground above the old well, endlessly justified the wisdom of the other croft folk who had stuck loyally by their bucket and windlass, for it went consistently dry all summer long, leaving Grannie Gavin to carry her water, pailed and yoked on her shoulders, from the old well a quarter of a mile away.

The privy though, like all Willie Gavin's biggings, was always in splendid order and that at least was something to be thankful for in a landscape where many such offices (where they existed at all) had fine slap-in-the-wind doors and were so full of draughts you could catch your death in them. Some had poor fastenings so that young bairns and shy lasses would have to sit hanging on to a string on a nail driven into the door. Even so, they might, thoughtlessly, be hoisted off the seat in a hurry before they had made themselves comfortable. Some privies faced the hill and some stared onto the road, with a peephole even at the right height in the door so that a man at his ease could take stock of the countryside (or what he could see of it). Most, like Willie Gavin's, sheltered behind their croft biggings and got busy about the dinner hour and in the earlier part of the evening. Willie Gavin, however, offered his folk and his guests the security of an inner bolt, which could also be inconvenient: bairns went in and could not be got out (without prising off the side-boarding) and other folk took to it selfishly as a retreat from the world for it was a comfortable, solitary place when things went wrong or for a lass suddenly forsaken – spotless always and the seat so well scrubbed that its only danger was splinters, not infection. The floor was as clean, and rich with a fine arboreal scab where the wood knots stood through against Grannie Gavin's obsessive scrubbings. Young Gavin boys in particular lingered there, entranced as they grew older by the spencered ladies from the mail-order catalogues already quartered-down for convenience; there was an education, a world of wisdom there on the nail that they were unlikely to learn any other way.

All the same, the John Gunn, with its nail, its swatch of absorbing interest, and its pail (removed and emptied once a week from below the seat) could be claustrophobic on a fine summer's day – so near to the midden.

The croft's biggings though were the best of it; there was little Willie Gavin could do about its eight and a half sour acres, where all friability was bedevilled by bad drainage and the sedge growing in the marshy part of the ley would be a reminder to him, if he needed one, that he could not call nature his friend for all his love of it. Like his mother, Old John had kept his beasts on the tether, an earlier, easier form of controlled grazing that was less tiresome than cordoning the corn. Willie Gavin, however, had not been able to rest until he had fenceposts into the ground and the paling wire strung three-stranded between them.

Raw and damp from the sawmill, they marched in rows down to the burn, demarcating the fields of his smallholding, each a little under an acre and a half. Poor though their soil was – 'strongish land but somewhat cold and damp', the laird's land surveyor had called it, circumspectly, when he had recommended raising the rent in 1885 – the old crofter man never grudged the price of them. Moderate in all his enthusiasms and never easily parted from his siller, he went willingly to his bank (the tin box he kept in the top shelf of the closet cupboard) as rent day came round. The croft cost him, in the 1930s, just £7 a year, less than £1 an acre, the same as it had cost his father fifty years earlier. For that recommendation of a rent rise from the start of John Gavin's new lease in 1886 was never implemented. By then that wide countryside of the great farmtouns had gone over the peak of its prosperity and begun its slide into the years of farming depression.

And the Gavins, whatever else they had been, had been lucky in their lairds. Today the list of entries in the estate's old improvements-and-repairs ledger is a litany of ceaseless wants that tell the story of a fight to better poor ground (500 2½-inch tile pipes in 1904) and, with cryptic 'wood and iron' entries, keep poor biggings standing. If the Gavins could not get fat on such a holding, neither could the laird, and there must have been years when his crofts were an accountant's nightmare.

As he got older and more respected in the community, Willie Gavin would more easily get the factor's ear to complain about a rotting door or a leaking roof. Likely the laird's man-of-business had always known that the excuse about a winter lull in the masoning trade was no more than the crofter man's poorly reasoned rationale for taking over the holding. After all, the same conditions precluded all but the most routine of crofting chores. The mason man had fooled nobody; what he and the other men

like him felt, has been aptly summed up by yet another of the
numerous royal commissions on crofting:

> Above all they have the feeling that the croft, its land, its
> houses are their own. They have gathered its stones and reared
> its buildings and occupied it as their own all their days. They
> have received it from their ancestors who won it from the
> wilderness and they cherish the hope they will transmit it to
> the generations to come . . .

It is a statement worthy of a better home than a bureaucrat's
report. Its sentiments were frequently as true of the North-East
Lowlands landscape as that of the Western Highlands. Written
long after Willie Gavin's day, it captures his creed entirely.

6

The Shifts and the Seasons

The seasons turned and Willie Gavin, like all the North-East crofter men, turned with them: from seedtime to harvest and through the dreich days of winter. The cycle of the croft year, the pattern of its crops, followed that of the farmtoun to whose skirts it clung, dependent always upon its goodwill. Though the old crofter man would never willingly let a Clydesdale set foot on his land, he was beholden like his neighbours to Laverockhill for the heavier working of his fields and for the spring cultivation of his soil in particular. That obligation, the contract work by the farmtouns for the crofter men, came out of the past though Old John Gavin had circumvented it by borrowing his neighbour's shelt to yoke with his own in the plough. But then, he himself had been a ploughman, as capable of setting up a *feering* and handling a Clydesdale pair as any man the big farm could send down to him. Many of the croft men, however, were tradesmen like his son and not able to speak to a horse without upsetting it, far less set up a respectable furrow – though that never made them any the less critical of the ploughman's work. Far from it. Many aired their views as though they had been match champions in their time.

In Willie Gavin's landscape the seasons of ploughing and sowing and harvesting held an ancient and comforting immutability, a rhythm that knitted the pattern of country lives to the needs of the fields, the old croft men's, whatever their calling, as surely as those of farmtoun folk. It was a pattern that linked a man with the past and there was hardly a year when the winter ploughs did not turn up an old hunter of that wind-scoured plain crouched still in his cold stone-kist; or a spring when the seed harrows did not draw their circle round the venerable ruin or pass through the long shadows of its history and that time when the sword, not the plough, held the land.

Though he might demur whiles, late-on though it was, that the ground was not right for sowing or that the hairst parks were not yet ready for the scythe, Willie Gavin fell in with that old country order of things, bowing to the need to work when the weather would let him, mindful that a late sowing brought a late hairst with all the hazards and loss that entailed. Like the rest of the Lowlands croft men he followed the ley-farming principles of the Scottish farmtouns, a system that had been a feature (and the sheet-anchor) of that northern landscape since the mid 1700s. He had no permanent grass for his beasts. His rotation of crops in his humble *shifts* (the crofter's name for his small fields) adhered to the old order (written into many an early farmtoun lease) of the improving lairds a century before: a six-year cycle that gave him temporary leys instead of fixed grazing and that had long made rotation grasses a part of east-coast arable farming. It was a pattern of cropping with many merits, and ideally suited, had the old lairds but known it, to what lay ahead, for it was a rotation with an enviable in-built elasticity: the lying-in ley could be lengthened or shortened according to what was paying best at the time, horn or corn. It was the system that enabled the fine Scottish farmtouns to weather the lean Depression years sometimes a little better than their English counterparts. Its use had taken them through to about 1880 before the importation of wheat from under a more bountiful sun started to affect them. Only then, and only gradually, in the leaner times that followed, had the permanent leys been laid down.

It was a cycle that suited the east-coast crofter man, with his concern for stock as well as crops, though unlike the farmtouns, which in the 1920s and '30s were letting their leys lie for four years (and maybe longer), Willie Gavin had little chance of extending the pattern. The old crofter men in that now-distant landscape preferred a six-shift system, giving themselves three years' grass, and Willie Gavin held to it. That pattern had been set by his ploughman father at the height of the boom farming days. He ploughed his ley after its third year – back into the *tattie corn* that helped to keep the crofter folk poor all their days for they clung to it, most of them, when they should have known better and when the farmtouns round them had long sown the improved varieties that would have better filled their barns and their meal girnals. The crofter man's limiting 'sixth-course shift' gave his fields their yearly changing cycle: ley oats; turnips; clean-land oats; hay; first-year grass; second-year grass. The ley oats got the rich humus of the ploughed-in grass that in an extended rotation might well have supported stock for another year. Their ploughed stubble in turn would lie winter-long and, with the weeds (the *growth*) gathered off, become next year's turnip ground. In the third year the shift would take the clean-land corn, undersown almost simultaneously with the grass seed for the fourth year's hay and the temporary pasture that followed it. It was a system as intricately linked and balanced as any Chinese puzzle.

Willie Gavin, like his father, meticulously followed its cycle of renewal and fertility but it never made him rich. The old man's sons-in-law, cottars at the big farmtouns with their mounds of fine dung and sacks of rich lime, claimed always that he was over-thrifty in manuring his shifts. Maybe he was. Yet it was not the spirit that was unwilling for he gave his oats as much bagged fertiliser as his pocket could stand and needed all the contents of his byre midden for his root crop, the yellow *neeps*, the only kind of turnips he grew (though many of the old croft men also liked a drill or two of swedes). With his oat straw, they would be the bulk of his beasts' winter diet. It was a sound enough judgement and his inability to do otherwise was no more than a bitter indictment of the straits of the life and the poverty that whiles gripped him, and others like him. And there was no certainty, anyway, that his poor-quality corn would have done any better supposing he had dowsed it in dung.

He made a little hay, as did all the croft men, to add to his milk cows' diet. The shift gave him some summer grazing as well as winter keep for with his hay crop off and ricked in the cornyard, he could run his beasts on it till they were housed in the autumn.

His crofting year – like that of the farmtouns – began late in the fall of the year in that ritual that was as old as farming time. With autumn well through and his own cornfields ploughed, Laverockhill would send down one of his horsemen with his plough and his Clydesdale pair to turn over the old crofter's stubble – though for all the long years of their acquaintance he dared do nothing till he was asked. The old man, he knew, was tetchy about being placed under anything that seemed like obligation, and the arrangement itself had a ritual that hardly varied from one year to the next. It was a sly observation of protocol that left the old crofter with his dignity.

If the mason man did not catch Laverockhill at the kirk gate on the Sabbath, he would step over to one or other of his ploughmen at work in a neighbouring field – or carting home turnips to the fine stirks the farmer always had fattening in his byre.

'Tell yer maister, laddie, that I would be obliged to him gin he could gie me a turn o' the ploo when he has man and beasts tae spare.'

'Fairly, I'll do that, Mister Gavin,' the young horseman would promise. 'As soon as ever I see him.'

So it would be fixed, and with the coast clear, in a week or so the same young ploughman might be setting up a feering in the old man's field one morning almost before it was daylight. The task of ploughing the croft shift would not take him that long: just a day and a half for an acre and a half, and he could have done better but for the shortness of the crofter's field for he had no sooner got the plough point into the ground than he was out and turning at the other endrig. He would have been a damned sight quicker still, Laverockhill always said, if Jess MacKendrick had not been forever stopping the laddie with jugs of tea and a *piece*, and certainly Grannie Gavin, minding her own farmtoun days and the bareness of the bothy lads' table, would be guilty of that. She was fastidious about visiting ploughmen.

The stubble ground would lie getting the good of the winter frosts and the ploughman would be back before the New Year was long past to get his dram (if it wasn't too late) and turn over the old ley land for half that year's oats, and later still, about mid-April when Willie Gavin had had time to pull and clamp the last of his turnips (for his beasts were still in the byre), to plough the ground for the clean-land crop, the other one and half acres or so of tattie corn that the old man would sow. Before April was out, and when Laverockhill's own fields were sown, the horseman would be back with the harrows to make ready the seed ground.

If he was a bit late it hardly mattered for the low-lying croft shifts were always behind the brae-set fields of the big farmtoun in their readiness to receive the seed. And even then, it was never in the state the old crofter man would have wanted it for he was as hard to please about that as ever he had been about masoning. The horseman could as easily have brought the broadcast-sower with him and finished the job. It would not have taken him long. But Willie Gavin would not have countenanced that and Laverockhill knew better than to anger him by suggesting it. For Willie Gavin had always sown his own seed corn (as had his father) from the hopper strapped round his shoulders. It was a ritual the years had hallowed and that took him into the world of the Scriptures and maybe closer to God. He did not speak of it but it was important to him.

The evening before, the bags of seed oats would be set ready in the croft barn and if the weather held, almost before light and as Grannie Gavin readied his breakfast, he would load his barrow to set the bags at intervals down the length of the shifts, assessing where the hopper would fall empty. From the nearest, when he stopped in the bout, the hopper would be refilled by Grannie Gavin with a small pail. It was a scene that looked back to an old landscape, to another time and an earlier folk. Feet and scattering fist absorbed the past of the run-rig and the centuries in a heavy symbolism, and set their rhythm on the day. For Willie Gavin it was a moment of commitment and dour though he looked, an aged patriarch striding his parks, that day his heart sang. Behind him would come the harrows, three times over the field, their burying teeth drawing the patterns of their own shallow ridges. In a week or so, ten days at the most, the crofter man would sow the grass seed that would be his next year's hay in his clean-land field, this time pinching the seed between the thumb and forefinger of each hand (not broadcast as before) and the farm-toun man would come down in the evening light with the harrows and stone roller. From the corner of the byre that night as he *muckit* his beasts, the old man would watch this final movement in the orchestration of the spring sowing, grudging the lone Clydesdale's hoofmarks on his land but thankful, all the same, that his corn was in.

The old stubble would lie till May, its furrows baked grey, before it came time to prepare Willie Gavin's turnip shift; to set up its drills and cart out the dung to them from the croft midden. That was not a horseman's favourite job and he would be glad to see the end of it. He would give the crofter man and his wife a day or two to spread the dung along the bottom of the rows before returning to 'split the drills' and cover it, and run the turnip-seed barrow over it. That, too, did not take him long and he would have time for a *news* with Grannie Gavin when she brought out his afternoon tea. He would leave a drill or two in the shift for the Gavins' potatoes: in the 1930s, the Duke of York earlies the old man liked would take half a drill; his maincrop, Kerr's Pink, equally well favoured in that old countryside of stark farmtouns and hardy men, or the great Golden Wonder. Willie Gavin had always had a good word on them, small in size though they usually were. He could hardly let you eat your Sabbath dinner without praising their quality so highly that the occasional guest might well go away believing he had invented them.

Like most of the farm and croft men, Willie Gavin liked his turnips sown by the May Term (28 May) and he was late, and a laughing stock, if they weren't. But that done, he was a happy man. He had seen the last of a Clydesdale on his land till the back-end of the year. For his turnip-singling and their second-hoeing (to keep the weeds down between the rows), the hay-making and the harvest were his own. Apart from his wife, his children and anybody who had been unwise enough to marry into the family and could filially be inveigled, he needed no-body's labour.

Likely he could little afford it. His bill from Laverockhill over the years between the wars for the contract work of the spring cultivations and the turnip-seed sowing had risen steeply, from £4 in 1914 to £20 in 1939. The increase may have reflected the hard times then hitting the farmtouns and even Laverockhill's need to turn a penny wherever he could, even if it was at the expense of the crofter men; it certainly did not reflect in the wage his horseman got: in the 1930s that was being cut with almost every six-monthly feeing market. And the crofter folk were no better off. The time now might be long past when after a bad hairst or on their entry into the tenancy of a croft they had to go thigging for the seed corn or begging from the kirk's girnal to sow their parks. But there were good reasons still why the croft shifts never got all the manure they needed.

The Bloo Coo Economy

A crofter's cow was squeezed for every drop of milk it would give, morning, noon and night, and that even into the 1930s, long after the thrice-daily milking had been abandoned by all but the smallest and most impoverished of the neighbouring farm-touns. But the reason was not hard to find, for his beasts, and his milk cows especially, were at the very centre of the crofter's lifestyle, and the basis of his economy. It had always been so, in the eastern Lowlands no less than in the Highlands: they gave him milk and butter and cheese for his household (and maybe to sell to the grocer when times were good) and, more important still, a calf apiece, every year. It was his stirks – his young steers – that paid the crofter's rent. That, at least, was the commonly held belief and Willie Gavin held hard to those old-proven principles. He kept two *bloo coos*, the North-Eastern crofter's traditional animal, slatey-grey beasts whose antecedents were as obscure as those of the crofter folk themselves but whose ability to give a calf each spring could never be despised.

Willie Gavin was mindful of that, as his father had been. When he had the longest day of the year behind him he would take his milk beasts up through the fields to Laverockhill on a rope halter. It was an undertaking hedged round with indecision and for a week or two beforehand he would be asking his visitors, as they took their stroll through the Sunday fields, whether they considered this or that beast sufficiently in heat. It was a delicate question for the middle of a Sabbath afternoon – and for a farmtoun lad who had come to see one of the old man's daughters and might be shy about airing a knowledge that in another context could be held against him.

In fact, it mattered little, for Laverockhill's bull was an accommodating beast at any time and always very willing. A docile animal, who would never have been allowed between the covers of any pedigree stock book, he had offspring in nearly every field in the parish. Laverockhill, maybe aware of the poor brute's lack of breeding, even in the 1930s was charging only a fee of five shillings or so for each service. Indeed, he said affably whiles, the beast was a damned disgrace and a constant embarrassment to him, charging good money for the likes of that when most folk did it for nothing. Sometimes he would waive all payment if Willie Gavin had been '*verra* reasonable' in his account for some small job about the farmtoun.

Old Hector rarely disappointed, and come the end of March or thereabouts Willie Gavin, if he had a young cow that year, might be as often in the byre at nights as in his own bed as he waited for the beast to calve. He was kind to his beasts; a lot kinder than he was to his family, folk said. If he was, he reflected only the hard calculating life of the crofter man and the wealth (no different from that of the African tribesman) that lay in his livestock. He might rise twice through the night, sleepily pulling on his *breeks*, pushing his bare feet into the chill of his heavy boots and throwing his jacket over his shoulders – and lighting the byre lantern, set ready on the kitchen table, on the way out. Going down the close, the cold night mist on his face would wake him, or worse still, the steady drizzle of a grey morning. But the byre would be warm with the breath of beasts when he stepped into it, shutting the door behind him. Edging up the side of his young beast in the stall he would swing the lantern over its head, rubbing its neck, his voice soothing.

'Foo are ye, lass, eh?'

In a moment the young cow would have swivelled her head, turning a large and docile eye up at him to reassure him: *Not yet.* And thus satisfied, Willie Gavin would pull the lapels of his jacket across the front of his flannel *sark* and head back for the house and his bed. Not always though. If the eye that looked up at him betrayed the slightest trace of alarm he would settle down on some straw in a dry corner of the byre, his back against the white limewash of its wall, and take his pipe and tobacco mull from his pocket, to wait. His vigil, even so, might be long and to no avail; in the morning Grannie Gavin would find him, fast asleep, his head pillowed in his bonnet against the wall.

Once, in his old grandmother's time, if not his father's, it had been a woman's job to calve the cow, whether her man was at home or not. But that had been in the time long past when the event had been veiled in superstition and as fraught with portent as the first furrow of autumn. Round the crofts and the small farmtouns then, they too had sat in the byre so that their bloo coos would not feel lonely. Up-country, where the past was dark and not always to be inquired into, the beast had been prepared for calving with the titbit of a *quarter* of oatcake dowsed in whisky (which was more than any croft wife got in a similar predicament) and rewarded afterwards with a helping of 'pottage'. And the tribute to the old gods did not end there: for the first milking a shilling would be set into the bottom of the milk pail and to compound the magic and keep the witches from the byre door the croft wife would remove her wedding ring to milk the first few 'strains' from each teat through it. If Willie Gavin had heard of such things and could smile at them now, he would have known their reason and their origin: they too were rooted deep in the crofter's dependence on stock.

The bloo coos, their care and their keep, dominated the crofting day and kept every croft wife in thraldom: Grannie Gavin's first out-job after lighting the fire would be the morning milking – and the milking was almost her last task at night. When she shut the milkhouse door in an evening, she said whiles, it was like putting the lid on another day of her life. Rain or shine, his beasts extended Willie Gavin's working day, the first and last concern almost of his waking hours. As a working mason, in the winter months he would give his byre beasts their breakfast before he took his own, leaving his wife to fill their troughs at midday. Home at night, he might feed them before ever going in for his own supper. And even the Sabbath brought no respite, as it did with the other croft work. Willie Gavin's father had compromised, whether from fear of the Free Kirk's wrath or due to his own natural indolence, it is hard to say: he milked his beasts but they got leave to lie in the filth they themselves had created until Monday. His son was less fastidious about the one, more concerned about the other: he muckit his bloo coos and their byre Sabbath or no.

For all but a short time in the spring, while one cow was ready to calve and the other had gone dry (when the Gavins would have to beg from a neighbour) there was always milk on a crofter's table, though there might be neither eggs nor fowl nor any of the other things his holding produced. There was milk in abundance just after the calves were born, a fine surplus that brought a spurt of butter- and cheese-making. The calves themselves would take about a half-gallon each in a day but that still left plenty and Willie Gavin, like most of the crofter men, would look round for an extra calf to get the good of it – one a day or two old from a nearby dairytoun perhaps, where they were hardly concerned about stock-rearing. In the 1930s, the calf would cost about £2 10s (£2.50) and so long as the milk yield kept up for three months or so, the gamble became a bonus, for at that age the calves would be *coggit* (weaned) and put on to a little hay and turnips chipped small with the *hasher* Willie Gavin had made (from an old scythe blade) or sliced, when he was in a hurry, with his knife. There might still be a little milk for them, too, for the crofter's system allowed a slower transition than the rougher world of the farmtouns.

The crofter man fed his beasts well, giving them some oilcake in with their feed when he could afford it. He was a great believer, too, in the properties of rock salt, and kept a slab always beside the beasts' trough. His belief in the salts was proverbial. They did harm, he claimed (forever seeking converts), to neither man nor beast, and though some folk would have violently disagreed with him, he set an example by dosing himself regularly – with salts for human consumption. They fairly cleaned out the system, he said.

He turned his cows out to grass about the middle of May, certainly not later than the Term Day at the end of the month, depending on the condition of his pasture, and took them back into the byre for the winter before the end of October. Now and then, in open defiance of both the law and the county council he would tether a beast at the roadside to take the lush abundance of the verge in advance of the roadman's scythe (it was a criminal waste otherwise), as most of the crofter men did. Housed, his beasts' feed was *neeps and strae* (turnips and straw) – the diet that fattened many a fine beast for the London dinner table – with a handful or two of hay pulled from the stack at the end of the day, to sweeten the milk and maybe boost the yield.

Not all the crofters' cows were bloo coos. Some were as black as Auld Nick and about as reliable and there were brown cows as well, all equally undistinguished by any sign of good breeding. It was getting into the 1920s before the pure-breds of the dairy-touns began to make their impact on the crofting scene and the crofter men considered what they could do with the yield of an Ayrshire or a Friesian, sometimes double the old bloo coo's daily one and a half to two gallons.

There was something sad about putting the bloo coos away after so many decades of faithful service, but even the most loyal crofter man, with all his conservatism, could no longer ignore the benefits of the pure-bred beasts. About any croft their extra milk was a godsend and for a time the neighbouring dairytouns faced a brisk demand for their heifer calves. Willie Gavin though was in no hurry to put his bloo coos away, and it was into the 1930s before he did so. Then, traditionalist though he was, he could no longer afford the allegiance. With stern patriotism he switched to Ayrshires.

Not all of them were as docile as his old bloo coos had been. Now and then a young beast, annoyed by Grannie Gavin's attentions, would flick a *shamy* tail round her ears, content with that as a protest. But some were less easily pleased, and at times milker, pail and stool would be sent flying by a kicker and Grannie Gavin's return to the house would be delayed while she searched for her glasses among the beast's bedding straw.

'Gin ye bring home another beastie like that, Willie Gavin,' she would threaten him whiles, 'ye will get tae milk it yersel.' Mostly, she would have little to say about it, or about the black bruise on her hip for a week or two after. It was a part of her life and always had been.

The croft men sold their stirks at a year old – certainly at no more than eighteen months – to any farmer who came seeking them and showed a willingness to pay something approaching their worth. Though the croft men might be in sore need of the siller and not always in a position to haggle, the dealing would be hard. Yet the farmer seldom got the worst of the bargain; he knew that always there came the time, a point finely judged, when the tide turned for the old crofter man and the beast would begin to eat him out of any profit he might have expected to show on it. It was not feasible to keep the stirk longer: he had neither the feed nor the siller for such a long-term investment.

But again, if he preferred to, the crofter could sell to the cattle-dealers who also came round to his door regularly with reasoned and quiet inducement; men skilled in the salesman's glib art who would give him no more in the end of the day than the farmer. For they, too, were looking for easy pickings in a hard-up society and if the time and the price were about right the crofter man could do nothing but strike a bargain. With the sale agreed, the croft men would let their beasts go when the drover men came round to collect them. Local droving continued for some years after the motor float was a common sight on the country road flitting the stock of the farmtouns, for the protracted gathering of the crofters' beasts would have made its hire for that purpose an expensive business. The float, for all that, was a fine innovation: it saved the leather of the servant lass's boots as she dragged an unwilling beast to market at the end of a rope halter and kept her where she was doing good, in her mistress's kitchen. In time it would put an end, too, to the drover men; though their droving was far different from those earlier times when the beef of that countryside had gone south on the hoof to the old trysts, they were the last of their kind and would become as redundant as the wandering packman.

But there was another reason why the crofter men had to accept the dealers' prices, and it was an important consideration: few could afford to take a day off from their regular work to take their stock to the market. And even there the crofter's stirk rarely made the price of a farmtoun beast.

With the hens that squawked in the croft ree – impatient to be let out to scavenge in the stubble or screich in the cornyard – his milk cows and his stirks were Willie Gavin's only stock. It had not always been so about the Gavin croft. Indeed, folk said, looking back to Old John's days, there had been a time when it had seemed more like a menagerie. Then the poultry was to be seen at any time of the day picking the titbits out of the roof thatch of the old dwelling and perched on its low chimneys getting their glossy feathers sooted with fire reek. One of his granddaughters who came to marry a banking man remembers the croft as it was in the early days of the century, with humour if not with affection:

> The stock consisted of a horse that did as it liked, two cows and a calf, the usual hens, and turkeys that laid away. They [her grandparents] also kept a pig or two . . . and my mother would walk to market with a pig in a poke slung across her back, presumably to be sold. To reach the byre from the field the cows had to pass in front of the house and they seemed to save up their excreta so as to liberate it as they passed the house door.

Well, there were many things about the crofting life that never changed, and even in Willie Gavin's time it was always advisable to take a lantern to light your feet through the dark.

The grandson who was Old John's constant companion through the summer months during that same time also remembers the old croft life, and Old John's livestock in particular:

> They had a couple of milk cows and they had a few stirks (steers we would call them today), half-grown beasts. When they got close to maturity they would sell them, of course, for beef stock. And they had two or three calves . . . They had a horse there, and a pig-pen, too, where they kept a couple of hogs and maybe a few pigs from time to time. They also kept a lot of poultry, my grandfather and grandmother. They usually had a bunch of turkeys. They were all for sale. And they had a whole bunch of chickens and they kept guinea fowl for quite a while – for their eggs.

And it hadn't ended there, for besides his collection of hoof and claw, some of the old croft's stock was on the wing. Old John's grandson again:

> My grandmother was a great bee-woman, really adept as a bee-keeper, and produced quite a lot of honey. She would prowl around amidst all her hives – she had quite a few, maybe fifteen to twenty, I cannot recollect exactly – and she would never wear a bee-veil or a glove on her hand. They would never sting her – her hands, her arms, would be covered with them – she would never pay any attention to them. My grandfather though, he wouldn't go near them; he was terror-stricken if he was asked to step inside where they were located.

Willie Gavin would inherit from his mother, along with much else of her character, her fearlessness of bees and when she grew frail he took over her skeps, keeping four or five right up to the end of his days. When the hardy old woman died it was he who went out to the bees to tell them.

8

The Heartbreak Life

A crofter's day was never-ending. If he were also the smith, the
tailor, a mason man or a dyker it stretched regularly to sixteen
hours or more through the summer months and was only
fractionally shorter during winter. Even then, many of the old
North-East Lowlands crofter men pulled their beasts' turnips
from the frozen drill when they came home from work, if not
by the light of the moon by the fitful gleam of an oil or candle
lantern. On any hillside crofting colony on a dark night their
lights could be seen, bobbing like will o' the wisps about the
brae-face, a sight that raised pity in the heart and poignantly
underlined the wretchedness of their lifestyle. For the poor
croft man had little choice, especially as he grew older and his
children moved away and his wife became frail with the
fullness of years and unable to help him with any but the
lightest of the work.

Always he was a man on a treadmill; he didn't dare stop. So
interrelated were all the strands of his simple agriculture – his
cropping and stock-rearing – that if he broke the momentum
even for a season, his fragile economy shattered. For his system
had, acutely, all the inherent disadvantages of subsistence farming; he was a man without margins, in land or capital, without
room to manoeuvre. His was a delicate structure, one part so
diabolically dependent on another: his crops fed his beasts which
refertilised his shifts which grew their feed . . . When his rotation
slipped or a crop failed his whole lifestyle faltered or was thrown

wildly into an imbalance whose outcome was unpredictable; for that, in turn, put him at the mercy of outside forces which were never favourable to him, that even, at times, viewed his self-sufficiency with antagonism, or outright enmity. There were in the North-East Lowlands no short cuts the crofter men could take in following the cultivation pattern of the proud farmtouns (incongruous though that parallel seems); there was no stream-lining possible that would successfully guarantee an on-going crofting viability, far less the maintenance of a modest stability – beyond the kind of speculation that took a holding right out of the crofting pattern and into a world entirely under the sway of those other, alien factors.

It was the stark understanding of this, perhaps unformulated and unreasoned but congenitally understood, that would take a croft man out of his warm bed and into the fields when society folk were hardly home from the ball, and drove him indoors on a summer night only as darkness fell.

There were times when Willie Gavin must have thought himself luckier than most for during the dark of winter when the fierce frosts settled in that pre-chemical age and made the lime-mortar unworkable, there would be few masoning jobs he could do. If he was working away the onset of deep-winter days brought him home to stay for weeks at a time – as it did all the other masoning men of that countryside, even those who had gone to America. They came home with all the siller they had made from their skills with stone. There are songs still in that bare countryside's ballad books that celebrate the return of those masoning men to their small village communities and the arms of their hopeful (and determined) sweethearts, lasses who spurned the ploughman and even the smith and knew the fine life they could have as the mason's wife – if he were not also a crofter man:

I winna hae the sailor
  That sails on the sea;
Nor yet will I the ploughman
  That ploughs on the lea;
But I will hae the mason,
  For he's a bonnie lad,
And I'll wash the mason's apron,
  And think it nae degrade.

I winna hae the blacksmith
  That burns a' the airn;
Nor yet will I the weaver
  That works the creeshy yarn;
But I will hae the mason
  And the mason he'll hae me,
And the bonnie mason laddie
  I'll mount the scaffold wi'.

On the dreichest days there would be little that Willie Gavin could do about his shifts or around his small steading, and there was little he would *have* to do unless winter came early and caught him unprepared. Then he might be out in the snow-covered parks, digging to find the neeps for his byre beasts, stopping from time to time to blow some warmth back into his mittened hands and stamp feeling again into his feet where the ground struck cold through even the thick soles of his tacketed ploughman's boots and their lining of straw, and the heavy woollen socks Grannie Gavin was constantly knitting for her menfolk. (For an outdoor man in a cold countryside they were a godsend and almost better than a bottle of whisky in your hip pocket.)

But Willie Gavin was a cautious man and it was seldom that winter caught him unawares. Usually, like the best-run farm-

touns around him, he would have a *fordel*, a cache, of turnips
barrowed home and clamped against the back of the house
(under the old thatch from a rick) before the days of storm came
on him. There were days, certainly, when he might look out
from the kitchen window to watch McCaskill foraging to find a
bite for his stirks in a steady *on-ding* of snow and be pleased at his
own careful nature. When the beige ribbon road to the kirktoun
had filled with snow wreaths quite beyond the conquest of short
legs, he would yoke Meggie, his father's old shelt, into the shafts
of the sleigh to take the bairns to the school and out of their
mother's way – and maybe, too, because he had a wonderful
belief in the 'learning' and all the doors it could open. (He had
been a willing scholar, encouraged by his mother; a clever boy
among country lads who had cared little for their sums and
already saw their futures clearly before them: the rough life of a
farmtoun bothy until such time as a lass might make a home for
them somewhere.) In the right humour the crofter man might
order a bag of bran or a roll of wire-netting from the merchant's
in the kirktoun for a harder-pressed neighbour, picking it up
when he returned in the late afternoon to fetch the children. But
he was not known as an obliging man and people thought twice
about approaching him, so savage was he about anything that
foresight might have avoided.

Yet gradually even a hard winter passed, its unaccustomed ease
marred for the mason man only by the worry that there was siller
going out and none coming in. He would be pleased enough to
see the spring when it came and to get back to his chisels and
trowels – cycling away by four in the chill dark of a Monday
morning to start his week's work at six, fifteen miles away. It was
the last his wife would see or hear of him until the Saturday
afternoon. Then with luck he might be home an hour or two
before dusk and in time to put the top of a rick through the
threshing mill to get straw for the Sabbath and the following

week. Like most of the crofter-tradesmen, however, Willie
Gavin preferred to work in his own parish, or failing that, in
the ones that adjoined it. That let him home each night to keep
up with his croft work, though doubtless there were croft men
who were pleased to be in their own beds for other reasons. It
would be a slack season of the year, or a night of driving rain, if
the croft man was seated by his fireside before eight in the
evening.

If spring brought the Clydesdales onto his ground, summer
brought its own kind of frenzy for the croft folk themselves.
There might be a pause in the year when the neep seed had been
sown and before the hoeing began, but not for Willie Gavin and
the other crofter men. There was never an evening when they
could not find a necessary chore in their shifts (repairing the
fencing) or round their biggings (maybe tidying the cornyard).

It was with the singling of turnips, the *hyowing* (to use the
word from that now-distant landscape) that the rush began,
towards the start of July. By then, the turnip seed of mid-May
would be well brairded, running (in those days of uncertain
germination) like thickening threads down the length of the
broad drills, burgeoning almost as you watched.

There were crofter men who rose at four in the morning to
hoe a drill or two before they cycled off to their regular work,
and there was hardly a creature about the Gavin croft – man,
woman or child – who could not handle a hoe, and who did not
have to. Sons who had gone to be *orra loon* at some farmtoun, or
were apprenticed away and learning trades where the future
looked brighter, would be summoned home for an evening or
two and given a hoe into their hands to hyow a drill or two;
cottared sons-in-law who had been hyowing all day would cycle
down with their hoes for an evening stint at the same job,
remembering that earlier time when they had come to see the
old man's daughters and been given a hyow into their hands

instead. For there had never been any doubt but that a lad's skill with the hoe had recommended him to the crofter's notice when it came to considering his lasses' future. Even the non-farming visitor could find himself enlisted (there was always time to news, the crofter man promised him, quite truthfully), and just as willingly a hoe shaft would be shortened for any grandchild who showed the slightest aptitude or the inclination to learn. Its sex was immaterial, as was its age. But that was no grandfather's indulgence; Willie Gavin wanted good work even if all he was paying for it was a pandrop from his pocket when they came to the endrig. Keen though he was to have fine neeps, however, Willie Gavin was never in a hurry to lift them; if his circumstances had permitted it he would have let them lie in the drill (fattening, as he believed) into the New Year. But they were ready by the end of October and unlike the farmtoun men, who could feed tares to their stock in the meantime, Willie Gavin needed his turnips from the moment his beasts were housed for winter.

Croft folk were hardly out of the hyowing before they were into the hay-making, which was almost as frantic. The crofter man made his hay in a hurry and while the weather held. By the time he was spotted on the road on his way home from his day's work, his supper porridge would be cooling on the windowsill so as to be about the right temperature by the time he reached home and set his bicycle against the wall beside it. There were nights indeed when Willie Gavin did no more than cry in at the window for the spoon to sup it with and for some quarters of oatcake and a hunk of cheese to follow it. He ate the porridge where he stood and took to the hay park with the oatcake and cheese in his hand, never setting foot in the house until the dusk drove him in. His hay-making, in that time before the machine-baler let alone the nutrient-sealing grass-drier, followed the traditional pattern: cut with the scythe, it lay for a day or two in the bout before being raked into wider windrows and dragged into small *coles* (haycocks) and finally into big coles before being ricked in the old man's cornyard. Though help was less urgent than for the hoeing, the old man could always find a visitor a spare hayfork – and there was always a bairn more than willing to *trump* a cole or a rick for him. If not, there was always Grannie Gavin, called from the house just as she settled with her knitting or with her behindhand sewing.

But then the croft life had always been hard on the woman. If Willie Gavin's day was long, his wife's was even longer; lengthier even than the working day of the servant lasses fee'd home to the farmtouns – and that was scandalous enough. Grannie Gavin was up and lighting the fire before the kitchen clock struck five and had her crofter man's brose kettle on to boil before he had swung his legs over the side of the closet bed. It was a high bed, and when she left it, over its bottom board, it was as a fugitive or an escaping prisoner. So as not to disturb him too soon, she stepped down first to a conveniently placed chair and then to the closet floor. For long enough her role, like that of all the other croft wives, took her back into the dark of history and the slavery of the old cot-touns of that earlier landscape where the women had sheared and stooked, carried the muck and the peat, and done a whole host of other duties through a day without end. The croft wives, too, did all those tasks, long after the censure of society and a new social awareness had outlawed their continuance even in the rough world of the farmtouns. If some of them became hard cases, as rough diamonds as any of their menfolk, that is little to be wondered at, for it was a life that turned the bonniest lass prematurely into the aged crone. In their lace mutches, most of them went grim-faced to the kirk, but in a life that robbed them so often of their womanly grace it would be surprising if some of them at least had not, long since, lost all faith in it.

With her man away all day – and often all week – Grannie Gavin did much of the everyday, outdoor croft work: hoeing, turning the hay in the swath, mucking the byre beasts, pulling the turnips from the drill and even bringing them home in the barrow, small woman though she was. Through the rush of her man's small hairst and while the weather held she came in from the fields only to prepare their simple meals. Her daughters, when they came of age, learned to do the same and never questioned it.

There was a job for everybody in that old crofting landscape with its ceaseless pattern of work, even for Daft Sandy. When the threshing mill came its croft rounds shortly before the New Year, his help was constantly sought. The night before, the croft men would walk along to his folk's place in the evening gloam to ask could he be sent in the morning, for Daft Sandy had that uncanny compensating gift of the weak-minded: a strength that could hurl heavy sacks of corn about as though they were feather pillows. They were damned glad to have him for they were all of them older men than they had been and not a few of them already broken with work.

Daft Sandy would work as though seeking pardon for his life, speaking continuously to himself – raging it seemed – in some high tongue of another time that nobody could understand. He carried the corn and sometimes cleared the chaff as well from the mill's dusty underbelly. And folk were careful to nod to him whiles (whenever he looked their way) to humour him, and would get the beam of his soft smile in return: they knew if he broke loose there was no one could hold him.

That need never arose though and at the end of a mill day Daft Sandy would go home like a king with a shilling or two in his pocket that the croft man had given him. That night, like many a night, when you passed his folk's place, he might be at the top of the close or hanging over the garden gate – singing to the moon.

Grannie Gavin had never liked the croft life; most of all, as a young wife with her children at school and her husband away maybe for the week, she had found its isolation and the silence of the countryside unbearable and terrifying. Long after, she would confess to the fear and loneliness of dark winter afternoons, a fear that had driven her repeatedly to stand at the head of the Whinfield croft-close in the hope that she might spot – somewhere on that grey landscape – another human soul (a tink on the road, some shepherd walking the hill fields) or, listening, hear the carry of a human voice or a dog's bark on the wind.

That had been in their earlier crofting days, when her man was not long into his father's croft. A grim poverty had stalked their days and want was the constant grey ghost of their lives. With the legacy the old man had left them – leaking biggings and the lack of fences, and a shelt that did as little as it could to earn its keep – it could hardly have been otherwise. From the moment of his occupation Willie Gavin's family had known what it was to be grindingly poor. There were times when they almost lost hope. 'It was nothing but hunger, misery and want,' Grannie Gavin would say, long years later and in widowhood, when she had left the life behind her. Good Christian though she was, even then she would be unable to keep the bitterness out of her voice. It was a life that had robbed her of all leisure, completely.

There were nights when, too tired to sleep, her mind had gone back to the days of her young girlhood and the times in the 1870s when she had visited her grandfather's place in the old crofting colony of Lumphanan's Perk Hill. Lying in the closet dark at Willie Gavin's side, she would remember her grandmother's advice as she had straightened her back for a moment in shearing her man's meagre corn with the old heuk:

'Never marry a crofter, lassie, for it's nae life at all. What comes in fae this year's hairst, will gang oot for next year's seed.'

And so it had proved; croft solvency was often that delicately balanced.

Willie Gavin's first harvests, threshed out, brought little more than the seed to re-sow and the price of just a little of the manure the sour ground so urgently needed. It seemed for a time that they might all be into the poorhouse, and to keep them out of it young Jess MacKendrick had fallen back on something she could do superbly: her sewing. With her croft chores done, inside and out, she picked up her needle, sewing till midnight by the feeble light of a candle – till she could no longer see the material and was ready to fall off the stool with exhaustion. It was a time still when men's shirts were hand-made in the countryside. Many a farmtoun wife augmented the family's income with such sewing and the young croft wife's skill soon brought her more work than she had time for. Yet she dared not turn it away. Glad of the money it would bring in, she would think nothing of the ten-mile walk that meant an afternoon's mending at the grieve's house on a big farmtoun. And when war came she would continue – making shirts for the soldiers. They were much like the shirts she had always made, except for their colour; maybe they went onto the backs of the same men, the fee'd lads of the farmtouns who had left their brown cords lying on some bothy floor to put on the king's khaki. But that was something she would never know. During the four years of war she made over 400 shirts in her spare time on the old German-made sewing machine she had earlier bought to help her keep up with the work that came her way. When it was over, the army gave her a medal and the Gavins were still in the croft.

9

The Weaver's Lass

Marriage to a crofter man was an indenture into slavery. It had always been so, and Jess MacKendrick had known it. Though she was come of weaver folk there had never been a time when, like Willie Gavin himself, she had not had a foothold in the crofting past of that North-East countryside and known what the croft life was like. She had come down into Willie Gavin's bare landscape from the Donside uplands where the air was fine and the Highlands began; there, even now, boarded and silent and high above the stream that once gave it life, stands the wool mill that her folk once worked.

The old mill ran in its heyday and for long after that on the skill of the MacKendricks and closed, some years since, almost as the last of them left it. It weathered the years better than most of its kind because the quality of its goods was exceptional, the best for many miles round, and they found a quick sale over the best London store counters, where the mark-up reflected the standard of the work rather than the standard of living of the folk who made them. Always the siller it made had gone into somebody else's pocket, but if its business from time to time took the MacKendricks away (maybe to London for a week to speak with storebuyers) they were as pleased to be home again.

With its sluice unworked, its sightless windows and rusting belt pulleys, the blue wooden mill has become the sad derelict of a newer industrial age, a reminder only of the former self-containment of that uplands countryside. Farther on up the hill is the old MacKendrick croft, Scrapehard, a pleasant cottage now, flower-garlanded on its knoll, with a view of the Highland hills. It carries no memory of bitterness, for Jess MacKendrick's father showed all the sound sense of an intelligent man – and a reconciliation with things as they were – by giving up his croft land to a neighbouring farmtoun, a renunciation of the old style of crofting existence that avoided the spiritual rupture of running two lives, and an action that brings him down to our time as a reasonable man and a realist to boot. He had not even kept his own cow, unusual in that time, and had been happy to carry his milk from the byre of the man who worked his land. The arrangement had suited the weaver man well: not for him the trial and the despair of that old dichotomy of cultivation and commerce which so blighted the lives of his cronies.

But not all the MacKendricks were weavers. Early sons, like Jess herself, had been forced out into the world and soon like their father showed some singularity or oddity of character: one was a sawmiller who flattened woodlands as other men sheared corn; one, a carpenter-turned-coffin-maker in London; and yet another, also in the metropolis, stood constantly tailed and frock-coated in the women's fashion department of a top Oxford Street store though later, for reasons that were never discussed in the family, he left hurriedly for the backwoods of Canada, to settle down finally as a market-gardener in Manitoba. There, he lost everything (including his false teeth) in a prairie fire. It was a blow that might have felled a lesser man, but not that bold MacKendrick. Out of the chaos (and the insurance), he returned to his original store-minding trade; he raised first one shop and then another, and then, in partnership, a whole chain. The good-looking weaver's lad had come a long way from his early beginnings in the old bigging above the mill and whatever had happened in that London store those long years ago (and likely the society woman had encouraged him, folk said), it had done him nothing but good. Only the later MacKendrick daughters and a delicate son whom the weaver had fathered as an afterthought had been needed to staff the mill. Their nephew would remember not only their skills but the old mill, its operation, and its reputation:

> They used to buy up all the wool from folk who brought it in from the country all round there. They would card it and tease it and do all the usual procedures needed to convert it into a good high-grade woollen worsted used in knitting and in the manufacture of all kind of woven materials. They were experts on the machines, these aunts of mine, they could do all kinds of weaving, any intricate pattern you could dream of. They made all kinds of Scots tartans – all the popular tartans. They were really adept in that particular field. They used to produce very good quality blankets, too, in this woollen mill and my crofting mother and father used to buy these from the mill periodically – though not that frequently, since they invariably lasted a lifetime. But the climate of that old countryside was such that a warm blanket was an asset and appreciated in any home.

Jess MacKendrick, as the eldest, had been less fortunate than her sisters, her childhood typically that of a country bairn of her time. Her humble academy was the *fummlers' skweel*, the girls' school, nestling its red-tiled roof among encircling trees where the broad farming strath began to draw in its flanks to become a landscape of smaller brae-set fields and the road took to the high Cabrach moorland. Miss Myers' school took twenty pupils at a time; like most of its kind it was unashamedly fee-paying and without hint of government envy or interference – which was as well, for the way Miss Myers ran it, it might as well have been a military academy. Fortnightly or monthly (depending on the social credibility of the pupil's family) she took from them the 6d (2½p) or 1s (5p) to pay for their learning and daily from each the peat from her father's peatstack or the lump of coal that would keep the schoolroom fire burning and on a wet day dry out their clothes before it came time for them all to go home again.

Weaver man though he was, there seems to have been some doubt about Jess MacKendrick's father's standing: his daughter carried her sixpence fortnightly in the pocket of her inmost petticoat, wrapped (in case she should lose it) in a page from *The People's Journal*, the weekly newspaper that served that uplands countryside and whose lum-hatted reporters tore round it regularly in their pursuit of every titbit of scandal it would yield (and that could be reliably attributed). It was the only news-sheet that MacKendrick allowed to darken his door and besides the obvious, its uses were endless, for every day of the week in another of its pages Jess carried her lunchtime piece: dry oatcakes.

If Miss Myers' regime was rigid and ultra-strict there was no doubt that it got the kind of results that would have gladdened any latter-day dominie's heart. It was what her customers were paying for. She hammered home the tenets of basic arithmetic with the thumping insistence of a big bass drum; hardened the outlines of history in the mind with the dates that only death itself would erase; and managed at times to lift the long recitation of a multiplication table in the dark of a winter's afternoon to the sonorous chant of high mass.

A little farther along the road, in the separate boys' school, Mr Pithy reigned like an emperor, ready to thrash any pupil within an inch of his life for a misguided subtraction, and it was here that the MacKendrick brothers were similarly prepared for the hard business of life in the same unrelenting routine. In the circumstances the weaver's family, aware of where their best interests lay, turned into excellent scholars and emerged more than willing to take on the world as they found it.

So, it had been neither lack of scholastic ambition nor ability that had ended the young Jess MacKendrick's education at the age of ten. Far from it. It had been that ancient necessity of a hard countryside: the need for the eldest of the family to earn its own crust (and maybe contribute to the economy of the home) at the earliest age. And the siller that paid for her schooling had been hard to find from her father's income with brothers and sisters rising behind her, all of them with an equal claim. Yet even then, it had seemed for a moment that the weaver's lass, though she might not realise her heart's wish of becoming a nurse, would at least escape the endless drudgery of the old farmtoun and crofting life.

Her first job had taken her as maid into the home of a woman who was herself a retired lady's maid. Miss Barclay was out of the same mould as Miss Myers; she stood as straight as a stick in her stays, severe and unbending, withering reprimand forever on her lips. Home safely at last from being a 'companion' to a lady of quality in Italy (where the hot blood had seemed constantly a threat to her spinsterhood), she paid the weaver's girl only 15s (75p) each half-year but, in guilt for such parsimony, gave her instruction – a fine finishing to her education, almost – in all the graces of the tea-table and the drawing room as well as a fine pronunciation of the Auld Queen's English and a liking for the higher caste of religion that was preached in the parish's little Episcopal kirk. This the servant lass attended with her mistress on Sunday evenings, imbibing the grace of its litanies and the gentler modulations of its minister, who saw sin in simpler terms than the Free Kirk did and plainly, in that direction, expected less of his flock.

But Miss Barclay's wisdom, after all, would do the Free Kirk weaver's lass little good. At the age of twelve she was needed elsewhere: to help on her grandfather's croft. Just when it seemed that her future lay in refined service and in the lifestyle of a different kind of society, destiny had turned Jess MacKendrick back to the crofting background from which her family had emerged. After the faded gentility of Miss Barclay's way of life, it was a harsh awakening.

On her grandfather's croft on the bare Perk Hill of Lumphanan, her grandmother, worn by the life and soured by its bitterness, had no wish to hear the Queen's fine English spoken in her kitchen, still less in her byre, and as for the Episcopal kirk, that was damned nearly halfway to Rome anyway. And lady of small deceits though she was, she thought a traycloth an extravagance far beyond the needs of common crofter folk, and maybe even, in its way, a kind of betrayal.

There had, after all, been no escape for the young Jess MacKendrick and even today it is easy to summon into the mind that grey landscape of her youth. The brae-face of the Perk Hill still betrays a little of its crofting past. Its fields, still, are somewhat small and awkwardly set, a reminder in a modern farming age of the days of the crofter men; beneath the trim and harled exterior of the low, single-storey dwellings – even those with the dormer windows of their cramped garrets poked through the roofs – it is not difficult to discern the shape of the old but-and-ben house that once occupied the site. But roof-thatch or red tiles has long been replaced by the cold conformity of grey slates and the seemlier sanitation of a more sophisticated age has added its agglomeration of bathrooms abutting and adjoining. And the years of attrition and farming progress have long driven the old-style smallholder men from the hill and dispersed what was once a colony typical of the North-East's crofting communities.

It was a countryside always where the past lay uneasily in wait for the future, its settlement long a staging post in the affairs of men, its inn as important as its old kirk. The kirk had long been there, bringing men in from the country far round on the

Sabbath for the good of their souls, but it was at its inn that the travelling folk of that old countryside sought their first sustenance and their succour after coming over some high pass of the Grampians or fording the dangerous Dee; they sought its shelter before night fell on them, before they pressed north on the old highway. To and fro down the years they had come and gone on their endless errands, the preacher, the packman (the one as vital as the other), the soldier and the wastrel, the thief on his way to grace the gallows tree. Whatever their station they had been glad of the old inn and the kirk that stood by it, a beacon lit in the dark days of the seventh century by Saint Finan as he passed that way, a seeker for the souls of men. His association with the lonely hamlet would descend the centuries in the tortured Gaelic that first gave the kirktoun its name. Among the many who came through on the old road, north and south as their destinies drove them, was another who was more sinner than saint and whose name would adorn the darker cloak of history. They called him Maelbetha; he was Mormaer of Moray. He was going north in a hurry, and with vengeance at his heels; though he did not know it then, he was nearing his journey's end. The man fleeing that fine summer day of 1057 was the chief that an English bard would pass down to our time as Macbeth. His crime was old but it had lain long in his mind: an old man's death, seventeen years since. It had gained him a crown but never the peace to enjoy it. Now the man they called the Red King, old Duncan's murderer, had pursuit behind him; in the words of old Wyntoun, the chronicler now of such far-off things:

> Owre the Mounth thai chast hym than
> Til the wode of Lumfanan.

It was 15 August and the warrior who engaged the 52-year-old usurper of a kingdom in single combat was Macduff. The district has, still, its memorials to that day and its encounter: though Shakespeare took the scene of that action to the woods of Dunsinane (captivated perhaps by their more mellifluous sound but cynically contorting history) he would hardly be able to transpose the wells or the burial cairn that carried the rebel king's name and where tradition had buried him long after he was at peace in another saint's kingdom. After that, the old kirktoun and its countryside had slept through the centuries – as serene as the old warriors in their stone kists below the run-rigs – till the railway came in the mid 1800s. It had carried with it a new kind of religion and a new kind of men who lived it; they called it commerce and there were folk who said it corrupted the soul far faster than the Devil ever did. Its temple was the station they built half a mile to the east of the old kirk; it had its own excitement and in no time at all it had all the appurtenances of trade clustered sycophantically round it.

The railway had reached Lumphanan a few years after James Geerie but there is no doubt it got the better ground, richer by far than the croft man's soil on the skirts of the hill little more than the length of a barley rig from where the Red King died. The battle that James Geerie fought there, too, was mostly single-handed, and like Macbeth's, it was one for survival. Years later, Jess MacKendrick would speak of her grandfather, the pioneer crofter man of the Perk Hill, from whom she would imbibe her fear of God's wrath and an abiding faith in the Word, with a warm affection:

> He was a hard-working, clean honest man. He kept rigidly to the laws of the Book, as he called the Bible, and woe betide any of us younger ones who did not do the same. Some time about 1850 he married my grandmother and bought a piece of land on the edge of the hill, built a house of sorts, trenched the bit of land, had it cultivated and grew corn and turnips and kept two cows.

Devout though he was, James Geerie had bedded his bride some time before their betrothal only to find her more fertile than his poor ground would ever be, for Jess's mother, their first bairn, had been born, as her daughter would wryly admit 'not too long after the marriage'. But then, in that lost countryside, there was nothing unusual in that.

Herself a grandmother, Jess MacKendrick would vividly recall the life of the croft hill of Lumphanan in the early days of her childhood, and in doing so provide a valuable record of the hard times the crofter men and their families of the 1860s and 1870s faced as they still broke in fresh ground:

> The whole hillside as I remember it was dotted with small crofts; every year they trenched some more ground and generally planted their potatoes in the little hollows they had dug and put the sod back on top – and they had just lovely potatoes! The Perk Hill did not grow turnips well, hence the whins that they cut on the hills. Everyone had their whin patch as well as their whin stone. But the whins were not like the ones you see at the roadside: they were stout, green, single strands and they were cut with a steel heuk, with a forked stick to keep them off your hands. They were taken home and chopped fine on the whin stone at the byre door. This was a built, stone erection with a flat top.

The whins that James Geerie's granddaughter brought home from the hill on her back were needed to augment the meagre diet of his beasts; they were 'threshed' on the whin stone with a wooden mallet the crofter man had made for himself from the stout log of a tree simply by fitting a shaft to it. Implement and procedure are at one in demonstrating the oddities and improvisations of the old croft men's agriculture.

On the Perk Hill croft, though still only twelve, Jess MacKendrick had been her grandfather's help more than her grandmother: carrying neeps home to his byre in a bag on her back (for James Geerie could afford no barrow); gathering growth from his clean land; gathering stones for his laying-down of drains in that time before the tile pipe took the poor man's agriculture by storm and drainage, such as it was, was achieved by arranging flattish stones in an inverted 'U' in the bottom of a trench, opened and then re-filled. Such jobs the crofter man could do himself; the heavier cultivation – ploughing, for instance – was done under the old contract system and in that uplands country-side by a team that yet again demonstrated all the awkwardness and elements of compromise that marked its agriculture: a shelt yoked in the traces with a cow.

James Geerie's crofting life, running in parallel with old John Gavin's in the lower landscape, was as bedevilled by that insoluble problem: the need for another occupation to keep want from the door. Geerie was a road foreman in that early time when the highway's custodians were the men who sat busily by the wayside beside their *birns* of stones, ceaselessly manufacturing the metalling that kept the countryside's beige ribbon roads passable. He rose at four each day to give himself an hour or two of the flail – threshing his sheaves on the barn floor – before setting out for work. All of her days Jess MacKendrick would remember the thump-thump heard all round the hill as day broke, and in the winter long before that as men worked by the glimmer of a cruisie lamp hung in a safe corner of the barn. Only the Sabbath stilled that insistent morning sound.

The flails of the crofter men were of the traditional type, their design as common to the North-East Lowlands as to the High-land kingdom that lay beyond the bare moors of the Cabrach and began in Strathspey, though their size and weight might differ from one region to the next and depend, also, on whether the man or woman of the croft would be using it. In the Highlands the woods used for the flail were usually ash (for the longer shaft) and hazel (for the shorter striker or swipple that threshed the corn). In practice though, it is likely that a hard-pressed crofter man was glad of any two suitable sticks that could be strapped together and other woods were almost certainly used. Its method of use was more of an art than a glance today at the crudely constructed implement might suggest, though the threshing principle was primitively simple, as Jess MacKendrick would so succinctly recall: 'The flail was just two sticks joined by a leather thong. You held by one, the other you twisted round . . . and it came down on the sheaves on the threshing floor – a square of wooden splits to let the corn through onto the floor below and keep the straw for use.' To get enough straw to put him over the Sabbath, James Geerie would have to be up betimes on a Saturday and maybe return to the barn when he came home at night if he thought his fordel was not sufficient to feed his beasts over the weekend. The straw he needed for his cows; his corn he took to the Mill of Kintocher, beside Craigievar's old castle, when the level of meal in his girnal began to get low.

The sweat would be dripping off the crofter man as he came in from the barn after his morning's threshing to the oatmeal brose Grandma Geerie made for him. She filled his short clay pipe as he supped them, lighting it with the dross from the peat fire and putting the tin lid on it that enabled an outdoor man to have his smoke supposing it came a downpour of rain. She would take half a dozen good 'pulls' herself, just to make sure that the pipe was 'drawing' properly and that the stem was unchoked, before pushing it straight into his mouth out of her own.

For a godly man, James Geerie was none too keen on cleanliness and went out to meet the world each morning (they say) with a kind of cat's-lick wash that would have made the laziest animal blush with shame. The crofter man's ablution was, to say the least, idiosyncratic. Without ever taking the well-lit clay pipe from his mouth, he filled the drinking jug from the water pail as he went out at the door and cupping a little of the water in one hand swilled one side of his face, repeating the operation on the other side with the other palm. He hardly paused even, and his back would no sooner be out of sight round the bend of the hill than Grandma Geerie would order Jess to let the hens into the barn for some rich pickings among the new-threshed corn, a deception that made the young girl think less of her grandmother and which she had later to cover up by gathering the hen droppings left in the barn after she had shoo-ed them out of it. Though it doubtless improved the quality of the eggs, it was a cruel trick, for James Geerie's crops were always poor, their return a promise bitterly unfulfilled. But the roadman's lifestyle allowed him little time for such reflection, or for the smaller pleasures of life, and maybe that was as well for his position, like that of the other hill men, would not bear thinking about.

It was a life, in spite of the croft man's faith – in himself and his ground and in his God – that never redeemed the hope it held out to those early croft men. For his young granddaughter, her days on his croft at an age when children today are barely embarked on their years of serious education, it was a bitter rehearsal, had she but known it, for her own future as a kitchen maid in the equally hard world of the farmtouns that shared the same landscape and sometimes the same disillusionment. Reluctantly, some days before her thirteenth birthday, and with regret even at leaving her sly grandmother, Jess MacKendrick said goodbye to the Perk Hill and her grandfather's crofting neighbours to fee home at the November Term to a farmtoun in her own up-country parish.

Rob Gibbon's was not a grand toun, nor, given Rob's own lack of drive, would it ever be; it was just a middling place that kept Rob and his folk this side of penury and out of the poorhouse, with maybe a bit put away from the fine hairst or two that had come his way in a farming lifetime. Mostly, by the time he had paid his fee'd bothy lads, his margins were fine. Not that it showed, for all that, for both Rob and his *gudewife* faced the threat of poverty, as the farmtouns began to go downhill from their production peak of the 1880s, with a pretension, in their circumstances, singularly unwarranted.

It was in the last light of a grey afternoon that Jess MacKendrick went home to her fee at the Gibbon place. Its track led up from the road through the sad November parks to the steading on its bare rise of ground, its bleak greystone biggings unsoftened even in the failing light. Its gaunt dwelling formed the fourth side of the farmtoun's quadrangular layout, a house so dour and chill that you knew at once that charity was mostly a stranger there. The weaver's lass fought down her desire to turn and flee its foreboding. Her knock was answered by the farmer himself, and not for the first time (nor the last) would her small stature tell against her.

'Is Mistress Gibbon aboot?' she asked the tall man who stood stooped and unsmiling under the door lintel, looking down on her.

'She'll be i' the byre,' Gibbon said finally, and after a further moment, as the thought occurred to him: 'And what would a littlin like yersel' be wanting with her?'

Hidden by the gloaming light the colour flew into young Jess MacKendrick's cheeks as she stood on the door flag. 'I'm nae a littlin,' she retorted hotly, bristling with quiet rage, 'I'm the new servant lass.'

Gibbon's silence had discomfited her, leaving her trembling and biting her lip, but his reply had not been the rebuke she expected. He had shaken his head slowly, wonderingly. 'Well, well, gin that be the case, may God preserve us,' he had said, shutting the door in her face and leaving her to find her own way to the byre.

All the same, Rob Gibbon had turned out a kindlier man than his sour countenance suggested and the weaver's lass had stayed with him for three years, doing all the kitchen chores for a mistress in insatiable quest of the unattainable – making butter and cheese, washing and scrubbing till her hands were blue with the cold and sometimes horribly chilblained, boiling hens' feed and making calfies' *stoorum*, or gruel, an oatmeal-and-water mixture little different from the brose that went into the bellies of the farmtoun's folk; it brought up the calves' strength after they had been *coggit*. As often, she might be summoned into the fields to break dung down the drills or help with the hairst, or maybe to drove one of Rob's beasts to the weekly market at Alford – something she did with an ill-grace (it was damnably wounding to the pride in your own parish) and in which she took her revenge by thumping the stirk's rump with her stick whenever it showed inclination to loiter. On the road back, likely she would not be unburdened and often enough her load would be a young sow in a bag, squealing on her back all the way home. For Rob Gibbon was a tattie-man, and like all potato-growers kept pigs to fatten on the *brock*, the damaged tubers; the one was unthinkable without the other and never more so than in that time of farming advance when men became fevered in their minds in their quest for new, fine-tasting potato varieties for the southern dinner-tables. In that, despite all his endeavours, Rob Gibbon was unsuccessful; he never evolved the potato that would carry his name into the future. What he could do was grow other men's discoveries to perfection: Grampians (inevitably, to show loyalty with his landscape), round and red; Lang Blues and Irish Cup and fine Glenbervies, another rounded variety; and Champions, floury and pure white and as strong then in the uplands fields and the crofters' shifts as in the Highlands, where they helped down the winter herring in that ancient marriage that has so long escaped the gourmet's good word but which sustained the Highlands through the vagaries of a troubled history.

The life, though, was a sad come-down for the young girl who had absorbed the graces of the genteel lady's maid; her days were long and their leisure moments few. On the Sabbath she went to the kirk with the Gibbons and sat in her master's pew; it was the day that brought all the parish's folk into the landscape, folk from places far round. Some of them had barely time to take their breakfast brose before they were onto the kirk road, and it might be nearly dark before they won home again after the sermon. It was a diverse society, one, unlike our own, with its fine sprinkling of worthies and dignitaries. It was rich in its lairds, men who ruled their own roosts and gave not a tuppeny damn, some of them, for anybody; their flying carriage shelts scattered the Sabbath folk to the roadsides giving you hardly the time to doff your bonnet before you had to step back into the ditch. Some were big men in the world of affairs, as much at home in the fashionable squares of London as on their own hillsides (some of them more so, maybe, for few of them had any great liking for mud on their boots). There was old Knockespock and Lord Forbes of Castle Forbes and Farquharson of Haughton, an affable man who had but lately risen dramatically in local esteem on the strength of a chance encounter in the English capital.

The interest now of such a meeting is not that it was remarkable or that it so eminently demonstrates the old laird's skills but that it fixes his paternal place in that old society. Chancing into Marshall and Snelgrove's one day, Haughton had found a familiar face staring at him from the other side of the counter: none other than a laddie from his own estate and the brother of one of his own, Big House maids. From a parish (or so it sometimes seemed) that supplied the world with shrewd merchants, the young salesman had known his place. Polite and courteous, he had shown no recognition and lesser lairds might have avoided the situation by clutching the cue that was offered them. But not Haughton: he seized the laddie's hand as though he were Stanley come suddenly on Livingstone; his purchases momentarily forgotten, one question followed on the other. What was the laddie's position? What were his prospects? How found he the capital and were his lodgings satisfactory and was he given enough to eat? and – oh! what a strange thing life was, wasn't it, and the world always smaller than you thought. Overwhelmed by the laird's goodwill and concern, the laddie had hardly been able to contain himself till the omnibus took him home to his Clapham lodging house and he could sit down and write home to his mother. Triumphantly, before going down to his supper egg and toast the lad had concluded: 'When Scot meets Scot in foreign land, it's equality for a'!' It was a catchphrase that might well have delighted his old dominie's heart and certainly it did Haughton no harm, though Rob Gibbon was less sure about it.

'Maybe so. And then again,' he said sourly, 'it is maybe damned little he kens aboot it.' But then Rob had to pay rent to him.

It was seldom that Rob swore or showed such disrespect for his betters before his young kitchen maid. The child who had come to his door on that grey November night three years before was now fifteen and beginning to grow into young womanhood, pert rather than pretty, a puritan with an impish sense of fun. It seemed, after all that time, that she might stay there until some farmtoun bothy lad took her fancy – or she his. That was the way of it about a North-East Lowlands farmtoun. But as that winter set in Jess MacKendrick became ill, too weak even to lift her head in the kitchen's box-bed let alone climb out of it. The doctor was sent for and came as soon as he could and as fast as his shelt and gig could carry him. He was an old man now and had long seen a side of that countryside far different from its bright fields and its acres of bonnie waving corn. When he had examined Gibbon's kitchen maid he took Rob out to the farmtoun close with him.

'It's nae the scarlet fivver, Mister Gibbon,' he said slowly. 'It's the diphtheeria.'

Their conversation was low, brief and punctuated by the nods and understandings of men. In the morning, a horse would be yoked into its farm cart and the cart-well filled with straw. The box-bed would be riven from its moorings on the kitchen floor and lifted bodily aboard, its doors shut and the small patient behind them muffled under a weight of blankets.

It took all the strength of Rob's four horsemen to load the box-bed onto its cushion of straw and to rope it securely for the four-mile journey. And when they had done so, Rob watched till the cart and its strange cargo turned out at the farmtoun road-end onto the turnpike.

'I doubt,' he said, the heavy folds of his face lugubrious, 'that the next time four lads have a hold of you, Jess, you will be more lightly handled.'

So, sadly, they had taken Jess MacKendrick home to die.

A Bride for the Mason Man

Mistress Sheriff, the merchant's wife, watched through her kitchen window as the men in white moleskin breeks unloaded their barrows and trestles and planks, their trowels and hammers and chisels – all their masoning equipment – from the long horse-drawn wagon that had brought them up from the station. They had come to build her man the new house he had long wanted and to modernise his emporium, the only substantial centre for trade in that broad and fertile countryside. Mistress Sheriff felt a vague unease she could not put a name to, as she always did at the sight of any sizeable gang of burly working men. For all that, their foreman looked a decent, civil man (little more than in his mid-twenties, she thought), fair-haired, the heavy Kitchener moustache maybe a bit elderly on his square young face. He seemed austere even, avoiding the jokes of his seven companions as he supervised them in the unloading; a man (she thought) not to be tampered with, for he gave his orders easily, expecting no contradiction. His reputation had arrived ahead of him, though now that she saw him he seemed young to justify it.

Even so, Mistress Sheriff remained fretful.

'Whenever the stonemasons come aboot the place, there's aye a wedding,' she said.

'Well, ma'am, ye need be nane feared it will be mine,' said her maid, most emphatically, pausing only for a moment at her wash-tub to glance out of the window. Jess MacKendrick had survived the scourge of diphtheria by some dispensation of destiny – and when her life seemed forfeit – to put her farmtoun days behind her and enter domestic service, at sixteen, in the merchant's genteel household. She was cook as well as maid.

Their years of confinement between the same walls since then – for the weaver's lass was now in her twenties – had given the two women a bond, an empathy that did not alter for one instant their social standing, one to the other. And in her way, Mistress Sheriff was as hard a mistress as Mistress Gibbon had been. The merchant's wife's washday was Monday and she had her maid out of bed by four, and standing to the tub on the kitchen floor, in case the day wore past before she had taken the good of it. The rest of the week though, Jess MacKendrick's day stretched only from six in the morning until eleven at night: seventeen hours. And certainly it wasn't her fee that kept her there for at 5s (25p) a week she would not have been worse off at any farmtoun in the district. But there was this consolation: there was never any outdoor work she could be sent to.

And the Sheriffs were considerate in other ways. Mindful of the position her man had to keep up in the community (and before the local gentry), Mistress Sheriff kept her maids presentable in black frocks that would be replaced before they got anywhere near to threadbare. These were worn with all the insignia of service, a white cap and white apron and (to lift the gloom round the face) a starched white collar.

There was no doubt about Sheriff's gentility, nor about his standing. A small man with thinning red hair and a rust-coloured tuft of a beard, he gathered pennies from every single transaction that took place over his counters with a skill and assurance that had long been proverbial (and regarded as inevitable) in the parish. It might have been unfair to say that the merchant

worshipped siller but he certainly made every penny pay its way
and the friendship was a close one.

He had the speculator's knack: if there was a single want in
the community, in the farming countryside, he filled it; he had
bran and maize and feed for all kinds of stock; oilcake that could
put a bloom on a fattening calf as well as the grass seed you had
to sow to graze it. He had scythes (hanging by day on the wall
outside) for your hay or your corn, hay-rakes and forks and byre
graips in profusion. Inside, the wooden *caups* from which the
farmtoun men supped their brose paraded in rows on his shelves
along with *spurtles* and *tattie-chappers* whose simple design-lines
drew your eye to the quiet taste of some country wood-turner.
He had galvanised paling wire, plain and *pikit*, and still something of a farming novelty in the northern landscape, the latter
coiled on its awkward rough-hewn reels that would soon fill
your fingers with splinters. He had wire-netting to keep your
hens out of mischief and trap mice round the rick-*foons* for
slaughter; *drogs* for man and beast (be sure to specify, he said
always; and not to be given to a bairn) and all the provisioning
that any farmtoun kitchen had need of – and a lot that some of
them never had heard of. He would sell you meal if you could
not get to the miller, eggs when your hens went off the lay. And
out at the back, in a corrugated-iron shed and with the kind of
industry that would today incite mutiny, men sat cross-legged,
tailoring on their tables, putting sleeve to armhole with the kind
of assured abandon that could put a suit out of shape even before
you had worn it and suggested that at times they worked more
from memory than the measurements. But there was this you
could say for such suits: if they didn't fit the man they were made
for it would not be long before another lad came along who
could be sized into them perfectly.

It was, in that upland strath, the last outpost of commerce
before you entered the wastes of the Highlands, and the little

merchant man presided over it in a spotless white apron drawn tightly round the lower depths of his watch-chained waistcoat and the considerable expanse of his own corporation.

Mistress Sheriff kept an orderly house, fearful of the havoc an amiable maid might cause among the menfolk, and the merchant himself, with a fine knowledge of his sex, met all attempts at courting his maid with a venomous 'No'. His permission, in the manner of that time, was needed to take her to the Oddfellows' Ball, a concert, or the tawdry, tarry-flared excitement of the circus tent, and his refusal was given at such times with such dour finality that the lad who had asked for her company knew better than do the like again. The choice, though, was not always Jess MacKendrick's.

Only on the Sabbath, and then briefly in the evening when they had washed the tea dishes, were the Sheriffs' maids allowed to see their lads in a moment or two of country dalliance and even then, only in the hope that the day would prevent the kind of deed that could bring shame on them.

All the same, and unknown to him, Sheriff's maid joined the lads of the shop (when her master and mistress were in their beds) on many of their midnight pranks – lending her shepherd's tartan bonnet to one of the shop boys so that he could look in, his face pressed to the window pane, on the travelling vanman down to his drawers as he prepared, un-curtained, for bed. The frolic had convulsed the pair of them for weeks after whenever they encountered the man who traded the merchant's wares round the lonely farmtouns; and the man himself was plainly embarrassed forevermore in the young maid's company. The same shop lad (and maybe he was a favourite before the mason men came) was her partner in another, older kind of ploy traditionally played at Yule or the turn of the year and against folk one little cared for. One dark night when the house was silent, they had sneaked out, the pair of them, to paint the front door of the Sheriffs' genteel residence with *sowens*, stifling their giggles as they slapped the mealy gruel onto the fine varnish of the wood till it ran in rivulets down the doorstep Jess herself had polished that morning, and which she knew, come daylight, she would be sent to wash yet again. It was perhaps, had she but known it, a necessary act of rebellion for the young puritan lass, caught between the merchant's careful gentility and the earthier world of the crofts. Again, it may have been the outcome of her irritation at her mistress's insistence on having the sowens barrel spotless, its girds or hoops clean and shining. It sat in a dark corner of the Sheriffs' kitchen, steeping the last grains of nourishment from the husks of the milled oats so that they would make a gruel supper for the merchant's shopmen, the bane of the young maid's life.

Jess MacKendrick would not have considered herself beautiful; not even pretty. But she was vivacious, her eyes lively and twinkling with fun. It is likely that she attracted the wrong men at times and for the wrong reasons. But Willie Gavin was an honourable man. The young mason, who had finally found lodgings in the married vanman's house, was well pleased with the trim figure of the merchant's maid, small and neat in its dark dress. If she had other offers from time to time, maybe she liked the mason's stolid, steady nature best, even enjoyed the prestige his job gave him as his skill became increasingly praised in their small community. Stone upon stone, the merchant's new home grew under his guidance at the side of the old shop and, with it, the early friendship of the mason man and the weaver's lass deepened into courtship. It grew, for once, with the merchant's goodwill for doubtless he saw in Willie Gavin a man as serious in his affairs as himself; a man who would not take life lightly. It was a judgement based on the two pillars of profound regard: trust and respect.

So, when the mason man's work drew to an end, they had been married with all the dignity that the Sheriffs' new drawing room could give to the occasion and within the walls the mason man himself had largely built, little knowing they would provide the setting for so personal a destiny. Out of his customary white mason's moleskins, Willie Gavin that day cut a fine figure in his black swallow-tailed jacket and bell-mouthed trousers that narrowed dramatically at the knee. His vest was bound with black braid and his wedding shirt, a lavender shade, with his tie – in the custom of that long-ago time – had been chosen and bought by the bride.

For the journey up-country from his father's croft, he and the guests he had brought with him had hired a brake with seating for two dozen or so folk on seats ranged down its sides. The early July day was with them, colder perhaps than might have been expected for that time of the year but dry, Godbethankit. Horses were changed at an inn in Inverurie, the halfway stage of their twenty-five-mile journey, and refreshments taken that markedly revived the company, kept the chill of the day something at bay and enlivened the rest of the way. The humour had been keen but not outrageous; there were well-aimed shafts about the staggering step that marriage betokened as well as quiet allusion to its comforts (and their consequences). Most of the party, excluding his own family, were mason men like himself – his friends, or as close as he ever came to making any. Willie Gavin bore the brunt of their broad humour that day and their barbs most amiably, a restrained smile shadowed under his black tile hat.

His bride was no less resplendent. Her dress was black, full-length and ruched round the hem, the height of fashion, bought through the merchant's influence and brought out all the way from Esslemont and Macintosh's in Aberdeen. The bridal hat, from the same temple of elegance, was trimmed with flowers and veiled to hide the blush of that small oval face. And though Willie Gavin might not yet know it, she wore blue silk hose and no drawers. There was, though, nothing scandalous about that, for neither did many other women assembled that day in that company; as yet the fashion for underdrawers had percolated north only to the most fashionable circles.

So they had stood together in the merchant's front room so that their bodies might be given one to the other in the embraces of matrimony. Inside, in the solemnity and silence, Mr Brander the Free Kirk minister's high and fluting voice, rising with sonorous grace, gave them God's blessing, and on the heels of each supplication came another, from outside the new sandstone walls, raucous and shrill:

'Herrr-in!'

'Fresh herr-in!'

'Herring tae sell.'

Between the prayers and the plain hymns, between the words that would unite Jess MacKendrick and Willie Gavin in wedlock for all their long years, the fishman's voice rose and fell in its own liturgical chant oblivious of the consternation it was causing. Nobody moved to silence him and it seemed to many that day that the omens were not as they should be. Others, however, determined to make light of it, for the young folk's sake, saw the comical combination of the high-minded Brander with lowly herring and would long remind them of it. Most were happy to sit down to the feast that followed and fell to drinking to dispel the memory of it. They danced late in the old storeroom the merchant had cleared for the celebration to a keen fiddle and an even higher-strung fiddler. And by then, they had all of them all but forgotten it.

If the drive up-country had been restrained, the humour of their return to Willie Gavin's low-lying countryside was less so. Now they had the bride with them, changed for the journey to her new home into another of her purchases from the fine Aberdeen store: a blue, tight-bodiced dress with a decorous high neck and a long wide skirt, and over it, a short velvet bolero. Against the nip of the night air she had a black cape with a Queen Mary ruched collar. The blue bonnet with velvet ribbons that tied under her chin had two brilliant yellow feathers anchored in front, like some proud cockade, by a massive buckle. The merchant's maid that day, folk said, was out of her box and dancing on the lid.

If the night air was cold, there were those who did not feel it; they sat, swinging easily with the sway of the vehicle, so well warmed with drams that even the dour presence of the bridegroom's mother could not dishearten them. The whisky, as always, had broadened the carnal horizons and as bottle after bottle emerged from under what had at first appeared to be singularly ill-fitting suits, the banter, too, became broader. As well as the bride, they also had the cradle with them, rocking gently with the motion of the brake between the two rows of folk, a temptation for every wag with a quick wit and, at that moment, with more whisky in him than was good for him. It was painted a pale blue on the inside, dark brown on the outside; its presence, one merry character suggested, showed more faith in Willie Gavin than he had.

The sallies brought shrieks of well-modulated shock from the womenfolk.

'Ye'll need tae ca-canny, Willie. That crib has only room for ane.'

'Yer sure it's gaun tae be a laddie then, Willie – painting it blue inside, like that,' one voice mused.

'Mair likely it'll be a lass,' said another, with the kind of quiet authority that brought silence to the buzz of talk.

'Why dae ye think that?' the first voice asked finally, its trailed wonder broken by the steady sound of the horses' hooves on the road. It trailed into further silence before the reply came, reasoned and clear.

'Why nae? He will hae the pattern in front of him at the time.'

Night hid the bride's blushes, but broad though it was, direct even in its allusion, the humour seldom added the offence of prurience. There was mock comfort for the weaver's lass from a woman's voice, matronly in the dark and wise in the ways of men.

'Never ye heed them, lassie,' it hinted, 'we'll see tae it that Willie disnae cause ye any concern this nicht.'

By that time they had taken Willie Gavin's folk home to the croft (where Old John, nothing loth, had broached his own bottle) and set off again on the final few miles to the little quarrytoun where the mason man had rented two downstairs apartments in a house with more tenants than it had room for. With the groom's formidable mother set down the mood was ever merrier and it was a raucous crew that entered the little village in the early hours of the morning, waking everybody in their beds.

The bridegroom was seized almost as the brake stopped and long before its unsteadier passengers could summon the courage to dismount (or fall off) and bundled bodily inside by his mason colleagues, followed by their wives and lasses, all of them now intoxicated if not with drams with the heady excitement that had suddenly taken hold of them. Bodies jostled each other in the constricted dark of the lobby where the bridegroom resisted peevishly, thrown against each other by the young mason's struggles. Lasses became pinioned for long moments against walls by dominant male forms, impromptu embraces that registered every contour and suspender. Things got worse as the struggle got keener; men who had descended finally from the brake to dry land (unaccountably unable to shake off its motion) followed on, colliding with doorjambs and with each other and eventually with the mob in the lobby. Grappling hands in the anarchic dark gripped velvet thighs and buttocks as men shaken loose from the mêlée slid down them to the floor. Finally though, they managed to drag Willie Gavin into his bedroom and the more high-spirited – lasses as well as their menfolk – fell in through its door after him. Bedding the bridegroom was still a common enough custom in that old countryside and it was an occasion, for all the Free Kirk's thraldom, that generated its own sweaty carnality.

'Aff wi' his breeks, noo,' a voice said, its breathlessness a tribute to the mason's ceaseless resistance.

'Haud him, then! Haud him!' cried another, querulous and impatient. Willie Gavin was instantly and ungently spread-eagled on the floor, two of his companions perching on his shoulders with a further two pinning his feet. A candle was brought to let them better see their work for the group encircling the bridegroom had cut off the glimmer of the oil-lamp.

'Lowse his galluses, can't ye,' the first voice instructed.

'His boots first, ye fool,' protested another. 'How in the hell are we gaun tae get his breeks aff wi' his boots on?'

Men, one at each foot, unlaced Willie Gavin's patent boots, their drunken fingers prolonging the excitement for the bolder lasses peering over their shoulders at the prostrated form, who squealed their delight as the groom's boots were flung under the bed.

'Now—' The first voice again.

'Wait!' It was as quickly countermanded by one of quiet authority. 'Have ye gotten the bolster case?'

'The bolster—?'

The men holding down the mason man looked up surprised – almost sobered – by their own stupidity. 'God, no . . .' They looked from one to another; in their drunken excitement the whole point of the custom had almost been forgotten.

But in a moment, women's hands had slipped the case off the bolster on the bed and dropped it over the ring of heads.

'And tow?' that authoritative voice demanded. 'Ye'll need string – strong string – for God's sake!' Exasperation laced the quiet tone. 'Ye'd think nane of ye had ever bedded a bridegroom afore.'

As suddenly, string was produced.

'Richt then—' The man who had unbuttoned Willie Gavin nodded to the men at his feet. 'Pull!' Simultaneous yanks slid the bridegroom's fine bell-bottomed wedding breeks from under him.

'Again!'

With the chorus of approval, the men took fresh purchase on Willie Gavin's trouser legs and heaved – and only then was it noticed that the loops that kept the bridegroom's drawers hanging, like his breeks, from his braces had somehow got caught round the buttons of his trousers. Lasses jostling to peer over their men's shoulders suddenly shrieked and turned to hide their faces in convulsions of excitement; and the best man, fevered though he was by the drams and his exertions, did what he could, seizing hold of the tail of Willie Gavin's shirt, dragging it down and holding on like grim death to it while the mason man flailed on the floor apparently unaware of his predicament – or his own excitement. Finally his drawers were again dragged over him and though he fought strongly against them, they got both his legs into the bolster case and pulled it up to his waist. A short further battle and both his arms, too, were inside it and the case brought up to his chest.

'Wha's guid at knots?' The quiet voice that had taken command registered a small note of triumph. A volunteer bored forward and soon the strong string was stranded round and round the top of the bolster case and the man it contained bound tightly and incapable of all movement to free himself. Thus, incongruously imprisoned and still in the wedding splendour of his swallow-tailed jacket, Willie Gavin was put into the bridal bed and the blankets drawn up to his waist. Satisfied, the members of the party gathered round to crow their delight and gape at the mason man's plight. They showed a deep mock concern for the bride, the weaver's lass come newly among them:

'There ye are, Jess – he will nae be a handful till ye this nicht. See till it that ye get a guid nicht's sleep noo.'

'I'd nae let him out of there the nicht gin I was you.'

'Gin ye do, lass, it's nae good kenning what could happen.'

Jess MacKendrick bore their sallies good-humouredly; finally, there was a drift towards the door, a last sly warning:

'Mind ye noo, Jess – prevention's aye better than cure.'

The remark lit a fresh wave of hilarity, and their laughter spilled out to the night and the quiet of the little quarrytoun, leaving Jess MacKendrick alone with her mason man. Though she might, reluctantly, tell the story of that night and the 'vulgar affair' of the bolster bedding when pressed to do so, she never told of the rest of that bridal night. But one thing we know: Jess MacKendrick at twenty-four had been little accustomed to the ways of men or indeed to the rough intimacy of their caresses. She was not a prude; far from it. But she was well versed in the precepts of the Good Book and had held to them as staunchly as her old crofting grandfather did. And then there had been Sheriff, overly protective of his servant maids at times and anxious for their reputation, so easily lost in that northern landscape (where, alas, it was seldom that no one was the wiser). Mistress Sheriff, too, had been strict: from the start of her service with the merchant's household – within a matter of days – the weaver's lass had been enrolled (at 6d a year) as a member of the Scotch Girls' Friendly Society, which did its best, in the long and sometimes uphill fight, to stave off ruin among the countryside's kitchen maids. When she went to Willie Gavin's bed eight years later it was with her virtue intact, innocent of lovers and with a certificate from the Society to prove it. It gave her bridegroom a written guarantee of her virginity though it is unlikely he would have asked for it and anyway, could not have been in doubt of it. Long years after, in her nineties and in a society long grown used to the indiscretions of young lovers and untroubled by them, she would speak of the Rules that had kept her pure until her marriage: 'I did not find the Rules hard, as I was just brought up to them from infancy. I won't say I've kept them all – reading the Scriptures every day – but even now I never begin my day, whatever I'm going to do, without first asking the grace and guidance of God for myself and some others . . .'

Her observances and her creed, all the same, came very close to truly reflecting the Scotch Girls' main injunction, set out at the top of its 'Rules for Daily Life' on the back of its member's card: *Seek ye first the kingdom of God.* The Rules themselves were six in number and in the religious climate of that earlier time by no means extravagant:

1. To pray morning and evening and especially to remember the Associates and Members of the Society every Thursday evening.
2. To read a portion of the Bible at least once a day.
3. To attend Divine Service, if possible, at least once every Sunday.
4. To avoid reading bad books and magazines.
5. To endeavour to spread no scandal and to repeat no idle tale to the disadvantage of others.
6. To dress simply, according to your station, avoiding all exaggerated fashions.

The Society's slim, white-lidded guide began with a prayer and ended with the words of the society's hymn and the chorus that encapsulated its simple message:

> True friends help each other,
> Gladly give and take;
> Bear with one another,
> For sweet friendship's sake.

And it explained, among other things, fearful of all the temptations the fashionable faced, how inadvisable was the stretching of a dress budget too far, instilling in the bygoing its Presbyterian precept of thrift:

> We determine to dress simply, according to our station. This does not mean that we are not to dress prettily and well; on the contrary, we are anxious that all belonging to our society should look well but we must not spend on our dress more money than we can rightly afford. Sometimes, for example, we may have to buy an article less attractive to look at than we would wish, because it will 'last well'.

It was good advice, just a little superfluous for any kitchen maid whose pay was only 25p a week and for one who would become a crofter's wife in a lifestyle where the lessons of thrift were brutally instilled.

According to the Society's guide the Rules were 'no more than any well-brought-up, high-principled girl is already trying to carry out in her daily life'. All the same, there was one thing, at least, in the Scotch Girls' Friendly Society's Rules that the young Jess MacKendrick would disagree with, which she felt appallingly lacking in Christian charity. The guide made clear its unbending unacceptance of those of blemished reputation:

> Those girls *only* are admitted as Members who have borne respectable characters; and should any Member unhappily lose her character, and therefore her right to be ranked with the

others, she would forfeit her card, and cease to belong to the Society. It is earnestly hoped that all will remember that they have a character to keep up, and will resist by God's grace, those small beginnings of evil, which, if yielded to, so often end in terrible sin.

For the backslider then there would be no forgiveness, no sympathetic hearing or understanding, only expulsion. And for Grannie Gavin, as well as the lass she had once been, that had never seemed right: 'There was just one thing I never liked about the Society. They expelled the sinner when she was most in need of kindness and help back to the right road.'

Besides her purity and the cradle, there were other things aboard the brake that summer night that the bride was bringing to her new home: the things bought in her employer's shop a short time beforehand. When the shop had closed for the night (and after she had given the merchant his supper and washed the dishes) she had been invited into the little man's emporium to purchase the simple plenishings she would need for her new home down the country. Sheriff himself, impressively aproned as though for the Lady of Haughton herself, had stood behind its counter, noting the items and their prices as she brought them to him, choosing from the cluttered shelves. He could hardly have thought that his account, preserved in an old woman's *kist* and proclaiming him James Sheriff 'draper, clothier, grocer, seedsman, wine, spirit and general merchant' and underlining the twice-yearly custom of that farming countryside with the reminder 'all accounts payable at Whitsunday and Martinmas terms' would one day constitute a document of humble history. Its fine Gothic heading gives the merchant himself some standing; it is from another age when commerce, still, had a touch of dignity. Its list reflects the wants of a kitchen maid when she came to move into her own domain for the first time, and in 1893, the young Jess MacKendrick's wants were few:

	£	s	d
1 bed cover 5/– 9/–	–	14	–
1 pr cotton sheets	–	4	–
½ doz dessert spoons	–	1	–
1 doz dinner spoons	–	1	9
½ doz egg spoons	–	–	6
2 pr blankets 15/6	1	11	–
1 watering pan	–	2	6
1 girdle	–	1	6
1 chamber	–	–	8
1 frying pan	–	1	2
1 pail	–	–	9
basin 6d bath 1/3	–	1	9
ladle 6d jug 1/6	–	2	–
scoop 1/6 spitoon 6d	–	2	–
9 tumblers 1/6 6 glasses 1/–	–	2	6
teapot 6d stew pan 1/8	–	2	2
boiler 2/6 basin 3½d	–	2	9½
pan 6d pie dish 4 by 8 1/–	–	1	6
lamp 2/3 6 bowls 6d	–	2	9
½ doz teaspoons and cream jug	–	3	–
2 jelly dishes 1/–	–	2	–
1 ashet 8d doormat 1/10	–	2	6
9 plates 2½d	–	1	10½
1 zinc pail	–	1	–
4 brushes 8d	–	2	8
10 yds bed tick 1/–	–	10	–
1 tin kettle	–	1	2

Besides demonstrating all that money could buy in that bygone age, the account reflects something else: the eclectic wandering of young Jess MacKendrick that summer night as she took the pick of her master's shelves. Some of the items now have their own piquancy, their reminder of another time: the spitoon, for instance, that great monument to the strength of thick plough-man's twist, and the chamber pot, a necessary convenience when the alternative was a cold walk in the night to the chill of the outside privy. Mr Sheriff gave them all his blessing with his 'Paid' on the old queen's head, to which he added his signature and his thanks, as well he might for the maid who had served him so loyally and for so long. Assuredly there *was* a fine dignity to trade!

In that first year of her marriage (with her man away at his mason work all week) Willie Gavin's bride had taken a *hairst fee* to help towards the rest of her 'providing'. It was at the small farmtoun, not far from the little quarrytoun, of her man's uncle and aunt: there she gathered and bound the harvest sheaves behind the bothy lad (who was hardly old enough to be in control of a scythe and would be lucky to finish the hairst with both legs). Kinship though was not strained, for she got leave to eat with him too at the noon mealtime on a side table in the kitchen, while the master and mistress had the main board to themselves. 'But now you're *related*,' folk said, incredulous when she told them.

'Aye,' she would say, impishly, 'distantly related.'

By the time the next year's hairst came round, Jess MacKen-drick was heavily pregnant and not able to take a hairst fee. Even so, some folk said, Willie Gavin had taken his time about it.

A Life without Luxury

A croft house was seldom comfortable and the human frame was never cosseted. In a hard world the chairs too were hard, though that bothered nobody for there was little enough time to sit on them anyway. It is likely that such mortification of the flesh explained why the crofts threw up more than their fair share of Free Kirk ministers, contentious and uncompromising and so strong on denial. It was an environment calculated to make its inmates cussed and that, undoubtedly, many of them were.

Grannie Gavin's kitchen was as much a part of the croft biggings as the byre or the barn, an extension of the croft life and never a 'home' except in the late hours of the evening or when the door was *snibbit* against the winter's night. At all other times it was a place where folk sat briefly (and usually only to food) before shrugging on their jackets again and going out to the fields. Its privacy was such that to be alone its occupants would take a walk ben the road or lock themselves in the John Gunn. Its stone floor, when it was not dominated by the wooden washday tub on its three-legged trestle, or the plump churn, was a thoroughfare through which much of the commerce of the crofting day passed: Willie Gavin himself to the girnal (the meal chest) to make the calves' stoorum; Grannie Gavin making passage to and fro with the hens' pot that dangled through most of the afternoon from the *swey* hook, hottering its hideous pottage of potato peelings, bad turnips, all manner of morsels the humans had not had the stomach for and heaven knows what else. By the end of a wet day, the floor would be swimming with water – the rain that ran off boots and oilskins unheeded as its folk came and went on their outdoor errands. And if the fire blazed, only the cooking pots got the good of it for folk were discouraged from sitting down not only by the lack of luxury but by the biting wind that whistled in through the ever-open door.

The croft kitchen's furnishings were minimal, mainly functional and ranged, usually, against the walls so as not to get in the way of the day's business. It had a dresser tiered with plates and cups recumbent in stacked saucers; a tall chest of drawers, recessed at one side of the chimney breast, a small table at the other; the main table, covered by the saving grace of frayed oilcloth, a token, in that day long before our own wipe-clean age, of crofting poverty, for tablecloths were so rare a sight you could hardly enjoy your food off them. They were reserved for grand occasions and the visits of richer relations, some of whom looked down from the walls. Heavily framed and silent in their faded sepia, their serious faces unblemished by life, they were the old and representative young of far sprigs of the Gavin family. Few of them looked like themselves for there was not a pimple or a blackhead between them and their appearance in the flesh was always an anti-climax and a sad disappointment. Among them was a stranger, as dour as the rest and so seemingly unyielding that he might have been one of the family. He was not; his name was Charles Spurgeon. It is impossible now to say where the Baptist pastor touched the lives of the folk of that bare domain but clearly his stern countenance had some dominion over them. From beside Willie Gavin's old shaving mirror near the window, he stared down, his gaze as austere as the old crofter man's own. It may have been that once there was a time, in the days of revival, when the Baptist man's sermons were read round the croft biggings for there would have been much in his creed that would have been relevant to the crofting existence.

The grey stone floor's only adornment was the *clickit* rug that lay before the fire, though that was mainly for the comfort of the evenings: during the day it would be rolled up and thrown against the wall for the fire was the focal point. A croft wife's day revolved round it. Washed – as it was daily – the floor gave off the aroma of soured dust, a smell, like the scent of the clover fields or the stench of the muck midden, that became one of the touchstones of a croft bairn's later life.

Though there was variety in its seating, the kitchen had only one substantial armchair, wooden and red-varnished, its armrests worn and smoothed by years of rubbing hands but its stature instantly recognisable. Even so, it was not a comfortable chair; its seat, painted black (the better not to show the dirt from a working man's breeks), was also wooden and as unyielding as the others in the room. It was called the Throne; it was Willie Gavin's chair and even in later life while its hard seat chastened the old man's work-weary frame, its straight back gave him a ramrod stiffness, as though he were on parade by the fire. Its design, its square-built lines, had affinities with the traditional wooden chairs of the Gaelic kingdom though the Lowlands crofter himself had none. The Throne was sacrosanct: it emptied as if by magic at the mere sight of Willie Gavin coming home over his shifts or as he passed the kitchen window on his way in to his supper. Indeed, there were folk who dared not sit in it by invitation even when he was known to be miles away in case he should come suddenly home and surprise them – far preferring the guiltless ease of one of the kitchen table's chairs, which were shaped to cup the buttocks. For all that, they were a 'hard sit' and folk did not overstay their welcome. Mostly, Willie Gavin's household made do with what they could get – stool or table chair – to drag in to the fireside in the evening.

The crofter man, like all the Gavin men in their own homes, and as James Geerie of the Perk Hill had done sixty years earlier, took the left side of the fire, though there may have been nothing traditional in that any more than seems to have been the case in the Highland landscape. But there was a parallel in other ways. As Dr I.F. Grant, in her delightful and authoritative record of that lifestyle, *Highland Folk Ways*, says: 'Whatever the seating accommodation might be, the man of the house always had his special seat by the fire while his wife occupied a lower one or a stool on the opposite side. I have never heard that the right or the left side was specially appropriated to either partner.' In Grannie Gavin's case, the millwright son who had made the Throne had, in the 1920s, made a lesser, female chair for his mother, a companion piece to the croft man's own seat, though the old stool she had so long occupied for her sewing and nursing remained also at her side of the fire and it was that, mostly, that she drew in to the fire between the byre and bedtime.

Reviewing Highland seating, Dr Grant continues: 'A charming feature is the number of very small children's chairs that one finds, some of them, elaborate, craftsman-made chairs with arms, others replicas of the local type.' In the Lowlands crofting and farmtoun landscape, too, there was a similar custom and many of the croft houses contained miniature versions of the traditional seating for the bairns. The Gavin household was no different: it included a child's seat that was an absolute model of Willie Gavin's own, a mini-Throne that a young Gavin male (on a night spent in his grandparents' care) could draw in to the edge of the kitchen's clickit rug between the old folk's chairs and, glancing from one to the other as he puffed solemnly at a 'pipe' fashioned from an old fir cone and a twig from the elderberry, assimilate the traits of the dour Gavin character and come to know the things that would be expected of him.

But it was the meal girnal (as also in every cottar house and farmtoun kitchen of that countryside) that was the most crucial piece of furnishing, as it had been for centuries. Inherited, like

the old croft itself, it stood under the kitchen's small back
window not too far from the fire, maybe as much for Grannie
Gavin's convenience as for the conditioning of the oatmeal in it.
The youthful companion of Old John Gavin's later years remembers still the tramping of the meal, the girnal's importance
and its place in the crofting economy:

> Oats were the main crop in that particular area – I don't think
> there was any wheat grown at all – and they used to be taken
> to the mill to get them milled or ground for the folk's own
> use. My grandfather used to take his crop to this miller named
> Watson – he was an old friend of my grandfather – and they
> would get enough oatmeal to last them for a whole year. And
> they had a special container, called the girnal. They used to
> pack the meal in and the kids would all have a bath the night
> before and they would tramp the oatmeal with their feet.

He recalls, too, the look of the old Gavin girnal. It is unlikely that
its constructional details were unique.

> It was about five feet high and a pretty fair width too. It was
> hinged at the centre front and you could lift the front down
> fairly low so that you could dump the oatmeal into it. But
> there was access, too, from the side to the meal, for the croft
> wife just taking some, a moderate amount, to bake oatcakes or
> make porridge or brose and such-like.

It was in the kitchen, too, that many of the old crofter folk kept
their sowens barrel, its shiny hoops scoured clear by the sea sand
brought round, by pony and cart, by a man from the little
seatoun where Willie Gavin sent his oats when he had any to sell
– the seatoun, they said, that his missing grandfather had come
from. The sea-sand was sold by the half-stone or the pound. The

Crofter folk *top*, the way they wished to be remembered. The itinerant photographer of the late 1800s brought them to their doors in their Sabbath clothes. And it was not only the people who turned out. Sometimes the result, *above*, was the kind of remarkable picture that encapsulated all the elements of a life of grim compromise. Hitched here in the plough, in 1888, are a horse and a cow, a pairing typical in the old crofting landscape.

Left. A hardy breed: the years and the work might take their toll, greying hair and beard, but they could not dim that shrewd steady gaze. This Turriff, Aberdeenshire, couple are dressed in the traditional heavy tweeds and the close-buttoned bodice of their time.

Right: Mutched and aproned, a croft wife of the old North-east Lowlands countryside pauses on her way to the byre in the 1920s. The milking of cows – central to the old croft's economy – morning, noon and night, was the great unrelenting tyranny of her life.

Left: How the crofter man won his crop: usually the scythe was the implement of his haytime and his harvest long after the sound of the machine-harvester was heard from the adjoining farmtoun fields.

Right: Stopping to sweeten the scythe-blade with the carborundum stone. Note the scyther's leather apron: was this the smith winning his croft's own small harvest after a day at the forge mending other men's machine-harvesters?

Proud toun: *top*, a North-east Lowlands farmtoun of the early 1900s, Barnton of Skene, typical of the farms the crofter men turned to for the contract ploughing of their few acres. Though the binder – *above*, at Denmill of Culter in 1912 – was by then becoming common in the countryside, few of the croft men came seeking it. Few, indeed, could afford to pay for its work and some diehards would not have let it on to their land at any price.

Croft *bigging*: *top*, a house of the later crofting landscape, two-storeyed and dormer-windowed and dourly overlooking its small fields. It was a vast improvement on the earlier dwellings, where the smell of the byre percolated through the end wall into the croft's parlour, and that time, *above*, when the plough and the drill-plough had brought together in the traces such an ill-yoked pair as the croft shelt and a bullock.

In the steep uplands fields of many of the old crofting colonies the ploughing – as *above*, much later, at Greystones of Lumphanan – was all one way, with the implement tilted on to the mould-board for its return to the top headland. It was with the plough that the crofter's year began, its ritual culminating in the spring sowing of his oats and, *left*, the compaction of the soil by the horse-drawn steel roller.

The kirk and the mill, perhaps the two most enduring pillars of the old countryside. The steam threshing-mill, *top*, was constantly on the winter roads, moving between one farmtoun and the next. The threshing, *above*, brought a feverish activity to a croft's small stackyard but when it was over the crofter had oats to take to the miller for grinding – and, subsequently, the oatmeal to refill his girnal or meal-chest.

Lost art of a lost landscape: rick decoration, the kind of embellishment that once proclaimed the triumph of another harvest gathered safely into the cornyard.

Modest neat stacks that show the criss-cross roping of thatch common in the North-east Lowlands before the dawn of the combine age robbed harvest of its ancient architecture.

Future ploughmen, farmers and crofter men? Perhaps, and already the boy pupils of this small school, paraded for the yearly visit of the photographer, show a stubborn individuality. Fashion ranges from the Puritan-style collar to bow-tied elegance; from tight, leg-warming breeches to short socks and bare knees. Yet all have the kind of sturdy, thick-soled footwear a country child needed for his long walk to school.

Meeting points: a typical North-east Lowlands smithy, at Lyne of Skene, Aberdeenshire. The smiddy, with its litter of worn wheel-rungs and forlorn ploughs, was where countrymen met while their Clydesdales were shod or an implement mended.

Meeting points: a country kirk in the Cabrach, in Banffshire, stands lonely amid the still fields. Folk came from far crofts and farmtouns to worship in its pews – and to lie finally in the quiet of its kirkyard.

Men of trade: *above*, a fine example of the old country emporium, at Bridge of Alford in the 1890s. It sold everything from sugar and soap to scythes and cattle-cake and accounts were settled twice-yearly at May and Martinmas. *Right*, the travelling country dealer of the same period, a trader in discarded trifles. He rendered no accounts; his deals were impromptu and if he bought rags he paid for them in chinaware.

Right: Country smith: an old smiddy with old-style chimney in Banffshire. For safety, the roof is tiled above the forge. The two-pronged hand-tool is a pluck.
Far right: Country wife: a quiet scene from the old lifestyle that seems idyllic yet poignantly emphasises the sometimes solitary life of the croft or cottar woman.

Country kitchen: folk did not linger here, and in this bare interior, probably of the 1880s, everything has been swept aside for the comings and goings of the day. Furnishing points: the deece, left, and the wall plate-rack right. The fireplace shows the links and the crook on which cooking pots were hung as well as the hobs on which black kettles sat. to the right of the fire, hanging on the wall, is the small hand-bellows, and, in the right-hand corner, a little wooden armchair for the child of the house.

Even where a crofter man or small farmer could afford a mechanical reaper, harvest still took his wife and daughters out of the kitchen and into the fields to bind and stook.

If the task was quicker than the long days spent with the scythe it was just as tiring. In time though, machines would end the old work patterns of harvest.

Left. Caught by the camera. The poacher was a familiar sight in the old landscape, a lone figure in the closing dusk, for a rabbit or hare was always a tasty addition to a diet based mainly on oatmeal.

Right. It was a time, the early 1900s, when the men of the farmtouns – like the horseman at Meiklepark of Oldmeldrum – would cook one in its skin in the hot ash under their bothy fire.

With both horse and farmtoun cart beribboned and garlanded with greenery, this North-east group, about the turn of the century, were probably on their way to a seaside picnic or the summer games. Wherever they went, they travelled light-somely, for they have a bearded piper as well as a young melodeon-player on board.

Meeting points: a country kirk in the Cabrach, in Banffshire, stands lonely amid the still fields. Folk came from far crofts and farmtouns to worship in its pews – and to lie finally in the quiet of its kirkyard.

Men of trade: *above*, a fine example of the old country emporium, at Bridge of Alford in the 1890s. It sold everything from sugar and soap to scythes and cattle-cake and accounts were settled twice-yearly at May and Martinmas. *Right*, the travelling country dealer of the same period, a trader in discarded trifles. He rendered no accounts; his deals were impromptu and if he bought rags he paid for them in chinaware.

Right: Country smith: an old smiddy with old-style chimney in Banffshire. For safety, the roof is tiled above the forge. The two-pronged hand-tool is a pluck.
Far right: Country wife: a quiet scene from the old lifestyle that seems idyllic yet poignantly emphasises the sometimes solitary life of the croft or cottar woman.

Country kitchen: folk did not linger here, and in this bare interior, probably of the 1880s, everything has been swept aside for the comings and goings of the day. Furnishing points: the deece, left, and the wall plate-rack right. The fireplace shows the links and the crook on which cooking pots were hung as well as the hobs on which black kettles sat. to the right of the fire, hanging on the wall, is the small hand-bellows, and, in the right-hand corner, a little wooden armchair for the child of the house.

Even where a crofter man or small farmer could afford a mechanical reaper, harvest still took his wife and daughters out of the kitchen and into the fields to bind and stook.

If the task was quicker than the long days spent with the scythe it was just as tiring. In time though, machines would end the old work patterns of harvest.

Left. Caught by the camera. The poacher was a familiar sight in the old landscape, a lone figure in the closing dusk, for a rabbit or hare was always a tasty addition to a diet based mainly on oatmeal.

Right. It was a time, the early 1900s, when the men of the farmtouns – like the horseman at Meiklepark of Oldmeldrum – would cook one in its skin in the hot ash under their bothy fire.

With both horse and farmtoun cart beribboned and garlanded with greenery, this North-east group, about the turn of the century, were probably on their way to a seaside picnic or the summer games. Wherever they went, they travelled light-somely, for they have a bearded piper as well as a young melodeon-player on board.

sowens barrel shared some of the girnal's symbolism; both were ever-present monuments to the importance of oatmeal (and a reminder of its dreadful monotony). But it was the girnal that was vital, the repository of the kitchen's largesse; where the space was tight, the *sowens bowie* would be relegated to the milkhouse.

The fire that Willie Gavin had installed in his new-built house had been determined by functional considerations more than any question of comfort for its occupants. It was a range, that rage of the farmtoun kitchens that put many a servant lass onto her knees before it – with the emery-cloth and the black-leading brushes – before the sleep was out of her eyes. All the same, it was a fine fireside by crofters' standards and many would have liked it. It had an oven built in under one of its two hobs, or *binks*, and the fire itself – set so high that you could get frostbitten toes while its heat took the skin off your face – was set behind three bars and closed on the three other sides by the fire bricks that helped to hold in its heat. From its glowing heart at the ragged end of washdays, Grannie Gavin plucked the red-hot 'bolts' for the box-iron that smoothed the creases of her man's Sabbath shirt. The dainty flat-iron might do well enough about the Big House for the governess's petticoats or for the frills of the laird's fine shirts but in a croft house it would have been an irrelevance and at Whinfield, as elsewhere, it was the heavy dreadnought box-iron that reigned unchallenged down the years, giving its users the kind of wrists that could thraw a chicken's neck without noticing it.

Willie Gavin had not stinted, thrifty man though he was. His high fireplace had a swey, swivelling out from one corner and into the room to allow the hens' pot and the black iron kettle to be lifted on and off without also consigning yourself to the flames. It was an impressive piece of ironmongery in its polished state; from it dangled not only the *crook* on which the pots were hung but also the *links* of the crook, the chain links into which the crook fitted. These were the unsophisticated Regulo of the croft and farmtoun kitchen: you could not immediately turn down the blaze, but what you could do was adjust the height of the pot above it by hitching the crook into a higher link.

There was hardly a moment of the day when the crook did not carry its burden: the *girdle*, the griddle, hung by the ring of its semi-circular handle, and the hens' pot in turn usurped the big kettle which 'sang' above the flames in instant readiness to make the kind of tea that shook strong men right down to their boot-tackets. On the bink alongside sat the teapot, warming its chipped enamel and waiting.

Above that, on the mantelshelf, sat the tea caddy, its kimonoed Chinese lady headless now where Grannie Gavin's thumb and her persistent hospitality down the years had worn the paint off – for she would have the tea into the pot before she knew for sure whose footfall it was on the step. Beside it, enflanked by the ornaments that had come from kindly folk and a day here and there at the sea coast, ticked the kitchen timepiece, one of the many clocks the punctual mason man seemingly could not live without and which whispered through the silent house with conspiratorial urgency, *Make haste . . . Make haste . . .* They were uncanny, the clocks of Willie Gavin's house; you could swear that at times they held conversations among themselves.

On one side of the fire's wooden surround hung its most important piece of furnishing: the small bellows that blew fresh life into it whenever it faltered.

For anything that came near to comfort you had to walk through to the ben-end of Willie Gavin's croft house, the *spence* or *horn-eyn*, as Grannie Gavin called it, using the words that came out of the past of that far countryside and that were, even then, all but forgotten. There the floor was wooden and black-varnished round the edges where its dull pink linoleum square reached unsuccessfully for the wainscotting. There, too, the furnishings were of better quality, sometimes even with a small hint of luxury. There was the black-rexined sofa where the semi-invalid could pine comfortably and lie out a day or two with the fire lit, or where anyone with a sprained ankle might seek sanctuary while it mended; the crofter man's own winged armchair, its armrests patched with bicycle solution, where the horsehair had been on the point of escape. Beside it, so that he had only to swing his head over it, was the spitoon bought all those long years ago in the up-country merchant's shop, its white enamel now badly chipped.

Around the room stood chests, deep-drawered and mysterious and seldom opened to the world; a glass-fronted tall cabinet with a selection of china figures, each a memory from a moment in Grannie Gavin's life; and, on a small table by the fire, the fine oil lamp with globe and elegant chimney that lit only the dark Sabbaths of winter, when its brass pillar gleamed in the firelight. Before the hearth, enclosing its long-handled poker, shovel and fire tongs, stood the brass fender and the footstool you were not to put your boots on.

Here, in the ben-end of the house the silence and the dust might be undisturbed between one Sunday and the next, maybe for months on end if the summer was fine. It was a silence presided over still by the woman whose iron will had long dominated that crofting household: Willie Gavin's mother. Turbanned with tulle, she looked down from her brown frame above the mantel with the same dour gaze on all who entered there, factor and fee'd laddie alike, a tribute to the terrible realism of the photo-portraiture of her time. Her eyes (you would swear) followed you all round the room and gave you good riddance as you left it.

It was a room, above all, that had its social nuances, for it was here – in the croft parlour – that folk got married for better and often for worse and where the minister came ill-willing, know-

ing the day could no longer be decently postponed and that he
would be back too soon to the christening that followed it. It
was, always, the place where serious business was done; where a
man with important proposals (or serious grievance) would be
shown to have out his speak. Not least of them was the factor, the
laird's man of affairs. When he came he would be conducted into
it, with Grannie Gavin scurrying before him to give the best chair
a wipe with her apron in case his fine tweed breeks should get
dust on them. And it was here, finally, that folk lay quiet in their
coffins for a day or two to say goodbye to their friends and put
their long croft days behind them.

The remaining ground-floor room was the closet – the *culaisd*
of the Gaelic landscape. It led directly off the kitchen and housed
the brass bedstead that was the matrimonial bed and the bed,
brought with them from the little quarrytoun and their young
married days, in which Jess MacKendrick had given her mason
man five bairns and, between-times, some moments of pleasure,
hurriedly taken. Its satellites, pushed under the eaves in the attics,
were black iron on whose ends there blossomed the black roses
that held together the tracery of their intertwining bars. Their
mattresses, like that of the closet's bed, were chaff-filled, the chaff
being renewed once a year when the steam mill came into the
district on its threshing round.

Throughout, Willie Gavin's fine house was panelled with
strips of narrow boarding varnished light brown to give the
patina of a seemlier grandeur; lace curtains graced the sashed
windows, but and ben, and on their broad interior sills geraniums
and begonias flourished as the croft folk themselves never did,
taking most of the daylight. At night, illumination down the
crofting years had been first the bog-fir taper, the cruisie lamp
with its rush-light and its lurching shadows, the tallow candle
(which took Willie Gavin's folk up to their garret beds still in the
1930s) and the type of small paraffin oil lamp that today

commands a fortune in the antique shop. In the circumstances, a croft bairn's greatest gift was to be born with good eyesight.

Even the porch, that architectural afterthought of a cold climate, did little by day to improve the warmth of the house for the steady foot traffic through it kept it as open to the weather almost as the close itself. But by night, with its outer door rammed shut, it almost succeeded. Built entirely of wood, the porch was the halfway compromise of stoically hopeful men who refused to believe that the weather was as bad as it seemed and who had resisted for years the need to incorporate some such functional structure at the doors of their dwellings.

Given its makeshift character, the porch could be said to be neither indoors nor out. It contained the thick mat that stopped some at least of the croft's mud passing into Grannie Gavin's kitchen floor. In it, too, stood the water pails filled from the pump, and near them the washbasin on its marble-topped table, its cold location a discouragement to protracted ablutions and beyond doubt typical of the kind of arrangement that threw up a race of hardy men who washed always with their shirt on and could run the razor round their chins without ever wetting its neckband.

If there was a semblance of cosiness at all in Willie Gavin's house it came from the welter of clickit rugs that littered its floors. They were everywhere and the collection grew yearly. Thick and strongly backed by further layers of the tough seed-corn sacks on which they were hooked, they absorbed all the old pairs of breeks and black stockings the house's occupants had no longer use for. They kept an agreeable distance between you and the stone cold of the floor.

Cutting the material into strips, Grannie Gavin hooked her rugs by the winter fireside, improvising the patterns as she went along. Given the preponderance of stockings in the rag-bag, they would invariably be bordered by black, but within that sombre outline would be an in-filling of fine swirling patterns of colour that soothed the eye. There was little doubt ever about where the pale pink *clippit cloots* had come from – or that the dash of equally pale apricot was the remnants of another kind of garment that was rarely joked about in Willie Gavin's house and never mentioned in front of the bairns. All the same, there would be the occasional wet Sabbath when a newly made rug would cause its moment of mirth where the menfolk sat, in the best room.

'You've surely been gettin' yersel some new pairs o' drawers, Wullie?' someone would say, all serious on it.

'Maybe then. Maybe . . . ' The crofter man, surprised for the moment, would be dourly non-committal, as in all things. 'But what is it mak's ye think so, man?'

The joker would look down solemnly at his feet and the pattern below them. 'Faith, man,' he would hoot, unable to hold in his merriment longer, 'I can see yer auld pair in the rug here.'

Yet, if the comfort of Willie Gavin's croft house at times seemed minimal, there were others much worse; his neighbour, Lang Andra, would take an earth-floored kitchen almost into the television age. And its panelled rooms were a far cry from the old walls Willie Gavin had been born into and the dark interior of the single-storey dwelling he had so remorselessly ripped down. The old crofter man's daughter, nearing eighty, remembers that earlier bigging still: 'It had three rooms – a kitchen, a closet and a room end. In that you got the smell of the beasts coming through from the byre, so it wasn't very healthy for folk . . . ' In the days of her girlhood the old croft house's living end had '. . . two binks at the fireside and a swey to hang the big iron kettle on, and a dresser and a *deece* – something like a settee – and a home-clickit rug, with a footstool, fender and fire irons.'

There must have been days when Jess MacKendrick thought, in her new croft bigging, of all the improvements the years had brought with them and remembered that old dwelling on the Perk Hill that had been her grandfather's croft house. Yet, amid all the changes some things had remained, ingrained and traditional, among them the importance of the meal girnal and the impregnability of the *gudeman*'s chair. They gave continuity to her crofting life.

The walls of my grandfather's house were built of stone and clay; very low they were. The house had a thatched roof and it was very dark inside. The roof had couples but no wooden roof, just boards – 'wattles', they were called – with strong stalks of heather intertwined with them, like the darning on a sock, and over that a thick thatching of broom. The house itself had just two apartments, a but and a ben, divided by two box-beds placed back to back to divide the rooms, with a press at both ends. There was a big meal girnal in the corner of the living end, filled with meal that came from the Mill of Kintocher, and a bench between that and the bed: it was a wooden seat, and it had a back. There was a *plat rack*, as we used to call it, with the plates all set in rows and spoons in front of them. There was, of course, the usual tables and chairs, with Grandfather's large one; a big blue-painted box at one side of the fire – the *saut backet* – bellows at the other, and of course the floors were earth. Grandfather's seat was called the Throne and nobody else sat in it when he was there.

There was a big wide fireplace; it was always well-filled with peat and turf. It had a wooden canopy – a hinging lum, they called it – that came over it. The grate had three smiddy bars and the *aise*, the ash, was pushed through a trap-door out at the gable. The windows were twelve inches by twelve inches and they did not open. The stones round them were white-washed to make more light inside.

Even the thrifty placing of peat with divot on the fire had its traditional pattern in the hard crofting world of the Perk Hill: just a single peat was set at the centre and the turf divots arranged around it.

It might seem now, these long years after, that the finer nuances of life would surely be absent from such poor and simple dwellings or that their folk might be lost to those small and gentle graces that have their enhancing effect on the quality of life. That was not always the case; far from it. Old John Gavin's daughter had played the harmonium that sat on the earth floor of his spence, his parlour room. If she played the psalm tunes on the Sabbath when the Free Kirk folk met in her father's barn, it is likely that through the week she played the tender songs of Burns as well as the rumbustious songs of that countryside. She would not have been alone in that. Throughout the crofting communities there were others who distilled the elements of a hard life into song and poetry, whose gifts indeed might in time lead them elsewhere. And comfortless though their lives were, for as long as the peat fires burned on the crofting hillsides there were hardy wives who never forgot to end their day on a note of grace, repeating the words of the *smooring* prayer as they 'rested' the fire to keep it burning through the still hours of the night:

> In the name of the Father,
>   the Son and the Holy Spirit,
> Thanks be for our life,
> For peace in our home,
> And for matchless grace
> This nicht and ilka nicht.
>   Amen.

The words are beautiful still in the sanctity they seek, the most moving perhaps of all the incantations that come down to our sophisticated time from the lips of the old crofter folk.

Kebbucks and Kail Brose

Want was something the croft bairn grew up with; he expected nothing better and he was seldom disappointed. And if, as was so often said, he was always willing to go to school because it was less arduous than staying at home, the lure of education was certainly, in the later days of the crofts, enhanced by the taste of early school dinners – usually rabbit, a benign laird's gift from his keepers' guns. The dinners were a boon beyond mere gratitude and if the croft child were fortunate too in having a chum with a fastidious middle-class stomach, he could even have two dinners and go home at the end of the afternoon with a full belly. Such charity had only one serious consequence: much as the stew might please the bairn, it could put the adult off rabbit for the rest of his days.

Yet that did not make his gratitude less, for want was as old as that landscape and ingrained in the folk memory of its people. Its dark shadow had haunted the hindmost days of the 1700s with a series of ill years that had taken a tragic toll and given musty grain the lustre of gold. And later still, other ill-hairsts had visited their own calamity upon the countryside, a constant reminder of its fragile ecology.

It was not that the landscape lacked good basic foods. Far from it: it raised the finest beef and oats, prize potatoes, and eggs and poultry as good as any, with partridge and pheasant on the hill and the moor and fish in the burn. But the crofter man, like the cottar folk of the farmtouns, enjoyed none of it; he got no game pie and but rarely a bite of the beef he helped to raise or the chickens he fed. The moor and the hill (and even the burn) were the laird's, and his hens were a part of his crofting economy. To kill one, outside of some important family occasion or reunion or the high festivity of Yule, would have been unthinkable. Though the Gavin croft at the turn of the century had been teeming with guinea fowl and turkeys that strutted and preened and gabbled their glottal chorus to the point of irritation as they scavenged round the old croft biggings, Old John's grandson and companion never tasted turkey until he was a grown man on the other side of the Atlantic. He recalls their importance, indignant now at the suggestion that they might have brought variety to the bare croft diet from time to time:

> The turkeys were all for sale. I never tasted turkey in my life till I was a married man. That was living – eating turkey, in those days. The croft folk would never even have *dreamed* of eating turkey. To do so would have been the most ridiculous thing you could possibly conceive of . . .

It was no different with the produce of Great-Grannie Gavin's considerable number of beehives. Though a little honey might be used to make the hairst's honey ale, most went for sale, Old John yoking his shelt to take it the seven miles to a merchant's near the railhead where it got a passing trade.

It was a landscape in which the recipes, some of them as eccentric as the folk, passed down with a careless abandon and usually without the benefit of a recording 'receipt book' from mother to daughter (the only dowry she was likely to get) compounding the kind of culinary disaster that gave many a croft house and farmtoun kitchen a bad name (and sent visitors home for their supper). Equally, it perpetuated now and then an inexplicable and exceptional excellence.

It was a landscape in which the Auld Alliance had left its legacy as surely in the home as in other areas of life. Though *velouté de volaille* would not have been everyday fare (since it took a chicken) there is little doubt but that it sometimes graced the croft table in the disguise of *feather fowlie*, a soup remarkably similar that managed to wreck the savour of the Frenchman's fine cooking in the process. *Stovies*, that stomach-filling dish that could take a countryman from his breakfast brose to his brose supper, and which fell so frequently into the croft menu, may have an equally illustrious affinity with that gourmet's cuisine: there are those who see the recipe's method – and the name – as deriving from *étouffée* (meaning to stew in a closed dish).

They may be right, but to be sure it was a terrible comedown. The dish the crofter's wife so adroitly concocted about the middle of the day would have sent any conscientious chef into a decline. Fat kissed the stewpan and was allowed to melt before a small onion was cut and added and allowed to brown in the fat. When the fat was very hot, sliced potatoes were added, laced with salt and with pepper and dowsed with a tablespoonful or two of water. The leftovers of the previous day's beef or mince (and that would be little enough) were spread on top of the potatoes and the whole permitted to simmer for about three-quarters of an hour. Then, stirred up with a spoon, the stovies were ready to eat with accompanying oatcakes and a glass of milk. There were wives, certainly, who abided by that North-East Lowlands recipe; others who *birsled* them so long in the pan that the silvers of onion shrivelled to cinders and usually took some of the burned bottom of the pan with them when they left it. When they didn't have leftovers of meat, the croft wives added a wry humour instead – and called the dish *Barfit Stovies* (Barefoot Stovies).

There was many a day, indeed, when a croft diet was so poor that it needed a bit of humour to help it down and there were other examples of culinary wit. One 'making' of broth, for instance, could go on so long you could imagine that you would never see the end of it: the second day it would be called Yavil Broth, the third day (with a frowned-on irreverence) Resurrection Broth.

Away from the sophisticated taste of France, Sheep's Head Broth was a lot closer to home, though undoubtedly it would have gone down better in a foreign language. It took the bit of the animal that nobody else wanted (or had the stomach for) and combined it with the kind of ingredients found in every crofter's kailyard. A vital preliminary, however, was the children's walk to the blacksmith's – to have the sheep's head singed at the forge. That was a necessity, the old folk said, for good broth of its kind.

Salt herrings came to the table without such ceremony and often from the crofter's own barrel if his holding was well off the beaten track. They were eaten with the fingers (as were most kinds of fish) and partnered by potatoes, traditionally boiled in their jackets. The *tatties and herring* had a strong following all through that old countryside, and sometimes even ascended the social ladder to appear in a modest gentleman's house, upgraded for his dining table by having the herrings set out on one *ashet* (from the French *assiette*), the potatoes on another. Then, in the kind of quandary that never troubled the crofter's table, the finger-bowls would have to be brought out to provide some semblance of refinement. There was no doubt about the dish's wide appeal: tatties and herring yoked together like a cart and a Clydesdale, the one unthinkable without the other, the potatoes' blandness taking off some of the strong flavour of the fish.

For long the red herrings (salted and smoked) were a staple in the poor folk's diet. Soaked overnight, to draw some of their sting, their raw saltiness, they were usually boiled on top of their accompanying potatoes. Bought regularly from the fisher lass who came round with her creel, and later off the fishman's cart,

they even found a favoured place on Jess MacKendrick's table –
in spite of the havoc they had wreaked on her wedding day.

There was little on the croft wife's menu that did not come
down from the distant past; that, like the old language of the
North-East Lowlands, did not find its last bastion, its final
foothold, in the croft house before fading forever from the
landscape. The basics did not change, though thankfully they
got slightly more plentiful. The food of the rural communities of
the mid 1700s had a close rapport with what was still coming to
the crofter's table 125 years later. Thus William Alexander,
looking back to the earlier time as he sat down in the late
1870s to write his *Notes and Sketches Illustrative of Northern Rural
Life in the Eighteenth Century*:

> So with only their porridge, their sowens and their kail . . .
> supplemented at exigent times by a dish of nettletops or
> 'mugworts', it is not to be supposed that the food of the
> common people was ever luxurious. Their favourite drink was
> home-brewed ale, which they manufactured to pretty good
> purpose . . .

The home-brewed ale gave way, even at the croft table, to tea,
earlier to be found only in the laird's house. But that was the only
difference the young Jess MacKendrick would have noted in the
1870s at her grandfather's Perk Hill croft. She would remember
the main dishes of the Sabbath dinner, the midday meal, the best
of the week: cabbage brose or *claith* broth made with barley. In a
variant, one of many on the brose theme, the cabbage was *chappit*
(mashed) small, mixed with milk, sugar and cream and eaten with
oatcakes.

Then, in that bare, wind-scoured countryside, as for many
years before and after, the oatcake was king. In its time it had
been eaten by bishops (with their morning dram) and it would be

found in the *aumery* (from the French *armoire*) of many a kirk manse up to – and maybe beyond – World War II, where the incumbent had grown up with it and formed an addiction. It was like a bad upbringing; a man could never get away from it. Oatcakes came to the croft table with everything; the first dish plumped down on the table oilcloth as the mealtime came round was the wooden oatcake *truncher*, piled high. Oatcakes accompanied saps, stovies, soups and broths of all denominations and practically any other dish you could think of. Most of all, they were quite inseparable from the crumbly blue-veined cheese all the croft wives made and whose bacterial content did not bear thinking about – and which had come to maturity (not to say over-ripeness) sitting chessilled and muslined in the stone cheese-press standing a few paces from the dung-midden.

The oatcake went to the school with the bairn for his playtime piece; with the tradesman as his dinner snack. When a man sat down to eat it, he took part in Scottish history. Its anvil was the girdle, the griddle, that followed the hens' pot onto the crook of the swey in mid-afternoon. Rolled flat and circular in its raw, newly kneaded mix of oatmeal and water that also mingled fat and a shaking of salt and bicarbonate of soda, one round followed another on to the griddle where it hung above the flames. On the griddle the 'round' was quartered into *farls* and these when baked were toasted to a dry crispness on the toaster that hung from the top fire-bar. With cheese, the farls followed the breakfast brose or evening sowens as a second course, the only one you were likely to get.

In the North-East oatcakes, singularly and collectively, were called *breid*, misleadingly but evocatively, for the word aptly sums up their role: the staff at the centre of northern rural life. As such, they were baked in croft kitchens throughout the North-East right up to World War II. Only then, with the end of that holocaust and the readier availability of the factory-made article, so uniform in taste and texture after the individuality of the past as hardly to engender anything like the same loyalty let alone excite an addicted palate, would the griddle be put away – banished, like so much else, to the gawping wonder and speculation of the antique shop. It is a far cry now from that time when the iron stalwart was hardly put away from one day to the next.

Maybe it deserved better, for the girdle too had an old and honourable role, its history stretching into the Celtic mists of Wales, Ireland and Brittany as well as those of Scotland herself. The word, in the view of some knowledgeable opinion, is from the French *gredil*, though equally there is room for supposing a descent from the Gaelic *greadeal*, the hot stones on which the old Gaels toasted their oat bannocks. But let none doubt its glorious past. The fourteenth-century chronicler Froissart, who would have known about such things, claimed that the Scottish soldier of that earlier time carried with him a flat metal plate and with it a small wallet of oatmeal. With a fire and a little water he had his sustaining oatcakes in no time. Give him a sword or a halberd as well and you had something unstoppable. If there were croft wives who baked dainty breid, thin farls that melted mealily on the tip of your tongue, there were more who baked in the substantial traditions of such hardy men. Grannie Gavin was one of them; on her thick oatcakes you could have marched for a day or more.

From the same source – the meal girnal, restocked yearly – came vital variations on the oatmeal-based diet: oatmeal brose, and the more occasional porridge that took the same ingredients and more time and with a kind of culinary savoir-faire put them on to a plate instead of into a bowl or a caup. And there was sowens, of course, which repeated the same basic trick with poorer constituents (the milled husks of the grain) but sought to disguise the fact by being sometimes pourable – into a bottle, for instance, to take to the hairst field.

The better the oatmeal, the better the porridge or brose, naturally, though there were folk of that far countryside who believed (with many another superstition) that good porridge could only be made by stirring clockwise with the spurtle. There was a belief even that porridge must be eaten standing up. For a treat, and usually for the supper, porridge would be made from bere meal, made from good barley instead of that more commonly milled, from oats. It was stronger to the taste, with its own very distinctive flavour.

Sowens, whatever they came in, arrived with a testimonial – Dr Johnson's no less. The jaundiced old man of English letters (with so little good to say of oatmeal), during his famous 1773 tour of Scotland, at Tobermory 'took sowans and cream heartily'. (He also had a good word on Scotch broth with barley.)

A croft's sowens bowie stood usually in the cool of the milkhouse dark. In it, the corn *sids*, the husks brought home from the miller's, steeped for a week or more until the residual grain was soaked out of them. Then the barrel's contents would be emptied, sieved into a pail. There were two kinds of sowens: supping and drinking, the latter sweetened with syrup, the supping variety served on a plate like porridge.

It was to the milkhouse dark, too, after the calves had been given their share of it, that the milk from Willie Gavin's bloo coos was taken, steaming and *yoaming*, hot from the udder to the chill of the polished stone shelf and the shallow dish in which the cream would rise. When it had done so it would be skimmed like a crust – into the big earthenware jar on the equally cold floor – to keep for the churn. For the butter for the croft table, like its cheese, was home-made long after both might have been easier bought off the grocer's van. Traditionally it was made in the milkhouse though more often a croft wife, with cooking pots to keep an eye on and a new bairn in the cradle, would take her churn into the kitchen.

Making butter sounds simple; in fact it wasn't. It might prove impossible even. In the days of the old crofts and farmtouns, there was difficulty with the temperature: both extremes, hot or cold, brought problems and in winter especially, to ensure success, many of the old crofter wives would warm the butter cream by the fire-range before emptying it into the churn. There were paddle churns (on which you turned the side handle) and plump churns with their plungers (older and traditional). Jess MacKendrick, all her days, stuck faithfully with the past and the plump churn made for her by her millwright son, but there were as many croft kitchens where its place was finally usurped by the smaller versions of the paddle churns used in the farmtoun dairies.

Near the end of the butter-making, the buttermilk was drained off, and many of the croft folk drank it as an ambrosial draught. Young crofting Cleopatras even saved it to later wash their faces in, believing that it enhanced the complexion. Finally, cold water was put into the churn to 'firm' the contents, and in with it went the dosing of salt that so often made a croft wife's butter as savage as her tongue.

But the abiding staple of the crofting families, as of the folk of the farmtouns, was brose, of one sort or another, relentlessly made to appease ever-hungry stomachs. Besides water brose, the basic concoction from which all other variants stemmed and grew in their bewildering complexity, there was milk brose – though this, because of the value of milk in the crofting economy, was less seldom seen on the croft table than in the farmtoun kitchens.

In its basic form, what brose did have was the merit of over-whelming simplicity: a few handfuls of oatmeal thrown into a caup (the wooden bowl from which it was traditionally supped), a little salt after it, all stirred with the spoon as water or milk was poured over it. Such an easily prepared dish could give a croft wife an extra half-hour in the harvest field – something never to be scoffed at as the weather held and the croft folk battled to bring in their crops.

Kail, as honourable as oatmeal, was for long years as central to the northern existence and kail brose, unappetising as it sounds, was at one time almost as universal as the midday meal, a sustainer as vital as the psalms of the crofter's Free Kirk and richer in vitamins certainly, if not in iron. It was always, in fact, more nutritious than palatable, which may be why the croft folk supped it one way and every way, trying anything that might mitigate its monotony. Again, in its basic form it was not difficult to cook, and God knows, the Scots had always had plenty of practice. In the popular way of the North-East Lowlands (though certainly it varied), the kail (colewort) was torn into pieces and put into a pan to boil in water for a couple of hours – maybe even longer, for that could only be for the better. Then the kail was 'pulped down'. Next, that older, stauncher standby, a *bicker* of brose, was made, adding butter and salt and pepper, with the bree (the liquid) from the kail pot. When the brose was made a further libation of the *bree* would be poured over it. Meanwhile – the way many of the crofter folk preferred it – the mashed kail was mellowed with a nob of butter and further mashed in the pot to be ready as the second course. This would be eaten off a plate, the brose having been supped from the bowl in which it was made. Just occasionally, the kail, mixed with butter, might be spread on a farl of oatcake, as a between-meals titbit. Turnip and cabbage brose, made on the same principle, allowed the same eccentric permutations. But kail was the standby, its hold on Scottish history practically as immeasurable as the oatcake's, and if once there were bishops who took an oat bannock with their morning drams there were, later, ministers of wilder evangelical fire who rejoiced in the name of 'kailpot preachers'. They got their name not from any dullness in their sermons, as they held the crowd in thrall at some great five-day communion, but from the fact that their impassioned oratory kept the folk of that countryside from their Sabbath dinner.

Though the culinary leap was hardly momentous, oatmeal *could* come to table in other forms: as *skirlie*, for instance. The cookbooks of today that give it countenance at all, lavished as they are with the sumptuous still-life feasts of fancier fare, will tell you with the kind of enthusiasm that is tantamount to recommending avoidance, that skirlie can be an accompaniment for meat or game, or even fish. In the old crofting kitchens, with its chipped onions first well birsled, mixed with oatmeal and the mixture cooked till it took on the lustre of dull gold, it accompanied nothing grander than boiled potatoes (often mashed) and came to you with the glass of milk you so desperately needed to get it down. Once, for the festive occasions that punctuated the year, even the shortbread was made from fine oatmeal. Indeed, the subsistence factor of the old crofting life would have delighted today's self-sufficiency pundit, even if he might have cared little for most of its dishes. Though beef (after that time when the killing of the mart beast had been a yearly custom) came from the butcher the rest of the household's food was home-grown. Out of Willie Gavin's carefully cultivated garden there came the carrots and the occasional cabbage that would partner field-grown potatoes and turnips. In the *yard*, too – its main provision almost – grew the strawberries, currants (red and black) and the green and russet gooseberries that became Jess MacKendrick's preserves, put away in the *press* to appear on the tea-table only when visitors came.

The croft eggs, though plentiful enough, were not part of that self-sufficiency; they were not eaten recklessly. They were part of the croft's produce, for sale to keep the bailiffs from the door. Often they were preserved for the winter, when the hens went off the lay, in waterglass in a big *pig* or earthenware jar. This method of preserving was practised also when egg prices were low; first, as a means of minimising the market glut; second, so that the family could later use the preserved eggs and offer the newly laid for sale when prices rose again.

Such was the bareness of the crofter's table that only the man of the house might have a supper egg occasionally. He ate as well as circumstances allowed and that was by no means lavishly. The reason was sound enough: it was on his strength that they all depended. If the breadwinner was not able to work for any length of time in those pre-dole days, they were all of them – the entire family – out of a home and into the poorhouse where the texture of charity was sometimes sadly thin.

The diet at Willie Gavin's table was no better than most, and considering his craft skills it was perhaps more frugal than it need have been. In the early days, as he took over the poor fields and rebuilt the old biggings inherited from his father, his siller had been sunk single-mindedly into the croft and his family got barely enough. His daughter, in her late seventies, recalls un-complainingly the want and the dietary monotony of those days in the early part of this century as Willie Gavin pursued his impossible dream: 'There wasn't much to live on at that time. We would have had kail and kail brose for dinner and peasemeal brose for supper – or maybe neep brose or sowens. My mother used to make cheese and we often had *crowdie*.' Crowdie was a kind of almost-instant cheese made by squeezing the curds in double muslin and then hanging the 'cheese' out to dry on a nail on the wall. For Willie Gavin's children that was a treat, like the top off his supper egg, which each of them received as their turn came round, or the small piece of his supper herring spread on a corner of oatcake (to make it last), which came round in the same rotation. If such want left marks on the soul, none of the Gavins showed it.

By the 1930s, the Sabbath, if no other day, brought beef to the

Gavin's table. Boiled to make the broth that went before it, it came on its ashet with a cordon of carrots and turnip segments plucked steaming from the pot and with the broth barley still barnacled on them. To follow there would be a simple sago or tapioca pudding made (like the broth) the day before and allowed to settle into rigor mortis in its enamel dish. It was a feast after the frugality of Lumphanan's Perk Hill colony.

Sabbath tea, after such largesse, was a simple affair: oatcakes and Grannie Gavin's blue-veined cheese or maybe the luxury of a boiled egg if the hens were laying; bread and butter and (if you were lucky) a smearing of redcurrant jelly; maybe even the special treat of a floury bap. A maverick big Abernethy biscuit might also appear on the plate from time to time, but since there was never one for every guest it gave the young Gavins their first lesson in ethics. Such was their reluctance to disgrace themselves (or their parents) that often, sadly and to their dismay, it went untouched back to the cupboard from which it had come, to become the mason man's dessert the day after.

Though the Sabbath meal might be more leisurely than most, folk did not linger at Willie Gavin's table; the croft's board was no place for social eating and the old crofter man himself had little time for that. As soon as he had finished his pudding he pushed his plate from him and if you were still putting away the last mouthful or two – forcing down the chill sago – his glance of displeasure was indication enough that you had not been in sore need of it. But that haste was the only unseemliness. At the crofter's table, as in his mason squad, he allowed neither bad language nor coarse stories and any man who did not realise it never got the chance to repeat his mistake. Having given the backslider a moment or two, the old crofter man would reach into his cords for his Stonehaven pipe and the round tobacco mull that polished ceaselessly in his pocket – a signal that the meal had ended.

Mutches and Moleskins

If the wedding folk saw the brief exchange between mother and daughter just before the bride boarded the brake that would take her down-country to the quarrytoun and into the midst of her man's folk, maybe they smiled to themselves, assuming the tenor of the conversation: a mother's last word on the ways of men and wifely duty; absolution in advance after all the years of sternly preached denial.

They would have been utterly wrong.

Jess MacKendrick's mother's advice that day concerned something much closer to her heart, an important matter in that now-distant countryside: family pride. 'See to it,' she had said, 'and mind and always put yer man oot tae his work wi' white breeches and black sheen.' A wife's reputation could hang on such things but Jess MacKendrick's was never in doubt for she did both nearly all the years of her married life and Willie Gavin set out each Monday morning as though he were going to an Odd-fellows' meeting and never less than a worthy example to the men of his masoning squad.

Every Saturday evening when he came home from his week's work, his mason's white moleskins, the hallmark of his trade, would be spread-eagled on the croft's kitchen floor almost before he had time to step out of them. And down on her hands and knees beside them, his wife would first smooth soft soap over them before beginning with the scrubbing brush. With the cleaning of the family's shoes, and for as long as Willie Gavin made his living from his trowel, it was almost her last task before the lull of the Sabbath. Appearances had to be kept up – all the more so if you had no siller in the bank and little meal in your girnal. And that had been true long before Willie Gavin's time.

It was the Sabbath still that drew the folk of the countryside out in their finery, as it had done when Willie Gavin's father was a boy. Then, in the 1840s, were the ploughmen 'free from the plough for one day . . . done up according to taste in rough grey tweeds, and with the ends of their brilliant neckerchiefs flying loose'. On the same kirk road trudged 'one sturdy old dame with close mutch, ancient shawl of faded hue and big umbrella implanted firmly under her arm, fine as the day is . . .' Beside her clanks a servant lass in heavy tackety shoes. The picture, so delightfully evocative of the fashion of the time, is drawn for us by William Alexander in his *Notes and Sketches Illustrative of Northern Rural Life*, written just over a hundred years ago. Fairs and market days too, among the very few holidays of the crofting and farmtoun year, were other occasions that brought the country folk out in their best attire. Few events drew them in greater numbers in the North-East Lowlands than Aikey Fair in Aberdeenshire, where there was practically nothing that was not traded between the drams and among the raucous cries of the chapmen. Again, the same author, writing of that slightly earlier time when the crofter man's grandmother had been a girl, gives some indication of the country fashions the folk of the mid 1800s had left behind.

The men appeared in the old-fashioned homespun, woven and tailored coat and vest, with big pockets and big buttons, knee breeches and hose all made of wool of sheep reared at home. They wore shoes with large buckles; and some of the rustic dandies came dressed in white trousers and vest. The women also were in their 'braws', and those of the fair sex who could afford it appeared in white. They generally wore high-crowned gipsy mutches. Then, as now, in matters of dress, the common folk trode on the heels of the gentry.

Clearly the craze for trousers was something new in the countryside and, quite predictably, the mood of change was not to everyone's liking. Thus, a minister, of the same landscape, about the same time, in that most remarkable series of Scottish records, the *Statistical Account*:

> The dress of all the country people in the district was, some years ago both for men and women, of cloth made of their own sheep wool, Kilmarnock or Dundee bonnets and shoes of leather tanned by themselves. Then every servant lad and maid had a quey or steer, sometimes two, and a score or two of sheep, to enable them to marry and begin the world with. Now every servant lad almost must have his Sunday coat of English broadcloth, a vest and breeches of Manchester cotton, a high-crowned hat and watch in his pocket. The servant maids are dressed in poplins, muslins, lawns and ribbons.

The minister was not well pleased. But the interest of his quaint lament lies now in its confirmation of the way the fashion wind was blowing. What irony, that it was always the kirk road that brought out the excesses of fashion!

Yet up to 1840 anyway, and into the days of Old John Gavin's childhood, there were folk of the North-East who still wore the linen and cloth spun by a woman of the family. And James Geerie, when he set out from his up-country croft in Lumphanan in the 1870s for Sunday worship (often alone, for his gudewife was not the ardent worshipper he would have wished) was still wearing the coat and breeches of the old landscape. But pious man though he was, there was one way in which he kept remarkably up to date with fashion: his heavy road-foreman's boots were thrown aside for the lightsome grace of elastic-sided ready-mades. His granddaughter would recall the rest: 'He wore a high Gladstone collar with a black silk neckerchief hanging down, long hose with garters, with white toes and white tops, made from strong mill worsted.' His weekday wear would have been that honoured garment of the northern countryside, the sleeved waistcoat with its back and sleeves of black jean (a cotton twill), worn with moleskin breeks. Women's fashion then, around the crofts and farmtouns, was as delicately poised – between the primness of the mid-Victorian age and an earthier past, for as Jess MacKendrick would remember, they wore two petticoats but nothing under them beyond their home-knitted stockings so heavily gartered on the thigh that they almost stopped the circulation. The petticoat worn next to the skin would be made from sark (shirt) flannel; that over it, fully pleated round the skirt, from wincey. Over both went a wincey skirt. The stockings worn through the week were brightly coloured, those of the Sabbath a sombre black. Topping everything was a *vrapper*, a kind of jacket with long sleeves.

Some thirty years later, about the turn of the century, croft fashion was well settled into styles that would pass down the years. By then, for sure, Old John Gavin was favouring tweed for the Sabbath and for all the other important affairs and occasions of life. His likeness about that time shows him as well-suited as any eminent Edwardian, the wide skirt of the jacket falling away from a high button. The photograph shows a small-built man with moustache and full whiskers and (despite his years) a full head of hair elegantly quiffed at the front – a man with some claim to be thought handsome had his lack of height not denied him. There is a dim and now-distant memory of him as a man with a liking for the old plush waistcoats that were once the rage of that northern countryside, and that would have been entirely in keeping with his jovial character. But it was a trait that could hardly have pleased his wife, for the velvet double-breaster with its pearly buttons was never seen on the back of a gentleman; it was the stamp of the rake, at best of the upstart. Blue was the favoured colour though red was more outrageous and just the thing for a man who wanted to leave his mark regardless of good taste. His granddaughter would remember quite definitely, though, the ill-assorted pair who set out for the kirk each Sunday from the Whinfield croft in the early years of the century and her grandmother's fashion in particular.

> My granny was a great tall lady and Granda was a real small man with a moustache and long beard. Granny wore a long skirt and a blouse and apron and when doing dirty or heavy work she wore a sack-apron. When going out she had a nice black dress, with buttoned boots and a black velvet cloak with bead trimming all over it, and a wee hat the shape of a mutch with lovely mauve flowers on it. She wore black knitted stockings. She only went to church with this on . . .

The mutch was a persistent fashion in the crofting countryside and among the lonely mud-girt farmtouns and, in a commoner context, lingered long in the language to describe the old scarf a croft wife might throw over her head to go out to the byre or to work in the shifts alongside her man, or more likely by herself in his absence. In its original form though it was a baby-shaped bonnet that tied with ribbons under the chin, and in its time its lace frills framed not only the sweet features of many a winsome lass but the face of many a matron where endurance was more strongly written than beauty and looks, where they had been early bestowed, had soon become sallowed (often) with peat reek. Frequently, in sepia'd prints from the past, the flinty gaze from under the frills is a reminder of the steely woman a croft wife had to be.

Crofter fashion changed slowly. Willie Gavin's mother looking black-browed down from her frame in the ben-end, besides
being heavily turbanned in tulle, wears a tight, dark bodice.
Many years later, her daughter-in-law, similarly framed – her
hair dragged back to a bun and her face made austere by the
photographer's flash – is similarly bloused. Without decoration,
the bodice is puritanical and Prussian-collared for in the close and
circumspect fashion of her day Jess MacKendrick showed neither
bosom nor barely an ankle to anyone but her husband and her
doctor. Though the 1920s would put her daughters into the
mass-made frocks of the flapper society, she never lifted her
hemlines more than would clear the mud of the old croft's close.

On the Sabbath, like all respectable men, Willie Gavin himself
quit weekday moleskin for the dark green tweed he so strongly
favoured and wore in defiance of the seasons with a waistcoat of
the same weight and colour (where else could he put his watch,
or anchor his watch-chain?). It was a suit made of as stern stuff as
the man himself, which was just as well, for in the great tradition
of Scottish tailoring it gave its occupant plenty of room to move
inside it. It seemed whiles that it would long outlast him, and
finally, it did – a testimonial to a thrifty countryside where folk
did not ask was a fabric fashionable but was it hard-wearing.
With it he wore brown boots of supple leather that made the
kirk-miles a lightsome walk.

Married in black, Jess MacKendrick, for all sober and Sabbath
occasions, never deserted it though after the splendour of her
wedding day, her croft life with its ceaseless chores was a decline
into drabber greys. It was all a far cry from the neat maid's
uniform of her servant days with the up-country merchant. Now
the most persistent fashion of her working day, like that of every
croft wife, was the sacking apron (made from a washed corn-seed
bag), which she flung round her waist when she rose from her
bed in the morning and removed, sometimes, only when she

went back to it at night. Her workaday bodices she made from her man's flecked wincey shirts when they could no longer bear the scrutiny of the masoning world, cutting their tails to make a new collar-band and piping that with binding so that it might wear even longer the second time round. Her seamstress's skill and ingenuity were endless, a byword (and sometimes an embarrassment) even in a society well used to thrift and making-do. She made all the family's clothes bar the new tweed suit her man might need, or be able to afford once in a blue moon (and only after a good hairst), and the dress that might be needed for some special occasion. In the threadbare days of their early crofting life she had cut down her own clothes for her daughters as they came to adolescence, causing many a bitter tear, for though she could easily transform the garment, she could never disguise the giveaway of the fabric. Bairns' clothes were adapted to meet the needs of rising Gavins; collars and cuffs were endlessly turned till everyone lost count, for in the crofting community, as in the cottar's house of the farmtoun, the hand-me-down was a way of life, as inevitable as the seasons. Indeed it was said that as brother followed brother into the classroom the woman teacher, though she might not know her new pupil, could instantly recognise the breeks. Understanding women that they were, they never gave the pupil less attention because of it. The breeks, anyway, would still have been a novelty to the bairn, for until they were four, Willie Gavin's sons in the early 1900s were kept in frocks (coming to no psychological harm because of it), graduating then to the usual small boys' attire for that time and region. Willie Gavin's daughter remembers the crofting child's fashions of that day just as vividly. The boy's outfits were 'breeches and long stockings, a sort of jacket with an Eton collar that you wiped clean with a cloth. They had strong boots in winter and went barefoot in summer.' The girls of the crofter man's family 'had on a frock and pinafore, real long, with black knitted stockings and buttoning boots'. It seems certain that they took the school-road better clad than their old grandfather had been in the days just before the mid 1800s. Here is a description of the country school-bairn of that earlier time, from *At The Back o' Bennachie*, whose author, Helen Beaton, has left us a remarkable folk record. The desperate saving on materials is evident:

> A boy from a cottar house was usually dressed in moleskin trousers, the legs made narrow and short. The coat was the same material, the sleeves being made usually too small, which, altogether, gave the child the appearance of having jumped out of his clothes. In winter the boy's hands were often bleeding through the dirt from chilblains and hacks. His hair was usually very long and always looked tooslet. He wore a red gravat round his neck on which the 'water mark' was plainly visible. The boys had no greatcoats in those days; but if the weather was very stormy, an older brother's jacket or an old plaid was donned.

A crofter man's working fashion, like the rotation of his crops, followed that of the farmtouns and the wincey shirt was king. Worn in the fields open-necked or closed with a stud, it had a collar-band so that in an emergency (or for a visit to the doctor) a man could go home from the parks and make himself presentable for better company simply by attaching a white collar with studs front and back, or more elaborately add a dickie front. His wincey shirt would be taken off for bed; it was just about the only thing that was, for the old countrymen spurned pyjamas – if they had heard of them at all – and slept in their flannel sarks and their long drawers, glad of the residual warmth as their feet left the clickit rug for the cold of the closet bed. (In stormy times there were men even who did not scorn the benefit of keeping their socks on under the blankets.)

With the factory-made shirt still the kind of luxury that a man would buy once in a lifetime, Jess MacKendrick made all her men's sarks. And like many another croft or cottar wife of that North-East countryside, she made them for payment for the men whose wives were less skilled with a needle (or less in need of the siller). Even in a parish where such a skill was by no means uncommon, she could sit in the kirk on the Sabbath and see never fewer than a half-dozen of the sarks she had made, not counting Willie Gavin's. One of them would be on the miller, so taut across the great barrel of his chest that there were times when she waited to hear the seams splitting. A big man, like a well-bred bull, the miller's twenty-stone bulk would have made a mockery of the stock of any draper's shop had he been at pains to step into it. But if he got his shirts made at the same price as other men (with maybe only a penny or two more for the extra bit of cloth needed), he milled Willie Gavin's oats at the same price as everyone else's. In the way of millers, north and south of the Border, he prospered well and retired finally to the house he'd built and called Millbank. The sly humour was not lost on his old customers. It had been that right enough, folk said, thinking little of his joke.

The shirting the young croft wife mainly worked with was the favourite of her day – wincey, which mixed wool and cotton and had ousted linsey-woolsey, combining wool and linen in an inferior fabric. But with equal flair, running her eye over the set of a man's shoulders and the tape measure round his chest, she made the half-sleeved flannel sarks, the undergarments that the men of that dour landscape wore next the skin in the days before the sophisticated *semmit*. (Not a few of them, in fact, continued to wear flannel sarks long after the semmit came round the country in the travelling draper's van: it was a poor thing against the comforting 'felting' of flannel, a garment for a man who could put a coat on his back on a day of storm.) Into old age,

Grannie Gavin knitted all the men of the family's socks, completing a pair in two or three evenings at the fireside and sometimes in less time if the need was urgent. She wove the kind of thick woollen socks that brought comfort to the feet encased the day long in heavy landsman's boots, genteel grace in cashmere for the shopman's ankles or for those in gentler occupations. Latterly, with her children up and away and her shirt customers at last seduced by the shop product, there was never a night (the Sabbath excepted) when she did not come in from the milking to pick up her knitting from her chair. It lay there ready to be resumed at any moment, assumed and set down almost without thought.

A croft wife's weekday wear was as little in the height of fashion as her man's. It was based on the kind of tight bodice that Jess MacKendrick made and the long skirt, in some heavy material. And if a wife cast her inmost petticoat on a winter's night before putting on her nightgown it would be only for reasons that need not detain us here. For the work of the croft shifts, and to keep the wind out of her hair, she might don one of her man's bonnets but, fearful of the warning of Deuteronomy that 'women shall not wear that which pertaineth unto a man', never his trousers. Mainly, for her chores round the croft biggings, it would be her shawl she would throw over her head and shoulders. That had long replaced the plaid, from which it descended, and had even odder uses. As her bairns came, Jess MacKendrick had worn her shepherd's tartan shawl in a way traditional in that North-East Lowlands landscape: folded lengthwise so that its two ends fell longer down the front of the body to conceal her pregnancy. The shawl, like the plaid, was a classless garment. Popularised by no less a figure than Queen Victoria herself, it endured round the crofts long after the cardigan came into its own, a practical fashion that would linger as surely in the Victorian ambience of the genteel sitting room till the shawls' old owners no longer had use for them.

If the Sabbath broke the weeks of toil one from another, it also brought with it another kind of regeneration. It was the day that the croft folk changed their clothes and in doing so looked back to obscure Celtic ritual and a lost past as relentlessly rooted in the folkways of the farming North-East, even in the 1930s, as in the Highland glens. That day a man set out on the rest of the week not only spiritually and physically healed but fresh-laundered with a clean flannel sark, clean drawers and clean shirt and socks. Only in the heat of summer would the drawers or the flannel sark be cast off, and even then, only until he had the hard work of hairst behind him. Summer and winter, Willie Gavin's last job on a Saturday night, before the Sabbath came on him, was to take off his working boots in the barn and pack into them a fresh lining of the straw that would cushion his feet through the week to come.

In all Jess MacKendrick's wedded years, croft fashions changed little – except perhaps in one notable area. On the day of her marriage, the mason man's bride had not worn knickers. Nor had she done so for some years after, for they were practically unknown in that old countryside except among women of quality and fancier ladies (especially the latter, folk said). It took a winter of storm and the quiet word of a neighbour to get her into them, and then, a long way from the stylish shops and working more from rumour than sample and taking her pattern from her man's, she made her first pair of cotton drawers. They had long legs feminised with frills.

Latterly, as the crofting years drew to their close in the 1930s, there would begin to appear, walloping on the clotheslines of the crofts and farmtouns, a garment that had percolated north with the flapper society and the headlong advance of the mail-order catalogue. Measured against the croft wife's early underwear, it

gave some indication of the way that sophistication had raced
north in the intervening years. It invoked indeed some of that
spirit of romanticism of the Auld Alliance and in our own time
would duly emerge, further abbreviated and lace-trimmed, as
French knickers. In those earlier days, however, they came round
surreptitiously in the battered suitcase of the Chapman–Sikh and
were known in that countryside of good oats and fine bulls by
the droll name of 'free-traders' – a calumny that resulted from
their most conspicuous lack: leg elastic. Their appearance was
enough to raise suspicion about many an innocent wife's character, and almost certainly, there were wise men even then – the
elders of the parish – who looked at them and foresaw the
downfall of a society.

14

The Pattern of Harvest

As the years came on him Willie Gavin's hairsts grew harder, taxing him more, so that he must have wondered whiles would each be his hindmost. Glad he would be each year to put the task behind him. For all that, it pleased him when it came, that high point from which the year hung. His crofting economy might be based largely on his beasts, but it was his harvest shifts in all their glory, bright with corn, that gave his life significance. It is difficult now to know the old man's mind, to understand his delight in his small harvest: it was something from another time, a thing of the spirit in a bare landscape.

It was part of the dream of the crofter men that each hairst when it came would bring them abundance, the yield they hoped for. It never did. Yet, having sheared his corn a man won a victory in his soul. Whatever the condition of his crop, he had then a month or two when he almost breathed freely, without responsibility, with nothing committed to the soil or the seasons except his neeps, still swelling in the drill, and they hardly counted. There was little hurt even the frosts could do them. And even if his hairst, after all, left him little to sell to the corn merchant, just to have staved off disaster was enough, itself a reason for rejoicing.

In that the old crofter men joined the mood of the farmtouns, for the hairst brought its onslaught of work all round the countryside in which their small shifts sat – a strange festival it was, part slavery and part thanksgiving. It was a time that united

men as did no other season; that more deeply renewed the bond
between folk and the soil, for its treachery as much as its bounty
could strengthen the chains. It was a time whiles when the mind
slipped the years to call up earlier harvests and the haunted folk
who sheared them, when one saw again the old patterns behind
the binder's technology. For the crofter folk, indeed, the pattern
of harvest was practically unchanging. If it immured them in the
past – divorcing them in the 1920s and 1930s from the machine-
modernity of the farmtoun harvests around them and accent-
uating their loneness in the agricultural landscape – it was a
pattern, none the less, that looked back more directly to the ritual
harvests of a lost countryside.

Willie Gavin's small hard hairst was repeated on every croft in
every parish throughout the North-East Lowlands; while the
clackity-clack of the mechanical cutter-bar carried to them on
the clear air of a fine harvest day the croft men wielded their
scythes in their patchwork fields, looking anxiously over their
shoulders in case the black clouds were massing behind them and
the weather should break before they were done. Maybe they
looked, too, at the worn women gathering and binding behind
them. They would stop, the weary lot of them, in the middle of
the long afternoon to seek the shade of a stook and ease their
backs against it as they *sookit* drinking sowens from the glass lips
of the china-stoppered lemonade bottle they had brought with
them; or sat, as thankfully, for the sweet reviving tea and floured
baps brought out to them under the folds of a teacloth in a
wicker basket. These moments were one of the delights of hairst
in the days before the lonely combine and the zippered beercan;
work paused briefly and there was banter and a high good
humour as folk got their breath back.

Yet the old crofter men were hampered in winning their hairst
in a way that would not be so today: the Sabbath then, the one
day of the week that was their own, was inviolable. A silence lay

on the still fields and nothing impinged on it; it was broken neither by the swish of the scythe nor the sound of the reaping machine. And even on his Sabbath afternoon stroll round his small parks Willie Gavin would not straighten a slipped sheaf in the stook without first glancing in the direction of the croft biggings to make sure Grannie Gavin was not watching him. He knew, should she see him, that he would be given his rascally character. But if she knew, or suspected him whiles, nothing was said – though the mason man's caution long caused sly merriment among his companions of the day and especially among the younger men who had come to look over his daughters. Only the fluting of Free Kirk psalms from some barn service, carried across the hush of the land, would disturb the quiet, their dolour at odds with the triumphal fullness of nature.

There were crofter men ill-placed to win their hairsts: the roadman (fee'd home for a harvest to some farmtoun in an attempt to make ends meet); the blacksmith (too busy by far at that time of year with the needs for other folk's hairsts to think of his own) and farmtoun horsemen and grieves who could not reap their own crops till they had gathered somebody else's. Sore was their plight and their loyalty torn as they toiled, wanting only to be home. Their hardy croft wives, nothing daunted, would go out with the heuk by themselves to shear the croft crops while their men were away; it was fine, after all, to have your own hairst in and the fee for the work of another.

Those days now are only a memory in old men's minds. But their activity was intense. Though the mechanical harvester was a practical reality in Old John Gavin's day – from the 1870s, anyway – it was always something for the farmtoun fields. Hired, it had to be paid for; and, of course, it was an impossible investment for any croft man even if he had the horses to harness into it. So, down the years, his scythe had been the crofter's best friend: it captured his hay when the clover was sweet, his oats when they came to ripeness and began to *reeshle* on the stalk. It had a name in that spare countryside – Rob Sorby, from the name on its blade. And if that particular make of blade had as good a following as any good whisky, there were also men who would hear nothing said against the Tysack. New blades were bought at the *smiddy*, where the smith fitted them to the *sned*, the wooden frame of the scythe, a job not nearly so simple as it seemed. It needed its own skills in alignment and adjustment if the implement was to be sweet to use, not cumbrous and unwieldy, a thing without grace.

With his oats coming to ripeness and the promise of a fine harvest hanging in the summer air (as it sometimes did) Willie Gavin would take down his scythe from its nail on the toolshed wall to check the truth of its blade and the strength of its stay. He would sharpen it and oil it and make a mental note (as he did before each harvest) to buy a new carborundum stone next time he went to the kirktoun. There had never been a time when Willie Gavin had not sheared his own crops and brought them in. It was a strange loyalty, a loyalty to his grun, that drove him. Beholden though he was to Laverockhill for a *yoking* or two of a Clydesdale pair and a plough and for most of the cultivation of the spring work, he would not let a reaper or a binder on to his land from fear of the harm the weight of the machine might do. A cottar son-in-law fee'd home one year to the big farmtoun on the hill, who had borrowed his Clydesdale pair and a binder one evening and brought it down to the old man's shifts to save him the long hours of slavery under the sun had been sent home again with damned little thanks for his pains, and fell so far out of favour that he knew never to do the like again. But maybe it was not the weight of the machine that worried him, only that it came between him and the hairsts of his ancestors. There is nobody knows now, one way or the other, for Willie Gavin, even to his friends, could be a close and secretive man.

The old crofter man began his hairst bouts at the top ends of his shifts, cutting across their width, walking back to begin the next bout, working slowly, inexorably, down towards the burnside. Old man though he was in the 1930s, he was still as tidy a man with a scythe as he was with a trowel. Bout after bout – each about four and a half feet wide – the rhythmic sweep of his blade, right to left, took the grain to the side of him, to fall neatly in a narrow swath. The blade's sound in the summer air fell sweetly on the ear, harmonising with the scyther's rhythmic movement. You could almost hear the changing note – feel the drag of the blade, as Willie Gavin did – as it became blunted and the crofter man stopped to sweeten its edge, setting the tip of the blade on the toe of his heavy boot as he *straiked* it.

Willie Gavin took all the straw he could get – he had need of it – leaving little more than three inches of stubble. Behind him, as relentlessly as Old John's formidable consort had once done, Grannie Gavin bunched the fallen grain into sheaves, her hands seizing the straws that would make the band, dividing them and twisting them with that deft assurance she had known almost from the cradle and certainly from the days of her girlhood in the Perk Hill croft colony. Quickly she enclosed each sheaf, tying the band and tucking the ends under, tidily. Row upon row, by the yoking's end, the sheaves would lie like the lines of battle dead, their eared heads in the direction Willie Gavin worked. When Grannie Gavin went in, about noon, to prepare dinner, he would lay his scythe against the fence and begin stooking.

Working again across the shift he would seize the sheaves where they lay, tucking one under each armpit as he strode across the stubble to settle them into stooks. If the old crofter managed to make it look easy, it was anything but that. It was hard work and it always had been. The hairst field had its pattern, like so much else in the seasons of that old countryside, and in a good year when the stooks stood proud it delighted the eye. In a bad hairst, it was something else again: a crying in the heart of you as the grain flattened and tangled under the constant *blatter* of rain till it was almost beyond handling. Then the bouts of harvest were haggard, their harmony and pattern lost by the harvester's need to scythe as he could, undercutting the twisted crop where it lay.

The steady swish of the scythe was a sound that echoed down the years in a croft bairn's mind; a memory that united the generations, as it did the Gavins. How little the old pattern changed! Here is Old John Gavin's grandson, the old man's summer companion when the century was new:

> My strongest recollections of my young days were in the time when I was aged between nine and thirteen or so . . . I used to spend the major part of my holidays with my grandparents, at which time they were usually busily engaged in taking off their crops. I recollect those days as being very, very happy and pleasant. There was no such thing as binders or even reaping machines for the croft folk and the crop was all handled by the scythe. My grandfather did all the scything and my grand-mother and I did all the making of the sheaf and binding it. After a fair bit had been accomplished I would abandon the gathering to work on the stooking. At that time, my grand-mother used to make a batch of honey ale every season. This was taken in a stone earthenware jar to the field, the jar being cast usually into a stook to keep the sun's heat away from it so that it would remain palatable. There was no alcohol in it.

By then, Old John and his spouse were both into their seventies, and needed a short nap after dinner before going out for the afternoon yoking.

Yet if that memory is of hardy folk, it is also of something else, that strange equation of harvest-time: hard work and happiness.

The years had changed nothing at the Gavin croft – except that with that formidable old woman gone where they brewed no honey ale, the drink taken to the hairst field was now sowens.

Blessed with fine weather, it would take Willie Gavin a week, maybe ten days, to cut and stook his three acres. He would cut his ley oats first, moving, immediately that shift was done, into his clean-land crop. Bad weather could make his hairst a fragmented and protracted affair. But it was never the straightforward operation of a farmtoun harvest, for into it had to be fitted the tending and milking of beasts as well as the odd funeral or two that might take the best part of an afternoon. It was a fine time though, for a man to go, with the hairst golden, or cut and standing tidy in the stook, and Willie Gavin had always thought so – though it was a damned inconvenience to his neighbours.

Yet slowly the stooks would rise on the cropped stubble of the old croft shifts, immaculately ranked, north to south in their ancient alignment so that the sun at noon struck along the length of their bunched heads. A week in the stook – ten days at the most – and if the weather was with him, Willie Gavin's oats would be ready to take home to the cornyard. In the early days, when he still had Meggie, his father's old shelt, as well as the cart to yoke her into, that had been an easy task; his hairst had come home in style in the manner of the farmtouns'. But in time the old beast, like its master, was gone, and Willie Gavin, like most of the crofter men, brought in his crop with his barrow, building a harvest frame on it to take the sheaves.

It was a method that aped the hairst carts of the farmtouns, where the Clydesdales bore home the loads. The croft barrow, however, rolled home under the power of human sweat and Willie Gavin was a tired man before he had his crop safe and into his small stackyard. A Clydesdale between the shafts of a Laverockhill cart could have done the crofter's *leading* in an evening at the end of its day's work, without tiring either its horseman or the beast itself. But Willie Gavin set his face as firmly against that as he did the trespass of the binder; he would not have allowed it. Even so, in the up-country folds of the hills, there were crofter folk worse off, and men so poor that they had to bring their harvest sheaves home (with a big rope sling) on their backs, the same way that they brought a young sow home from the market.

So, like a fulfilment, Willie Gavin's sheaves came home. He tipped them, one barrowload after another, in the cornyard until he had a sizeable birn, a heap he judged enough to be the beginnings of a rick. For a start he managed by himself, building from the *foon*, the stack foundation, of springy spread brush-wood, throwing the first sheaves into the centre, building up the 'heart' of the rick before he began to splay them, heads inwards, round the circumference of the foon. The stack grew, tier upon tier, the crofter man still keeping up the 'heart' of the rick so that outer sheaves would run the rain *out* not *in*. Layer was kneed upon circled layer, until it was no longer possible for him to continue unaided. Then, magically (because she had been watching from the small back window) Grannie Gavin would appear round the corner of the barn (mutched and aproned even on a day of heat) to fork up the sheaves to him.

Willie Gavin was a careful man; he built slowly, laboriously considering his trade, coming down the ladder she would prop against the stack to walk round and round his work. Taken from her butter- or cheese-making, she would lose patience with him at times:

'Dyod man, what needs ye tak' such pains about it? It will stand tae the wind and keep oot the weet, and what else is there that matters?'

But Willie Gavin would not be hurried; he biggit to satisfy something deep in himself. Yet the truth of it was that the crofter man for all his skill with stone could never manage to give his

cornyard the kind of simple grace he could so easily bestow on a
new farmtoun barn or byre. He never biggit a house with more
care, but his stacks were neither proud nor handsome. Waterproof he could make them, certainly, but that symmetry that
marked a master's skill eluded him and in his later years he never
biggit his stackyard – got all his crop in – without one of his ricks
being thankful for some prop to lean on. His small hairst would
raise three or four ricks in the cornyard behind the croft barn,
poor things beside the stacks that filled the farmtoun yards and so
modest in stature as barely to lift their heads above the height of
the barn roof: ten feet, little more, to the *easings*, the point at
which the builder began to draw them in to their conical points.

Their thatch would be ready and waiting, the last of the
straw from last year's harvest. On one or two wet mornings
the old crofter man would have been in the barn *drawing thack*
– straightening the straw – in readiness till it faired enough to
let him out again with his scythe. Crofter men in other
parishes might use *sprots* (rushes) from the bog or the burn
bank as thatch, but whatever the thack, it would be lashed
down with rope criss-crossed in the traditional tracery of that
North-East region.

Grannie Gavin would be glad to see the hairst sheaves home
and into the cornyard, for then too Willie Gavin was a happier
man: he had (in the language of that farming countryside) 'gotten
winter'. His crop was secure and his crofting year had ended.
And that was a matter for congratulation among the crofters no
less than in the world of the encircling farmtouns. To have your
hairst home dry and in good order was a small triumph.

'I see you have winter, Willie,' folk would call, meeting him
on the road as he brought his beasts in for the milking.

'Aye, just so,' he would cry back at them, jovial almost, well
pleased to be at one with farming men. And then, for modesty's
sake: 'An' nae afore time.'

It delighted him, all the same, to be among the first of the croft men to have his harvest in, though in that he was handicapped by his cautious nature and was never the leader. He would not cut a corner here and there as some men did or risk a hot rick – and maybe a fire – in the process. But he was never the last, and there was little chance of his being so, so long as Puir Angus was among them.

So the pattern of harvest passed down the years, giving its continuity like the kirk with the crofting past. But if that gave a kind of reassurance, it was also a bitter condemnation. It showed the croft for what it was: an anachronism, a unit out of its farming time. And that, in turn, was never more deeply demonstrated than when it came time to thresh out the corn stacks. Here, more dramatically than in anything else, the years *had* brought crofting change.

Old John Gavin had been early at the flail, every morning bar the Sabbath, turned out of his bed by his strong-willed wife to give them straw for the day when by all accounts he would sooner have lain there quietly at her side. Like James Geerie of the Perk Hill, Old John had threshed on the barn floor, stripped whiles to his under-sark and no doubt cursing, unkirk-like, the necessity that drove him to it. But by his son's day it was different: the steam mill – the contractor's portable threshing mill, moving winter-long between one farmtoun and the next – had become a part of the country scene, a thing of wonder and a terror to every Clydesdale in the land, for they would sooner leap over the dyke (cart and horseman and all) than face it. Even so, with their threshings so small, the crofter men would have to approach the mill's owner in a body to have any hope of raising his interest. And even then, Old Henderson would grumble and *girn* at them: there was not one of them with anything more than a yoking's work to his machine. Forbye, it took him longer to manoeuvre the mill into their small cornyards than ever it did to do the thrash, always supposing he did not tip the whole caboodle – engine, mill and bogie – into the roadside ditch in attempting it! But Henderson was never a happy man for all the siller he made (folk said) and was ill to please with lesser work so long as the big farmtouns wanted him. He complained bitterly when he did come: it was as well that his crofting customers, like all his others, had to buy the 'firing' for his traction engine (he said) or he would have been bankrupt long since.

If the steam mill caused a stir about a farmtoun, its half-day at a croft was pure upheaval. It turned the normal routine upside down and caused claustrophobic congestion in its kitchen for it was the practice, as well as common Scots hospitality, to feed the mill crew – twelve men at the fewest. Lumps of beef would be brought from the butcher's the day before to make broth in the washday pot, wiped round for the occasion. Trestle tables were set up in the kitchen, or sometimes in the barn, and to augment the worn kitchen spoons the best cutlery was ripped out of the canteen where it lay bedded in silk between one christening and the next. In the excitement of it all, in his early crofting years, Willie Gavin had been able neither to sit nor stand; and Jess MacKendrick's kitchen would have come to a halt completely had not both Puir Angus and Lang Andra had the good grace to go home for their dinners.

Later though, the Gavin croft would avoid the disruption of the steam mill's visit. Willie Gavin would have his own barn-mill, something unique in the crofter community and a blessing that put him beyond the bargaining and the desperate petitioning and gave him, perhaps, his only real measure of independence as a crofter man. His son, Old John's young companion, recalls how the croft got its mill:

My younger brother took up threshing-mill construction as a livelihood. He was quite good at it: he had a great reputation for building the threshing machines that were installed in each farmtoun's barn.

When the croft crop was harvested they would build it all into stacks in the cornyard and these would be made more or less waterproof against rain, to an extent like the roofs of the buildings, which were thatched. And as they needed grain or straw they would bring in one of these stacks at a time, into the barn. Mostly, when they started to move the stack there would be a considerable number of rats, running in every direction . . .

And my brother, he built a threshing machine . . . and it did a good job and it was certainly a step much beyond that of using the old flail. It was powered by a motor and the grain would all be bagged, of course, and subsequently taken to the miller for grinding.

In fact, Willie Gavin's little thresher, an ingeniously sized-down version of the bigger mills that huddled in the dark of the farmtoun barns, was the envy of every crofter man in the district. With its drum, corn riddles and conveyor belt and two straw shakers, it did everything that the larger barn-mills would do. And though a few of the other croft men, by the 1920s, might have the kind of small portable thresher that was pedal-driven furiously by the croft wife as she also fed the sheaves into it, that needed a strong purse as well as a strong spouse! Mainly, the croft folk would continue to wait upon Mr Henderson, hopeful of soliciting his sympathy.

Willie Gavin enjoyed his independence, and maybe not only because it went against his grain to ask favour. There was a feeling (remembered still) among his family and neighbours that just because he had a mill he had also a bee in his bonnet about threshing, as strong in its way as his insistence on winning his own hairst. Certainly it was the view of his sons that he sometimes put on the mill when he had no need to. In retirement, it is admitted by all who knew him, the old man's decisions to thrash became increasingly eccentric, taken hurriedly and unpredictably between his morning brose and stepping in for his dinner. But, his mind made up, there could be no gainsaying him.

'Wumman,' he would say, coming into the kitchen and hanging his bonnet on the back of his chair as he sat down at the table, 'we will need to thrash this afternoon.'

It was fair warning that, whatever other arrangements she might have made, Grannie Gavin would be needed in the barn to feed the sheaves into the mill-drum.

The power for the little thresher mill came from the old Ruston oil engine, housed in the shed behind the barn and transmitting its drive by a shaft through the dividing wall. It had been bought cheaply, second-hand, and it was not long before the old crofter man knew why. Crouched and waiting in the dark, fume-filled engine house, it was a cantankerous thing. It took Herculean strength – much more than the old man should have exerted – to crank its heavy flywheel into motion. More than that, it took an accomplished sleight of hand, not to say magical adroitness, to slip the cranking handle free of its engaging 'dog' as the engine finally 'fired' and careered into motion. Such encounters blanched even the features of hardy men. Failure to achieve the dissociation in the critical instant could put the cranker in peril of his life as the handle whipped round and round in an ever-increasing frenzy on the spinning flywheel – ready to be hurled off at any moment. Once, it had gone through the roof unhindered by the worn corrugated sheeting while the starter huddled petrified in a dark corner. Understandably, there was a tension about the Gavin croft whenever the mill had to be put on; when a volunteer had been selected (on a Saturday afternoon, say, when extra hands were available) he stepped into the engine house alone while his companions gave what good advice they could from the safety of the shed door.

All the same, there were times when Willie Gavin's famous engine stayed silent and sullenly unresponsive without even the encouragement of an occasional chuff–chuff. Men panted at it in relays, taking off their bonnets to wrap round its handle and so prevent themselves getting hand blisters. Fear heightened the responses so that over the years Willie Gavin's oil engine achieved a notoriety that matched the fame of his little mill, and with it, a number of names, none of them the maker's and few of them that Grannie Gavin would have approved of had she heard them. But she never did. Starting the engine was men's work; the womenfolk stayed in the house, waiting for the first steady thump–thump of it – and ready to attend to the injured.

The day, at times, might be well done before the threshing was begun but at the end of it Willie Gavin would have a barn full of fine fresh straw and in his small loft, where the mill's conveyor cups had taken it, there would be a quarter or two of oats ready for bagging to take to the miller's or the seed corn merchant. That night, as he stepped in for his supper and the plate of bere-meal porridge Grannie Gavin would have waiting him, he would be a man well pleased with the world and all the folk in it. There was no doubt that the threshing heightened his blood. Nobody knew why, for the old man's hard hairsts never gave him anything near the yield he had hoped for. But then, there was nothing new about that; the croft folk were long inured to it and took its inevitability stoically, as they did so many other misfortunes.

It was, after all, no more than they expected: the grand hairsts grew in other men's fields, in the parks of the fine farmtouns where, in the days before hairst a man might bury himself to the armpits in the golden waving grain. All the same, the crofter men often connived at their own failure by sowing tattie corn year in,

year out. Always it was a poor yielder, giving only seven quarters
or so to the acre, a poor return against that of the farmtoun fields.
Well into the 1930s most of the crofter men clung with cussed
insistence and misguided loyalty to the old strain when there
were improved varieties, long-strawed at that, which would have
bettered their yields by at least half again. But then, the crofter
folk were like that: as unwilling to change their seed as they were
to put away their bloo coos. Some, shackled by tradition,
compounded their plight by keeping back from their own crops
their next year's seed, so weakening the sad strain further. Willie
Gavin was no different. Only the quarter or two he did not need
either for seed or for household oatmeal went to the feed-and-
grain merchant. Maybe they just about paid for the oilcake he
needed to fatten his stirks.

The Summer Folk

The late end of summer brought another crop home to the old crofts: the visitors who came, drawn by the season or driven after a year's sterility of city streets by the need to renourish their roots, gulp lungfuls of good air and a desire to rest the eye on a green and remembered landscape. They were the folk with connection in that old countryside; who could not live in it and could not leave it, their loyalties now so strange and torn. Their yearly pilgrimage emphasised the *raison d'être* of the old croft dwellings: their appeal as a home and the family's hub.

Sometimes a man would return briefly from Canada or the States with a cultivated drawl to buy a bull at the sales and take a wife back with him, sure of the pedigree of both. Sons came home from southern police forces to help with the hairst; lasses who were nurses or teachers brought intended husbands from Edinburgh and Glasgow and Dundee and from their respective professions to be looked over: poor lads most of them, hapless in their Argyle socks and Aran pullovers, for they could neither bind a sheaf nor set a stook and were of no mortal use to anybody, except maybe the croft daughters who had taken a liking to them. Clever sons, too small of stature for the country life but with the kind of pernickity minds that made them masters of other men's siller, brought home womenfolk, socially superior, from far counties and some of them English, sophisticated *jauds*, knowing and teasing; they smoked and they drank and they painted their faces (and God knows what else) and wore short flapper frocks that showed sometimes a portion of knicker-leg. They called everybody 'Darling', small boys included (to their eternal embarrassment) and demanded hot kisses at bed-time. For all that, they would be invited to come for their supper some evening and just for once Willie Gavin, when he came home, would wash his face and his hands before sitting down to an unaccustomed fine spread. Later on, the lad (and sometimes the lass, too) would take a dram with the crofter man and not know that it was a hint to go home. They would sit on, with their speak of the southern ways, so that the mason man would have to get out his bottle again to give them encouragement.

'Ye'll hae another nip afore ye go,' he would say heavily, hoping this time, surely, the allusion would not be lost on them.

It was a sociable countryside then, at that time of year, while the *rowth* of hairst went on. It was fine to have the young folk back for a while, to re-cement for a week or two the close texture of the old society, and the croft kitchens about the end of the day would ring again with their humour – boisterous, abrasive and slyly allusive but never foul-mouthed. Willie Gavin enjoyed their company; liked it, without resentment, for the view of the world it brought to his fireside. In the course of a summer he might discuss the disaster of an English hairst, the problems of building with bricks as well as the rubber plantations of Malaya and (with some young missionary who spoke still in his own broad Doric tongue) the cropping rotations under a hot Swaziland sun. Given the right man and the right topic the crofter might talk well into the night, as absorbed as though he were bound there himself come the morning.

The young McCaskills who had done so well at the school were regular yearly guests. Known since the days of their childhood, they came home, the three of them in turn usually, for the haytime and to help their father put past his harvest – to scythe and bind and stook, tasks as natural to them still as breathing. When there was a lull in the work or the weather broke they would be invited to Whinfield for their supper at six. They were allowed to stay late and have out their speak, for with their clever minds they were interesting folk.

One year Angus, the youngest, a Metropolitan police-sergeant, brought a lass from the Shires, all rosy and dimpled and with a shingled bob that showed off her delicate neck to perfection. For a fortnight she was the speak of the parish as she billed and cooed about him, not able to keep her hands off him even in decent folk's company. It was 'darling this . . .' and 'darling that . . .' and 'Isn't that so, darling?' Poor Angus (folk said), to have landed himself with such a *limmer!* For days on end the older croft bairns trailed them surreptitiously through the landscape, hoping they could learn something to their disadvantage. But desperate though the lass looked, if young Angus got a roll in the corn there was none of them saw it.

That was unusual, for it was a countryside without cover, unkindly to lovers. Hardly a year went by without some of the visiting young folk being found in a grassy lie, at the edge of the corn by some old crofter man who had gone out in the gloam (with the gamekeeper gone home) only to set his rabbit snares.

Fiona McPhee was a nurse and as bright as a button. She came regularly home with the hairst to rekindle old passions and flirt with the menfolk and spoke of the body and all its parts (even in front of the bairns) as if it were no better than a binder. She was *verra clivver*, folk said – and strong on high heels and displacement of the uterus.

But there were years when her oldest flame, Geordie McCaskill, never won home. He was a mission helper and it was the Depression years. Down in Liverpool's dockland, his mother said, things were so bad that he could not be spared. The croft folk believed it: from what Geordie had decently been able to tell them it was a *byordinar* place, a bit like Hell, with its women all painted and powdered, ill creatures all of them, waiting on sailors; they did *that* for a living. Geordie could not get away for they were all of them in sore need of the Word.

The Gavin croft too had its family guests, most of them Grannie Gavin's relations, for the MacKendricks had always been sociable folk. Rob, the second eldest of her brothers, came, a regular refugee from his own grim hairst in the Home Counties, and no sooner was he there than her youngest brother came down-country to meet him. The one was manager of the wool mill the MacKendricks had run for so long, the other sold coffins in Harrow.

They came as fugitives from their respective responsibilities and their social positions – into the freedom of Willie Gavin's landscape. Without loss of dignity (or trade) Rob could enjoy his ale at the inn in the kirktoun; Will could swill the dust of the looms well and truly from his throat without fearing any loss of authority. Together, they came home late to keep the crofter man out of his bed ('Where the devil can they be till this hour, wumman?') or at least make sure he did not lie easy in it.

Rob had a strange charisma for an undertaker: he was no sooner known to be in the countryside than folk flocked to see him, filling Willie Gavin's house from all corners of the parish. He was Somebody and enjoyed it: he was worth a penny or two folk said, and he never denied it. The pomp of his arrival, indeed, would hardly have disgraced royalty, for he travelled north not by the rigours of rail but in the cabin'd ease of the steamship *Caledonia*, which he left in Aberdeen harbour not a moment before he had sighted the hired car sent to meet him. From its window, as it sped the turnpike road, his eye drank in the countryside; he would be ready to give his verdict whenever he was set down at the top of the Gavin close, and as soon as the crofter man had shaken hands with him and taken charge of his cases.

'The hairst will be late this year, Willie.'

Some years maybe: 'The oats are looking well, Willie.'

Or chancing his townsman's arm, as he looked down the old croft's shifts: 'You'll have a good crop there, Willie.'

A stocky, black-moustachioed man with the unfortunate pallor of the burial parlour, he wore his bonnets as broad as those of any ploughman and set squarely on his head – a habit that at once gave credence to the thought that they were not his normal headwear and but newly out of some London draper's drawer. His soberly refined suits had the kind of cut you could not find in any fifty-shilling tailors, and his patent shoes were unblemished by even the smallest wrinkle.

His appearance betokened what everyone so strongly suspected: a more than passing acquaintance with siller. That, the young Gavins were told (when Rob had gone home), he'd made by burying the English in large numbers when they were taken off by the big 'flu epidemic. He had worked night and day, all the skills of his carpentry stretched, till he was forced into ready-mades to keep up with the demand. Poor Rob: he had taken ill himself after the epidemic was over, out of sheer exhaustion of body and spirit. And when he had some come to himself and squared his accounts, he found himself a rich man, set for life. On the strength of it, he had taken a wife late in life and now had a daughter, neither of whom he exposed to his northern relatives.

There was little doubt but that his brief summer sojourn was an escape, a time from the world and his affairs about the sedate streets of Harrow, where he was known to wear the genteel bowler and maybe even that higher badge of public service, the striped breeks. Besides his broad bonnet, there would be croft days when he would come down to the informality of shepherd's tartan trousers, worn with his funeral-black jacket. When he took through the countryside thus attired, he was an impressive –

if alien – figure. There was hardly an afternoon that did not find him on the road for he was asked to tea here, there, and everywhere. He took leave to look over many a roadside dyke in the passing and be quite cantingly critical of the work going on beyond it. He would be scathing about the stooking, the capability of the man on the binder. Yet his presumption was soon forgiven him, for there was this you could also say for Rob: if he was quick with his opinion, he was not slow with his siller, in the inn or elsewhere. Short of that small talk that beguiles a bairn, it would not be long before he was reaching his hand into his pocket to compensate the child with a silver coin. The children of the countryside soon came to know it and went far out of their way whiles to encounter his goodwill.

In other ways, too, he was a man of singular habits, and almost all of them played hell with the croft morning. He would not sit to his (late) breakfast till he had washed and shaved and put on his collar and tie – a ridiculous refinement in any croft kitchen. And when he was ready to sit down, so to speak, he would insist on eating his porridge standing up, his back to the fire, in spite of all the inconvenience it caused.

'Sit ye doon man, an' tak' yer pairritch in comfort,' Grannie Gavin would advise him (in the interest of avoiding further delay), trying to get at the pots on the boil behind him.

'No, Jess, thank you,' she would be told solemnly. 'I'm fine as I am. It's the straight sack that fills the quickest.'

It was a truism that any fee'd farmtoun laddie could have vouched for but typical of the droll aphorisms the Harrow undertaker would hurl about him during the course of his fortnight's stay. His personal-cleanliness habits especially, drove the old crofter man clean out of humour at times, especially if the hairst was bad.

'It's as weel, wumman, that he did not bring his family wi' him,' Willie Gavin would say, when the coast was clear.

'God be thankit for it,' his wife would reply, in fervent agreement, her gratitude for that overwhelming for the moment her horror of vain usage. 'Gin I had them here as weel, among my feet, I would never get a cow milkit nor a hen meated.'

Yet the sovereign or two he would set down on the garret's chest of drawers when Willie Gavin had taken his cases out to the car wonderfully softened the memory of his visit, and when he left it was always with a cordial 'Haste ye back' ringing in his ears. Since he was paying for the car and it had to come back to the parish anyway, he was never short of a send-off. All the Gavins who could get away were inclined to pack into it, to make his departure something of an outing.

Aboard the *Caledonia* for his voyage home, they marvelled at the way he spoke to the crew and to the steward who took his cases below. And they marked his sadness.

'Ach, it is a pity that all good things have to come to an end,' he might say as they all stood on deck taking a look from the harbour round the fine granite town.

'I'd like fine, Willie, to have an acre or two of ground . . . Some small place, when I retire. It would be fine to be out from among the coffins for the last of my days.'

Maybe he truly wished it; we cannot know now, one way or another. He was held by a position, a woman and a bairn; yet he may have hungered for that old countryside he had known as the weaver's laddie. Or maybe it was only a dream that he had; a dream in his head. But Rob MacKendrick never came back to his native landscape to stay and put down roots again. Nor did Fiona. Nor Geordie, who spent his life helping folk who were even poorer than the crofter folk themselves. Not even Angus and his shingled lass from the Shires, for she had gotten Angus in the end. There was word for a time that Angus *might* come back. But he stayed away and bought a fine house and his bairns spoke nothing but school English.

So, yearly, the young croft folk went back to their city beats and their matron's rounds, their lathes and their ledgers; to stronger suns and darker continents. When they had gone the country would be quiet, the hairst sheaves home and a stillness on the land as it came into the fall of the year. They were the summer folk; they had broken that old continuity of family and landscape, broken away from the crofting dream. Though they might feel the pull, they would not be coming back to re-people the old crofts. That had saddened Willie Gavin and Lang Andra McCaskill and, for all we know, Puir Angus McPhee. It seemed they might be the last of their folk to work the small patchwork fields.

A Thread from the Past

The Gavins, like the rest of the croft folk, shaped no destinies, not even their own. Their lives were dominated by the prices of meal and corn and what a stirk would bring in. Yet their crofting years would bring undreamt-of change. On the land the machine age would transform the old patterns of agriculture; travel would move from shank's mare to the threshold of the jet age.

Old John Gavin had been a man in his prime in the days of railway mania, yet he never boarded a train in his life. His grandson and favourite companion was with him in the early 1900s when the first motor car was seen approaching along the narrow beige road that ran past the croft and the old crofter had to be persuaded not to run for his life. His turkeys and guinea fowl, equally terror-stricken, scattered in all directions and did not come home for days. When the first motor-bicycle came to the Gavin croft the old woman who so fearlessly faced the bees brought out a box of matches when it came time for the guest to leave – and then quickly retired from the scene to await the explosion. Grannie Gavin was twenty-two and maid at the up-country merchant's before she saw her first bicycle, a wooden bone-shaker. The shop boys who later bought iron-made models would be forbidden to take them out on the Sabbath . . . Train, car – the ubiquitous bike most of all – would bring a rural revolution as far-reaching as the one that had first brought the crofts themselves into being, bringing an end to country life as the Gavins had known it.

Yet there would be continuity of a kind: it came down at Grannie Gavin's fireside on the nights when she kept her grandchildren to let her daughters and their men to a harvest supper or the bacchanalia of a Hogmanay ball. These were the nights that knit the generations; when story and legend passed down from the lips of the old to the credulous, receptive minds of the young.

The past came vividly alive at Grannie Gavin's knee; she was a great tradition-bearer – to use a modish and pompous word that had no currency in her own time and even now takes away the warmth of her recollection. Painstakingly she untangled the crofting past, never tired of answering a bairn's foolish questions. It was a fragile thread but she spun it with fine colours and the kind of striking detail that would stick in the mind and come back to you long after she had gone. Though she had worn black for best for as long as any of her grandchildren could remember, she was by no means in mourning for her life (though God knows, she had reason enough). She was a merry story-teller and her grandchildren listened, silent and wide-eyed. On such nights, in the 1920s and 1930s, in the hushed glow of the oil lamp and the dance of firelight, it was the spell of a hard landscape that passed down and with it the lore of the Gavins and the MacKendricks and all their folk, imprinting identity. Often she would return to the days of her own childhood and to her grandfather's small place on that windswept hill where the early crofting life had been at its most primitive.

'Where was that, Grannie?'

'On the Perk Hill.'

'Far's that?'

'Up the country, lassie. In Lumphanan.'

'Is yer grandfather's hoose still there, Grannie?'

'No, lassie. It is gone these many years noo – like nearly all the folk.'

'What were they like, Grannie? Yer grandfather's folk?'

'They were just poor crofter folk, like oorselves.' With a chuckle she would glance at Willie Gavin seated at the other side of the fire, herself enjoying the joke, her listeners as yet too young to catch its irony. But they would listen as she told of the Hill and the old croft life.

Later, scarfed and bonneted against the night air, they went out to the byre in a body as milking-time came round, the little ones going down the croft close on Willie Gavin's hand, as yet barely able to stand and apt to sit suddenly down in its mud if released. They stood quietly against the byre's limewashed wall while Grannie Gavin milked the beasts, their voices stilled for once by the leap and menace of the shadows brought to life in every corner by the flicker of the candle lantern. Outside the wind haunted the old croft biggings but inside it was warm with the breath of beasts, a solitude made mesmeric by the steady slurp-slurp of the bloo coos' milk rhythmically hitting the side of the enamelled pail.

Coming back up the close, if the night was not chill, there might be time to take a look at the full moon, a yellow disc that hung in the sky over Lang Andra McCaskill's chimney.

'Is that God's lantern, Granda?' It seemed, on the face of it, not an unreasonable supposition.

'Dyod laddie – likely it will be, then.' The old crofter man would see no need to refute it.

'They say there's a man in the moon, Grannie.'

'An' sae there is, laddie. See ye . . .' The milk pail would be put down for a moment while the young Gavin was lifted to get a better look. 'D'ye nae see his een an' his side-whiskers?'

Long he might look, the young Gavin, unwilling to accept defeat. Finally, though, he would be forced to admit that he could see neither eyes, nose nor dundrearies – caught, as he was, between the desire not to disappoint his grandmother and the honesty in all things that was constantly preached at him. Yet even that young, he knew the value of compromise.

'I think, Grannie, that must be the back o' his heid.'

Indoors again they were in the private world of Granda and Grannie Gavin. Coats were hung on the passage nails, not to be needed till morning. Now night folded in on the croft biggings. Grannie Gavin took off her outdoors apron (finally) and found her knitting and the old folk settled in their chairs at each side of the fire while the bairns played (and as frequently squabbled) on the rug between them. There were minor emergencies in which the smaller children were excused the cold trip with a lantern to the John Gunn. All the same, the proprieties would be observed. Little girls were seated behind their grandmother's chair, shielded from curious glances; small boys took cover behind their grandfather. Both parties would be asked, repeatedly, had they done 'their business' and if not, advised and instructed, their grandfather in particular counselling pressure should it be needed.

'*Birss*, laddie. *Birss!*'

Decorum came to disaster only when a young bairn, feeling ignored, so far forgot himself as to rise and bring pot and results on to the rug.

Here was the softer side of the hard mason man, one that the world never saw, as he and his wife, between the wars, again surrounded themselves with children. Willie Gavin liked his grandchildren, folk said, better than he had ever liked his own. But maybe it was only that he had more time to give them.

In the young Gavin laddies who might keep him company in his small fields, he inculcated the old ways, maybe judging whiles the man the bairn would become. What he passed down was a landsman's skills. A likely lad would be given a light spade to assist the old man on some crofting task and would be reminded as they came home again and into the croft close: 'See til't that ye clean and oil that spaad, laddie, afore ye put it awa'.'

If the boy showed aptitude, he would be allowed to quarter the beasts' neeps with the spade; he would be taken to the hoeing with a cut-down hoe and encouraged to walk home from his yoking's work like a man, the hoe's shaft across the small of his back and his arms crooked round it. He would be invited to pat cow rumps and hold stirks by their halters, and in time to judge crops for their ripeness. He would be given a hay fork to turn the hay in the swath and when he was older and stronger, the *smiler*, the hayrake, to pull the swathes into windrows. And on a day when the old crofter man took it into his head to thrash, he would be given the same fork back again and put into the barn corner to clear the straw as it came off the little mill's shakers.

For such a lad, Willie Gavin, hard man though he was, could make concessions: coming home from the hoeing the lad might have his boots brushed for him with the besom at the croft door before they both stepped in for their supper; a blind eye might even be turned were he to be seen for a moment among the garden strawberries. In time, it might be that the laddie would absorb some of the old man's compassion for dumb beasts and for those folk whom life had maimed.

And there was something else their old grandfather taught the young Gavins: that to survive you had to win. In those long winter evenings with the milking done, he would bring out the *dambrods*, the draughts, that he loved so much, to take on all-comers. In that he made no concessions: he had to be beaten fair and square. It was not that he lacked pity, far from it; only that in a hard world he saw no point in pretending it was otherwise.

With his wide antiquarian interests, it was Willie Gavin who re-peopled the historical past of the countryside for his grand-children, making them understand how close they stood to the men who had once walked its old baulks and its burn banks.

'Fa was it bade in the auld castle, Granda?'

'The Forbeses, laddie. Gey cheils all of them.'

Excitement would dance in young *een*. 'Did they hae fechts, Granda? Battles, like long ago? Folk fechting wi' swords and suchlike?'

If Willie Gavin was not the man to tell lies, neither would he willingly have stunted a young imagination; he would get round it neatly. 'Well, I never heard tell o'that, laddie, but maybe . . . They were sair times lang syne.' In truth it was not only its history that took the mason man still on a walk to the castle on a fine Sabbath but his admiration for the men who had biggit it; he went to marvel at the way its mortar had weathered the years. He would have liked fine to have built a castle in his time.

'Did they fecht at Harlaw, Granda?'

'I kenna gin they did or no'.'

'Didnae the king himsel' come once to the castle?'

'Long syne, I believe. Jeemes the Saxt, not long after they had biggit it.'

'They say that one laird saved a king's life.'

'Aye, and so he did, laddie. The tenth laird. He was a colonel of horse at the Battle o' Worcester. Doon in England that was, in 1651 or thereaboots. The poor king had his horse shot from under him . . . The laird, he swung his whole troop around him—'

'Was the king kil't, Granda?'

'Na, laddie . . . The laird does nae mair but pit the king intill a sodger's coat and pits a bleedy rag roond his heid to make him look wounded-like – and then sets him on his ain horse an awa' tae safety, aff the field!'

Strange they thought it that history had brushed so close to them there by the fire on a winter's night; strange to think now of that laird, who had lost all his siller in the disaster of Darien; or the one who came after him, bankrupt but defiant, entrenched behind the old castle's wall till the Redcoats came to evict him.

'Was it a ruin lang syne, Granda?'

'No, when my father was a young man there were folk still bade in it.'

Bedtime came always too soon for the young ones, for under Grannie Gavin's roof they had expected indulgence. Again there was discretion as long cotton nightshirts were donned behind either grandfather's or grandmother's chair. A song was sung to forestall tantrums and dispel a few tears, the old crofter man joining in as he took their hands and *convoyit* them as far as the foot of the stair.

> Wee Willie Winkie rins thro' the toon
>   Upstairs and doonstairs in his nichtgoon.
> Chappin' at the windae, crying at the lock
>   'Are a' the bairnies in their beds
>   – it's past echt o'clock?'

Tiny feet tramped their thumping accompaniment, one step after the other, their disappointment forgotten – and suddenly found themselves at their bedroom door. Prayers were said on clickit rugs before they climbed under the blankets – muddled orisons that made appeals in their own behoof and for all known and remembered Gavins and all others believed to be deserving cases, the tones of supplication slipping from the school English into the lurching Doric of their own landscape as vocabulary failed them. It is impossible to say what the Almighty made of these garbled messages but, their penury apart, He never did badly by the Gavins and for all their mishanters they never lost faith in Him.

Under Grannie Gavin's care the young ones slept three to a bed under the panelled eaves of their grandfather's garrets, a small Gavin girl between two Gavin boys whom she would cuddle in turn, all innocence yet in her bedding. High on its shelf above them, sconced in its black-enamel holder, the candle was allowed to burn till sleep had claimed them.

The older Gavin grandchildren sat on with their grandparents. Secrets were shared, confidantes made as the firelight dwindled. The speak now would be 'grown-up', almost between equals. Affection kindled laughter and even Grannie Gavin herself might be quietly teased. Willie Gavin, they were led to believe, had not been Jess MacKendrick's first love. There had been another, whose name had never been dropped in their hearing, though the reason for his fall from grace was known: he had attempted liberties with Grannie Gavin's young person. Knowingly unknowing, her older granddaughters slyly abetted such revelations.

'But did ye nae take him back, Grannie?'

'No.'

Quiet pressure would elicit that the poor lad, thus disappointed, had gone on to misbehave elsewhere and had been immediately banished from the young Jess MacKendrick's circle.

As often, it was her adventures that seized them: her escape, once, from a blazing attic, her journey home in the kitchen's box-bed in Rob Gibbon's cart.

'Ye was goin' tae die, Grannie, wasn't ye?' Endlessly, insistently, they would need confirmation of that.

And there were other things too, known darkly of Grannie Gavin's past, that were rarely spoken of and might be gleaned only from the guarded gossip of her daughters as they sat round their own firesides. Among them was her encounter with The Convict. Now and then, as the fire wore down and Willie Gavin filled his stump of a Stonehaven pipe for the last smoke before bedtime, a spirit, emboldened, would say:

'Tell us aboot the convict, Grannie – when he captured you and ye didnae ken what tae dae. And he made ye sew a button on till his troosers.'

Grannie Gavin, her head mutched still from the byre, would nod gently, staring into the last of the fire, her voice quiet as she told them.

It had been the gloam of a winter's afternoon and only herself about the croft, busy in the kitchen. Sensing his presence, she had turned from the fire to see him, half-hidden in the lobby's shadows. There had been news round the country, word from the kirktoun; she had known. He was a dangerous man, so they said. And maybe he was, for all that. But what the young croft wife saw that day was a man driven to the end of his tether by days on the run and exposure; a man in draggled clothes, stolen like enough in the night from some farmtoun that had unwittingly sheltered him – a need and a necessity that had immediately pin-pointed his flight. They had stared at each other, gauging their fright, one of the other.

'You're by yourself?' he asked finally.

'Aye, man.' If he sensed the fearless spark in the little woman facing him, he saw also her pity.

'Have ye food? I've no' eaten for days.' His accent was from somewhere in the South.

'Little enough, but ye're welcome. Sit ye doon.'

Cautiously, listening for noise in the house or in the gathering night outside, he drew the chair out from the end of the kitchen table, between her and the door. It had not troubled her. From the meal girnal she brought the trencher with its piled farls of oatcakes; from the press she set down kebbuck cheese and watched him wolf into it.

'I hiv second day's broth . . .' she offered. 'It will tak' but a moment to heat.'

'And tea?' he said. 'Wid ye make tea?' It was more plea than command. She picked up the iron kettle from the fireside and went to pass him into the porch when he seized her wrist in a desperate grip.

'Where're ye gaun?' He had half-risen from his chair.

'Tae get watter man, from the pail.'

'Oh, aye.' He sat slowly back onto his chair.

Close to him she saw the state of the clothes he had stolen: the misshapen heavy jacket that some bailie maybe kept behind the byre door to take him across the farmtoun close on a day of *dinging* rain; the breeks, buttonless and held by twine, from God knows where, but likely from some shepherd's bothy and used only for the dipping.

'Yer claes are sodden man. Ye'll catch yer death.'

Reassured, he released her wrist and when she returned from the porch and filled the kettle she saw he had hung his jacket to dry on a chairback, close to the fire. He broke oatcakes into the broth she set before him, supping it untidily.

'Warm,' he said.

She nodded, watching him. 'The tea will be drawn in a meenit.'

'Hae ye threid?' His broth finished, he had stood up and was looking down at his buttonless trousers. 'And a button? Tae mak' me decent.'

'Aye, man. But ye'll need tae come near the fire to let me see.' She took a mug down from the dresser and poured his tea.

So, in the firelight of that darkening room, Jess MacKendrick had sewn on the button that would save the convict embarrassment, he in that moment, more her prisoner than she his. As she stuck the needle back in its cushion on the mantelshelf and put her thimble away, he had shrugged back into his jacket, still damp but at least a little warmer. Under the growth of beard the face had seemed that of a decent man, without evil in it; it was hard to think of the ill he could have done.

'Ye've a barn?' It was the most tentative inquiry.

'My man will be home directly,' she said.

In a moment he had been gone, into the deeper dark of the croft house lobby, a shadow an instant later flitting past the kitchen window.

'God be wi' ye, man,' she had said, not knowing if he heard her. It had seemed wrong that any human should be hunted so – like a beast.

When Willie Gavin himself came home she would tell him what had happened to the second day's broth she had been heating for him, and though the poor convict's other crime was never known, he went into the Gavins' folklore forever as The Man Who Ate Willie Gavin's Supper.

In the last blink of firelight, from the skeletal account and their knowledge of their grandmother's ways, the young Gavins would fill out the portrait of that encounter in an old country-side. They would be the last generation to gather through those long winter evenings round the old croft's fire – the last to know the old crofting life and the ways of the folk who lived it. For all their grandfather's encouragement and his dour discipline, some of them would not be able to tie a hairst band or know the need to clean and oil a spade. But they would remember an old man's steely character and a croft wife's charity. None would choose to work on the land. Their only inheritance would be the memories of the crofting Gavins. It was a past binding on the soul.

The Bonds of Friendship

Crofter friendship was a fragile thing; it could be ruptured abruptly by your cow in the other man's corn. Yet deeper down there was an underlying unity in crofting society that drew folk together. That it was so was less than surprising: theirs was a community in which self-help, though constantly preached, was a fallible commodity and mutual aid more frequently the hard necessity of a hardy lifestyle. Differences there might be but, for all that, a man would not willingly stand by and see his neighbour lose his crop or in desperate want. Bad illness would bring help, a willing spade or a scythe from along the road, from somewhere else on the hill; death itself, where a man without sons had gone without gathering his hairst, the kindly aid that would tide his widow over until such time as she decided her future. The womenfolk, when family tragedy took them from home, or childbed claimed them, would milk each other's cows and feed each other's men. It was more than mere neighbourliness for sooner or later they knew they would need repaying in kind. For the same reason a man was careful not to too far outrage his fellow crofters; though he might not himself be a regular kirkgoer (and there were few who did not owe allegiance somewhere), however rough his character or his crofting, rarely would he provoke censure by blatantly working his shifts on the Sabbath.

The New Year traditionally was the time – as in the world of the farmtouns – when the crofting community came together to resolder old friendship and bury (for a time) ancient vendettas; when passions cooled and all debts were acknowledged. It was a festival in that harsh landscape – like old Beltane and Lammas and All Hallows – that for all their kirkgoing came perilously close to the pagan. It had to do with the earth and the soul, with nature and portents; its theme was renewal, the rebirth of the year and through that the rebirth of the spirit. Like most of his kind, Willie Gavin held to Aul' Eel (Old Yule). It was the trait of a persistent man, and one widely shared in a region where the elderly, refusing to nod to the calendar's change of a century and half earlier, still counted their days by the old feasts, Handsel Monday, and Fastern's E'en (with its bannocks and brose) and lovely old Candlemas among them. It was a calendar, that old one, whose seasons and days more closely marked their everyday lives (and their backward agriculture); its customs at times had long roots in the past that didn't bear scrutiny. It was a calendar richer than ours, with its grey insistent days, and it is strange to think that it died without a conservationist's whimper. Aul' Eel had been its anchor-point and it was still, in the 1930s, one of the festivals from which the old crofter man dated events. His speak would be reflectively punctuated with 'Just afore Lammas, that would have been . . .' or 'That would have been about Aul' Eel'.

Hogmanay, like Halloween, had once been a festival to older and darker gods, all of them now long forgotten; the last day and night of the year, it drew to it in the old landscape much of the spirit of modern Christmas (then a normal working period); its goodwill and good fellowship certainly, if none of its religious observance. As the year drew to an end straw would be fordeled, stored ready, so that none need put a hand to the flail all the days of the holiday. Willie Gavin, in his time, put on his small mill and threshed beforehand: his beasts would share in the season's goodwill. If, as in his father's boyhood, the *clyack* sheaf, that totem to future fertility, no longer came down from the barn's rafters as a treat for the shelt, the mason man would make sure, all the same, that his bloo coos had a turnip or two extra in their troughs on New Year's morning.

As the last night of the year drew in and all work stopped on the land and in the farmtouns of that far countryside, visiting bairns would hang their stockings from Grannie Gavin's mantelshelf and become increasingly anxious as the evening wore on: had Santa been notified of their temporary change of address? With endless patience, their old crofter grandfather reassured them. In the night outside, older children came to ring the croft-house door, swinging leering neep lanterns (a ring of toothy faces, when you opened the door), and cry the old orisons that linked that night with the guiser's past and an earlier, unChristian time:

> Rise up, gudewife, an' shak' yer feathers,
> Dinna think that we are beggars.
> We're only bairnies come tae play –
> Rise up and gie's oor Hogmanay.

On a night of storm the pleas would be torn from their lips and lost on the howl of the wind. That, or the failure to stir the gudewife's heart at first, would lead to a further supplicatory chorus, chanted with urgency. Often enough on such a night it had a literal truth that gave it point, and at times maybe poignancy:

> Wir feet's caul', oor sheen's thin.
> Gie's a piece, an' lat's rin.

A piece it seldom was, for the gudewife of the croft or farmtoun, frantically preparing for the holiday, would not have time to make them one. But apples and oranges were as well received, or a slice of seedcake that could clog your jaws for days after, and with them, perhaps, pennies would be handed round with the old salutation: 'A happy Hogmanay tae ye'. Few were refused on that night of nights, though folk should go begging in the morning. Yet by the 1920s and 1930s, as Willie Gavin came near to the end of his crofting days, the neep lanterns and the old chants were almost part of the past; they would largely die out round the countryside as the old-style cottars and crofters left it.

When their voices had faded on the night, a quiet would come down on the old croft dwelling and in that hour or two before the turn of the year, its hush was filled with the whispering of Willie Gavin's clocks in their conspiracy to end it.

Though he had no ill will at a dram, it was only about the New Year, the end of hairst or a threshing or in the social climax to a wedding or a funeral that the old crofter man himself would take one. It was only at those times too, and maybe for the summer guest, that the croft's bottle was taken from the cupboard. But at Old Yule he bought goodwill as willingly as the next man and with a good grace received the first-footers of the year, taking a dram from their bottles and giving one from his own. The New Year was like the day of a fair or a feeing market, a kind of lighthouse in the year that men looked to from time to time as they charted their way across it. It was a point of destination, a landfall they reached when they had sometimes doubted it, and there were times, with relief in their souls, when they celebrated it with all the gratitude of folk who had just survived shipwreck. Poor though the croft folk were, the bottles went round with abandon, for theirs was a hardy voyage and the wind never with them.

Cottared sons-in-law (on a spree by themselves or bringing the old man's daughters with them), neighbours and folk whose degree of relationship was tenuous but would not that night of the year be inquired into (even if it could have been determined) came in from the dark for their glass and to give seasonal greeting and stayed to make fools of themselves by forgetfully trying to tell the coarse kind of story that would put them clean out of countenance for years to come. Old soldiers whose only battle-ground now was their small croft shifts stepped in off the road worsened by drams and drank on till the old scars of war re-opened like raw, bloody wounds inside them and they marched Grannie Gavin's stone kitchen floor with her besom (seized from the porch) at the slope, shouting and shouldering and presenting arms as it all came mercilessly back to them, nearer to them still than the old acquaintance of the folk who sat round them; till the memory of it all shook them shivering cold sober.

More cheerful, peace-loving men wandered in on nights of *blind smorr* (just in the bygoing, they insisted, shaking the snow from their whiskers and their coats) to give the old crofter man and his wife that old salutation:

'A guid New Year, Willie. Tae yersel' an' a' yer fowk.'

And, catching Grannie Gavin's eye, from some man, well liked: 'A guid New Year tae ye, Jess – you're keepin' weel?'

'A guid New Year – and many of them,' Willie Gavin would wish his guests, that response as ancient, as ritually deep in the old pattern of the occasion as the greeting itself.

'Please God, she will be a better one than the last.'

That, always, was the fervent wish, the glimmer of hope: that next year's crop and next year's stirks might bring better prices and some relief if not comparative prosperity (which was too much to ask for). With the last harvest now well behind them they could look back, stoically.

'She was an ill hairst, this year by-past.'

For a moment amid the conviviality of that night, the heart-break of it came back to them, the memory of the laid crops, the way the stooks had stood long and *drookled* in the farmtoun parks till they had taken root where they stood, the rain never-ending.

Other men, too, stepped in from the dark – uncertain of

whose house they were in as their heads swam and the cogs of
memory slipped – to spout toasts that were doggerel pure and
simple and yet in a crofter's world were profoundly relevant.

> Here's tae the warld that gangs roon' on wheels,
>   Death is a thing that ilka man feels.
> If life was a thing that ane could buy
>   The rich wid live and puir wid die.

Or, from the ecological panjandrum, and parodying the poor
crofter's plight:

> Here's tae the tatties
>   Far e'er they be.
> The skins feed the pigs
>   An' the pigs feed me.

Neighbouring croft men brought their womenfolk with them,
their country first-footer's gift of a quarter-pound of tea, a half-
pound of sugar or a jar of preserve, something they could well
have done with keeping for themselves. But as they so often said:
'A friend's gain is nae loss.'

By the 1920s and 1930s, the old women who had taken a
dram (and the smoke of a clay pipe) along with their men were
long into the kirkyard and their daughters more genteelly
welcomed in the New Year with circumspect sips of port or
the last home-brewing of elderberry wine. All the same, there
were times when they might have done better to follow the old
wives' example for there were croft women in that old countryside who made home-made wine more damaging than bad
whisky. Innocents who supped it unguardedly might soon have
to be helped home the worse for it – or so unaccustomedly
flushed and chattering as to be in imminent danger of letting out

in loud whispers all their family's secrets. Favourites – kin and
close friends – might sit sociably through the night-long traffic.
When they had swallowed their drams they would be given tea
while the folk came and went: out to get home, or to go to the
edge of the midden and be sick and get over it.

Bonnets, politely doffed, dangled from slippery serge knees
and fell periodically on the floor where, as the night went on,
their retrieval became increasingly perilous. Men unaccustomed
to the drawing room graces juggled tea cups in their saucers in
one hand, a slice of seedcake on a delicate plate in the other, an
art so diabolically difficult that only the socially gifted could
manage it and the older croft and farmtoun men would wave the
cake plate away with an imperious:

'Na, na . . . I'll tak' it in my hand just.'

But in time even friends went home, out into a northern night
hung with stars, their cry coming out of the dark as they headed
up the croft close:

'Guid nicht and Guid be wi' ye.'

It would be morning, and milking-time, soon enough.

It was a night that took its toll; with such a surplus of goodwill
that was inevitable. Men did a mischief to themselves and to folk
who were with them, and some had the kind of luck that could
only be marvelled at and made them a legend in the land.
Munro, long in the smiddy, had a journeyman smith whose
bowing of an old Scotch fiddle was second to none in that long-
ago landscape. Such was his artistry that folk passing by his
roadside bothy on a summer night would stop to listen to the old
airs that he wrung so sweetly from the strings. But Montgomery
had two other loves: the drams (like fiddlers all) and his motor-
bike. There was never a New Year's morning when he was not
found – slightly the worse for the one but safe in the saddle of the
other – in the ditch into which he had ridden it. Sober, he was a
shy man and a fine smith.

With the New Year past, the croft folk looked forward, with hope, to the spring. The mason man's thoughts would be on the work he would be starting as soon as the frosts would let him. The evenings given to his children, playing draughts and dominoes and snakes and ladders or maybe hide-the-thimble, would be taken up with the men who came to see him – building men like himself, wondering would there be work with him again that year. They would time their arrival to find Willie Gavin, the milking done, still in the byre. It was, after all, a warm place to do business and the two of them would stay out there long after Grannie Gavin had gone into the house. A man whose work the mason man regarded as competent (provided he was not a troublemaker or addicted to bouts at the bottle) would get a fair hearing and a likely starting date; stronger favourites or other master masons, some agreement reached, would be brought to the house for a cup of cocoa and a biscuit before cycling off again into the night on the wobbly glimmer of a fitful gas lamp. For business, in that old landscape, fused strongly with friendship.

For all its hardship, it was a sociable countryside. Croft wives found time (between feeding beasts and men and hens) to go visiting and in some of the old croft kitchens indeed there was a social graciousness that would have surprised the outsider. Many of the croft wives, after all, had been in service in their younger years, like Jess MacKendrick herself – at the manse maybe, or even the Big House – and when they put away their sacking aprons for an hour or two in the middle of the afternoon the tea-tray they laid lacked little but the sheen of the laird's silver sugar-bowl.

Their dress aprons then would be black with a brightening of broderie. Even so, these would be removed before they answered the door. To have done less would have been impolite, and the apron could always excusably be donned again when it came time to make the tea. Given that it was almost their only recreation, the gossip was less genteel. Inevitably, it concerned the countryside and its folk; few escaped with a clean character. Like the frail, babies were visited and welcomed into the world and invariably had silver coins thrust into their small clutching fists, not in the hope that it would set them on the road to much-needed riches (though that was better than crofting) but to bring luck to the donor, who might have more immediate need of it.

Still summer nights were enlivened by the occasional feet-washing, that ancient prenuptial rite that took on, at times, all the character of a human steeplechase as the victims were run down and plastered from head to toe by black-lead, black axle-grease (whatever might cause the most havoc) and sprinkled with flour. It was a ritual as old in the Highlands, an indication perhaps of how close the landscapes once had been, but less vicious there than in the farming North-East Lowlands, where it stopped just short of taking life.

It was a landscape in which rank got the respect it deserved, and in which the laird, with his old house, stood at the centre of rural life, a considerably greater figure then than now. If he went from home for a time, his welcome back could be effusive – maybe in the hope he would not put the rents up, but as often with a genuine response that betrayed the interdependence of a close-knit society. Here is such a reception, described in *We Twa*, the combined memoirs of Lord and Lady Aberdeen, a well-loved pair, published in 1925 after a lifetime's lairdship. It was a chilly November evening towards the close of the 1800s, but even a monarch could hardly have made a more triumphal progress. When the laird and his party reached their home station it was ablaze with light and most of their tenantry awaited them.

As we drove home every cottage and every farm was illuminated. Bonfires blazed along the route and groups of cheering spectators and children seemed to spring up at every corner.

An arch of fairy lights had been erected at Raxton Lodge entrance, and within half a mile of the house the carriage was stopped by a party of 170 torch bearers, who insisted on taking the horses out and dislodging the coachman, replacing him by a piper. So, to the tune of 'The Gordons hae the guidin' o't', our carriage was dragged along by a stalwart band and escorted by a torchlight guard of honour to Haddo House, where every window was illuminated, fireworks being let off, and a great bonfire burning.

It was an occasion, of course, that neatly stratified the estate's tenantry, and though they carried no torches, put their shoulders to no carriage or spoke any word of welcome, there were crofter men on the fringe of that vast assembly who raised their bonnets and cheered with the rest. Among them were Old John Gavin and his mason son.

Yet rank never held the monopoly in friendship and the man selling besoms, or the tinker wife, would be 'Hallo'd' on the road and as warmly greeted and given a drink of milk on the doorstep. Many of the wandering folk of the old countryside came round the crofts year after year till the people would ask after the wife's man and all her bairns. Willie Gavin all his life had a weakness for the packman who hawked his wares round the country doors. Just the sight of the pedlar turning down the croft close was enough to make him drop his hoe in the drill and come home to buy more bootlaces than he would ever have need of and more collar studs than a careful man like himself was ever likely to lose. And the sight of a good pocket knife in the old man's pack never failed to excite him like a school laddie.

The arrival of the rag-and-bone man's pony and cart, too, would take him home to the croft biggings in a hurry – just for a news of the 'ragger' and maybe to see that Grannie Gavin got a fair deal for the rags she had not as yet hooked into the heart of a rug. The deals with the rag-and-bone man were about the last bastion of barter in the old landscape for coin never came into it. Old John's grandson remembers the visits of Raggie in the early years of the century as well as the disability that had first turned him to his trade:

> He used to go round all over the countryside, picking up old bottles, rags – anything that would be regarded by the average person as scrap. He picked up all this sort of stuff. In exchange for a fair-sized bag of rags he would give the housewife a couple of bowls or a cup and a saucer or a few plates, or something like that – it was all china that he carried.
>
> He was a kindly old soul, well liked by the children and adults alike. But he had only one arm. He must have lost his left arm some time early in life – I never heard how. But he was quite adept at using his one arm; he would grab a bag of rags and toss it on the hook scale without bother. He was a noted character all over the countryside.

That the croft folk's welcome should be so cordial is little to be wondered at, for their own circumstances in life were little better. Old John Gavin, with his own shelt and cart, was on the road almost as often as any rag-and-bone man and frequently with less errand. He had been a sociable man, the old farmtoun horseman, easing himself through life without worry and occasionally with the help of the whisky bottle, and in his old age especially he had been most ably abetted by his sociable shelt. Whenever the croft work grew sore on him, he would yoke Meggie into the cart – his rig no different from the 'ragger's' – and find a need to go somewhere: to deliver honey to the railhead shop; to fetch hens' feed; cow's oilcake; netting wire for a new hen's cruive; *backs* (those first bark off-cuts of the tree-trunk) from the sawmill.

In the little kirktoun he had many convivial friends, notably the innkeeper, who liked nothing better than a dram with cronies about the middle of the day (it was trade, after all). The two of them would sit well into the afternoon till the shelt, with more sense than its master, would come to the inn window to look in on them, knowing it was time they should be home. There were times when Old John was so low he would have to go to the sawmill several days in succession and years, as a result, when he had so many backs about the croft that he could have built the OK Corral. As for the shelt, its behaviour was a disgrace and an embarrassment to the abstemious son when the old man had gone, for it stopped always at every inn they came to.

In that old landscape entertainment had been rustically simple, a pattern of ease, centuries old, that slotted neatly into the farming calendar: a once-a-year visit from the travelling circus about the end of hairst (in its small tent, lit by flares, a man walked tall on stilts stealing the sad clown's laughter); concerts of sorts later on in the deep of winter that brought faded sopranos out from retirement in Aberdeen (most did not travel well); the Oddfellows' Ball (and for that a lass, the maid at the manse or the merchant's, had to be asked for and went only with the kind of lad who could be relied on to return her in the condition he found her). It was a calendar that fitted its gatherings and its shows into that lull before the hairst.

The games had been the delight of Old John Gavin's year. If he could not travel like his laird to see the world it was this yearly event – in the grounds of the laird's Big House – that brought some of a changing world's wonders to him, for a day. The old crofter attended them until he had almost to be carried there. His grandson, who would read the programme to him to whet his excitement, recalls the wonder of that country occasion:

The games were on a big scale and they had something really outstanding every year . . . Something really significant to draw the crowds. One year they had a lady go up in a balloon . . . after a considerable time had elapsed she came down again.

The next year they had an aviator – this was in the infancy of aviation – an aviator of considerable repute, one of the pioneers, and he flew round the park where the games were being held in his aircraft, barely above the treetops. And that was something sensational to see in those days.

That would draw a big crowd: they would come by the thousands and there were no motor cars in those days – they were all horse-drawn vehicles that used to be identified as charabancs; they could accommodate anything from twenty to fifty passengers on board and they would be drawn by anything from six to a dozen horses . . .

For all the wonders of that day though, the daily round of that far countryside was still one which was read for sign and portent; where the tea leaf circling your cup brought a stranger to the door, as did the knife that fell to the floor; where a blue gleam in the fire-flame foreshadowed the storm to come, like the ring round the moon; and the spark flying out from the fire to you meant a letter in the post ('Yer gaun tae get news'). If belief at times was thin, it mattered little, for those were merely the things that added dimension to the days.

It was a society – that of the old crofting hillside – in which friendship knitted deeply with the social hour, much more than in our own time, and understandably enough. Though suburban man can ignore his neighbour (and usually does), the croft man could hardly afford to; the time came soon enough when he had to rely on him. If the crofter men at the end of their hard hairsts held no meal-and-ales, those orgiastic harvest suppers of the big farmtouns, that is not to say that they did not invite near-neighbours for a dram and their supper when they all had 'winter'. To end such an evening, Willie Gavin liked the *cairds*, the cards, an unexpected weakness that must have come down in his father's rakish blood; there were few things he liked more – having trounced a few folk at the dambrods – than a hand or two of whist with worthy adversaries. But the play was for pleasure alone: nobody played for stakes at Willie Gavin's table, no more than they played on the Sabbath.

Like the land itself, friendship had its rituals. In all but the most savage weather, visitors to the Gavin croft were convoyit, accompanied a little of the way home, when it came time for them to leave; that was the custom, anciently observed, and departure with less ceremony would have told the thickest-skinned guest that he had overstayed his welcome and to be in no hurry back. Willie Gavin himself convoyit the menfolk (it was the moment for the quiet confidence, the private word, something they had not been able to exchange at table); Grannie Gavin accompanied the women at about a fifty yard' distance, out of earshot, taking stock of such female affairs as could not be mentioned in mixed company. It would have been insult pure and simple not to have been convoyit past McPhee's on the one side or McCaskill's on the other, and on a summer night the custom could be extended for so long that a man wanting home to feed beasts would think he was never going to get away.

For all its poverty it was a society in which care was deep and rooted; unlike our own, it cared for its old and kept them in the bosom of the family even if it sometimes tired of their opinions. The heat of a summer's day would bring the aged patriarchs of the croft hills and colonies from their winter ingles to look over the landscape and the burgeoning fields their sweat had created. Frailer still, they would be brought to the croft doors in their chairs to sit heavily jacketed in the sun as their last days slipped from them. What saw they then, you would wonder whiles, as they sat looking out on that countryside that stirred with the shades of Dane and Highlandman, Royalist and Covenanter, Jacobite and Redcoat, that unquiet land where the old gods stalked and the past was not still.

And there was yet another side to friendship: the sorrow shared. Grannie Gavin was no stranger to it: death, like birth or disaster, could bring a knock to her door. When tragedy struck or an old person eased out of this world, whether in the croft community or among the encircling farmtouns, it was often to the Gavin croft that folk came, sad-faced, to seek after her to wash and dress the corpse and lay it out for the coffin. It was something she would do without question, as a matter of duty, never refusing however tenuous the friendship or family connection and whatever her own health at the time. Frail though she seemed whiles as the years came on her, she would sit with the dying through the dark regions of the night (so that their folk might get sleep) and be in her own byre for the milking in the morning. In the death room so strong was her faith that she bore up others in their grief; weighed down with its indignities, she scrupulously kept its secrets. Afterwards she would stay a night or two with a new widow till she got used to the terrible silence of her house and never the scrape of her man's foot on the door flag.

Providence was Jess MacKendrick's staff and her consolation and she advised everyone to put their faith in it; it was her own caution in the everyday affairs of life, so strongly felt that even an invitation accepted would immediately bring its proviso: 'Gin we all be spared', or 'Gin Providence spare us'. A merry woman, it seemed whiles that her life was hedged round with the knowledge of death; its shadow brushed her, saddening her for a day or two. In condolence she wrote letters expressive of a loss deeply shared, her penmanship (even into her nineties) in the scrawny

Gothic of her day such that it was impossible to believe that her schooling had ended at the age of ten; her sentences never offended against the rigid tenets of the dominie's grammar and often caught deep and poignant truths in their simple grace. Equally, as unstintingly, she counselled mothers in their new-found maternity, comforted occasionally lasses facing confinements without being sure of the father and doubtless, in the bygoing, asked God to forgive them. For the greatest sin in Jess MacKendrick's book – as it had been since she had seen the backsliders cast out of the Scotch Girls' Friendly Society – was a meanness of spirit. That alone could kindle her eyes with anger.

The Sabbath Road

The Gavins were kirk folk and always had been: the psalms were their rod and had sustained them through many a bad hairst and the kind of crofting catastrophe that two or three sick beasts could bring. The Sabbath was holy and they kept it. Boots that were going to the kirk in the morning would have to be cleaned the night before; broth was made, ready for reheating; potatoes, pre-peeled, were potted and set down at the side of the fire ready for salting and setting on to boil the moment the croft's folk came in from the sermon. Not a needle stirred from its case, not a darn was done, and if you were too late in discovering it you went to the kirk with a hole in the heel of your sock uncomplaining rather than break the Lord's Commandment. Bairns were kept in their best suits all day to discourage the temptation to play; no newspapers were glanced at (for fear of eternal damnation) and the only book read was the Bible. About that old countryside, it was said, there were small places where uncompromising men, well up to the turn of the century (and maybe beyond it), carried the neeps to their byre beasts that day in muddy armfuls in their best suits (and sometimes in their best patent boots) rather than turn a barrow wheel and defile the Sabbath, though on any other day they would bow to nobody.

On Saturday nights Willie Gavin shaved the frail grey stubble from his chin, a week's growth that would be unless there was an Oddfellows' meeting or a funeral intervening. It was a pre-Sabbath ritual. His cut-throat came out of its thick cardboard case

in the closet drawer to be stropped sharp on the strap that hung
between Spurgeon and the kitchen mirror and had, it was hinted
darkly, been put to other uses. Latterly, when the years had
shaken his hand, there was hardly a time when the old man did
not nick the thin skin of his cheek, or his chin, and on winter
nights he would need the closet mirror on the table, and the
small paraffin lamp beside it, to see his work. Unless he was
bedded with illness, Willie Gavin went unswervingly to the kirk,
and unless you were at death's door you were expected to go
with him. For when he took the kirk road he carried his brood
with him: as many of his kin and cottared daughters as could be
conveniently assembled at the croft beforehand – and as many of
their bairns as were reasonably presentable and could be relied on
not to disgrace him.

For long after coming to the croft the Gavins had kept faith
with the Free Kirk, the crofter's kirk, in the small quarrytoun. It
had been Old John Gavin's kirk and likely his mother's kirk
before him. Each Sabbath the Gavins had walked up through
Laverockhill's fields to cross the old ridge track and strike on to
the Cadger's Road that led all the way to the sea and brought the
herring from it still, creeled on a lass's back. In Willie Gavin's
grandmother's time – she had been forty at the Disruption – the
Free Kirk had been strong in the land. Its fiery and demanding
God had been taken round the countryside like a beacon and
even Old John, strong though he was in the faith, had been later
discomfited whiles, as he sat in his pew, by the unexpected
announcement:

'Brethren, there will be a service this afternoon in Mister
Gavin's barn, at three.'

Old John had gone home in high dudgeon, ill pleased at not
even being consulted and as ill suited at having to gulp his kail
dinner to get out and make the barn presentable. The old crofter
had not been sorry when they found a new man for the Free Kirk

pulpit, an easier man with his own kind of indolence. But those days that had divided a countryside and its folk were by with now; dogma had diluted to allow the men of the breakaway kirk to come again, all rancour stilled, under the roof of the laird's church and with that Willie Gavin had taken God at his nearest point, the kirktoun's Congregational.

The crofter man had paid a half-crown in the year for his Free Kirk pew and never counted it money ill spent: it did a man no harm to hear the Word whiles, he said. But the Congregational was good for his credit and kept him in the laird's eye (which was another form of insurance). He was never more the patriarchal figure than when he turned out at the end of his croft close onto the road with his best walking stick (taken down from behind the kitchen door) and his tribe trailing him. Willie Gavin had always walked to the kirk: that was the custom – maybe it would have been unseemly to approach Him on a bicycle. For all his years, he stepped the road in style, setting the pace, discussing the close-lying parks with those of his cottared sons-in-law who had seen nothing for it but to accompany him. On a fine summer day, heady with the smell of clover, or with the hedges hanging in hawthorn or the verges clouded with wild parsley, it was like an outing almost. Though the rest of his folk might be ignored, Willie Gavin himself would be saluted from every passing gig and 'Hallo'd' and 'Fine morning'd' from every bicycle, and if the old man had his own reservations he showed no ill will towards them, raising his staff in acknowledgement of the greetings. It was possible to say whether he was early or late on the road by taking note of the point at which Laverockhill's phaeton passed them for Laverocks was a grand time-keeper and folk that day would set their watches by him for the week following.

Unless the party caught up with a slower assembly and had to adjust its progress (for to nod and pass on would have been unthinkable) Willie Gavin would have allowed time for them all to get their breath back and for a turn round the kirkyard. There, indeed, was a whole history of the countryside ('Their folk were long in Braeside,' as you passed one stone; 'Your cousin's folk,' at another). There, also, was an ancestral past that haunted the present and family scandals long buried but not forgotten.

It was Willie Gavin's inviolable rule to go in at the kirkyard door and there, unless it was a day of storm or driving rain, there would be a word with old neighbours, exchanges with other sprigs of the family. Among the immediate gravestones, where the grass was always well trampled and unlikely to wet your ankles, Willie Gavin usually met his sister Mary and her husband who had almost overnight become a man of substance and some celebrity. His rise was a byword about the parish and Willie Gavin was never sorry to be seen in his company. From farmtoun strapper, driving the phaeton of a considerable cattle-breeder, he had risen on the unstayable tide of his master's success (and wealth) to be his chauffeur and the driver of almost the first motor vehicle in the district. Folk without family connection thought it an honour just to say 'Hallo' to him and he had come to enjoy as much esteem as the Great Man himself. In fact, Johnny Gordon had so far come up in the world that on a weekday as he took past at the wheel of the Great Man's Model T he had to avoid nods to the lesser placed of his relatives and they in their turn soon forgot to salute him and so save him the embarrassment of their acquaintance. Wherever the Great Man went, Johnny Gordon went; together they went south to the sales where, it was said, the Great Man even took Johnny into the exhibitors' tent for his lunch with the result that Johnny found it increasingly hard to call common folk his equal. His master, it was hinted, had become so dependent upon his man during their ceaseless travels that he would hardly dare buy a bullcalf without Johnny's good opinion. Out of the sober grey of his weekday livery and the official severity of his chauffeur's cheese-cutter hat, Johnny Gordon had lately succumbed to the flamboyance of crotal tweeds and almost peach-coloured boots, polished till they matched his roseate complexion. He was an affable man at a kirk door.

In the gallery pew the Gavins filled, each Sabbath there was social as well as tactical advantage: you were, so to speak, up there for all the folk to see and at the same time looking down on them, the minister included, for his pulpit was just below you. For an ageing man Old McCaid was still in vigorous command of the Word, much given to exhortation and the fistic utterance. There was never a Sabbath when he did not beat hell out of the Book in front of him. Indeed, a shrewd mind might have thought Willie Gavin had selected his pew with unusual care for it was, as it were, also behind the old preacher's back and one got peace to sit there out of range of his watchful eye – except when he swung suddenly round, his face uncomfortably close, as though demanding your personal indictment for some sin or slip of behaviour. Willie Gavin was less discomfited usually than his folk, for he sat at the far end of the pew, a sentinel against all escape and handy for the collection plate when it came round. For all that, his interest was not deeply engaged; before long he would have slipped into that gently comatose doze that is ill to define and harder still to detect, and would rouse himself only to pass his bag of pandrops along the pew now and then with a glower that said 'Choke on that, gin ye dare!' In fact, there was not one of his grandchildren who, having lined a small cheek with the big sweet, would not have spluttered quietly and died in silence rather than risk his wrath. It is probable that, unlike the rest of his brood, Willie Gavin, with his dour and scrupulous integrity, had little need of God's correction.

If Daft Sandy came in you were bidden not to stare at him for he might catch your eye and call your name, shaming both of you. Poor Sandy was a terrible affliction too, to his own folk, for he would sweep a wild and piercing eye round the pews, fixing his gaze savagely at times where he felt he was being too studiously ignored. Once, to relieve the tension his irregular appearances invariably caused, his mother had remonstrated with him:

'Why d'ye keep lookin' roon' ye – annoying folk?'

Sandy had looked at her straight and unsmiling.

'I was wondering gin God had come in.'

Folk that day had not known whether to laugh or pretend not to have heard him. And nobody knew what to tell him.

As the kirk filled the levity of the kirkyard was forgotten; nods were circumspect, the greeting *sotto voce*. Inside there was a holiness, a sanctity; maybe there gathered there still all the long-forgotten souls of that countryside. The first notes of the organ sprang resonant and deep from the pipes ranged behind the pulpit, a prelude to plain worship amid the bare brown pews and within plain, whitewashed walls. Hymn and psalm were sung with solemn faces; prayer penetrated the simple heart; few there would be that day who were not moved, who did not have someone to think of, some private grief they could not tell. In the kirk on the Sabbath you felt the long continuity of God in that hard landscape that broke men whiles and sometimes inspired them; it passed down like a cloak, the spirit of those long-forgotten folk and the dreams of men whose names were outside on the tombstones – with old Grace in her lair, shrouded in secrets. The organ notes filled your throat, bringing a lump that refused to go away. Through a veil of tears you saw for a moment that long and painful past: the surprised cry of the Covenanter as the Royalist's steel ran through him; the witch's shrieks on her burning scaffold; the swollen belly of the weeping lass on the penitence stool. What had come over folk then, you would wonder; what fear gripped them that made sweet reason a stranger?

Always the kirk had been there, for good or for ill. The pull had been strong. From all corners of the old countryside folk had flocked to the great kirkings and conventicles of the past – to the five-day Sacraments when first the Free Kirk was born – in their threadbare plaids and their poor shoes, and likely Grace among them. A plurality of preachers had wrestled in relays for souls on the bare hillside and the psalms, precentor-led, had been sung line by painful line. Folk then had not needed the Book for many could not read. At the end, and in their excesses, the big preachings had left folk weeping and unstable, prostrated at times among the gravestones. For all that, the kirk had been good to the crofter folk, with the seed corn from its girnal, the siller for a milk cow from its session funds. Folk did not forget: that lived long in the memory of the crofter men.

There was a continuity, too, as they came out from the Benediction to linger at the kirk gate and get the news of folk they had missed going in; that was the tail-end of a tradition that stretched back to the days of the *scries boord*, the noticeboard, at the kirk gate. It had carried the news of the parish and its projected events like a wall newspaper, though now it carried nothing but the name of the minister and where that man of kirk business, the session clerk, could be found.

Cut-throat commerce had once flourished at the kirk gate, to the wrath of the session for all the damage it did to men's souls, and even in Willie Gavin's day inquiries were still discreetly made – for this or that kind of work. If you were on the lookout for a hairst man or two or hands for the threshing mill there wasn't a better place to find them. And still, coming out from the psalms, there was the occasional deal quietly done. His soul succoured, a man might take care of his earthly needs. A farmer man, looking for stirks to fatten and bring on for the mart, would watch for his chance among the crofter men, waiting till he saw that the coast was clear.

'Ye will have naething for me i' the noo, Willie?'

The negative, back-handed inquiry was a part of the bare North-East Lowlands landscape, at the centre of its lifestyle; its negligent offhandedness avoided any bruising of egos; the bad refusal; obligation of one to another – and, totally, anything that smacked of outright commitment. It was the careful weapon of men who were maybe the finest cattle-dealers the whole breadth of the country, a disinterest at times so studied that it profoundly shook a man's belief in his own beasts and invariably took a pound or two off the price of them.

Willie Gavin though was a careful man.

'Naething much i' the noo, Charlie. Unless—'

Men baited and laid verbal traps for each other with quiet guile.

'I could look in-bye.' The response would be suitably guarded.

'Aye, surely then, gin ye happen to be on the road.'

Willie Gavin, the old crofter man, loved the gambits, the careful nuances, and hardy old card-player that he was, he could play his hand as well as any. He would set away home from the kirk well pleased with himself, stepping out in silence as he worked out in his mind the price he would be asking – and the one he expected to get.

On the Sabbath grace was said at the Gavins' dinner table with all the meaning and added solemnity that day gave it, for hard though things were there was a memory of those earlier times when the crofter folk had been at their wits' end to provide. That was something else they did not forget in a hurry; and if they did, the next bad hairst would be a salutary reminder to them. There would be a hush and Willie Gavin, at the head of his table that day and with his folk around him, would wait for its silence before he bent his head into his hand.

'For that we are about to receive, O Lord, make us truly thankful, Amen.'

The simple words were written deep in the hearts of many of the old crofter folk, and though the fashion for saying grace was fading by the 1930s the Gavins held to the past that they knew. The only time the old crofter man would give up his duty was when the minister, maybe after a christening, was bidden to stay for his supper. Then he would ask his guest to say a few words. And so he would, fine words to be sure, graciously said and pleasing to God no doubt if He had a feeling for the felicitous phrases a fine education could bring. Still and all, it was the grace of a man (honest soul though he was) who had never himself faced want or wondered where the rent was to come from. For all the unctuous concern he gave it, it seemed that it never equalled the old crofter's plain words or the dignity he gave them.

When Willie Gavin straightened, it was to reach to the table behind him, where his huge Paisley-patterned red napkin lay on top of the family Bible. He knotted the napkin round his neck for every meal, though table napkins were as much strangers to the Gavins as to the tables of any of the croft folk. (When you were old enough to do without a bib, you were grown enough to do without a napkin.) That napkin was the most colourful thing in Willie Gavin's life. Its brilliance – brighter even than the faces of the playing cards he favoured so much – in the high noon of his masoning days had enclosed his piece dinner: his oatcakes and cheese and the penny Abernethy biscuit (or the apple) that would be his dessert. Lying, its dazzling colour on the black cover of the Gavin Bible, it was as though the two of them held the key to some point of tension in the old man's days. Maybe they did. Or maybe they were no more than the totems of Willie Gavin's life: the spirit and the toil.

Grace said, however, the Sabbath dinner got into its stride, noisy with the sound of quarrelling bairns. It was the family highlight of the crofting week when sons fee'd away to the farmtouns or apprenticed to some trade came home with their news and daughters cottared and decently married brought their children. On a busy day Grannie Gavin might have as many as three sittings, with the men and children first so that the womenfolk could linger over the dirty dishes and have out their speak. Only family or special friends would be invited for their Sabbath dinner; where the acquaintance was anything less than warm intimacy, folk came to their supper.

There would be talk round the Sabbath table – news of family, for it was here that the Gavins took a look at their dirty linen and washed it. There was referral and cross-referral, a reporting back on previous problems: pleas might be made and listened to, backing sought for this or that course of action and quiet blackmail levied where one felt a majority sympathy among others round the table. Willie Gavin listened and gave his opinion against which there was no appeal unless you had Grannie Gavin's ear. Then the table divided: among the men at its head there would be talk of beasts and mart prices, crops and outgoing sales; at the other end, news of births and deaths and marriages and the whispered aside (that the bairns could not understand) about what some women (they understood) had to put up with. Giggles would get the better of well-feigned astonishment as the women bobbed up and down to refill the potato dish or restock the oatcake trencher.

When the cold pudding had gone down and been given time to settle on top of the boiled beef, Willie Gavin would produce his pipe and tobacco mull and rise from the table, and if you were a man or a man-child you did the same; only the womenfolk got leave to sit on. In summer the men would step out to take their smoke and take a turn in the sunshine through the cornyard where those in need, and sometimes the entire company, would relieve themselves against the blind side of a corn rick without ever interrupting their flow of conversation. Wind would be broken (permissible in all-male company) and when everyone was comfortable again Willie Gavin would lead them through his shifts to get their views about this or that stirk, the progress of his ripening oats or the condition of his grass. He was a great man for asking advice was Willie Gavin, but as his counsellors constantly complained, in the end of the day he was just as damned likely to please himself – which was true. He had never been a man to hand down his responsibilities.

For the chill of a cheerless winter afternoon, the ben-end fire would be lit the moment the Sunday meal was ended. Even before the men had put down their pudding spoons Grannie Gavin would have risen from her seat at the end of the table and, with the tongs, begun piling glowing red coals from the kitchen grate onto the ash shovel. Thus prepared, she set sail for the parlour with her smoking cargo. Having deposited the hot coals in the ben-the-house grate and piled logs on top, she would return to announce, in what had also long been a Sabbath ritual:

'Well, sirs, gin ye wid like tae gang throo and tak' yer smoke.'

They went, as they were told, out of the way, taking out their pipes as they walked through. Ploughman's twist as thick as liquorice sticks, bought from the grocer and made in an up-country town, was rubbed and rolled in work-calloused palms ready for the pipe bowl, an art so ingrained in that countryside that long after you could pick out a man on a London bus and know he was raised there from the way he did it. But if it took strong hands to make the twist suitable for the pipe, it took even stronger lungs to get it alight. This indeed was so difficult that seasoned, wizened smokers who lived on practically nothing else had perfected a special technique. A little of the aise, the ash, would be saved from the previous smoke and balanced on one edge of the palm while fresh tobacco was rubbed on the other – a trick so fiendishly difficult that you could be an old man before you had mastered it. The ash was then sprinkled over the fresh tobacco to help to kindle it.

It was a tobacco for strong men but even so, the most fearless, with a cast-iron stomach, would have shortened his life by swallowing its juices. The result was that most of the hard-smoking crofter and farmtoun men had cultivated yet another ancillary art: that of spitting. It is fair to say that Willie Gavin was always very good: on weekdays he could hit the heart of the kitchen fire without ever touching the grate bars. In the ben-end and on the Sabbath, though, such behaviour would not have been seemly and there the big white-enamel spitoon was beside his chair. For his guests, however, the problem was unrelenting; its positioning was less favourable for others seated round the parlour fire so that a pipe-smoker beginner of but a few years' experience faced an awkward dilemma: whether to go for the fire with safety, but with social loss, or to try for the spitoon and risk getting the shiny toecap of his host's boot.

It would have to be an afternoon of blind smorr or lashing rain to keep Willie Gavin happily by the fire and even then he would spend the greater part of it wandering to the window, looking for some break in the clouds.

'A coorse nicht,' he would tell his guests huddled at the fire. 'I doubt gin it will fair the nicht.'

He would hardly be able to wait till it came time to put on his oilskin jacket and go out to the byre. For the Sabbath night, like every other of the week, brought its evening milking and in winter the mucking-out of beasts.

When he followed Grannie Gavin in from the byre, it was time to pick up the big Bible lying with his bright napkin. Riffling its pages, the crofter man would select the chapter he would read aloud to his family and as many as were in its circle and round his croft fire that night. For all his complexities and contradictions, they said, he could give them the Word deeply and movingly, so that it made a mark on all of their lives. When he had finished, the young men who had come courting his available daughters and been bidden to stay for their supper took the hint and went home.

The Old Speak

The croft folk of the North-East Lowlands had the old speak, the language of an older Scotland. Not just the homely diminutives of later time that softened the impact of a harsh landscape and the guttural tongue that grew out of it, but a host of the words that old Jamieson had so assiduously harvested for his dictionary in the early 1800s but which languish now for want of the men who can speak them, far less understand them. Their meanings are as lost to us now as the words themselves. More's the pity, for the old speak had nuances that revealed the sin but spared the sinner, subtleties and inflections that were inexpressible in the precise English that would replace them. And we could have done with them now, for often they were quiet words with guile in them that could slip round the outright confrontation. The croft folk, with the farm-toun cottars, were their last repository and the old speak died with them and took with it some of the dignity of that countryside.

There died then, too, much of the old culture. Like the old balladry of the landscape, it could not continue without the medium that gave it colour and life. The old words would fall silent on the lips that once had sung them to remain enshrined only on the fading page where the ear imperfectly attuned to the past could pick up again a little of their music, the shades of their old enchantment. Now that audience, too, has largely been lost; the old voices are stilled.

It would be impossible in any work that deals with the old landscape not to lament them. What was lost was a strong link with the land, for the two were closely related. The country-man's culture grew out of the soil and the seasons; many of the words in his rural society had agricultural connotations and came out of the dark past of the farmtoun hamlets, the early farmtouns. They had, some of them, a relevance to the work of the old run-rigs in those days before the hedgerow and the margined field; yet most were still in everyday use among the North-East crofter folk of the mid 1800s and a great many would remain on the lips of old men right up to the 1930s.

Sadly, the old speak of the crofter's Lowland landscape was without the strong roots of the Gaelic that would sustain and nourish it; its words, expressive and telling though they were, were regional. Refined and sifted into an art form, they would delight the knowledgeable ear – and at once narrow the performer's appeal; if they travelled on the folk singer's lips it was as much on the strength of a ballad's vigorous, earthy beat as from any understanding of the words themselves. This was the dilemma: though the words were nurtured in an area that sent a large number of its young folk out into the world, they could not carry the old words with them. They might hold a pub audience captive for a moment or two but a sophisticated society had no use for such words; no more than it had for the crofter men who used them. Their day was over and done with, their homely sound made redundant by the catchphrases of a glib society where the spectrum of communication was narrowed and channelled and where the brief and precise shades of response were increasingly rehearsed.

It is not difficult now to see why. It has to be admitted: Doric, the dialect of the North-East Lowlands, with its dementia for diminutives, its contortion and distortion – of the French and the English (and the tampering with the Gaelic) – and its guttural explosions, is not a genteel language. It was graceless in the drawing room and no doubt damnably alarming at times in the

English boudoir. It was – as, in its remnants, it still is – a language of the land and its folk: brusque at times and rough round the edges. Yet few now, even if they feel little grief at its loss, would doubt its relevance in a hard countryside. It had a quality the old speak, an aptness, that the words of pure English could not encapsulate, even at times a tenderness in the affairs of life that not even the gentlest southern tongue could convey. It had, withal, a richness, that slow speak of the farm and crofting men that could surprise you. And given the nature of such men – and the bitterness, sometimes, of their days – it was a language full of cautionary aphorisms that drew their images from the land:

A drappy May mak's the hay. (Rain in May makes good hay.)

He that lippens till a lent ploo will hae his land lang in leys. (He who depends on the loan of a plough will have his hand long in grass.)

Ye've the wrang soo by the lug. (You have the wrong sow by the ear – meaning: you are indicting or criticising the wrong person.)

Ye've ca'ed yer hogs till an ill market. (You've driven your pigs to a bad market – meaning: you have not got a good bargain.)

It was a language as full of instruction for the landsman as any in the length and breadth of Britain:

> *Fin the meen's on her back*
> *Men' yer sheen an' strap yer thack.*

> (When the moon's on her back,
> Mend your shoes and prepare your thatch.)

There was news of what a community itself could expect from the seasons, not exclusive to crofting society or even to the region but never more pithily expressed: *A green Eel mak's a fat kirkyard.* (A green Yule makes for a full cemetery.)

There were saws that took care of social occasions and came into their own about the New Year especially. A man needing a drop of water with his dram (when his stomach that night had already taken enough) would stay the water jug and his host's hand with the injunction: *Dinna droon the mullart.* (Don't drown the miller.)

Wrongdoers that night or any night, for whom retribution seemed imminent, would be advised to *Mak' yer feet yer freen'* (Make your feet your friends).

With its underlying belief in salvation through work, it was a landscape – and a language – strong on incentives to personal industry: *A gangin' fit is aye gettin'.* (A going foot is always acquiring goods.)

There were maxims that ring down to our own time, redolent of the hardiness of life in the crofter colonies and of the need for the contents of the broth pot and the porridge pan to go round: *Pairt sma' and sair a'.* (Part small and serve all.)

Warnings abounded, most likely to lasses: *Dae naething through the day that'll mak' ye greet at nicht.* (Do nothing through the day that will make you cry at night.) More than a few embodied that most important of considerations, the need for good health: *Better tae weir oot sheen than sheets.* (Better to wear out shoes than sheets.)

There was an abundance of advice for folk who never had enough siller, and that was most of them: *Short accounts mak' lang freens wi' the merchant.* (Brief accounts make friendship with the grocer easier.) And there was in a chauvinistic society scant sympathy for the woman who was a dedicated follower of fashion: *If yer warm eneuch, yer braw eneuch.* (If you are warm enough, you are fashionable enough.)

It was a landscape with humour as dry as the proverbial Martini, one in which droll stories (sometimes with a sexual undertow) circulated without unforgivable offence. They reflected only the astringent wit of Willie Gavin's spare countryside and the deep layer of human awareness that lay just under the skin of its hard-bargaining consciousness. It was a humour, often, that allowed the slow-spoken countryman to score slyly off his neighbour or folk who might have considered themselves as intellectually superior. Above all, it had a wryness to be found rarely in any other landscape.

In a community of good masons, so many of whom went to America for a season of work, it was dryly said of one who had hardly arrived there before becoming homesick and returning: He gaed owre and lookit the time and cam' hame. An old millwright of that same countryside, a craftsman who could turn wood to any purpose under the sun and had the kind of engineering skills that further enhanced his reputation round the parish – maybe because he had spent so much of his time acquiring such skills – reached middle age a bachelor still, one of the best catches of several parishes but without even a housekeeper's bed to climb into. One day, when all hope had gone, he was invited in by a neighbour for his Hogmanay dram and to see the new baby that had arrived just in time to see the old year out. His host, the father, was understandably a man well pleased with himself.

'I'll bet yon's something ye'd like fine tae make, eh Sandy?' he said, with a wink to his wife and a nod in the direction of the bundle in the cradle.

Sandy considered for a moment only. 'I doubt,' he said, quiet and unsmiling, 'that it is oot o' the question. As ye ken, I hae nae wife and am therefore withoot the material.'

The man's wit, like the reputation of the fine threshing machines he built, would pass down in the folk memory of the countryside to be remembered and repeated (whenever the bottles came out) long after he had left all drams and 'mulls' behind him. He took it all very well (since he had little chance to do otherwise) and even into old age would be nudged gently as a bonnie lass flew past on her bicycle and asked: 'What think ye o' yon bit o' material, Sandy? Could ye dae onything wi' that?'

That such drollery lived on, perpetuating itself, implied no paucity of humour. It was simply that life itself, like the land, turned to a pattern and in a close-knit society had a rhythm to its days. For twenty years, it is said, the Free Kirk minister of one parish met daily in the street one of his flock, a mason man whose leg had been crushed by a stone, and for all of those twenty years had daily inquired: 'And how's the leg, the day, John?'

And as regularly and as unvaryingly for the same twenty years, the reply had come back: 'It's jist aboot the same, minister. I am jist aye hauding it forrit.'

Neither had considered the exchanges remarkable and though sympathy undoubtedly prompted the concern, it is as likely that the droll response it occasioned had a deeper therapeutic purpose: it hardened the scars and healed the bitterness.

In many ways, it was a speak of surprising kindnesses. A man near the end of his days did not decline into senility but got just 'a little bit raivelled', that softness of phrase taking all the indignity out of the muddle his mind had become. And death itself was as gently approached and prepared for:

'Old Gordon is nae verra weel, I doot.'

Or:

'Willie is a gey puir cratur, I hear.'

In such announcements there was a studied avoidance of anything that might come near to the categorical, a concern that kept open a man's option on life even as he slipped out of it. Death when it came brought regret as softly expressed, as gently voiced:

'Puir man, he didna lie lang.'

Or:

'Puir man, he was taken away in a hurry' – an indication that the deceased had not been expected to succumb so quickly or perhaps that he had not been allowed a fullness of years. And even then there could be the subtler nuances that only a native ear would register:

'It's a pity yon man was taken away in such a hurry' – a regret that obliquely recorded the fact that a man's passing left something unaccomplished or a promise unfulfilled.

Understandably it was a landscape in which appeals to the Almighty were not infrequent, though with its horror of blasphemy, they had to be couched in the careful terms that avoided taking His name in vain. Surprise and astonishment were accordingly muted, exclamation watered down to: 'Dyod be here . . .' or 'Guid be here . . .' or even 'Guid fegs!' though the heedless spirit might come close to vain usage with the explosion of 'Michty be here . . .!' an utterance that never failed to darken Grannie Gavin's brows. Strangely, there were no problems about disbelief; then, amazement or the kind of consternation that would not call a man an outright liar to his face might be expressed by summoning a more appropriate Being: 'De'il be here . . .'

God's name, however, might be invoked on matters of some moment ('God hae pity . . .') or in qualification of some serious compact ('God willing . . .').

And there were other sly words of doubt in that old countryside that avoided the direct confrontation yet as surely indicated the strain of a statement on belief. 'Dammit' was often a prelude to doubt that could be transmuted to 'Daggit' in delicate company. It introduced the merest *soupçon* of suspicion. 'Dag the bit . . .' was a stronger doubt that could be strengthened by inflection to the level of outright disbelief without ever so much as saying so. Such careful phrasing had a further advantage: in bellicose company it left you a path of retreat.

Always the speak of the old croft folk was ruminative; opinion emerged, it was never jumped at. Inevitably, it wildly eschewed anything that seemed remotely to ring of commitment. Question, as often as not, took the form of statement, to the confusion of the outsider, with only the note of curiosity rising in the tail of it to tell the experienced listener that it was in the interrogative.

'You will be going to the meeting the morn's nicht, Andra?'

'Likely,' would be the rejoinder, its meaning as near to certainty short of flood or disaster you were ever likely to get but still and all, this side of definite, categorical commitment. A man did not parade his intentions.

Nor was endorsement given lightly. The most ordinary and sociable of greetings, civil to all whether it was the laird or the passing tink on the road, could verge on the careful hesitancy of high diplomacy.

'Fine day,' a ploughman might cry over the dyke to the croft wife passing on the road to the kirktoun. 'But cauld—'

'Aye – caulder nor yesterday.'

'Aye – but better nor last week.'

Nearly all the old landscape's responses were as finely measured, as cautiously hedged.

If it was a society with its fair share of rude rhymes (at the expense of bald men and cripples), it had others that had long been a part of that landscape, traditional and fit even for the ben-end on a bad Sabbath. They were the repertoire of the crofter's and the cottar's wisdom, the couplets that related to crops and to weather, their belief often ill founded. Though Willie Gavin in his keen mind must have known otherwise, he gave credence still to their warnings, as had his father before him. Some, indeed, were as important to the mason man as they were relevant to the crofter he also was:

> Gin Can'lemas Day be dry an' fair
> Half the winter's tae come an' mair.
> Gin Can'lemas Day be weet an' foul
> The half o' winter's gaen at Yule.

The crofter man knew their old words and their portents as well as he knew the old psalms and as the days came on him – St Swithin's for instance – he would turn them over on his tongue as earnestly as a sinner counting his beads. There were other couplets that prophesied what each day would bring:

> The evening reid an' the mornin' grey
> Is aye the sign o' a bonnie day.

The landmark of Willie Gavin's countryside was the lonely hill of Bennachie, where some of the bitterest chapters of the North-East's crofting history had been written. From the very start of his days, from his first wetted *hippen* in the old croft dwelling, it had been a factor in his life, and in his old age it was to the blue saddle of the hill that he looked each morning to see whether it was hidden by cloud or whether its peak was raised proudly in the clear air.

> When Bennachie pits on her tap
> The Garioch lads will get a drap.

If the old crofter man had the lore of the countryside on his lips, his speak was rich too in the old words that described the human condition. Obscure though their origins now are, their guttural sound gave colour and texture to the daily round and expressively recorded its calumnies and disasters. The folk of Willie Gavin's countryside rose in the morning to their *bickers* (wooden dishes) of brose, to *trauchle* (toil) through the day until they became *foisonless* (tired) and came home girning (complaining) with *teem* (empty) stomachs. Folk did not tinker with things, they *fichered*; they did not delay for an instant, they *dauchled*; they did not fall headlong, they *gaed clyte*; they did not go head-over-heels but went *heelsterheid* or maybe *heelstergowdie*; they did not deafen each other with gossip, just *deaved* one another. Ungainly persons with a capacity also for the eccentric were *halyrackit*; add to that anything further in the way of outrageous behaviour and they could be called *glaikit*, or, pushed to extremes, go *clean gyte* (demented).

And there were the words that signified and marked distress: *feuch!* for the unsavoury smell that assailed the nostrils; *fich!* for the anguish of stinging your fingers on a hot pot-handle, the nuance so slight that no stranger would hear it.

It was a society whose menfolk were inclined to go on the *splore* (on the spree) and with drams in them took to *stravaiging* (wandering) where they shouldn't, or *stoitering* (staggering) and even likely to *tummle doon* (fall down) before eventually reaching home, no doubt to be upbraided for their lack of *rumgumption* (good sense). There were old words that described a man in somewhat better shape: in his prime and dignity, for instance, or his *potestatur*; or in a more affable and amiable mood, as a *furthy cheil*. There were words equally old and just as enchanting that grouped folk in their gatherings for ball, kirk or market: a *boorich* (a confused assembly and a small crowd); a *hantle* (smaller, but still a fair number): and a *pickle* (a small cluster), all of them words, like so many more, that would never make a liar of you.

A man, like as not, would take the terminology of his fields into the croft or cottar-house kitchen as the hunger gnawed at him and ask, in the middle of the afternoon, for a *sheave o' loaf* (a slice of bread) to stay him till it came supper-time. It was indoors, too, that such French as had once filtered into the language came to grief on the rocks of guttural corruption and threw up such offshoots as aumery and ashet. Both had a home still in Grannie Gavin's kitchen in the late 1930s, along with such native survivors as *thieval* and *spurtle* (the stick that stirred the porridge) and tattie-chapper (potato masher).

Old words would linger on old lips as descriptive of the fashions as of the contents of the kitchens. The scarf the old crofter man wound round his neck on a cold morning before going to the field to pull turnips for his stock was his *gravat* (the early Scots spelling of cravat); a jersey or pullover when he wore one, which was seldom, was his *mauzie* or *gansey*, words more from the fisherman's world than the crofter man's though they had percolated inland and into the speak of farmtoun and small-holding.

When a man of that old landscape had to replace his Sabbath suit, something of a major investment, he kept the old one as a *scuddler* – to wear on less important occasions till he had finally had the last thread of wear from it. In speaking of their tweeds, crofter men would refer to their *shute*, a word not exclusively of the North-East for it was known in the Border country in 1802, when Susan Sibbald wrote her *Memoirs* and used it to distinguish a coachman's rig.

In any discussion of *claes* (clothes) the old words surface like bubbles in a porridge pan: *worsit* was worsted; *gartens* were garters (a fine word indeed for those bands of thick black elastic); and *breeks*, for all its couthie sound, came down from a grander past than one commonly supposed – from the days of the courtier and doublet, when it early described the breeches that kept the rest of the grandee warm and decent. History would give the word a terrible come-down – to describe a mere crofter man's trousers. Shank, though it had latterly designated the knitting that leapt like a kitten into a croft wife's hand every time she sat down, came surprisingly out of a similar and illustrious past: in that time of doublet and hose, the shank had been the lower part of the attire. It was natural that in the land of the factory stocking-knitter it had descended in the dialect to describe the piece of work itself. *Hose* was as reluctant to fade from the scene and endured among the lonely farmtouns and the crofts right up to

World War II and the lure of nylon to describe the stockings the womenfolk wore, whether woollen, lisle or sinful silk.

And if it held history, that old speak, it could also spring its surprises. Who now would believe that in the mid 1800s in that bare landscape there might be such modern-sounding sayings as 'I'll bet ma beets (boots)' or 'Like me, like ma dog'? Yet there were. Or that the crofter folk, Grannie Gavin among them, would speak regularly of getting 'a terrible aggravation' long before television filtered that expression from the dark corridors of villainy into the staid suburban sitting room?

There were delightful words that survived not only from their everyday use for the things they described but for the sheer flavour they could give to a conversation; like rare birds they fluttered into the talk of men whiles as they met in old age, in the mid-afternoon, to speak of earlier times. They rang in the mind, defiantly in the face of their English usurpers, their past as much a mystery as the dark side of Hogmanay: *forhooiet* (deserted, forsaken); *tootie-mootie* (whispering); *disjasket* (worn out); *galshich* (a tasty titbit). There were many more. Odd were their sounds and strangely they fell on the ear; but anything that followed them in the years to come, you knew, would be poor counterfeit. And so it would prove.

One might suppose that the packaged American TV serial – if not the increasing oil industrialism of the landscape that Willie Gavin trod – might be bringing an entirely new speak to the old crofting countryside. That assumption would be less than correct. Long, long before the oilmen came and even before John Logie Baird was born, one crofter man might ask another: 'Foo are ye makin' oot?' ('How are you making out?'). The same men, indeed, would be as likely to complain to one another about the *on-gang* of work or the on-ding of rain – years before the parlance of the space age gave a kind of lugubrious respectability to such grammatical leap-frogging. Had the New World, you would wonder whiles, plucked its phrases from the lips of some emigrant Scots ploughman?

Standing now, at a distance of years, one hears in the mind the language of a lost landscape and of a lost people, piquant and loveable words that fell once so easily on the ear, the old chants that took the croft folk through the seasons. Sometimes one hears the poetry unintentional in them. Is there anything now that holds the haunting melancholy of the *fa' o' the year*, that season that brought down the curtain on all green and growing things? Certainly not the English of 'autumn'. Is there any other phrase that proclaims so exuberantly that prelude to summer, the *gab o' May*, the interlude that as surely lifts it? Both were part of the calendar that Willie Gavin lived his days by. Sadly they no longer spring spontaneously to the lips and their loss diminishes a landscape (and maybe a nation).

But perhaps, after all, that was inevitable: the schoolroom with its dementia for the English took the old words out of a croft bairn's mouth before he had time to savour them – and almost rendered him speechless in the bygoing, for in his educational years he dwelt in a divided kingdom, going home from his desk (surreptitiously vandalised) to a home where the slow Doric described the day, the work, the seasons, in turn a refugee from both.

There were other factors, also, that would put the old words out of common usage, not least the rapid changes in the countryside in which they were nourished and had their roots; the increasing urbanisation of society; and the encroachment of alien cultures. In the 1920s and 1930s, as society settled itself again and resharpened the old class distinctions, those young folk taking the old words with them to become part of it soon thought the better of it, for they were neither the words of commerce nor social advancement. Their utterance would have been as dreadful as being caught in the fraudulence of passing bad currency. Even in their homeland, tradesmen's wives who took to the sophistication of wearing French knickers and making coffee, became guarded with a language so steeped in the past, so certain to betray a provincialism in its homely phrases.

So the old speak faded from the land like the folk who used it. Few would regret it, still fewer make a fuss about it. Yet it would have its champions: a dour northern newspaper editor or two loth to let the past slip so easily away, an occasional poet, a writer or two working determinedly and with a persistent integrity in the clay of childhood, an inner ear forever tuned to its old rhythms and cadences, striving to sustain the old patterns of speech that synthesised soul and landscape. There would be Jamieson's old dictionary, a hairst of fine words that his successor, the diligent Dr Longmuir after him had bound and stooked anew. Now and then, in the time to come, folk might turn to mull and mourn over the treasures that lie buried there and wonder that something so rich in its texture – so near to a separate language – should have died so quickly. Hearing the old words – a thin crackle perhaps on the recordist's tape – they might turn, to see how they fitted in the old landscape, to Helen Beaton's *At the Back o' Bennachie*, where they are spread like a feast. Yet already her sentences would need a translator to unlock their secrets for the young. And that would be nonsensical, an act of literary vandalism, for like the old ballads of the farmtouns, sung in the stables and bothies of that old North-East Lowlands countryside, it is only in the old speak that they come truly alive.

Willie Gavin's Last Hairst

Willie Gavin was struck down between the hay-time and harvest, while he was giving his turnips their second hoeing with the old Highland croman he had long kept for the work. Laverockhill would have been willing enough to send down a man with a horse and a *shim* for the half-yoking that was all it would have taken. But he knew the old crofter man would not hear of it, for Willie Gavin had long lived with the belief that the horse hoe tore down the drills too savagely, leaving not enough soil for his neeps to *boddam oot* and get fat in the row. He was seventy-five and had been frail for some time. A decision had been made: he would be out at Martinmas, the end-of-year term for the hiring of men and the ending of things, a time (like Whitsunday) when men shut the book on long and eventful tenancies and broke finally with the soil. It was a decision Willie Gavin had made with a sore heart; and since making it he had become quiet and withdrawn.

It was Grannie Gavin, going out to cry him in when he did not come home for his dinner, who found him: sprawled helpless between the drills, his old steel-rimmed spectacles splintered where he had fallen on the shaft of the old implement. He was not dead, but neither could he move nor speak to tell her what had come over him. Only his eyes could appeal to her. She would remember them, like the gaze of a sick beast that had lost its reason for living. She took off her apron to make a pillow for his head and then ran for Lang Andra McCaskill, never more glad of him. Together they took Willie Gavin home to his croft biggings for the last time, in his own barrow, his legs lifeless over its end-shelving. Lang Andra, a resolute man, wheeled the barrow indoors unthinking, negotiating the turn of the porch with some difficulty, but then into the kitchen and finally the closet, where they lifted Willie Gavin gently into his bed.

He would not rise again. He lay through the harvest and the stooking, rallying a little to turn his head on the pillow to see the sheaves come home past the closet window and into the cornyard – led in by one of Laverockhill's horsemen – before the second stroke killed him. It was a fine hairst, the best he had ever had, for he had finally let himself be persuaded and changed his seed corn. Still and all, it did not take the horseman that long, and when he had finished he stepped into the croft house to see the old man. It was a fine end-of-hairst day with a strong sun and a light breeze that siftered round the corners of the croft biggings.

'We will have gotten winter?' Willie Gavin said to him, the words slow and no more than a whisper, as though he had husbanded his strength just to ask him the question.

'Aye, yer hairst is in, man,' the young horseman had said quietly, taking his bonnet off, ill at ease in the sickroom and sad to see the old man so sorely come-at at that time of year when men stood for once in the benign shadow of nature, the one at peace with the other.

Tears were shed for Willie Gavin, hard man though he was, and his family mourned him. The croft folk came to see him in his coffin, laid out in the ben-end in his best nightshirt, his face new-shaved and strangely serene as though his eyes beheld still the bounty of that last harvest, his long moustache spruced up. It was the custom. Simple folk, they put their regrets into stumbling words and walked through to see him.

'It was the worry of leaving the croft.'

'It was the way he would have wantit it,' they said one to
another, knowing the man. 'He would not have wantit to be
long an invalid-body, not able to step round his parks whenever
he had a mind to.'

They spoke too for themselves.

On the day of the funeral folk came from farther afield, not
only from the crofts but from the farmtouns far round where
they remembered him still as a good mason man. His family and
its immediate friends, the McCaskills and the McPhees, gathered
in the ben-end for the service round the coffin; outside in the
end-of-hairst sun the men of the crofts and the countryside broke
their news and took off their bonnets and stood bare-headed as
the words carried out to them through the widely opened
windows. By and by, when the lid of the coffin had been
screwed down, they stood back to let it come out through
the ben-end window to be loaded into the motor-hearse. With
that special stealth that is the art of undertakers, it had eased down
the croft close during the service, the purr of its engine all but
inaudible.

It was all of it now a far cry from that cold wintry day when
Willie Gavin's father had made the same journey. Then the shelts
yoked in the horse-hearse, fretful in the cold, had stood and
champed on the bit and scraped their hooves, anxious to be
home again and into the warmth of their stable. Mettlesome
black shelts they had been, high-steppers, jingling their bright
harness. They took some holding on the rein as the cortège
moved off, tossing the black plumes of death in their hames; who
can say now but that they gave death a greater dignity. It was a
grand rig; in life Old John had never ridden in such style. Great-
Grannie Gavin (for it was not then the custom for the womenfolk to go to the graveside) had set her foot on a chair by the
kitchen's back window and her chin into her hand, to watch the
hearse go ben the road, trailing its black ribbon of men. Old John

had gotten a good turn-out, though it had not been respect that brought them that day but honest friendship, for they had all of them known him for the crofter he was. Dry-eyed she had watched their solemn dignity as they convoyit her man and straggled from her sight round the corner of the Pairtrick Wood behind his glass coach.

'God, Johnny,' she had said – her last words to the little, likeable man who had slept so long in her bed – 'you micht well think something o' yersel' this day, wi' sae mony fowk trailing ahint ye.'

Old John, certainly had been a different man from his son, a different man entirely. He had been a man putting his days past easily. Willie Gavin had been a man with a dream and it would be hard, now, to give meaning to it. He had believed that his croft acres would be his kingdom, supporting him and his folk, bearing his crops, rearing his stock in a harmony of man with the seasons. It was a fragile dream, an impossible dream, and it had been old long before Willie Gavin's time. But he had invested in it – good money after bad, every penny he had earned from his craft skill that could be scrimped from feeding his bairns and buying their clothes. His croft biggings, built by his own hands, were better by far than those of most of the estate's farmtouns. But what good had that been, when the soil had betrayed him? It is likely that each poor hairst fed the roots of Willie Gavin's disillusionment; that in his soul he knew the heartbreak of it. Quietly, he had come to bury that dream, telling nobody, not even Grannie Gavin – though maybe she guessed it – for even with her there would be times when he was austere and distant. But then, Willie Gavin had never had the gift for sweet words, not even when they were young.

Jess MacKendrick took her man to the little kirktoun's cemetery to lie with his own folk in the family lair, as she herself would do when the time came. There had been no rain and the grass was dry; nobody slipped as they walked him slow down from the kirkyard gate into the shadows where the manse trees overhung the wall. The stone would be cleaned before Willie Gavin's name was chiselled to join those of his ancestors: his father and mother, his old grandmother Grace, husbandless still in her last sleep.

Slowly the kirkyard would gather his children.

21

A Break with the Land

Old Jess MacKendrick auctioned herself out of the croft at Martinmas that year, for it had been clear enough that none of her family – neither the sons long away and settled in a different way of life nor the cottared men of her daughters – wanted it. The croft line would be broken, but she could not blame them for that: for as long as she had known it, it had been a millstone round the necks of her menfolk. It had taken the best of her married years and though she had never complained she never had liked it; without her man she had no stomach for the life.

Not all the folk who came to see Willie Gavin sold up had known him, for the roup, the auction, had been widely advertised in the newspapers – in the slender columns, beside the mart prices, that the farmtoun eye reaped daily about dinnertime like the bouts of harvest, gleaning event and time and place. Nor were all of them croft folk. Far from it, for it was deep into the depression days that hit the farmtouns and not a few of their poorer tenants were there for the bargain or two that might come their way: a barn fork or two or a byre graip would be easier bought there than new from the merchant.

It was a dry and sunny day for the middle of November but with a chill in the wind that sent the first-comers into their coat collars and eventually into the shelter of the byre and the barn. Mistress McPhee and Mistress McCaskill came shawled for comfort, to be with their neighbour. The three of them watched from the kitchen back window as the waiting folk regrouped in the cornyard. Suddenly they were attentive: the auctioneer was up on his rostrum, Jess MacKendrick's old kitchen table. He was the man of the moment, on whom everything depended; his quick tongue would give repartee and riposte where it was wanted, his guile bring a guinea where only a pound was expected. For Jess MacKendrick (and the future of the mart company) he would bleed them for every penny.

That day they sold all that remained of Willie Gavin, all his long past and his hopes, lock, stock and barrel: his milk cows and his stirks, the stacks newly into his cornyard and his hayrick with them (after all the lean years his oats would thresh-out at twelve quarters to the acre); his picks and shovels and his shaving mirror; his old oil engine and his small barn-mill; the muck of his byre midden and his yellow turnips still sitting in the drill. A young mason's apprentice inspected his hammers and trowels and chisels, turning them over carefully on their frayed canvas bag before bidding for them, as though he had known their reputation, bringing a tear to Jess MacKendrick's eye.

The bidding was brisk (as it was always on a fresh afternoon) and the sell-up hindered nobody long. Soon the folk with the farthest to go were putting on their bicycle clips, keen to be home before night came on them, and the auctioneer came down from his pulpit (sold from under him) in the shelter of the corn ricks to walk the croft shifts and value the grass and the fences where they stood for the in-going tenant – if ever they should find one.

'Willie would not have made muckle siller oot o' the croft,' folk said, cycling home round the bend of the Pairtrick Wood in groups till such time as their roads diverged and their separate croft and farmtoun tracks claimed them.

'Verra little . . .'

'She was always poor grun.'

Only the old crofter man himself would have known for sure for like most of his kind he did not keep books. His accounts were in his head, where no one could see them.

'Aye, she was always poor grun,' a lone voice would say, the words torn away on the wind, an epitaph for the crofting dream.

Though he never admitted it, Willie Gavin's croft was more loss than profit. In the depressed 1930s lockjaw could clear the stirk stalls of his small byre in advance of the hard-bargaining farmer, losing him £30 in one swift, savage blow. It was the kind of loss a crofter man could never afford – or absorb. He grew poor in the life and his folk will tell you so. Arguably, his crofting returns were poorer than his father's had been for Old John's economy had been more strongly based on stock – those stravaiging turkeys and wandering guinea fowl (that were as often feeding on his neighbours' shifts as his own), pigs and stirks, to say nothing of the honey from twenty hives. With his shelt, and the borrowing of someone else's, the old horseman saved himself the cost of contract ploughing as well. And in the years up to 1880 he would have shared in the general prosperity of the farming countryside before the bubble burst. How else could he have afforded a harmonium with which to pace the Free Kirk's psalms?

It is unlikely that his son could have done so. When the auctioneer finished his work that day, there would be enough for Jess MacKendrick to rent a house in the little quarrytoun she had come from those long years ago. The irony of it could not have escaped her.

That end-of-year too, Puir Angus McPhee, with a resolve unexpected and never shown before, put his head in the calfies' trough and almost managed to drown himself before they found him. Poor man, he would have no more sheep to herd, no more lambing ewes to keep him awake in the long reaches of the night while other folk slept. Two men, sternly overalled, came in a blue van disquietingly anonymous and Angus went with them. Thus and forever was he taken out of the crofting life to dwell in a world of lucid fantasy and high conversation. He was happy, folk said, when they went to see him, as though his soul had found release from the utter loneliness of his life. His wife would continue in the croft house, letting Laverockhill rent the ground to graze a few stirks.

The Gavin croft sat empty for long enough, till finally the estate lost hope and let Lang Andra McCaskill take in its land with his own, realising his age-old ambition. But even for Lang Andra it was too late. Suddenly, like an old horse, he had gone wrong in the legs. He would not be able to work the grun after all. He put it all down to grass, breaking its old rhythms and rotations, running sheep through the war years and turning a fine penny or two. Then Lang Andra too would pass from the crofting landscape – to a street in the city and the trim little house that Mistress McCaskill always had wanted. It had a low stone wall that drew Andra up short every time he stepped on to his own doorstep and sharply demarcated the end of his interests and the point where the corporation's commitment began. He had only a small back garden and he had filled it with gooseberry bushes and very little else. From time to time, at the end of a mart afternoon, or between buses on his days of hospital treatment, an old crofter man might still go to see him: he looked lost, folk said, and sad and bewildered.

For long the old Gavin house stood lonely as a ghost beside its still acres, empty of life, its land undisturbed by the plough and so sadly unadorned by the stooks of harvest; silent now of all the voices that once had filled it. In time, maybe on a bad winter's night, some wanderer of the roads broke down its door to claim the shelter it could afford him in an uncomfortable countryside. Soon, too, the sheep found their way in and out, unfrightened by its presences, leaving their droppings in the kitchen, in the ben-end where the Gavin men had smoked their thick twist on a wet Sabbath and taken the affairs of the farmtouns throughhand – even upstairs in the garrets where the grandchildren slept on ball nights, and in the back closet-room where Willie Gavin had lain long a-dying. When its window frames rotted and its loose slates became a danger to adventurous bairns; when it was little more than a shell and had begun to smell like a sheep fank, a townsman bought it. With grant and government subsidy he ripped down the walls of Willie Gavin's old dwelling and built in its place a pretty little house with picture windows and an integral garage where the old crofter man had once had his byre.

It was a fine house, no doubt. But it had no business there. It was a trespasser in that bare cloud-capped landscape. He was a fine enough man who built it, for all that, a quiet man who brought his worries home in a briefcase; a man with a crisp city walk and a crisp city suit. His children ran sandalled all summer long.

22

The End of the Old Croft Folk

In that dour landscape they have forgotten Willie Gavin's dream
and the hopes of the men just like him. It is long years since the
old crofter man went slow past the gold of the autumn stackyards
to meet his implacable God, and it is all of it by and done with
now. The old croft folk have gone from the land and their old
ways with them. A few here and there might endure for a time,
too stubborn to change, too proud to admit defeat, but it was
unreasonable to suppose that their small and pitifully unprofitable
holdings could survive the revolution of the machine-farming
age. With them (though something of the kind would remain,
unchanging, in the Gaelic kingdom) there closed an era and a
lifestyle that endured against the odds. Theirs was already an
ancient landscape; their qualities and their agriculture those of a
vanished time. For the croft on the bare hillside or the lonely
moor had been outdated from the moment of its inception. It
geared the crofter man to that old subsistence agriculture that the
laird's improvements were set in supplanting. That was the irony,
the tragedy, of the crofts. The question, still, is: were they ever
meant to be viable, self-sufficient; intended to succeed? Or were
they, in the land-owning mind – since his few acres could give
the crofter so little – a way of allowing an illusory freedom while
effectively trapping a pool of pliable labour for light industry,
estate or farmtoun? It would be sinister to suppose so and their
rise may simply have been a spontaneous thing that coinciden-
tally gave the laird some advantages. In the North-East Low-

lands, certainly, there was never anything approaching the cynical and calculated exploitation that marked, say, the kelp-gathering communities of the Western Highlands and Hebrides.

The old crofts would largely die out with World War II, but even before the end of the 1930s their lifestyle had lost its appeal, like that of the farmtouns that ringed them. Indeed, their decline during the Depression years was in tune with that of the farm-touns though their story, by comparison, was one of failure, of a long betrayal by the land. It could hardly have been otherwise. Its span of development may have been fractionally longer than that of the farmtouns, but certainly from the late 1880s, if not before, the crofter's world was hit by the same forces and beginning its long slide into extinction. His stirks, those young beasts in his byre that paid the rent, were fetching poorer prices. His econ-omy, if one can invoke such a grand word for such a basic agriculture, was on the ebb; no longer was there a clamour for crofting ground.

For a time it had seemed that the self-sufficiency that was at the very heart of his simple lifestyle might protect the crofter man, and isolate him from the grip of the factors – fluctuating prices being perhaps the most important – that were beginning to have their disastrous impact on the countryside. But gradually, by the 1920s if not earlier, the old croft folk started to lose that self-sufficiency. The traditional life began to break down and in that came the old crofter's undoing. Ready-mades ousted the croft wife's shirts; the draper's van, where the road was anything reasonable, brought breeks that were a feeble imitation of the trousers the country tailor made, but were part, nonetheless, of the disposable lifestyle that would make his old moleskins redundant. The basic diet could now be varied with the visits of the grocer's van – even the occasional odyssey of the fruiterer's cart round the countryside. But at a cost. And again, the self-sustaining life of the crofts took a further knock as it became more convenient for the harassed croft wife to buy a loaf from the baker's passing van than put on the girdle for the making of oatcakes, that earlier breid. Hawkers on a summer night even brought linoleum squares round the croft doors that lessened the need for a scattering of clickit rugs.

None of these factors helped to keep the old crofting way of life alive. And there were others that would speed the crofting decline and the demise of an intriguing lifestyle. One was that general decline of the old countryside itself. Willie Gavin was living in a region that had passed its population peak somewhere about 1880, the last tide of the farmtouns' prosperity; thereafter, as machinery came increasingly into the fields, the numbers needed (even on a casual or seasonal basis) for the running of the big touns diminished and the country folk began their migration – to the towns and a different pattern of labour, even to other continents and new lives. Their ranks were swelled by the drain from the old crofting communities. Even the kind of folk who were the backbone of the old crofting society became fewer as machines began to push out the Clydesdale and the factory-made implement closed the village smiddy as surely as the ready-made suit shut down the tailor.

So, sadly beaten by progress – or rushing to embrace it – the folk who had taken in a piece of land, with or without the laird's grace initially, and tamed it, began to drift away from the hill and the edge of the moss into lives unrelated to the soil. As they moved away, the heather and the rushes that had thatched their stackyards repossessed their fields and gradually the old stones of their dwellings tumbled into decay. Who but a crank could want them?

There was something else that hastened the end of the old crofting life in the North-East Lowlands: the reluctance of its womenfolk to toil all the long hours that its way of life demanded, for the hardy old pioneers in their lace mutches had long passed from the scene. The crofter lad likely to ascend his father's Throne began to be shunned matrimonially, however handsome. And where it was not the work that frightened a lass, it was the isolation – on the edge of some broad moor far from any centre of civilisation, any cinema or place of entertainment; and with nothing remotely approaching travel facilities and only the most basic sanitation. A crofter man, poor in cash terms but geared to the old style of self-sufficiency, might indeed be richer than he thought. It was the lack of cultural and social contact that often engendered the feeling of poverty.

True, in the latter days of the old crofting there were shrewd and speculative men who forsook the old patterns and traditional ways entirely to keep hens or pigs under an intensive system and managed to leave the stench of both behind for the headier heights of a farmtoun tenancy, or even ownership. The times were always right for such men: they were the entrepreneurs who saw the chance of a penny long before it became apparent to others, and knew how to turn it. But they were not men of Willie Gavin's kind: they took no soil into trust to be deceived by it. And in any case, their success had no relevance in a wider context and offered no hopes for a revival. The drift from the crofting life would go on.

Where the old crofts stood cheek by jowl with the farming land – where they existed in the niches of the landscape rather than as colonies – the future was simple enough. As their folk moved out the dividing fence was flattened by the bulldozer and the old shifts surrendered to the machine age and the multi-furrow plough. It is all of it now a far cry from the old days. Today the machine-harvester, the leviathan of farming's increasing technology, encompasses the long days of anguish of Willie Gavin's hairst and those of his near neighbours, McPhee and McCaskill (their shifts now merged into the convenience of one modest 24-acre field), into one swift operation and the space of a brief afternoon. Willie Gavin, so adamant against letting the ungentle binder onto his land, would not have liked it and maybe it is as well that he did not live to see it. The combine cares nothing for compaction of soil; and it has made the whole operation so void of meaning – compared with those long days of the heuk and the scythe – that the old crofter man would have felt it a kind of betrayal.

Even now, perhaps because of the excesses of the Clearances of the West, crofting is still an emotional subject. Lairds have been blamed for their lack of sympathy with the crofting dream. Their attitude is understandable: from the landowner's point of view it was always more economically sound to hitch the land of a dilapidated croft, if not to its neighbour's, to that of an adjoining farmtoun than to put money that could never be recouped into rebuilding the croft's biggings. Yet this was not the only factor that came into such a decision and lairds were not always blind to that. Recalling his fifty years of lairdship in 1925, in *We Twa*, Lord Aberdeen, a former governor-general of Canada, came nicely to the nub of the problem as it affected not only the crofter's fragile economy at that time but the laird's own:

> On the one hand it is admitted that the crofters have, in the past, formed in large measure the backbone of the population. On the other hand, there has been a steadily increasing difficulty in placing small holdings on a satisfactory footing, except when the tenant has also a trade. In that case it is plain sailing; otherwise the question of erecting and maintaining the buildings presents serious difficulty.

Alas, even where the crofter man did have a trade or the kind of regular work that gave his economy some stability, his way of life was on the wane.

Those early squatters of Bennachie, moved on by legal might and the lairds unless they paid rent, penned a song to that loss of crofter freedom:

> Oh ye were once a monarch hill,
> To freedom's footsteps free,
> But now unless their honours will,
> We daurna tread on thee.
> Alas, the heather on thy broo
> Will bloom nae mair for me:
> The lairds aroon' hae ta'en ye noo,
> Ye're nae oor Bennachie.

If that was the first defeat for the crofter men, there were many more to come. All that would remain of that enterprising, 'outlaw' community on the old commonty was a patch of green in the heather and the unbroken sound of the wind. Its last resident, a mason and dyker, left the hill in 1939, in his coffin, having grown strange in his loneliness. For all the oddity of his later years though, his was the true crofter's creed: 'I beg and bow to no man and no man begs and bows to me.' It was a proud dictum, bizarre in its independence, for in their vulnerability few of the croft folk could live up to it.

Yet still for many people the croft and its simple way of life represents a dream, an escape route from the disenchantment of city streets and (worse still) the depersonalisation of a complex industrial society. At a distance it seems a life of enviable freedom, a model for the self-sufficient existence far from the tensions of ordinary life. It isn't. Nothing has changed: the crofting drop-out (discounting the assistance of social aid) still needs a secondary source of income to make anything meaningful of the life. What the croft does hold is the challenge of raw reality and an environment that reestablishes elemental values. Few folk now are fitted to cope with either.

When we look back, it is into a different landscape. What, one wonders, did the old crofts and the crofter folk accomplish? What did they add to the sum of farming knowledge? What was their contribution to the structure of the farming landscape beyond filling in its odd corners and, for a time, the high marginal land of its hillsides? The answer is: very little. For the croft was never a farming unit; what it produced was folk, hard men and sometimes hardier women, resilient and dour; determined folk whose children were scattered by life like windlestraes to the ends of the world, taking with them their uncompromising creed of thrift and hard work and the expectancy of little.

The grandson of that laird who had come home in gilded youth all those long years ago to refashion the landscape in which the Gavins had lived their crofting years, in recognising that, would display yet another awareness not always shown by his kind, and with it, in *We Twa*, reveal the reason why he had persisted in retaining so many of the crofter homes of his estate:

> . . . the type of person who seems to be produced by such homes as these is something that may well be described as a national asset. I am sure that any schoolmaster in Scotland would say that his most promising pupils, and those who have been the greatest successes in after life, have been those who have had the advantage of having been brought up not only in a home but a homestead, amongst all the surroundings of rural life . . .

The old crofts, certainly, were always more than the sum of their sour acres. Sometimes their names can be picked out, even now, on the Ordnance Survey map: isolated outposts where the meal mill once stood or the smiddy forge or the old country souter's bigging so far from the centre of trade but once in the middle of the farmtouns with their teams of men. (He too had put away his awl and his last as the population of that old landscape dwindled.) But as many – and maybe more – of the old names have been lost from the map as well as from memory. In 1936, as the old crofter days drew to a close, in uplands Lumsden – born of the moor and cradled in the hills between Strathdon and Strathbogie – a local historian would stop to take stock of the past. In one small area of just three square miles, sixty of the old holdings had gone. Such had been the congestion in crofting's high noon. Their names were redolent of a time and of a wiry folk who had once embarked on a dream but without illusions: Bogmore, Murchybrae, Staneyslack, Littlemill, Birkenbrowe, Linthaugh, Willowbush . . . In some there is a poetry that shows the affection of the folk who named them.

Mostly, though, the old crofts are forgotten now, except maybe by those who once had connection there. In their later generations they return yearly (taking a hired car from Inverness or Aberdeen or Montrose) to a green patch of the hill or the site of some ruined dwelling to plant co-respondent's shoes in the heather and ponder the lie of the land and absorb its contours – carried long in the mind and passed down, once, from the lips of an old man in a house at the prairie's edge or in the snow fastnesses of some trapper's wilderness. It is a strange fealty that draws them: a need to identify with an older culture perhaps, a quest for simple kinship far from the air-conditioned world and the concrete canyon. It may be difficult for them to relate to the past as they pick out again the outline of the small fields and the site of the old croft bigging. It matters little; that they come at all is testimonial enough to the old crofter folk and their bare lifestyle. Poor and driven though they were, they had a kind of dignity.

Select Glossary

ablins: perhaps; if able
aboot: about
ahint: behind
airn: iron
aise: ash
ane: one
ashet: assiette
aumery: armoire
aye: always

bade: stayed
ben: along; ben-end, best room
bere: barley
bicker: large wooden bowl; large quantity
biggings: buildings; biggit, built
binks: fireside hobs
birns: heaps
birsle: to burn; birsled, well browned
blatter: downpour (or rain)
blind smorr: thick blizzard
bloo coo: blue cow, a slatey-grey animal much favoured by crofter
    folk in North-East at one time
boddam oot: bottom out, grow fat
bourtree: elderberry
bowie: cut-down barrel
bree: liquid, juice
breeks: trousers
breid: oatcakes
brock: fragments, usually of potato
byordinar: extraordinary

ca–canny: take it easy
cairds: cards
caul': cold; caulder, colder
caup: wooden bowl from which brose was traditionally supped
cheil: young man; gey cheil, a young man worth taking notice of
claes: clothes, attire
claith: cloth
clay biggings: dwellings built with stones and clay
clickit: hooked; clickit rug, made by hooking rags through sacking
clippit cloots: cut-up rags
closet: small room, traditionally formed by backs of box-beds in
  but-and-ben dwelling
clyack sheaf: last-cut sheaf of harvest
coggit: weaned
coles: haycocks
convoyit: conducted, accompanied
coorse: coarse, dirty-minded
couthie: homely, cosy
creeshy: greasy
croman: Gaelic hoe
crook: hook
cruive: hen's pen

dae: do
dambrods: game of draughts
dinging: lashing
dinna: don't
disnae: does not
drogs: drugs
drookled: sodden
dyke: stone wall margining field

een: eyes

fairmer: farmer
farl: a quarter-portion of oatcake circle
fechts: fights
fee: engagement of an employee, agreed term of employment;
  fee'd, hired

feering: first furrow of plough-rig
foons: foundations
fordel: cache, store; to fordel, to store
forrit: forward
fowk: folk
frae: from
furls: whirls

gae: go
galluses: braces
gang: go; gaun, going; gangs, goes
gin: if
girdle: griddle
girn: complain, whine
girnal: oatmeal store-chest
girss: grass
graips: farmtoun forks
gravat: scarf; from cravat
growth: weeds
grun: ground; bit grun, bit of land
gudeman: crofter, farmer, head of the house
guid: good
gurr: growl

hae: have
hairst: harvest
hakes: hayracks
hasher: turnip slicer
haud: hold; hauding, holding
heuk: sickle
hinging lum: hanging chimney; canopy structure over fireplace,
    jutting out into room
hippen: nappy
hiv: have
hoast: cough
horn-eyn: best room, croft ben-end
hough: calf, leg
hyowing: hoeing or singling of turnips

ilka: every

jaud: knowing lady; a tease
John Gunn: privy
kens: knows
kist: chest

lang: long
lat's: let's
leading: taking sheaves home from field by cart or barrow
leys: leas; grass
limmer: troublesome lass
littlin: little one, child
lookit: looked
loups: jumps
lowse: loosen

mair: more
mak's: makes
marriet: married
mart: weekly livestock auction
meenit: minute
midden: dung-heap
morn (the): tomorrow
muckit: mucked-out

nae: not
nane: none
neeps: turnips
news: gossip, conversation; to news, to chat
nip: tot of whisky, a dram
noo: now

on-ding: downfall
orra loon: youngest member of farmtoun crew
o't: of it
owre: over

piece: snack; packed lunch
pig: earthenware jar; sometimes stone hot-water bottle
pikit: piked; spiked

pish: piss
press: cupboard
puir: poor
puirman: candelabrum for bog-fir taper

quarter (of oatcake): farl or quarter portion of original griddle round
    of oatcake

raivelled: confused
rantle-tree: crossbar built into either side of the chimney from
    which cooking pots were hung
rattons: rats
ree: hens' cruive
reeshle: rustle
reesin: reason
richt: right
riggin', rigging: couples, rafters
rimrax: ample sufficiency
rin: run
rodden: rowan
roup: auction sale
rowth: a plenty, a frenzy
rushen cords: rope made from rushes

sark: shirt; flannel sark, flannel undershirt
saut backet: salt bucket; old-time container for salt
sedge: rushes
semmit: undervest, singlet
shak': shake
shank: knitting
sharny: shitty
sheelin': winnowing; removing chaff from grain
sheen: shoes
shelt: light horse
shifts: small croft fields
shim: horse hoe
sids: oat-husks from miller, steeped in sowens bowie
siller: silver; money generally
skirlie: oatmeal-based concoction eaten to keep boiled (or mashed)
    potatoes company

smiddy: smithy
smiler: hayrake
smoor, smorr: suffocate; to smoor fire, to 'rest' it overnight
sned: wooden frame of scythe
snibbit: latched
sookit: sucked, drank
souter: shoemaker
sowens: a gruel of water and oatmeal, sweetened for human
   consumption
spence: best room, croft parlour
sprots: rushes
spurtle: stick for stirring porridge
stirk: steer; young cattle beast
stook: shock; to arrange sheaves in shock
stooking: work of setting harvest sheaves into shocks
stoorum: a gruel of oatmeal and water
stovies: potato-based dish for which the Scots have always been
   truly thankful
strae: straw
straiked: sharpened
stravaiging: wandering
swey: swee-frame on fireplace

tae: to
tattie: potato; tattie corn, potato corn
tattie chapper: wooden utensil for mashing potatoes in the pot
thacking: thatching
thigging: begging
thrash: thresh
thraw: wring, twist, strangle
threid: thread
tow: string
traviss: partition between beasts' stalls
trochs: troughs
trump: tramp
truncher: trencher

vrapper: female jacket-style garment

warld: world
wha: who
whiles: sometimes, occasionally
wi': with
windlestraes: straws blown in the wind
wir: our

yard: vegetable garden; presumably from ancient kailyard
yavil: second crop
yoaming: foaming
yoking: harnessing; period of work, morning or afternoon

BIRLINN LTD (incorporating John Donald and Polygon) is one of Scotland's leading publishers with
over four hundred titles in print. Should you wish to
be put on our catalogue mailing list **contact**:

Catalogue Request
Birlinn Ltd
West Newington House
10 Newington Road
Edinburgh EH9 1QS
Scotland, UK

Tel: + 44 (0) 131 668 4371
Fax: + 44 (0) 131 668 4466
e-mail: info@birlinn.co.uk

Postage and packing is free within the UK. For overseas
orders, postage and packing (airmail) will be charged
at 30% of the total order value.

For more information, or to order online, visit our
website at **www.birlinn.co.uk**

Birlinn Limited
Other Imprints – JOHN DONALD • POLYGON

KT-131-505

PENGUIN BOOKS

NO WAY DOWN

'A fitting shelfmate to the modern classic *Into Thin Air*'
Sunday Times

'Artfully and assiduously pieces together an account of a fractious day in brutal
real time. Fatality by fatality . . . devastating'
The New York Times

'Heartbreaking. Bowley writes convincingly about both the horror and magic
of extreme altitude' Rebecca Stephens, *Mail on Sunday*

'A tour de force of a book, a triumph of storytelling' Associated Press

'Brisk and engrossing. Bowley reveals a deep sympathy for his characters and
their quest' *Wall Street Journal*

'Thrilling and wrenching. Bowley is a gifted storyteller' *Kirkus*

'Riveting and powerful; an extraordinary story of an extraordinary tragedy.
Reading *No Way Down* is the closest you can come to being on the summit
of K2 on that fateful day' Sir Ranulph Fiennes

'A page-turning, utterly fresh take on the mountaineering experience, an *Into Thin
Air* for a new century of adventurers, about a mountain even more treacherous
than Everest' Doug Stanton, author of *Horse Soldiers*

'One of the best books I've ever read. But take it to the beach at your peril – it's
impossible to put down. Sunburn is guaranteed' Outdoor Science

'Both a gripping read and a clear-eyed investigation of the hubris, politics and
bad luck that brought on one of the worst disasters in modern mountaineering
history . . . an essential addition to any mountaineer's bookshelf, and [equally]
compelling for readers who have never tied into a rope'
Michael Kodas, author of *High Crimes: The Fate of Everest in an Age of Greed*

'A refreshingly unadorned account of the true brutality of climbing K2, where heroes emerge and egos are stripped down, and the only thing achieving immortality is the cold ruthless mountain'
Norman Ollestad, author of *Crazy for the Storm*

'A fascinating account that does justice to the history, allure and heartache of K2'
Kurt Diemberger, author of *The Endless Knot*

'A gripping story, full of hope and heartbreak, folly and heroism'
David Roberts, co-author with Ed Viesturs of *K2*

'I read this book in a single, sweaty-palmed sitting, and not because I intended to. I simply couldn't put it down'
Nick Heil, author of *Dark Summit*

ABOUT THE AUTHOR

Graham Bowley was born in England in 1968. He is a reporter for *The New York Times*. He lives in Manhattan with his wife and their two daughters and son.

No Way Down
Life and Death on K2

GRAHAM BOWLEY

PENGUIN BOOKS

The front cover photograph, taken by Norwegian climber Lars Flato Nessa shortly after sunrise on summit day, shows Italian climber Marco Confortola (front) and Irish climber Gerard McDonnell ascending the Shoulder of K2 at an altitude of close to 27,000 feet. They are at the end of a line of more than 30 mountaineers who are within 2,000 feet of the top of K2.

PENGUIN BOOKS

Published by the Penguin Group
Penguin Books Ltd, 80 Strand, London WC2R 0RL, England
Penguin Group (USA), Inc., 375 Hudson Street, New York, New York 10014, USA
Penguin Group (Canada), 90 Eglinton Avenue East, Suite 700, Toronto, Ontario, Canada M4P 2Y3
(a division of Pearson Penguin Canada Inc.)
Penguin Ireland, 25 St Stephen's Green, Dublin 2, Ireland (a division of Penguin Books Ltd)
Penguin Group (Australia), 250 Camberwell Road, Camberwell, Victoria 3124, Australia
(a division of Pearson Australia Group Pty Ltd)
Penguin Books India Pvt Ltd, 11 Community Centre, Panchsheel Park, New Delhi – 110 017, India
Penguin Group (NZ), 67 Apollo Drive, Rosedale, North Shore 0632, New Zealand
(a division of Pearson New Zealand Ltd)
Penguin Books (South Africa) (Pty) Ltd, 24 Sturdee Avenue, Rosebank, Johannesburg 2196, South Africa

Penguin Books Ltd, Registered Offices: 80 Strand, London WC2R 0RL, England

www.penguin.com

First published in the USA by HarperCollins Publishers 2010
First published in Great Britain by Viking 2010
Published in Penguin Books 2011

7

Copyright © Graham Bowley, 2010

The moral right of the author has been asserted

All rights reserved
Without limiting the rights under copyright
reserved above, no part of this publication may be
reproduced, stored in or introduced into a retrieval system,
or transmitted, in any form or by any means (electronic, mechanical,
photocopying, recording or otherwise), without the prior
written permission of both the copyright owner and
the above publisher of this book

Printed in Great Britain by Clays Ltd, St Ives plc

A CIP catalogue record for this book is available from the British Library

ISBN: 978-0-141-04406-4

www.greenpenguin.co.uk

Mixed Sources
Product group from well-managed
forests and other controlled sources
www.fsc.org Cert no. SA-COC-1592
© 1996 Forest Stewardship Council

Penguin Books is committed to a sustainable future
for our business, our readers and our planet.
The book in your hands is made from paper
certified by the Forest Stewardship Council.

To my mother and father,
and to Chrystia

Beware of the man whose God is in the skies.

 —George Bernard Shaw, *Man and Superman*

Take care to fly a middle course.

—Daedalus' advice to Icarus, Ovid, *Metamorphoses*

I long for scenes where Man has never trod.

 —John Clare

CONTENTS

AUTHOR'S NOTE

The story of how a multinational group of climbers became trapped by a falling glacier at the top of K2 flashed across my screen at the *New York Times* on August 5, 2008. Once it was confirmed that eleven climbers had died indulging a private passion for their expensive sport and three had finally come down frostbitten but alive after surviving several nights in the open, my immediate reaction was, Why should we care?

When my editor suggested I write about their ordeal for the newspaper, I balked at the idea—mountaineering had never interested me—although the next morning my story appeared on page one of the paper.

It was only after the *Times*'s website was deluged with comments from fascinated readers and after I took a trip abroad a week and a half later to the memorial service of one of the climbers that I began to entertain the possibility that there was more to the story. I interviewed some of the still-haggard survivors of the accident, saw their injuries, and, I must admit, was inspired by the charisma of the adventurers who had stepped into a world I could not understand and had faced down death.

I set about interviewing as many climbers as I could from the expeditions, as well as their families, and the mountaineering experts who had spent time on K2. As I talked to the survivors, I found their stories were often disturbing, painful, and occasionally incomprehensible. On the face of it, a thirty-nine-year-old reporter who had never been to the Karakoram range was an unsuitable candidate to comprehend the fascination and dangers of modern mountaineering. However, some of the considerations that might seem to have disqualified me actually played to my advantage. Already, by this point, the accounts were contradicting one another and it was clear that memory had been affected by the pulverizing experience of high altitude, the violence of the climbers' ordeals and, in a few instances, possibly by self-serving claims of glory, blame, and guilt. I realized one of the advantages I had in making sense of the story was my objectivity and distance from the events. And some of the climbers seemed to agree. In Stavanger, Norway, after I had strolled for three hours around the city with Lars Nessa, a remarkable young Norwegian climber, he turned to me to say, "We think you are the one to tell our story."

Anyway, by then I was hooked. I had stepped with these men and women into a foreign world somewhere above the Baltoro glacier and I could not turn back.

When I began working on this book, I wanted to write a story that read dramatically, like fiction only real. I would bring K2 alive through the eyes of the courageous climbers who were pursuing their dreams on this incomparable peak in the Himalayas. Re-creating the final days of eleven people who would never return from K2 posed some challenges. The book I have written is based on hundreds of interviews with the many dozens of people involved directly or indirectly with the tragedy. If I couldn't determine exactly what happened on the slopes, I interviewed the climbers who had been close at pivotal moments, or experts who had been through similar situations, or families or friends who knew the climbers well. Never did I rely on conjecture; in cases where firsthand accounts were not available, I drew on my knowledge of the characters of the climbers and on as much evidence as I could gather over a year.

As my goal was to write a book re-creating the experiences of the climbers caught up in this tragedy, I needed to report dialogue. With only a few exceptions, the dialogue was quoted to me directly by the speakers involved. In many of the important scenes I checked back to ensure accuracy and this often jogged memories or caused people to rethink. Right from the start I knew it was essential to interview the climbers early on, before memories faded, but in a very few cases, primarily those in which climbers did not survive, I have re-created the dialogue based on my impressions of the people involved as gleaned from my interviews.

I conducted the majority of the interviews in person, with follow-up conversations by telephone or email. Drawing on these resources, I have written as complete an account as possible of a narrative that involves multiple points of view. In the end, though, there are certain questions that I found impossible to resolve. My approach has been to set out as accurately as possible each climber's account, even where the accounts conflict. Some of the most crucial aspects of the tragedy turn on those points of conflict. The full truth of what actually took place in those August snows at 28,000 feet may never be known.

One June day, I followed the trail of the climbers to K2 and stood for a few hours in the cold sunshine on the Godwin-Austen glacier. I stared up more than two miles at the South Face, then climbed two hundred feet to the Gilkey Memorial, K2's monument to the dead. Seeing up close the peak, the Great Serac, and the Bottleneck, contemplating their beauty and their challenge, I could start to understand why this brave group of men and women would risk their lives to climb it.

CLIMBERS

Those names marked in bold denote climbers who made a serious summit bid on August 1, 2008.

NORWEGIAN K2 EXPEDITION 2008

> **Rolf Bae**
> **Cecilie Skog** (leader)
> **Lars Flato Nessa**
> **Oystein Stangeland**

NORIT K2 DUTCH INTERNATIONAL EXPEDITION 2008

> **Wilco van Rooijen** (leader)
> **Cas van de Gevel**
> **Gerard McDonnell**
> Roeland van Oss
> **Pemba Gyalje**
> Jelle Staleman
> Mark Sheen
> Court Haegens

ITALIAN K2 EXPEDITION 2008

> **Marco Confortola** (leader)
> Roberto Manni

SERBIAN K2 VOJVODINA EXPEDITION 2008

> Milivoj Erdeljan (leader)
> **Dren Mandic**

Predrag Zagorac
Iso Planic
Shaheen Baig
Mohammed Hussein
Mohammed Khan
Miodrag Jovovic

2008 AMERICAN K2 INTERNATIONAL EXPEDITION

Eric Meyer
Chris Klinke
Fredrik Strang
Chhiring Dorje
Paul Walters
Michael Farris (leader)
Chris Warner
Timothy Horvath

SOUTH KOREAN K2 ABRUZZI SPUR FLYING JUMP EXPEDITION

Kim Jae-soo (leader)
Go Mi-sun
Kim Hyo-gyeong
Park Kyeong-hyo
Hwang Dong-jin
Jumik Bhote
Chhiring Bhote
"Big" Pasang Bhote
"Little" Pasang Lama
Lee Sung-rok
Kim Seong-sang
Son Byung-woo
Kim Tae-gyu
Lee Won-sub
Song Gui-hwa

BASQUE INDEPENDENT CLIMBER

Alberto Zerain

FRENCH-LED INDEPENDENT K2 EXPEDITION

Hugues d'Aubarède (leader)
Karim Meherban
Qudrat Ali
Jahan Baig
Nicholas Rice
Peter Guggemos

SERBIAN INDEPENDENT CLIMBER

Joselito Bite

OTHER INDEPENDENT CLIMBERS

Nick Nielsen
Christian Stangl
George Egocheago

FRENCH "TGW" 2008 K2 EXPEDITION

Yannick Graziani
Christian Trommsdorff
Patrick Wagnon

SUNNY MOUNTAIN CHOGORI EXPEDITION

George Dijmarescu (leader)
Rinjing Sherpa
Mingma Tunduk Sherpa
Mircea Leustean
Teodora Vid

K2 TALL MOUNTAIN EXPEDITION

Dave Watson
Chuck Boyd
Andy Selters

SINGAPORE K2 EXPEDITION 2008

Robert Goh Ee Kiat (leader)

Edwin Siew Cheok Wai
Ang Chhiring Sherpa
Jamling Bhote

ITALIAN BROAD PEAK & NANGA PARBAT EXPEDITION

Mario Panzeri
Daniele Nardi

PROLOGUE

Friday, August 1, 2008, 2 a.m.

Eric Meyer uncurled his tired body from the Americans' tent into the jolt of the minus-20-degrees morning.

He was decked out in a red down suit and his mouth and nose were covered by his sponsor's cold weather altitude mask. A few yards in front of him stood the Swede, Fredrik Strang, Meyer's colleague in the American team, his six-foot, two-inch frame bulbous in a purple climbing suit, and his backpack weighed down by his thirteen-pound Sony video camera.

It was pitch black. There was no moon. Meyer put on his crampons and whispered a prayer. *Keep me safe.* "Let's do our best," he said out loud to Strang.

The two men nodded to each other, then kicked their boots into the tracks in the firm snow. The tracks led up the mountain, where they could see the headlamps of the twenty-nine climbers from the eight teams, bright spots on the steadily rising Shoulder.

"Don't let your guard down," said Strang. He tossed his ice axe in the air and caught it, just to make sure he was awake.

For nearly two months, they had waited for this moment. Now they were ready.

More than two thousand feet above them, the summit was still hidden in the night, which was probably a good thing. Soon the sun would rise over China. As the two men filed out onto the line above

Camp Four, at about 26,000 feet the final camp before the summit, their breath rasping in the low-pressure air, the winds of the past days had vanished, just as their forecasters had promised. It was going to be a perfect morning on K2, and Meyer, a forty-four-year-old anesthesiologist from Steamboat Springs, Colorado, possessed confident hope that his skills in high-altitude sickness and injury would not be needed.

Meyer's team was one of eight international expeditions that were setting off on the final day of their ascent of K2, at 28,251 feet the second-tallest mountain on earth. K2 was nearly 800 feet shorter than Everest, the world's highest peak, but it was considered much more difficult, and more deadly.

It was steeper, its faces and ridges tumbling precipitously on all sides to glaciers miles below. It was eight degrees latitude or 552 miles farther north than Everest, its bulk straddling the border between Pakistan to the southwest and China to the northeast, and, far from the ocean's warming air, its weather was colder and notoriously more unpredictable. Over the decades, it had led dozens of mystified climbers astray into crevasses or simply swept them without warning off its flanks during sudden storms.

Yet K2's deadliness was part of the attraction. For a serious climber with ambition, K2 was the ultimate prize. Everest had been overrun by a circus of commercial expeditions, by people who paid to be hoisted up the slopes, but K2 had retained an aura of mystery and danger and remained the mountaineer's mountain. The statistics bore this out. Only 278 people had ever stood on K2's summit, in contrast to the thousands who had made it to the top of Everest. For every ten climbers who made it up, one did not survive the ordeal. In total, K2 had killed at least sixty-six climbers who were trying to scale its flanks, a much higher death rate than for Everest. And of those who had presumed to touch the snows of its summit, only 254 had made it back down with their lives.

Waiting in his tent at Camp Four the previous night, Meyer had experienced a few dark hours of disquiet when the Sherpas cried out that the other teams had forgotten equipment they had promised to bring; he could hear them hunting through backpacks for extra ropes, ice screws, and carabiners. Although ropes had been laid on the mountain from the base to Camp Four, the expeditions still had to fix the lines up through the most important section, a gully of snow, ice, and rock called the Bottleneck. The Sherpas had only just discovered that one of the best Pakistani high-altitude porters (HAPs), who was to lead the advance rope-fixing team, had coughed up blood at Camp Two and had already gone back down.

Eventually the Sherpas quieted down, and Meyer assumed they must have found what they needed. By now, everyone was waking up. In the surrounding tents, alarms were beeping, there was the sound of coughing, stretching, zipping of suits, ice screws jingling, headlamps snapping on. The panic was over.

Yet when the advance team eventually left, it seemed to Meyer, listening to the swish of boots over snow outside his tent, that they were already late, and time was the last thing they wanted to waste on the mountain.

It was past 5 a.m. as Meyer and Strang pushed ahead together up the Shoulder, a steadily rising ridge of thick snow about a mile long. They prodded the snow with their ice axes to test the way. The snow, hard-packed, didn't crack. They skirted the crevasses spotlighted in the arcs cast by their headlamps, some of the crevasses a few feet wide. Several yards off in the dark was a row of bamboo wands topped with ribbons of red cloth. The poles had been set out to guide climbers back to Camp Four later that night. But there was only a handful.

The two men didn't say much, but every few minutes Meyer made a point of calling out to Strang, checking for warning signs of high-altitude effects: a trip, or a mumbled answer.

"How you doing?"

"I'm fine!" said Strang loudly.

After half an hour, they came to the start of the ropes laid by the advance team. The two men were surprised to find them placed so low in the route. *Weird*. The Bottleneck was still a long way off and these slopes were not dangerous for an experienced climber. The ropes had obviously been put there to guide the climbers on the way back down. The lead group must have calculated they would still have enough rope to reach where it was truly needed.

Meyer was carrying his own quiver of bamboo wands, which he had intended to plant at intervals for the return journey. Strang had brought three thousand feet of fluorescent Spectra fish line to attach between the poles. But now they left the equipment in their backpacks. *Not required.*

Exchanging shrugs, Meyer and Strang walked on. At 6:30 a.m., the sun rose, revealing the Bottleneck. It was the first time either of them had seen the gully up close. It was awesome, more frightening than they could have anticipated. About nine hundred feet ahead of them, its base reared up from the Shoulder, rising another few hundred feet later to an angle of 40 or 50 degrees and narrowing between stairs of dirty, broken brown rocks on both the right and left sides.

It was, Meyer could see, an unreliable mix of rock, ice, and snow. Another five hundred feet on, it turned up to the left toward a horizontal section called the Traverse, a steep ice face stretching a couple of hundred feet around the mountain, and exposed to a drop of thousands of feet below.

Directly above the Bottleneck was the serac—the blunt overhanging end of a hanging glacier—a shimmering, tottering wave frozen as it crashed over the mountainside, a suspended ice mountain six hundred feet tall, as high as a Manhattan apartment building and about half a mile long. It was smooth in places but large parts of it were pitted with cracks and crevasses.

This was the way to the summit, and for the whole of the Bottleneck and most of the Traverse, the mountaineers had to climb beneath the serac. There were other ways to the summit of K2—via the north side from China, for example, or on a legendary, nearly impossible route on the south face called the Magic Line—but the path up the Bottleneck and beneath the serac was the most established route, the easiest, and possibly the safest, as long as the serac remained stable.

The glacier moved forward slowly year by year. When it reached a critical point, parts of the ice face collapsed, hurling chunks down the Bottleneck. No climber liked to imagine what would happen if they got in the way. In past decades, there had been many reports of icefalls from the glacier, but in recent years the Great Serac on K2 had been quiet.

The strengthening daylight revealed the changing shapes and textures of the glacier, transforming its colors from gray to blue to white as the cold shadows receded. It revealed to Meyer and Strang the serac's true nature, something the earlier climbers would have missed because they had entered the Bottleneck in darkness. It looked to Meyer like giant ice cubes stacked on top of each other, and the ice had pronounced fissures running down it.

"Man, that's broken up!" Meyer said in awe.

They had studied photographs in Base Camp taken a month earlier, which had shown cracking, but this was far worse.

As the outline of the mountain emerged from the dawn, Meyer could also make out clearly for the first time the snaking line of climbers up ahead. He had expected to find an orderly procession of bodies moving up the gully and already crossing the Traverse. Instead he was met with a sight that stopped him short: an ugly traffic jam of people still in the lower sections of the Bottleneck.

Only one climber seemed to have made good progress. He was sitting near the top of the Bottleneck in a red jacket, waiting for the muddle to resolve itself below.

What had caused the delay? As Meyer and Strang approached, there were distant calls from above for more rope.

"The rope is finished!"

Eventually it became clear: The advanced group had not yet managed to fix rope to the top of the gully, and the climbers following behind had already caught up to them.

During the previous two weeks, the expeditions had convened cooperation meetings down in the tents at Base Camp. They had made an agreement detailing the sequence of who would climb when. The crack lead group of about half a dozen of the best Sherpas, HAPs, and climbers from each team would fix ropes up through the Bottleneck and the rest of the expeditions would follow rapidly through the gully without delay. The arrangement was meant to avoid overcrowding in the Bottleneck. They knew it was critical to get out from under the serac as fast as possible.

Well, thought Meyer, *so much for that.*

Everyone seemed to be staring at one another and wondering what to do next. After a few minutes some of the climbers at the bottom began bending to cut the ropes and pass them higher. Soon the wait was over and the line was edging on up again, though still slowly.

Until that moment, Meyer had not appreciated the sheer number of people trying to climb the mountain: one of the highest concentrations of climbers to attempt a summit of K2 together on a single day. A few were already turning back, because they were feeling cold or sick or today was not to be their lucky day. Probably about twenty-seven or so were still heading for the summit. It looked like being another busy day, like the ones in the 2004 or 2007 seasons when dozens reached the top. Meyer imagined the conditions up there. Everyone getting in the way. Koreans, Dutch, French, Serbs, and a string of other nationalities. Few speaking the same language. And they were probably so intent on avoiding one another that they were not focusing on how late it was nor were they looking up at the glacier to study it properly. *Damn.* They were not seeing how dangerous it looked.

Meyer watched the line of climbers struggling higher and had an uneasy feeling in his stomach. Beside him Strang said it out loud.

"Shit, it's late."

They took off their backpacks and sat in the snow, staring up at the serac and, below it, the Bottleneck.

"There's no way around that crowd," said Meyer. "We're going to get stuck behind them."

They made a calculation. At the expeditions' current speeds, they would reach the summit in the afternoon, perhaps early evening. Sunset. The climbers would be coming back down through the Bottleneck in the dark.

As far as Meyer was concerned, that multiplied the risk a thousandfold. It was already the most dangerous climb in the world. Descending in darkness through the Bottleneck was a no-no. He knew that everyone up there had a deadline for reaching the summit no later than three or four o'clock in the afternoon. What were they thinking?

He felt his courage drain away.

Yet turning back was hard, so bitter after the weeks of toil on the mountain. Like everyone else, he had invested thousands of dollars and nearly a year of his life preparing to come to Pakistan.

He might be able to return to Camp Four and try again the following day. But in reality, climbing up to these altitudes sucked so much out of a person, exposed a body to such pain, that they would have to descend to lower camps to recover before trying again. But the climbing season was ending. They had already pushed back this summit attempt because of bad weather. There was no time left. It was probably going to be the only shot Meyer had. If they failed today, they would have to wait another year. And who knew if he could ever return?

Together, he and Strang went through all the scenarios. They had made it to the Shoulder of K2. Were they throwing away a lifetime's chance to climb the mountain of their dreams?

Strang unpacked his camera and started to film the serac and the climbers beneath it. Meyer took some snapshots. The climbers in the Bottleneck were still barely moving.

They remembered the rain that had fallen in their first week in Base Camp, an odd event for K2 in June. Then there had been the weeks of winds and the overcast sky and snow piling up. And today the sun had risen into a clear blue heaven. It would be baking hot up there soon. If the serac was going to crack, it was because gravity was pulling it lower. The ice was also susceptible to the differences between the heat of day and the cold of night, which could cause the ice to expand and then contract, making an avalanche more likely. They didn't trust the serac.

They packed up and slogged one and a half hours back down through the snows of the Shoulder to their tent at Camp Four. It was around 10 a.m. The day was perfect. Around them, hundreds of mountains stretched away in all directions, white and shining in the sun.

The camp was still and quiet. It perched on a flat part of the Shoulder and, relatively speaking, there was enough room for all the tents here, more than in some of the lower camps, where space was rationed and tents hung on ledges or were reinforced against the winds by ropes and poles.

They had expected to find a dozen or so climbers milling around the colored domes of nylon tents, taking in the rays, sharpening crampons, waiting around. Down at Base Camp, some mountaineers had said they thought the good weather was going to hold and so they had planned to climb up to Camp Four a day later than everyone else to avoid the main crowd and try for the summit on August 2. The second Korean team would be coming up soon, along with two Australians: one of Meyer's colleagues, and another from the Dutch expedition who had been left out of the first summit ascent by his expedition's leader.

But the other climbers were either inside their tents or still grappling with the slopes up from Camp Three. Meyer and Strang saw only one other person, an Italian. He had turned back earlier because of altitude sickness. Now he stuck his head out of his tent, next to theirs. His climbing jacket was plastered with "Fila" and other sponsors' logos. He waved and then closed his tent.

Meyer could not help but peer back at the Bottleneck over his shoulder. Nearly a mile away, the climbers were distant dots, filing upward. They were higher on the gully now, about two-thirds of the way up. They were still crowded together dangerously. From this distance, they seemed to be not moving at all. Surely they would turn around soon. Did they have a death wish?

The two men ducked inside their tent. It was only four feet high, with no room to stand. They peeled off their down suits, the linings damp from sweat. They took out the radio, as big as a large cup of coffee, and crashed on top of the two sleeping bags that were spread parallel on the floor. They gulped at a bottle of melted water. It was hot in the tent. They didn't feel like talking much. Soon they would have to start thinking about descending. It would take them a full day to get down.

About twenty minutes later, they were resting when they heard a faint cry outside. It came from far away. Strang thought he heard it again.

They went out of the tent to check the mountain but nothing had changed from when they had last looked. The line of climbers was still stuck in the Bottleneck. The radio was quiet.

Then the Italian stumbled over. His name was Roberto Manni.

"I see!" he said, pointing at the mountain, his face red. "I see!"

Half a mile away, at the base of the Bottleneck, about six hundred feet below the main chain of climbers, a body was tumbling down the ice. A climber had fallen.

The small black figure slowed down and came to a stop just beneath some rocks.

Meyer and Strang ran a few yards and stared up intently at the Bottleneck.

The figure lay with its head pointing down the slope.

Immediately, excited chatter started up on the radio.

"Very bad fall!" Meyer heard someone say. "He is alive. He is still moving. It is one of the Serbs."

Part I

SUMMIT

Friday, August 1

"I wish everyone could contemplate this ocean of mountains
and glaciers. The night will be long but beautiful."
—Hugues d'Aubarède, K2, July 31, 2008

"K2 is not to be climbed."
—Filippo de Filippi, from the authorized account
of the Italian 1909 expedition

CHAPTER ONE

Walk east along dusty tracks from the village of Askole and within three days you will glimpse in the distance a wonder of the world, the rock-strewn Baltoro glacier and a giant's parade of ocher and black granite mountains, topped with snow and wreathed in clouds.

Eric Meyer and the other teams traveled this route in 2008, entering the inner Karakoram, the heart of the tallest mountain range in the world. The Karakoram range is part of the western Himalayas and forms a watershed between the Indian subcontinent and the deserts of Central Asia. Here, four peaks higher than 26,000 feet stand within fifteen miles of one another. Walk deeper into this dominion of ice and moraine and finally, after another three days, above all these lofty giants suddenly appears K2, the second-tallest mountain in the world.

K2's naming has become legend. In September 1856, a British surveyor of the Great Trigonometric Survey of India, Lieutenant Thomas G. Montgomerie, laden with theodolite, heliotrope, and plane table, climbed to a peak in Kashmir, his job to fix the imperial border of the Raj.

One hundred and forty miles to the north he glimpsed two formidable mountains, which he sketched in his notebook in ink, above his own wavy, proud signature. He named them K1 and K2. Montgomerie's "K" was for Karakoram. (He would log K1 through K32, and recorded K2's height at 28,278 feet, only about 30 feet off.) KI was later discovered to bear a local name and became fixed on the maps as Masherbrum. But K2 didn't and so Montgomerie's name stuck.

Five years after Montgomerie's visit, another tough, steely British empire builder, Henry Haversham Godwin-Austen, came closer to K2, becoming the first European to ascend the Baltoro glacier. In recognition of his feat, in 1888 a motion was proposed about K2 at the Royal Geographical Society in London that "in future it should be known as Peak Godwin-Austen." The motion was rejected but the name persisted, even into the middle decades of the twentieth century on some maps and in newspaper accounts. It carried colonial overtones, however, and in the end, "K2" won out, although Godwin-Austen's name still marks the glacier at the foot of the mountain.

After the imperial surveyors, Western explorers and travelers soon followed, encroaching ever deeper into this wondrous realm in hobnailed boots, tweed suits, and skirts. Two prominent visitors—an American couple, William Hunter Workman and his wife, the New England heiress and suffragette Fanny Bullock Workman—were making a bicycle tour of India in 1898 when they decided to visit the Himalayas. Years later, they explored the Siachen glacier to the southeast of K2, and they made first ascents of several Karakoram summits. The couple was notorious. William was a retired surgeon who believed no one could survive a night above 22,000 feet, and Fanny had an irritating habit of carving her initials and date of passage on mountain walls, as well as clearing foot traffic with whip and revolver.

In 1902, a six-man expedition made up of Swiss, Austrians, and Britons made the first serious summit attempt on K2. Among them was the English climber and occultist Aleister Crowley, who a few years later would assume the name "666," and whose wild-haired antics earned him the title "Wickedest Man in the World" in the British press and a place years after his death on the cover of the Beatles' album *Sgt. Pepper's Lonely Hearts Club Band*.

Following a nine-week trek, undertaken while carrying three tons of luggage, including volumes of Crowley's library, the expedition made as many as five attempts at the summit. Crowley preferred a route up the southeast spur of the mountain but the other climbers argued for a switch to the northeast ridge. They reached about 21,000 feet on K2's side. But the effort broke down when, among other things, one of the Austrians collapsed with pulmonary edema—an acute mountain sickness involving a buildup of fluid in the lungs. A disappointed and semidelirious Crowley, suffering himself from malarial fevers and chills, threatened one of his colleagues with a revolver and was disarmed by a knee to the stomach. The expedition made its retreat in disarray, although they had climbed higher on K2 than anyone before.

The mountain cast a wide spell. In 1909, seven years after Crowley's attempt, it was the turn of Prince Luigi Amedeo of Savoy-Aosta, Duke of the Abruzzi. A son of the king of Spain, and grandson of a king of Italy, Amedeo was a mountain climbing fanatic who a decade earlier had carried ten bedsteads up onto Alaska's Malaspina glacier. (He also hailed from the part of Italy that two decades later would be made famous by Ernest Hemingway in *A Farewell to Arms*.) When the duke visited the American Alpine Club at the Astor Hotel in New York, the ballroom was decorated in his honor: "great blocks of ice fashioned like mountains, with men roped climbing their steeps," according to a report in the *New York Times*. He chose K2 because it was relatively unmapped, but he had another objective. He wanted to set the world altitude record, which at the time was held by two Norwegians.

Surrounding his trip in great secrecy, he traveled incognito to London for supplies. Presumably the secrecy was due to the fact that he didn't want anyone to reach K2 first. But he may also, according to some history books, have been fleeing a very public (in the American press) romantic entanglement with Katherine Elkins, the rich, auburn-haired, horse-riding daughter of a United States senator from West Virginia, Stephen B. Elkins. The duke had likely met the Elkinses in Rome, where they traveled in the summer to buy antiques, but the romance was opposed by both families.

The duke set sail from Marseille on the P&O steamer *Oceana* with six and a half tons of luggage, bound for Bombay and thence to K2, for the glory of Italy and the House of Savoy. He was accompanied by a fifty-year-old mountain photographer, Vittorio Sella, whose glass plates and emulsions would yield some of the most beautiful pictures ever taken of K2.

The duke's ten-man team passed through Srinagar, where he was seen off by the local British governor with a royal escort of brightly decorated shikaras, or riverboats, each rowed by fifteen oarsmen. He traveled in luxury: The expedition's four-layered sleeping bags consisted of one layer of camel hair, one of eiderdown, one of sheepskin, and an outer layer of waterproof canvas. He first caught sight of the mountain from Concordia, a junction of two sweeping glaciers a few miles away at the center of an amphitheater of peaks. The duke's awe shines through his description. It was, he declared, *l'indiscusso sovrano della regione:* "the indisputable sovereign of the region, gigantic and solitary, hidden from human sight by innumerable ranges, jealously defended by a vast throng of varied peaks, protected from invasion by miles and miles of glacier."

Supplied from Urdukas, a camp several miles away down the Baltoro glacier, with a stream of fresh eggs, meat, water, fuel, mail, and newspapers, the duke and his entourage ascended partway up the southeast ridge, a rock rib rising directly above what would be named the Godwin-Austen glacier. The route he followed would become the main path for future ascents of the mountain and would forever bear the duke's name, the Abruzzi Spur. In his wake as he passed, he named other K2 landmarks in his expedition's honor, like a modern Adam discovering a new world: the Negrotto Pass, after the duke's aide-de-camp; the Sella Pass; and the Savoia Glacier.

The duke eventually set the world altitude record by climbing partway up another, nearby peak, Chogolisa. But he was frustrated by K2's seemingly insuperable steepness, and turned back at 20,000 feet, declaring that K2 had defeated him and it would remain forever unconquerable.

"After weeks of examination, after hours of contemplation and search for the secret of the mountain, the Duke was finally obliged to yield to the conviction that K2 is not to be climbed," wrote Filippo de Filippi, a biologist and doctor who accompanied the duke and authored the expedition book.

It was up to another Italian expedition to prove the duke wrong, years later.

In the years immediately following World War II, military hostilities may have ended around the world but national rivalries were still playing out in the arena of the Himalayas. In 1950, an expedition of French climbers was the first in the world to scale a peak above 26,000 feet when it reached the summit of Annapurna I in Nepal. In 1953, Mount Everest, the highest of them all, fell to the British, news of the event reaching London on the eve of the coronation of Queen Elizabeth II and prompting national celebration.

In the spring of 1954, it was Italy's turn to embellish its national standing, and recast its postwar funk, when an expedition arrived in Pakistan to lay siege to the slopes of K2.

The expedition comprised eleven climbers, four scientists, a doctor, a filmmaker, ten high-altitude Hunza porters, and five hundred additional porters. Altogether, they shouldered more than thirteen tons of supplies, including 230 cylinders of supplementary oxygen.

The expedition's autocratic leader, Ardito Desio, was a geographer and geologist from Palmanova, in northeast Italy. An ambitious man, he was nicknamed Il Ducetto, or Little Mussolini, by the team's members. To signify his serious intent, before approaching on foot Desio and three companions circled the mountain in a DC-3. The Pakistani army aided his approach by building bridges across ravines, and, in an echo of the preceding war, through his radio in Base Camp he urged his climbers on the slopes to become "champions of your race." On the trek in, through the unpeopled terrain of the surrounding valley, some of the porters went snow-blind after Desio refused to issue them proper sunglasses. The porters later staged a revolt but were placated by the Italians' cigarettes and baksheesh, and by the intervention of the military liaison officer, Colonel Ata-Ullah, although some of the porters then stole the team's flour and biscuits.

The climb itself was notable for the use of a steel windlass and a thousand-foot steel cable to winch heavy supplies up the mountain. And after sixty-three days of preparation—and the death of one climber, Mario Puchoz, thirty-six, a mountain guide from Courmayeur, due to complications that were initially diagnosed as pneumonia but were later accepted as pulmonary edema—by the evening of July 30, 1954, two climbers had reached 26,000 feet and were within a day or so's climb of the top.

At first light, the two men, Achille Compagnoni, a forty-year-old climber from Lombardy who was Desio's expedition favorite, and his partner, twenty-eight-year-old Lino Lacedelli, from Cortina d'Ampezzo, climbed up toward the summit. At one point Compagnoni slipped and fell but he landed in soft snow. At another, Lacedelli, removing his gloves to clean his glasses, found his fingers were white and without sensation. The two men were carrying heavy oxygen canisters. Within six hundred feet of the summit, however, they felt dizzy; the gas had run out and they wrenched off their masks.

They believed that life without oxygen above around 28,000 feet was impossible beyond about ten minutes; they waited for the end. When it didn't come, and they found they could breathe, they trudged on, though they were plunged into a hallucinatory state, both men believing their late colleague, Puchoz, was following close behind.

At a few minutes before 6 p.m., the slope flattened, they linked arms, and with a "Together" they stepped onto the summit. K2 had been defeated. The *New York Times* ran the story on August 4, 1954: "Italians Conquer World's Second Highest Peak; Mt. Godwin Austen in Kashmir Is Climbed in 76-Day Effort."

Back in Italy, the expedition was predictably greeted by a wave of patriotic fervor, a postage stamp was issued in the climbers' honor, and they were received by Pope Pius XII. There also followed decades of acrimony over the manner of the summit victory.

On the evening before their summit attempt, Compagnoni had pitched the final camp higher than had been agreed with the rest of the team and concealed it behind a rock. He did this because there were limited oxygen sets and he did not want another climber, Walter Bonatti, who was coming up from below with a Hunza porter called Mahdi, to take his or Compagnoni's place. Bonatti was a talented, younger mountaineer, less favored by the leader, Desio, and the Italian climbing establishment.

As a result of the concealment, Bonatti and Mahdi were forced to spend the night out in the open on a small ice shelf on the side of the mountain. They had actually carried the oxygen sets for the summit and they left them in the snow. Mahdi, who was without proper climbing boots, ran back down desperately at first light. He survived but lost half of both his feet from frostbite and almost all his fingers.

The rancor lasted for years in Italy. Bonatti went on to become one of the most successful and respected climbers of his generation, and mountaineers generally side with his version of events. In the 1960s, Compagnoni fought back, claiming that Bonatti had siphoned off oxygen from the tanks, thus endangering the lives of the two summiteers. He said that Bonatti had also convinced Mahdi to accompany him to the final camp by falsely promising him a crack at the summit. Bonatti won a libel victory in court against a journalist who had aired Compagnoni's claims. Desio would return to Pakistan in 1987 to settle finally the question of which peak was higher, K2 or Everest. (A University of Washington astronomer had announced that new data from a navy satellite showed K2 might be 800 feet higher than previously believed and taller than Everest; using better technology, Desio and his colleagues found otherwise.) He also faced questions about whether he had concealed the truth about what had happened on the mountain.

Despite the rancor, the Italian team's achievement still stood. Nearly one hundred years after the first sighting by Thomas Montgomerie of the Royal Engineers, men had finally reached the snows at the top of K2.

CHAPTER TWO

10:30 a.m.

It was so crowded near the top of the Bottleneck that Dren Mandic was nervous.

The lone mountaineer near the top, the Basque Alberto Zerain, had climbed in front of everybody up the steep gully, then disappeared quickly around into the diagonal passageway of the Traverse. A few Sherpas and a line of South Koreans had followed behind him. But the Koreans had gone so slowly and after half an hour they had stopped moving, causing this backlog down the Bottleneck.

Mandic was waiting near the top of the gully. He stood on a little rock shelf on the right-hand side while he waited to cross over to the mouth of the Traverse on the opposite side. Standing stiff and impatient in a black down suit and a red coat, he waited amid a small group of climbers—four, five, six, more—who were resting, some sitting, their coats unbuttoned and their harnesses unclipped from the rope, basking in the mid-morning warmth.

He glared up at the backs of the mountaineers lined up ahead of him in the Traverse. After the Traverse, the teams would have to climb up onto a long snowfield at about 27,500 feet, which after another three or four more tiring hours would bring them to the summit.

Mandic turned and looked below at the longer line of climbers stretching down the Bottleneck like dominoes. The climbers wore big jackets, clutched ice axes and ski poles, and had backpacks weighted with phones and radios. They were strangers to each other behind shaded glasses and frosted beards and eyebrows; some were wearing oxygen masks.

Mandic noticed that the crowd was making the Sherpas uneasy. In one place, they had thrust two axes into the rocks above an ice screw and wrapped two short rope lengths around the axe handles and down to the screw to take some weight off it.

The climbers at the bottom of the queue a few hundred yards below were still moving slowly higher. They stabbed their axe handles into the snow and moved their jumars—metal ascending devices that bit into fixed lines—up the rope. But soon the inevitable happened and they ran up against the crowd. Everyone's frustration was boiling over. The leader of the Dutch expedition, Wilco van Rooijen, snapped.

"What's going on?" he yelled. A professional mountaineer, Wilco had been one of the dominant figures over the past few months at Base Camp, one of the chief organizers of the cooperation between the teams. He was dressed today in an orange down suit, a thin, broad-chested man with spiky silver hair, blue eyes, and a silver earring in his left ear. This summer represented his third attempt to climb K2. He had first tried to climb it in 1995 but had been knocked unconscious in a rock fall; he broke his shoulder and lost one and a half liters of blood. This year he had returned with an eight-strong team and a 100,000-euro sponsorship deal from a Dutch water purification company, Norit. He was an impatient man and wanted success.

"Hurry up!" he hollered, in his Dutch-accented lilt.

Above them all, not fifty feet from Mandic's head, loomed the brow of the serac, blue and sweating in the heat. It was barely the middle of the morning and the sun already blazed above them in the blue sky.

The thirty-one-year-old Mandic had come to the mountain with a regimented five-man Serbian team with their three Pakistani HAPs, one of the first Serbian expeditions to K2.

There was Predrag, or Pedja, Zagorac, and Iso Planic, who was probably the most experienced among them. Zagorac was from Belgrade and Planic from Subotica. Then there was Milivoj Erdeljan, their gray-haired leader, who didn't climb but guided his charges like a father from Base Camp. His calming voice was always on the radio. A fifth member of the team, who helped with sponsorship, had joined them in July.

Of the three Serbian climbers, Mandic had the least experience. At home he belonged to the "Spider" Subotica mountaineering club. He had climbed Mount Ararat in Turkey, and the previous summer he had summitted Broad Peak, K2's big neighbor, but that was his only Himalayan achievement.

None of the Serbians was a professional climber—few people in Serbia were. Mandic worked as a carpenter in Subotica. But they had prepared well, he was convinced. They had financing from the Ministry of Sport as well as from private companies in Belgrade. They had a mobile weather forecast station, and back in Serbia two meteorologists were on call. They felt they couldn't be in better physical condition. After all, their fitness had been tested and approved at the Provincial Institute for Sport in Novi Sad; and in Base Camp, Erdeljan had sent his men out most days to keep fit by climbing up and down the steep cuts of the Godwin-Austen glacier. The Serbs had brought ten tents to the mountain, and 5,600 feet—more than a full mile—of rope.

Like most of the teams on K2 this year, the Serbs had traveled five hundred miles from Islamabad, the Pakistani capital, to Skardu, a dusty town in the country's northeastern territory. From there they had gone on by cramped jeep for another day to Askole, a mud-brick village and one of the nearest habitations to K2. After that they had trekked in for a week by foot over gushing streams and brittle glaciers, forever craning their necks to glimpse the distant peak. On the Serbs' trail in from Askole, one of the mules broke its leg.

In the following weeks, the different national expeditions had gotten to know each other well. They had worked side by side on the slopes, enduring rock falls and storms, loosened ice screws, scraped shins, and snow-crushed tents. In the Base Camp at the foot of K2, a small town of multicolored tents perched on the Godwin-Austen glacier at 16,400 feet above sea level, they had shot the breeze over yak's meat and the Hunzas' sweet tea. They had learned techniques from one another, bragged and swapped stories of conquests of lesser peaks—Annapurna, Chogolisa, Masherbrum—while the frozen tides of the Godwin-Austen shifted outside and cracked.

K2 had provided blunt reminders of its dangers. In Base Camp, one of the Pakistani military liaison officers—each team had to have one to qualify for a permit—got fluid in his lungs from the altitude; one of the Serbians' porters had had to push him by wheelbarrow to the military camp at Concordia. Then on a practice climb to one of the higher camps, a rockfall had showered down on the three Serbs. Mandic had simply lain down and put a knapsack over his head as the biggest stone—at least a hundred pounds— bounced over him.

Mandic and Zagorac were often in the kitchen tent, where they cooked Serbian specialties, Vojvodinean homemade plum dumplings and doughnuts, without plums, however; they had to make do with strawberry jam. It was still delicious. In the evenings, Mandic was invariably at the mess tent table, playing cards raucously with the Pakistani porters. Mandic, who had a special love of nature, told them about the volunteer work he did at the local zoo back in Subotica. He kept spiders, birds, all sorts of exotic creatures in his apartment, where he lived with his girlfriend, Mirjana. He had completed military service in Serbia. He had never moved away from Subotica, but he was restless and liked to travel, especially to places like K2.

Over the weeks, the Serbians and the other teams had established higher and higher camps so that they gradually became used to the altitude and felt more comfortable breathing the rarefied air. Then the altitude headaches were not so debilitating, at least when washed down with a cup of pills.

During the days, the teams fixed thousands of feet of rope to the rock and ice like a handrail so that they did not have to face the mountain unassisted. They followed two routes up—one on the Abruzzi ridge and another called the Cesen route, both of which met near the Shoulder. The teams bound the mountain, just as the yaks the porters led in from Askole had been bound in rope by the Pakistani cooks, their throats slit on the ice, the meat stashed in ice holes in the glacier for the mountaineers to eat. And the dance of the Balti porters in the glare of the torchlight on the festival of Aga Khan was like the celebration of the vanquishing of some mythic beast.

Then the leaders of each expedition team had convened the co-operation meetings, held in the Serbians' and Koreans' mess tents, to discuss logistics. The climbers knew they were too many to ascend in an uncoordinated rush. Around a large green table, they worked out who would bring the ropes, even who would supply what precise number of ice screws or bamboo sticks or lengths of fish line.

"We are working like one team," said Pemba Gyalje, a Nepalese Sherpa in the Dutch team who attended the meeting. They had turned the crowd to their advantage, it seemed. It was quite an achievement among so many competing languages and egos.

Gyalje banged his fist for emphasis.

"One team," he said. *Not many.*

On the way up the mountain during the final summit push to Camp Four, the teams had climbed up the ropes and rickety aluminum wire ladders suspended in House's Chimney, a 150-feet-high crack in a huge red-rock cliff below Camp Two. It was named after an American, Bill House, who had climbed it in 1938. And they had scaled the notorious Black Pyramid, a large promontory of broken rock and shingles below Camp Three.

Around this time, unforecast winds had swept in. In the night the gusts had nearly lifted the flapping tents off the ground. The climbers had clung to their sleeping bags, convinced they were going to die. The winds had ripped open one of the tents to toss a backpack full of equipment belonging to another independent Serbian mountaineer into the chasms.

It was the Serbian team's lead guide, a man called Shaheen Baig, who had vomited blood in their little tent on the narrow ledge at Camp Two. While some of the teams, such as the South Koreans, had flown in Sherpas from Nepal, the Serbs had hired three local HAPs—the HAPs were generally drawn from nearby northern areas such as Shimshal. During the storm, the Serbians listened, above the roar of the wind, to Baig's hacking cough. Baig possessed the valuable experience of having summitted K2 four years earlier. But there had been no other option; he had had to climb back down.

The rest of the Serbian team pushed on but the next morning the Serbians' two other porters, Mohammed Khan and Mohammed Hussein, slyly admitted that during the storm they had forgotten to pack everyone's food, so then there were no sausages or biscuits for Mandic and his colleagues, though they found candies and soups in a rucksack and borrowed a bowl of pasta from Alberto Zerain. At that altitude, though, they discovered they were not really hungry after all.

Then, on the steep mountainside at Camp Three, Khan complained of a headache. They gave him ibuprofen and he reached Camp Four; and he had set off with the Serbs this morning. He was to carry two bottles of oxygen for them to the top of the Bottleneck and then turn around. The Serbs were using supplementary oxygen—the breathing apparatus was a Russian-made system—and each climber had two five-kiloliter bottles. But Khan had stopped about 150 feet before the top of the Bottleneck and refused to go on, complaining he could not breathe. Planic insisted he had to continue, but Mandic and Zagorac took the two oxygen bottles the HAP was carrying and divided his backpack between them so he could descend. The Serbs were two HAPs down. That left just Hussein.

Mandic felt the extra weight he was carrying now as he shifted on the rope at the top of the Bottleneck. He and Zagorac had agreed they would change over to the full oxygen bottles somewhere at the top of the gully. If Zagorac ever made it up there. Mandic's friend was stuck below in the line in the Bottleneck.

Why was everything going so slowly? These were not hard slopes. Steep, yes. Fifty, sixty degrees. But no more difficult, really, than the ones the Serbs had scaled on Broad Peak.

It was the altitude that made the climbing tough. This was high, 27,000 feet. They were in an area climbers called the Death Zone, the region at or above about 24,000 or 25,000 feet where the air pressure is much less than at sea level and a lack of oxygen rapidly depletes human muscle strength and mental functioning. Human life can barely be sustained up here. Many climbers dared venture into these altitudes—well into the stratosphere—only with the protection of oxygen tanks in their backpacks and the nozzles of masks fixed over their mouth and nose. Others, like the American and Dutch teams, chose to confront the mountain unaided. They wanted to take on the mountain on its own terms. Otherwise, why do it? Even those climbers like Mandic who used supplementary oxygen were aware they had to be up to the summit and down in just a few hours. They could not delay; there was a ticking clock before their oxygen ran out. The altitude affected some people more than others, but after a short while even the hardiest found it difficult to think more than a few steps ahead. Bodies shut down. You could no longer trust your own mind.

And besides simply being in the Death Zone, you couldn't rely on the snow up here. Mandic looked at the rough surface beneath his boots. You could see blue ice shining under the snow. If a climber was unprepared, he could slip, easily, and it was a long way down. Probably sensible to go slowly. But then again this delay was ridiculous. The Serbian team had calculated they would be on the summit by 9:30 a.m. That is what Shaheen Baig had told them was possible. Mandic wished Shaheen was still with them.

Mandic checked his watch. It was already 11 a.m. In his down suit, he could hardly stand the warmth of the day. He stared out at the sea of white mountains around him, their slopes striped by brown and black rock and coverings of snow, with trails of clouds spreading between the peaks.

It was so hot, Mandic noticed, that a Norwegian climber called Cecilie Skog, who was standing only a few yards away from him, had taken off her purple jacket. Diminutive and pretty, the Norwegian woman was wearing dark sunglasses, and her long hair curled from beneath her helmet down onto her shoulders. From Norway's western oil coast, the thirty-three-year-old climber had come to K2 with her husband, Rolf Bae, who was not far below in the line on the rope in the gully.

About twenty or thirty feet below the little rock ledge where Mandic was waiting, three climbers finally let their frustration get the better of them and took matters into their own hands. They unclipped from the rope and began free-climbing in a snow channel up the side of the Bottleneck—as if there were no ice to worry about, and no drop below them.

"What the hell's going on?" Wilco van Rooijen called, as he clambered up the side, passing some of the climbers still on the rope. He made it clear to anyone who would listen that he had invested a lot of time and money to get to K2 again, and that he didn't think highly of the expertise of some of the other expeditions.

In his rush, he tried to pass Mandic's colleague Iso Planic. As he did so, he fell off balance and slipped backward, catching the Serbian's jacket with the sharp crampons on his boot. He was stopped by the arms of a Sherpa standing behind him who grabbed Van Rooijen's jacket around his waist. Open-mouthed, Van Rooijen stared up in shock at Planic, whose coat had been ripped on the left shoulder; the inner lining was coming out. The Serb's skin was also cut.

Mandic noticed the small confusion below and tried to see what was happening. But the next second his attention was diverted away when the line of climbers suddenly began to move ahead across the Traverse.

He saw his chance at last and scrambled across from the rock shelf where he had been standing, then moved up onto the tall ice wall. Then, to his frustration, within a few minutes the line of climbers stopped and he was blocked again by the knot of bodies in front of him.

Looking back, he saw that his friend Planic had climbed up onto the ledge among the waiting crowd. Instead of turning left toward the Traverse, his colleague had climbed over to the opposite side to a free space where it looked like he was going to try to change his oxygen bottle. He had already begun to wrestle the cylinder from his backpack.

Mandic decided that was a good idea; he would escape the crowd and join his friend. But when he turned around, he immediately came face to face with Cecilie Skog. There had been calls for more rope from the Traverse, and Skog, who was carrying a length of rope over her shoulder, was marching toward the Traverse like she meant business. Two thin oxygen pipes looped from her backpack to her nose. She said something about wanting to stash the rope in her backpack while she climbed across.

"I'll help you," Mandic said, mouthing the words through his frozen balaclava and indicating with his hand.

She nodded. *Thank you.*

Mandic unclipped his carabiner from the line so Skog could get past him. He stepped gingerly behind her while she turned her back to him to offer her rucksack. He pulled his sleeve across his forehead, which was damp from sweat.

As Mandic took another step to pass her, he felt his boot slide on the ice beneath the snow and suddenly his leg flew from under him. He fell forward onto Skog, pushing her down onto the ice, his body slumping heavily on top of hers.

Shouts of alarm filled the air around them. From below, Skog's husband, Rolf Bae, cried, "Hey Cecilie!"

Bundled together on the ice slope, Mandic and Skog began to slide. They were on a steep slope and within a few seconds they would be going too fast to stop themselves. Below them was the three-hundred-foot drop of the hard Bottleneck and its sharp rocks.

Skog fell for about three feet but her harness was still clipped to the rope and it stopped her. Mandic, however, had unclipped. As Skog stopped, he continued to slide, quickly.

Out of the corner of his eye, Pedja Zagorac saw something falling. It shot along the side of the line of climbers and down the gully like a bullet.

Then he heard the yelling, "That's Dren! Dren! Dren!"

He watched as the figure slipped farther down the Bottleneck, turning around and at one point cartwheeling all the way over, head over heels. After about four hundred feet, Mandic slowed and stopped.

Mandic was going to be all right, one of the climbers assured Zagorac; in the Alps, people fell like that all the time. It was no worse than a tumble on a ski slope. A few said they would climb down to help the fallen climber.

But as they were talking, Mandic stood up. Was he waving at them? Zagorac's whole body flushed with relief. Thank God! On the way down, his friend hadn't hit any rocks or anything.

The next moment Mandic seemed to fold over and he slid again. Not so far this time, maybe three hundred feet, but he went down over some rocks and when he stopped he lay on the ice and didn't stand up.

Zagorac strained his eyes to see. Someone on the line shouted, "He's moving! He moved his leg. I saw him."

He could hear people shouting into their radios. *He's moving.*

Zagorac felt himself shouting too, but he wasn't sure what he was saying. He was crying. The Serbians' HAP, Hussein, who was standing near him, was also shouting at the top of his voice. Zagorac wasn't going to waste any more time. The climbers waiting around him moved aside, and he turned to face the mountain and rappelled down, praying under his breath and hoping he was not too late. He focused on breathing steadily and moving his legs fast. *Let me be in time.*

It took him about fifteen minutes, but he eventually reached the end of the second length of fixed rope, where Mandic lay in the snow, his body pointing down the mountain. Panting heavily, Zagorac knelt down beside his friend. He stared at Mandic's gray face. His head was beaten up. There was a lot of blood.

"Dren!"

He couldn't believe that this was what had become of his friend. Zagorac quickly turned Mandic over and gave him mouth-to-mouth. *Oh God. Help me. Help Dren.*

Mandic's skin was warm. Zagorac waited for him to breathe. He put his mouth over the open lips once again. *Come on, Dren.* He pressed his fingers against Mandic's neck, searching for a pulse, but he could feel nothing. As soon as he had seen him, Zagorac had known his friend was dead.

After a few minutes, Hussein and Planic rappelled down to join Zagorac. They all stared blankly at Mandic's body, catching their breath, looking at one another.

What do we do?

They felt sick. They got on the radio to tell Erdeljan the news. Erdeljan knew right away what to do.

"Down now!" His voice crackled on the radio. "The expedition is over! Get down!"

From a backpack, they unfolded some sponsors' flags and a Serbian flag they had intended to take to the summit and laid them over their friend, trying to cover his injuries from view.

Zagorac and Planic knotted a thirty-foot rope to Mandic's safety belt. They were going to get him down and give him a decent burial. It was unusual and dangerous to lower a corpse from a 28,000-foot peak—a first rule of mountain rescue was never allow an injured or dead person to become the cause of multiple casualties. But they were not leaving him there.

Preparing to set off took longer than they had expected. They felt so numb and shaken. They always knew death was a possibility on the mountain, especially on K2. But they never imagined it would happen to them.

Hussein took the backpacks and they stepped down the slope toward Camp Four, Zagorac and Planic carefully letting the rope out before them. It was hard work and they said little.

It was not long before they saw a figure walk out from Camp Four and begin moving toward them over the Shoulder.

Meanwhile, up on the Bottleneck, a single climber in yellow emerged from the people waiting on the ropes and began to climb down. He was a Balti HAP working for the Frenchman, Hugues d'Aubarède. Up close, it looked to some of the climbers on the ropes as though he was slightly disoriented, like he might have had altitude sickness. As the HAP passed the teams on the line, opening and closing the small metal clip of his jumar ascending device, he elicited calls of protest from some who said the jumar should really only be used for climbing up.

He replied tartly that he did it all the time, and carried on awkwardly down the gully toward the group surrounding Mandic.

CHAPTER THREE

11:30 a.m.

Since the record for climbing the tallest mountain on each of the seven continents had already been claimed, Fredrik Strang had traveled to K2 from Sweden as the first stop in an attempt to climb—and make a documentary about climbing—the *second*-tallest summit on each continent. Up at Camp Four, one of the first things he did, as news of Mandic's fall spread, was set up his video camera and point it toward the Bottleneck. He zoomed in, trying to locate the fallen mountaineer.

A few of the other climbers who rushed out from their tents also felt compelled to capture the moment, including a twenty-three-year-old American from Los Angeles, Nicholas Rice. Nick Rice had turned back from a summit attempt five hours earlier after he spilled melted water on his socks and had never warmed up again, and now he began snapping photographs. Other people held up their digital cameras, peering through the lenses to get a better look.

Swearing in the zero-degree air, Strang interviewed Eric Meyer in front of his video camera.

"People are dying up there and we are doing nothing!" Strang said.

He and Meyer took a break from filming to gaze up the long, slanting avenue of the Shoulder. Mandic had tumbled down the Bottleneck and was lying prone at the bottom tip of an outcrop of rocks.

If he was dead, they knew, they were not going up. But if there was hope he was still alive, they would try to rescue him.

"Looks grave," said Meyer.

He waited and watched. The doctor's climbing coat was unzipped and he was chewing gum. He said he thought he could see movement in Mandic's arms and legs.

A voice came on the radio from up in the Bottleneck. It was Chhiring Dorje, the Sherpa from the Americans' team.

"Yes, Chhiring, this is Eric at Camp Four. What's happened?"

Like Pemba Gyalje in the Dutch expedition, Dorje was in his thirties and an established Sherpa, with his own guiding business back in Nepal. He had come to K2 as a climber in his own right and more or less on equal terms with Meyer and the other members of the American team, although Meyer had loaned him several thousand dollars to get there.

"One of the Serbs, he fell down," said Dorje over the radio. "His leg is still moving."

Meyer had the radio pressed to his mouth and communicated the news to everyone on the frequency. "We can see a lone figure down at the bottom of the Bottleneck. He is moving, over."

After a few minutes, however, the body appeared still. Voices on the radio were now saying he was probably dead. But Meyer thought they could be mistaken since it was possible to miss a pulse if it was low in these temperatures.

They tried to figure out what they should do. *Should we go up?* They had already climbed out toward the Bottleneck once today and they had to think of their own survival at this altitude. Yet on the other hand, a human being was out there and needed help.

Strang got on the radio again and spoke with climbers still down at Base Camp whose minds were not as clouded as their own by altitude. He asked them whether a rescue attempt was wise. He was told they should try to help. *Go fast. Take care.*

They knew it was the right thing to do.

"If he is alive, he won't be ambulatory," Meyer said to Strang.

They packed extra rope, oxygen, tubular nylon webbing, and a mattress pad for a sled to drag Mandic down. They also threw in a flask of warm water with electrolytes, a foil sleeping bag, and some energy bars. Strang packed his smaller lightweight Canon camera. Meyer spent a few extra minutes in his tent getting his medicines together—amphetamines, to help against the altitude, pain pills, suture supplies—so Strang set off first.

He was in good shape and moved fast up the Shoulder, blowing out his cheeks, feeling the cold ripping through his lungs. Some people, when they reach the Shoulder, see the Bottleneck and then the serac and the upper mountain beyond, and say it looks like another mountain stacked on top of the first below. Strang was glad he didn't have to go any higher than the Shoulder to drag the Serb down.

After about half an hour, he noticed the three climbers from the Serbian team who had descended from the Bottleneck. They had already reached their fallen colleague. Strang hoped he would be in time to help the poor guy.

———

It took Strang one and a half hours to ascend from 25,600 feet to 26,600 feet. When he was less than two hundred feet away from the group, he realized they were already dragging the Serb down.

He was breathing hard when he reached them. The two Serbians, Predrag Zagorac and Iso Planic, were holding a rope, which was tied around Mandic's harness, and they were sliding the body down the mountain in front of them, or sometimes behind. Their faces were mostly covered in balaclavas and goggles. Two yards to their left, their Pakistani porter, Hussein, was keeping his distance, unable, it seemed, to look at the corpse.

Strang told the Serbians who he was but they reacted dully. He also took out his camera to film the scene. When the Serbs looked up questioningly, Strang said he needed the film for the record.

"So we don't repeat this!" he said. "So we learn about human nature." He also wanted to avoid being accused later of doing something wrong. "Everything is recorded now," he said. "Every single word."

The group took a rest, drinking some water and eating the chocolate the Swede gave them. Strang asked what had happened. He knelt down and felt Mandic's cold skin but it was clear the Serbian was dead. A terrible fracture cut across Mandic's skull. He was only half covered.

One of the Serbs said they wanted to take the body at least to Camp Four, and perhaps all the way to Base Camp.

Strang thought he must have misheard him, or that the Serb was delusional. Getting the body to Base Camp would be next to impossible. He would rather have left the body where it was but the Serbs were insistent and he felt sympathy for them. Their friend had died. They were in shock.

"Look, you guys are tired," he said, trying to reason with them. They stood in front of him, while beside them Hussein crouched in the snow. They were on a steep slope and the mountains were beautiful all around them.

"You are on oxygen but I am not," Strang said. "Let's just focus on reaching Camp Four and we can give him a proper burial there. Even that's dangerous."

The two Serbians agreed. Strang took out the pieces of rope and the mat and the nylon webbing and the foil sleeping bag to wrap the body.

He looped the ropes around Mandic's chest. He told the others they could take one end of the rope and he would hold the other. But he warned the Serbs that if there was any sign that Mandic was slipping out of control, they had to release him, unless they wanted to be dragged off the mountain.

"Guys, if you do fall, you release. Okay? It's our lives too. Okay?"

As they had been resting, a figure dressed in yellow had approached slowly down the slope from the Bottleneck. The Serbs said the lone climber had been following them for some time but that he had stayed about 100 feet behind them. From the way he was dressed—hand-me-down hat and boots, secondhand suit, it seemed—they thought he had to be one of the Pakistani HAPs. When he came up to them, they saw it was Jahan Baig, a thirty-two-year-old HAP, one of three who had been working for Hugues d'Aubarède.

Baig was a farmer, with two sons and one daughter. He was a cousin to Shaheen Baig. He came from the same village, Shimshal, as Shaheen and several of the other HAPs. It was such a small village that Jahan, Shaheen, and d'Aubarède's other porters, Qudrat Ali and Karim Meherban, shared the same grandfather. Qudrat, the most experienced, had started a climbing school in Shimshal, which his cousins had attended. Shimshal was about one hundred miles from K2, close to the Chinese border. Baig had been taken on by d'Aubarède after a Singaporean expedition fired him for refusing to carry equipment up to one of the high camps in bad weather. No Nepalese Sherpas were being asked to climb up, which Baig had said was unfair.

Commercial mountain guiding had less of a tradition in these western flanks of the Himalayas than it did in Nepal, where the Sherpa reputation had grown over the years. But HAPs like Baig and Qudrat Ali were trying hard to develop a local industry and make it pay. It was a chance to make a decent living, and bring in foreign currency, in what was a poor region. Still, the HAPs were generally regarded as inferior to the Sherpas and sometimes there was rivalry between the two groups.

Unlike most of the other HAPs, who often seemed overeager to please their clients, Jahan Baig was less accommodating. He rarely ate with the mountaineers in their tents, though that may have been because his English was poor; he spoke mostly Balti or Urdu.

His job for d'Aubarède had been to carry oxygen cylinders up to the top of the Bottleneck, and once he completed his task, the Frenchman had allowed Baig to climb back down again. He now looked as though he had altitude sickness. Earlier that morning, even before the teams had left from Camp Four, Baig had complained of feeling sick.

At altitude, as you climb higher into the Death Zone and air pressure diminishes, the amount of oxygen in the air drops. For human beings, the shortage of oxygen results in a condition called hypoxia, which has a range of debilitating symptoms. These include headaches and insomnia, vomiting and stumbling, loss of motor skills and cognitive ability, poor judgment, even hallucinations.

That morning, one of the other HAPs had pointed out that Baig was acting strangely. D'Aubarède, who didn't know his new porter well, noticed nothing out of the ordinary. Then, in the dark tent at Camp Four, Baig announced he had a headache. D'Aubarède gave him aspirin and Diamox, a medicine to combat altitude sickness. Baig said he felt better. But when they were hastily preparing to leave for the summit, he took forty-five minutes to attach his crampons, even with the other HAPs' help. "Why is it taking you so long?" d'Aubarède had demanded, standing above him and becoming increasingly impatient. "Do you even know how to climb?"

Now, as Baig joined the group gathered around the dead Serb on the Shoulder, he stared nervously at Zagorac's jacket, which was blotched with Mandic's blood.

"I am sorry," Baig said, shaking his head. "I haven't come to help."

Zagorac said that was fine. "We're okay. We don't need your help. Thank you."

"I never saw a dead body."

Zagorac shrugged, and the others ignored the Pakistani porter. But just as the group was setting off, Baig stepped forward and said he wanted to help after all.

Strang looked at him suspiciously. "Sure you are okay?"

"I am fine!" Baig said, nodding. He spoke quickly, proudly, as if afraid to admit to a Westerner that anything was wrong.

Strang stood on the right side of Mandic's body. The Swede was a dramatic man, whose self-aggrandizing antics on the slopes with his camera sometimes irritated other climbers. He was a self-declared Indiana Jones fanatic. What he liked about mountaineering was that actions mattered; here in the crucible of the wilderness decisions had consequences. Now he had found a situation where a man had lost his life and the safety of those bringing down his body was still at risk.

There were two ends of rope on either side of Mandic. Zagorac and Planic held the ends on the left side of the body and Strang and Baig held them on the right side. This arrangement left the Serbs' porter, Hussein, free to carry their bags. Strang put a loop in the end of his rope for his ice axe handle and issued precise instructions about taking it slowly, keeping a safe distance between each of them and pulling in a balanced fashion. Their lives depended on the four men working together. They nodded enthusiastically, especially Baig.

The slope was about 30 degrees, although farther ahead it grew less steep on a saddle of ice. This part of the Shoulder was about 650 feet across and on either side it slanted away and ended abruptly over a sheer drop, to the east toward China and to the west.

The crunchy ice crust was like glass and the men took it one measured step at a time. Strang spat out commands, plainly irritating the Serbs. But the Swede was satisfied that everyone was working as a team, staying level so that the body didn't slide to the left or right. Behind Strang, Jahan Baig kept a distance of about sixteen feet, just as Strang had instructed him.

The four climbers were silhouetted against the big blue sky as they edged slowly down the white Shoulder. They slid the body down for thirty feet to test things out, then they stopped to eat some more chocolate. Their system of descent seemed to be working, and they set off again.

After about fifty yards, Strang felt something snag on his boots. It was Baig, who had suddenly come up close.

"You trying to push me off the rope?" Strang shouted, pushing Baig off him forcefully.

"Not my fault!" said Baig, stepping back and beginning to argue.

Strang turned around but there was something strange, he felt, something out of place, in the porter's voice. Before Strang could remonstrate—*Whose fault is it, then?*—an extra weight seemed to fall onto Strang's rope as though Baig were no longer pulling on his rope.

"Get behind me!" Strang shouted.

Without the equal pressure on all of the ropes, Mandic's body began to slide slightly faster and move to the left.

"Stop!" Strang shouted. "Stop!"

The Serbs were pissed off at Baig, too, and they shouted at him, but the porter didn't seem to register any of them. Something was seriously wrong with the HAP, they realized. He had obviously been in worse condition than he had admitted, than he himself had realized. He was trying to do the right thing, but the altitude had gotten to him. Or he was also in shock after Mandic's death, as they all were.

Strang saw that Eric Meyer was now only about sixty yards away down the Shoulder. As soon as he reached them, he thought, his American colleague could take Baig's place on the rope.

Suddenly, however, Strang was jolted forward as Baig tripped in the snow and crashed into the Swede's back. When Strang swung around, Baig was sprawled on the ice.

Strang had had enough. "Get up!" he said. "Get up!"

As Baig began to slide, Strang expected the porter to flip over and stick an ice axe into the ice or do something to stop himself but he remained sliding on his back. The rope he was still holding snagged around Strang's legs and began to pull the Swede over.

"Let go of the rope!" Strang shouted.

The Serbs were now shouting at the HAP as well but Baig merely looked up at them with a bewildered expression.

"Release the rope!" Strang shouted again. He didn't care what happened. He just wanted him to let go. "Release the rope!"

Baig dropped the rope. Within a few seconds, he slipped away ten feet, then eleven. He was sitting down and slid boots first. The ice was slick and he traveled fast. Strang couldn't believe it. Why didn't he stop himself? Why didn't he do something?

"Stop yourself!" cried Strang. *Jesus Christ. Stop. Stop.*

Instead, Baig's crampons caught and he flopped over awkwardly onto his stomach. It seemed he would lose momentum as the saddle evened out. But Baig slid down the slope to the left, shedding his equipment, his oxygen bottle, gloves, and then his rucksack, all the while picking up speed.

The others could see that Baig was heading toward the eastern side of the mountain. At the end of the slope was a well-defined lip. Beyond that, they could see the glacier far below.

Everyone was yelling, urging Baig to stop himself or pull to the right in the direction of Camp Four. Meyer had almost reached them by now and he was standing there, yelling manically, too.

"Turn!" Meyer shouted. "Over there!"

But Baig kept on going. At the edge, he screamed. Then he was gone and silence engulfed them all.

———

Strang, Zagorac, Planic, and Hussein stood around Mandic's body and stared at the space between the lip of ice and the blue sky where the Pakistani porter had fallen. They were breathing hard, coughing, and trying to work out what had just happened.

They were all dazed. No one wanted to believe that now there had been two deaths on their K2 expedition.

"What the hell is this?" said Strang, weakly, his voice tightening.

He began to shake. He covered his face and started to cry. "One guy died. I came here to help you guys."

When Meyer joined them, they considered going to search for Baig but they realized straightaway it would be suicide. It was a drop of about a thousand feet to the glacier below.

"Let's go down," Meyer said. His voice was tired and resigned.

But he first had a duty as a doctor, and he examined each of the Serbs in turn, peering into their eyes as he asked questions about how they felt. They had been through a lot and he wanted to make sure they were not showing signs of cerebral edema. They nodded. They were barely coherent. He rifled through his backpack and handed everyone a vitamin energy bar, then he lined them up and gave each of the Serbs a four-milligram tablet of dexamethasone, a quick-acting, anti-inflammatory steroid. It would reduce any swelling in the brain and be enough to to get them down.

The Pakistani porter, Hussein, walked out toward the edge of the slope to collect the gloves, rucksack, and other equipment that Baig had dropped. It was dangerous, and if he had slipped he would have disappeared over the edge before the others could have stopped him, but Hussein wanted to collect his friend's belongings and the others let him go.

There seemed no question now that they would leave Mandic's body where it was. Strang tied the rope attached to Mandic's harness to an axe and stabbed the axe securely into the ice. Mandic would stay there forever at 26,000 feet, or until the storms swept him away.

Meyer got on the radio to Base Camp and announced somberly that Baig had died. Then they followed each other in a line down toward Camp Four. The Americans wanted to tie a rope between themselves and the two Serbs but the latter said they could manage on their own. Hussein, however, was uncertain on his feet and so for a while Strang strung a rope between his own harness and that of the HAP.

They reached the tents near the bottom of the Shoulder at about 4 p.m. A number of people were milling around. The South Korean

B team and their two Sherpas had climbed up the Abruzzi and were waiting for evening and their chance to leave for the summit after midnight. There was the Australian climber from the Dutch team and Paul Walters, the Australian from Meyer and Strang's expedition. They wanted to hear what had happened.

Strang was overcome. He threw his rucksack on the ice, knelt in the snow, and cried.

"It's meaningless!" he said.

But then he saw the Serbs sitting down just a few feet away, silent and stony-faced, and he felt ashamed. They had more reason than he did to be upset. When one of the HAPs brought him a cup of warm tea, he waved him away guiltily.

The Serbs trooped off to their tent to make calls on their satellite phone and radio, to talk to Erdeljan in Base Camp; he would telephone Mandic's girlfriend in Subotica. Strang and Meyer debriefed the other teams.

It was still a warm afternoon, warm enough that they could stand outside in their Windbreakers. Up on the mountain, the line of climbers still heading for the summit had moved on and was stretched across the Traverse and up into the diagonal ascent to the summit snowfields. The mountaineers were a line of black dots against the white snow.

Even after the deaths, Strang and Meyer felt a pang of envy and wondered whether they had done the right thing by turning back after all.

Their teammate, Walters, pointed to the distant line of climbers and remarked on what good time they had made.

Meyer shook his head. "They are still going up," he said.

Walters couldn't believe it. He was surprised and disappointed. After fourteen hours of climbing, they were still hours from the top.

In their tent, the two Serbs, Pedja Zagorac and Iso Planic, sat alone. They couldn't rest, couldn't help staring at Zagorac's jacket, stained with Mandic's blood. Their friend was dead. Never again, Zagorac resolved, would he go on such a long expedition, so far from home.

CHAPTER FOUR

At dusk on July 19, 1939, Fritz Wiessner, a thirty-nine-year-old German-born American and a superstar climber of his era, put one hobnailed boot in front of the other to reach 27,500 feet, within three or four hours of K2's summit.

Wiessner was seemingly close to the end of a single-minded quest to become the first mountaineer to conquer the world's second-highest peak and the first to scale any mountain above 26,000 feet.

It would have been a stupefying feat for an American, and a German-American at that, just as most of the world spiraled toward war. It was not to be—it would take another sixteen years before Achille Compagnoni and Lino Lacedelli climbed to the summit. Instead, Wiessner's benighted expedition would come to illustrate the folly of relying too heavily on complicated logistics, including teams of unsupervised porters and Sherpas. It would have echoes in the 2008 expedition, in which, among other things, too many climbers relied on a seemingly foolproof cooperation agreement only to see it fail. Wiessner's expedition ended with four deaths, the first known casualties on K2.

Though night was falling, Wiessner wanted to continue to the summit. He believed he could get to the top, wait for dawn, and return in the morning light. But his climbing partner, a Sherpa called Pasang Lama, was already tense and warned Wiessner that going on at such a late hour risked waking the fury of the mountain gods that he believed inhabited the summit snows.

When Wiessner began a traverse that would have taken him up onto the summit snowfields, the Sherpa refused to play out his rope.

"No, sahib," he said. "Tomorrow."

Reluctantly, Wiessner climbed back down to their tent, which was pitched on the top of a rock pillar at 26,050 feet. He was confident he could make a second try the following morning or at some point over the next few days. Over the course of the previous month and a half, he had established a series of nine well-stocked camps below him. The camps were tended by a team of nine Sherpas and stretched the entire way to Base Camp. This elaborate network, he believed, would ensure he would continue to be well supplied and sheltered. He took the next day off, and as he rested in the sunshine, naked on his sleeping bag in the open tent, he expected a porter to appear at any hour carrying fresh food and supplies.

That did not happen.

Wiessner, a chemist, was born in Dresden and left for the United States in 1929. He was an inspirational climber but also domineering, autocratic, and single-minded—traits common to many of the world's most successful climbers and perhaps especially mountaineers who have been attracted to K2.

His difficult character was one reason why he struggled to gather the best of America's climbing talent, though he was also trying to put together an expedition during years when America was suffering the economic effects of the Depression and few mountaineers were willing to invest money to join. In the end, his indifferent K2 team was selected mainly for having the private wealth to finance the adventure. It included two twenty-year-old Dartmouth undergraduates, along with an independently wealthy, middle-aged New Yorker named Tony Cromwell, and, most curiously, a large, clumsy, but rich playboy called Dudley Wolfe. At the last minute, the American Alpine Club also added Jack Durrance, a twenty-seven-year-old Dartmouth medical student, who was also a powerful and competent climber.

Wolfe was a man who frequently required the help of guides to push or pull him up easy ascents. But despite his apparent lack of ability he was determined and strong and devoted to Wiessner, and he had doggedly managed to follow his leader and Pasang Lama near to the top of K2, until he was stopped by the deep snows covering a bergschrund, or crevasse, at around 25,300 feet. He waited at Camp Eight, below the Shoulder, while the two other men had gone on to Camp Nine for the summit attempt. (The early K2 expeditions had as many as eight or nine camps, but modern attempts have tended to employ an established system of four camps up the main routes as knowledge of the mountain has grown.)

Although Wiessner did not know it, his expedition had begun to fragment and communications between the lower and upper mountain had more or less broken down. Even while Wiessner, Pasang Lama, and Wolfe were waiting up near the summit, some of their disaffected colleagues in Base Camp were preparing to depart for the United States (and the fall semester at Dartmouth). Cromwell, the second in command, was giving orders for the lowest three camps to be dismantled. Ostensibly this was so that the climbers up above would have less to carry when they descended, but the prevailing sense was that they wanted no more part of Wiessner's personal summit quest. They were already thinking of home.

Although the lower camps were being put out of action, the Sherpas were still manning the higher tents. As the days dragged by, however, they heard nothing from Wiessner. When a Sherpa ventured up a few hundred feet past Camp Seven, he called out but received no reply, even though Dudley Wolfe lay asleep inside one of the tents at the camp above him. Seeing no trace of footprints in the storm-blasted snow, the Sherpa concluded that Wiessner, Wolfe, and Pasang Lama had been lost under an avalanche. He retreated down the mountain with the remaining Sherpas, and they gathered up everything they could carry—mattresses and sleeping bags, food, anything worth salvaging—or threw equipment away in order to avoid carrying it down. The elaborate supply chain Wiessner believed stretched below him was in fact a tenuous line of abandoned or broken tents blowing emptily in the wind.

In their first summit attempt, Wiessner and Pasang Lama had avoided the couloir—the gully that would later become known as the Bottleneck—thinking that it looked too dangerous, and had instead climbed an amazingly difficult route up the broken rocks to the left of the gully, a route that no one would dare try again. For his second attempt, Wiessner was thinking of climbing directly up the Bottleneck. But after waiting two days and with no new supplies having shown up, Wiessner and Pasang Lama descended to Camp Eight. They expected to find either porters or bountiful supplies. Instead they discovered Wolfe, still alone, and with only a few days of rations remaining.

"Those bastards," Wolfe told them. "They never came up here."

He had no matches to light his stove and had been forced to melt snow in the folds of his tent.

The three men roped up together and started down, but Wolfe tripped on the rope, pulling Wiessner off his feet, and the three men began sliding. They were only saved when Wiessner slammed the pick of his axe in the ice just sixty feet short of a 6,000-foot drop onto the Godwin-Austen glacier. It was an amazing rescue. They had, however, lost Wolfe's sleeping bag, and Wiessner had left his at the higher camp. They spent the night beneath a single bag, thinking unkind thoughts of their teammates farther down the mountain.

The next day, Wiessner and Pasang Lama left Wolfe in a tent at Camp Seven and descended rapidly to get help. They found camp after camp deserted until a day later they finally lurched half dead into Base Camp.

A rescue mission was decided upon for Dudley Wolfe. Wiessner was too exhausted to go up himself, and the first rescue attempt involving Jack Durrance was aborted when one of the Sherpas fell sick. Five days later, three brave Sherpas—Pasang Kikuli, Pasang Kitar, and Phinsoo—reached Wolfe at Camp Seven. They found him barely sensible and lying in his own excrement. He had been above 21,500 feet for forty days. They managed to get him outside his tent and gave him tea but he refused to descend with them and they felt they could not challenge him.

The three Sherpas retreated to a lower camp, vowing to return the following day. Delayed by a storm, they climbed back but neither they nor Wolfe were ever seen again.

Fourteen years later, after the interruption of World War II and the partition of India, another American team would become the first expedition to venture up the slopes since Wiessner's fateful quest. At the site of Wiessner's camps, they discovered torn tents, three neatly rolled sleeping bags, and Ovaltine, along with a stove, fuel, and a bundle of Darjeeling tea wrapped in a blue handkerchief, some of them the poignant remains of the Sherpas' last effort to save Wolfe.

CHAPTER FIVE

1 p.m.

The nineteen climbers in the tightly pressed line beneath the serac had spent an uneasy few minutes considering whether they should go on in the wake of Dren Mandic's fall.

Below them, the Serbs were distant specks dragging Mandic back toward the Shoulder. The Americans were climbing out from Camp Four. What more could *they* be expected to do? If they descended, they were only going to get in the way of the rescue operation.

Some thought Mandic was still alive. And if he was dead—well, they were used to death. Every one of them had good friends who had been killed in the mountains.

Among them, an Italian climber named Marco Confortola was determined to continue on. The determination seemed to shine in the thirty-seven-year-old professional mountain guide's sharp triangular face, in his brown eyes.

Confortola had grown up in Santa Caterina Valfurva, a ski resort town three and a half hours north of Milan in Lombardy, on the Swiss border; he came from the same valley as his hero Achille Compagnoni, and naturally Confortola had chosen to climb up on the Abruzzi route. Strong as an ox and flamboyant, he had come to K2 to burnish his professional curriculum vitae, but he also wanted to conquer the peak again for Italy. He said he wanted to "bring it back" to his valley.

Before coming to K2, Confortola had worked at a meteorological station on Mount Everest for fifty days. He had flown back to Milan and spent a week in Valfurva before hopping on another flight to Islamabad. From Askole, he had trekked to Base Camp with a team of eighty porters and their chickens and other supplies.

The ascent from Base Camp had been tougher than he had anticipated. His boots had gotten wet. His HAP had forgotten some of the rope Confortola was expected to supply as part of the cooperation agreement. But still, now, in the group on the ropes beneath the serac, he was determined to go on.

Some of the other climbers shifted uneasily on the lines. The Sherpa in the Dutch team, Pemba Gyalje, said Mandic's fall was bad karma. For him, as for Dorje, the American team's Sherpa, reaching the summit of K2 was going to be a significant marketing coup for his business—these two commercial rivals wanted to beat the other to the top. But the teams were late and Gyalje said he was prepared to turn back if anyone else wanted to.

When he saw the others still looking pensive, Confortola said they had to decide quickly whether to continue higher or go down, but they couldn't simply stand waiting beneath the serac.

As the line turned away up into the Traverse, those who heard him felt a little bit stupid to have harbored any doubts in the first place.

They arrived now at what in some ways was the most challenging part of the day's ascent. The Traverse was a band of steep ice and snow at a slope of between 50 and 70 degrees. It cut directly and horizontally to the left for 200 feet and then, after it, the route rose diagonally for a further 400 feet on a less steep slope of between 35 and 50 degrees covered with deeper snow. As the climbers stared up at the Traverse, they could see that the ice itself was hard and shiny, and when they touched it, it seemed almost alive under their gloves.

The serac hung above, while down to their left were humps of brown rocks, past which was nothing but thin air and, nearly two miles away, the lower gullies and buttresses of K2.

To go across the Traverse, the teams clipped on to the rope with the carabiners on their belts and heaved themselves along the face. The looping rope was secured into the ice at intervals by ice screws. There was the occasional place to rest, a jutting rock or ice lip to lean against. But when the line of climbers was moving, the mountaineers chopped in their ice axes, kicked in the front points of their crampons, and stepped—axe, crampons, step—their breathing coming hard. As they shuffled along, they avoided staring up at the serac directly above or the tiny lines of the Godwin-Austen glacier 10,500 feet below.

By this point, some of them had been climbing nonstop for nearly twenty-four hours, except for the few hours' rest at Camp Four. The midday sun was high in the sky. The Traverse was exposed, and though they had gauged their clothing carefully to avoid overheating and dehydrating—dehydration meant they would need water, and they had left their burners behind at Camp Four—they were dripping with perspiration inside their jackets.

Yet though they were hot and tired, they couldn't dwell on their problems for long. The view was just too beautiful. It made everything right. To their left were the heads of mountains, shining in the sun or wreathed in little trains of cloud. The world was on a gigantic scale. They could see the curving line of the earth's horizon. *They were on K2.*

This view, this feeling, this achievement is what they had come for. Despite the nagging anxiety about how long things were taking and the frustrations caused by the crowd, the climbers felt a sort of inner transcendence, an inner peace. When space opened up on the rope and they could start marching up and across the ice wall, they felt truly alive. The summit was a few hours above them. Now at last, after weeks, months, years of preparation and toil, they were closing in.

About one hundred feet across the Traverse, the line stopped again. Up at the front, four climbers from the South Korean team converged in pairs to change their oxygen tanks. Helping one another to unbuckle the empty cylinders, they started to refix full ones.

With fifteen members, the South Korean expedition was the largest on the mountain this year. Its proper title was the "Korean Flying Jump" team and its tents, national flag, and sponsor flags had dominated Base Camp.

It was divided into two teams—an A and a B team—and they were in the process of trying to bag all fourteen of the world's 26,000-foot peaks. The expedition was led by a prickly, ambitious mountaineer named Kim Jae-soo and his star woman climber, Go Mi-sun. The forty-eight-year-old Kim was president of a company called Power Heat, which manufactured heated mattresses and insoles for shoes.

There was no doubt a distinction between the Korean and the Western—American and European—teams. In the modern mountaineering age, the Western expeditions no longer climbed for their country—that belonged to a different, old-fashioned era. Their teams were sometimes organized along national lines but more than ever they were a loose multinational collection of friends.

But for the South Koreans the idea of bearing a national responsibility in these mountains resonated. They recognized a broader cultural mandate, and success was essential. Failure was to be avoided as humiliating.

They generally climbed in bigger groups than the Europeans and Americans and, certainly in the eyes of the other expeditions, they were more aggressive and took greater risks. Mr. Kim had told some of the other climbers his departure date for leaving K2 was whenever he climbed it.

He was a man who believed in protocol and the superiority of his climbers. Go had earlier moved swiftly and easily up the rocks beside the Bottleneck, shadowed by Kim like a bodyguard. But some of the other Flying Jump climbers were struggling in the Traverse.

The painstaking maneuver with the oxygen bottles caused another backup down the rope. The climbers waiting behind found places to perch and catch their breath. They expected the Koreans would resume climbing any moment, but it was as if they were moving in slow motion. The minutes dragged.

Eventually the South Koreans hung the empty orange oxygen bottles on an ice screw and moved on up. The other teams climbed past the bottles, which dangled delicately and precariously on the side of the mountain.

They were climbing once more but it was still slow going, and the delay allowed resentments to simmer, repeating the frictions that had arisen during the months at Base Camp. The truth was that climbing attracted strong characters, egos, oddballs, and they rubbed up against one another. Some of the climbers cursed the tardiness of other foreign expeditions. Outwardly they had respect for each other but in truth each considered the others slightly ridiculous—inferior, unprofessional, ignorant of the kind of monster K2 could be.

Now, they cursed the state of the ice screws, or the condition of the rope or the way it had been tied. Some in the big groups resented the small teams for parachuting in at the last moment on their weeks of preparations, while some in the smaller independent teams resented the space the larger expeditions occupied on the mountain and the way they had tried to dominate the slopes.

Some had brought only one ice axe, rather than the usual two, because they knew the fixed ropes would be in place to help them descend. This practice earned the scorn of other climbers, who believed two axes were essential, not least because you might drop one.

Those climbing without the help of supplementary oxygen quietly looked down on those who were relying on it; and the teams that climbed alone without Sherpas or HAPs believed they were purer climbers than those who were paying thousands of dollars for help. The HAPs could have a bad day. The oxygen could run out. A person who relied on aides like that, some thought, should not be tackling K2.

As they continued to wait, most of the climbers on the Traverse realized that the cooperation agreement, which had filled everyone with hope about teamwork and sharing, had in reality reduced them to the lowest common denominator. The ones waiting behind could pass the slower climbers but the ice made it dangerous. If one person stopped for a drink, or to adjust a backpack, they all stopped. Yet despite these misgivings, a kind of groupthink had set in. They continued anyway—because everyone else was still going on. They resented the other teams and at the same time felt protection in numbers. There was a manifest lack of leadership, no one to tell them to go back.

Rolf Bae had been more shaken than Cecilie Skog by her collision with Dren Mandic when the Serb fell.

The fair-skinned, red-bearded Bae was a good rock climber and experienced polar explorer. Yet, today on the Traverse, for all of his prowess, he was having a difficult time. Sweat glistened on his red beard and he looked pained.

"Not a good day for me," he said to the others around him on the line, wincing. "I am having problems."

Like his wife, he was breathing supplementary oxygen. The thin pipes from a new British-made system—it released oxygen on demand rather than piping it constantly—curled like transparent straws around the side of his face to his nose.

He had spent the early summer rock climbing on Great Trango Tower, a 20,500-foot spire of rock about twenty miles down the Baltoro glacier from K2, and so he had arrived at Base Camp a few weeks after Skog. Maybe Trango had taken it out of him or maybe he hadn't given himself enough time to get used to the height on K2, though Skog knew he was never really comfortable at extreme altitudes.

He and Skog had tried to summit K2 once before, in 2005 on the

Cesen route, but they had turned back, and they were eager this time to reach the top. Still, Bae said he was thinking of turning around, although he would try to go as far as he could with Skog.

The two climbers had been husband and wife for little over a year. They had met in Russia in 2003 after an expedition to Mount Elbrus. She had trained as a nurse and guide and Bae was working as a professional guide. He was a well-traveled man. He had lived in the United States; when he was seventeen, he had spent a year in Amherst, Massachusetts, living with a local family and studying. Between 1999 and 2001, he had spent seventeen months in the Antarctic in a naval base on Queen Maud Land.

Skog had soon learned that this was the sort of thing Rolf Bae did. He was also a serious bird-watcher; he knew the Latin names and most springs took the train to northern Norway on special bird-watching trips. When they were on an expedition, he loved to sing Bob Dylan songs as he walked along the trail. In the camp at night, he sat and played his guitar or his harmonica.

A week after they had got to know each other, Skog and Bae flew to the Himalayas and spent three months climbing in Tibet and Nepal. When they returned to Norway, they moved in together and started their own travel company, Fram Expeditions, named after the ship that took Norwegian explorers to the Arctic and Antarctic in the late nineteenth and early twentieth centuries. They began a life of guiding, writing books, and giving talks about their expeditions in the wilderness. It was a wonderful way of making a living, doing what they loved. They had a little apartment in Stavanger but they were rarely at home. In 2005, they traveled together to the South Pole. In 2006, they reached the North Pole.

Skog, dubbed the Polar Princess in the European media, had become the first woman to stand at both poles and on the tallest peaks of every continent, including Everest. She had wanted the achievement of climbing Everest; Rolf hated the crowds on Everest these days and had chosen not to go with her. Their fame at home in Norway was just taking off, Cecilie's especially.

———————

Ahead of Bae and Skog on the line, the dark-haired Frenchman Hugues d'Aubarède crouched on an ice ledge beside his Pakistani HAP, Karim Meherban. Both men were concerned about d'Aubarède's condition.

D'Aubarède, who was wearing a dark yellow climbing suit, was getting tired. The sixty-one-year-old was a stubborn, proud, noble man, neat and cultured, and he had invested a lot in his expedition to get to K2. He had left behind his partner, two daughters, and a grandchild in France to pursue his dream in the Himalayas. It was his third attempt to reach the summit of K2, and he thought it would probably be his last try. He was not the oldest to climb on K2, but he was close—a sixty-five-year-old Spaniard had summitted in 2004.

It had been a long climb up from Base Camp. When the storm hit around the night of July 29, some of the other expeditions had waited at an intermediate camp, forcing d'Aubarède to wait, too. He had used up valuable energy, food, and also gas for melting snow for water. The wind had whistled up inside his glasses, the slopes too steep even to stop to put on his goggles. He had had to wade through snow that drifted around his knees, by carving a corridor with his hands.

But then finally, at Camp Four, after the long ascent up the Cesen, he had climbed onto a flat space on the Shoulder on the afternoon of July 31, pitched his tent, and gazed down on the gallery of peaks around him. Taking out his satellite phone, he had sent a text message to his family in Lyon. He had been keeping a blog of his days on the mountain so that all his friends could follow his progress.

"I wish everyone could contemplate this ocean of mountains and glaciers," he had written, impressed by the beauty of what lay below him. "I drooled it was so beautiful. The night will be long but beautiful."

In the twenty-four hours since then, however, things had gone less well. D'Aubarède was feeling the effects of the altitude and heat. He told the climbers who passed him that, like Bae, he was also thinking of going down.

"My oxygen bottle has run out," he said, shaking his head sadly.

———————

Farther along the rope, the Dutch expedition was making better progress. For Wilco van Rooijen, climbing was an obsession. When he first met the woman who would become his wife, Heleen, he told her his ambition was to climb Everest without using supplementary oxygen, a feat he considered one of the most difficult in the sport.

She replied that she would never marry him while he was trying to do it, or have his children.

In 2004, when Van Rooijen finally sat on the summit of Everest, he called Heleen on his satellite phone—"Will you marry me now?"—and they wed the following year. But as soon as their honeymoon was over, he began to dream of the next challenge, which was K2. Just seven months before he left for Pakistan in 2008, his son Teun had been born.

Van Rooijen complained there was never enough money in the Netherlands for mountaineering. Not the sponsorship available for football players or skaters or sailors. But he was sponsored in the Netherlands by Bad Boys, a Dutch clothing line, and for K2 he managed to raise money from Norit. The company manufactured water purification systems, and so the K2 expedition adopted the slogan "In Search of the Source of Clean Drinking Water," the source in question being the pure water glacier on top of K2. From North Face he got tents and sleeping bags; from Canon the team received high-definition cameras.

Van Rooijen tried to climb K2 in 2006 but had turned back in storms. However, there he had met a an Irishman named Gerard Mc-

Donnell, who worked as an engineer in Alaska, and the two men vowed to return with an expedition this year that would be assured of success.

While Van Rooijen had focused on the financing, the thirty-seven-year-old McDonnell had assembled more of the equipment for the mountain from his home in Anchorage. The Irishman hailed from a dairy farm in County Limerick, southwest Ireland, but in 1994 he had won a visa for the United States and moved to Baltimore. After trying to settle for three years, he took a motorcycle trip across the country to Alaska and liked what he saw. He realized he could be near wild places and the mountains. He found a job as an electronic engineer in the Alaskan oil industry on the North Slope. He made a new life, met a girl, Annie, and played the bodhran, the Irish drum, in an Irish band, Last Night's Fun. One day, he said, he would return to Ireland. He dreamed of starting a mussel farm in County Kerry. After the big Himalayan climbs he went back home. His family was waiting for him now, in the green fields beneath the gray skies: Margaret, or Gertie, his mother; his three sisters, Martha, Stephanie, Denise; his brother, J.J.

He had visited Ireland after he conquered Everest. He was treated like a hero and later met the Irish president. When he drove into Kilcornan and stopped near the church, hundreds of well-wishers greeted him. He had walked along the main road, accompanied by the parade and a bagpiper, past the shrine to the Virgin Mary, to the Kilcornan school and community hall where McDonnell gave a speech and everyone tried to understand why their Ger was so in-tent on leaving them to climb into the clouds. He didn't climb to be famous. He normally preferred not to talk much about what he achieved in the mountains. But later, at a big hurling game in Munster, the announcer declared on the loudspeaker that Ireland's climbing hero was in the stadium and thirty thousand people applauded.

His father, Denis, had died when McDonnell was twenty. McDonnell had told his mother that his father was one of the reasons he climbed to the top of the world's tallest mountains. On the summit of Everest in 2003, he ran his father's rosary beads through his fingers, and later he said, "I felt close to my dad up there." At 26,000 feet, below the peak on Everest's South Col, he took out a *sliotar*, or Irish hurling ball, and pucked it from the mountain with a hurley.

On K2, he had taught Van Rooijen and the other climbers in the Dutch team some Irish sayings, such as "Tiocfaidh Ar La," which was pronounced as "Chukky Are Law," an old Irish Republican Army phrase meaning "Our day will come." Climbing the slopes, Cas van de Gevel and Wilco van Rooijen shouted it back at him in fun.

From Alaska, communicating with Van Rooijen by email and Skype, McDonnell had found a special 5mm white, lightweight rope for K2. It was stronger and lighter than the so-called plastic 10mm or 11mm ropes that expeditions usually picked up in Pakistan or Nepal. Its white color meant it reflected sunlight and so was less likely to melt grooves in the ice. He also found himself a strong helmet. In 2006, he had fractured his shull in a serious rockfall on K2, just above Camp One, and after descending was airlifted off the mountain.

As they put together the other members of the team, McDonnell insisted on including Pemba Gyalje, the trusted Sherpa he had climbed with on Everest, an erudite, traveled Nepalese. Van Rooijen advertised in the Dutch climbing press and circulated an email to Dutch Alpine climbers, and recruited two young mountaineers in their twenties: Roeland van Oss and Jelle Staleman, a former Dutch marine. They were the *jonge honde*, or young dogs, of the expedition.

They also included Cas van de Gevel, a tall forty-two-year-old mountaineer from Utrecht. He had made many expeditions with his friend Van Rooijen but he had never climbed above 26,000 feet before.

Years earlier, after university, Van Rooijen and Van de Gevel had started out in business together, mainly fixing up houses. Van de Gevel was a carpenter, Van Rooijen an electrician. They earned enough money to take off regularly together to the Alps in Cas's

Citroën 2CV or Van Rooijen's Volkswagen. One day, Van Rooijen found himself beneath the floorboards and realized he couldn't do that sort of work any longer; he began a career as a professional mountaineer, courting sponsors and the media, showing slides, giving talks to companies about mountaineering as a metaphor for business leadership and teamwork, and eventually writing books. But carpentry was enough for Van de Gevel—it paid for his trips to the mountains and for a monthly visit to his girlfriend in southern Spain.

Van de Gevel, McDonnell, Van Rooijen, and the rest of the Dutch team had enjoyed the weeks in Base Camp in the big strip of tents on the rocks. The cooks ran down to the right over the mangled ice of the glacier to fetch water for the kitchen. The toilet tents dotted the rocks to the left, closer to the mountain. The climbers hung clotheslines between the tents. Their camp was a few yards away from an independent Serb climber who had mounted a goat's head on a pole outside his doorway and a sign that read, "Come Please Slowly Slowly Inside."

Van de Gevel liked the simplicity of the work, the up and down, the carrying and making camps. Life was straightforward. There were eight climbers in the Dutch expedition, as well as their three Pakistani cooks. They were divided roughly into two teams, alternating the working days so there was always one team on the slopes. Learning how to "sniff" the route: That was how Van de Gevel thought of it. If it was your day on, you woke up early and worked on the mountain. On your rest day, you got up later, drank coffee, had a laugh with Gerard McDonnell, and gazed through your binoculars to see the progress the other men were making.

Such a life gave the Dutchman a lot of satisfaction. Their team worked well, he thought. There was pride in their efficiency, even if sometimes that pride turned into a sense of superiority over the other teams, which they did not always try to conceal. Occasionally, he admitted, there was niggling between the expeditions of the "you-are-doing-less-than-me" variety, and also within the Dutch team itself. But that was part of mountain life. Van Rooijen expected a lot of his climbers and he made the rules. Van de Gevel was content to leave the organization to his friend. If he, Cas, had been in charge, he knew, things would start to fall apart. He just wanted to climb.

During the bad weather, the Dutch teammates had crammed together in the mess tent to watch DVDs. And they had Isostar protein powder to keep Jelle bulked up; you simply added water for a protein shake. Olives, anchovies, or peanut butter on crackers for Van Rooijen. They taught the cooks how to fry hamburgers, and the cooks also made a tasty pancake mix. They had the dried food you simply stirred with boiling water, such as chili con carne or chocolate mousse. These actually didn't taste too bad. Up in the higher camps, they had soups and sausages.

Then there was the yak, bought for fifty-five thousand rupees in Askole and herded by the Balti porters up the dusty tracks past the great rock at Korophone, past Julah and Paiju and over the blasted glacier below Urdukas. The animal came unwillingly, tugging at its rope. When the expedition tired of dal or chicken and hungered for red meat, the porters bound its legs one day and, as it lay on the ice, they slit its throat.

The blade was blunt, and it took several minutes to hack through the skin. The climbers who had gathered around to watch the ceremony cringed. One of them, Rolf Bae, offered his own knife but the Sherpas warned that no man should give away his knife unless he wants to invite bad luck. Spilling the blood of an animal in such a fashion was disrespectful to the mountain, the Sherpas said; instead they should butcher the yaks and goats at a lower altitude, farther down the glacier, and carry the meat up for the climbers. In the end, the yak bled to death and was skinned and its head was mounted on the rocks outside the cook's tent.

The Dutch expedition was well organized and ambitious and when one of the *jonge honde*, Roeland van Oss, collapsed from carbon monoxide poisoning while he was using a burner in a tent at Camp Two and had to be helped down, there was no question that they would stay. The weeks of preparation were not all smooth going, however. Van Rooijen was a master organizer but he was not a very beloved leader. He was ambitious, competitive, demanding, and dismissive of others. His abrasiveness and self-focus had seemed to intensify the higher he climbed on the mountain. Some of the other members might be useful to Van Rooijen for ferrying supplies up the routes, but he did not hesitate to rule them out of the final summit group when he thought including them jeopardized his plans. This caused frictions, and even upset his friend McDonnell.

One day in Base Camp, Van Rooijen had clashed with Hugues d'Aubarède, marching into the Frenchman's tent to demand that he lend his two HAPs to the Dutch team to carry and fix ropes all the way to Camp Four. "There is good weather and we are going to go for the summit," Van Rooijen had said, determinedly.

D'Aubarède had declined, insisting that the porters were not used to the altitude yet and that in any case he needed them for himself. Van Rooijen felt the porters were not doing their share of work but d'Aubarède resented Van Rooijen's presumption that he could just use other people's HAPs. The Dutchman had already charged d'Aubarède and Nick Rice five hundred dollars each for using the ropes the Dutch team had fixed on the route.

"We will carry the ropes up when we are ready," d'Aubarède said. "We need to conserve their energy for our summit bid."

Afterward, d'Aubarède felt that Van Rooijen ignored him on purpose sometimes when they passed on the route and he feared he held a grudge.

While Van Rooijen possessed qualities that didn't endear him to everyone, most of his teammates accepted that those were probably what it took to be a great climber. As part of his effort to ensure the expedition's success, Van Rooijen had hired a support team back in the Netherlands, including a doctor, webmaster, press spokesman, and a high-end weather forecaster. He wanted good forecasting to avoid a scenario such as the notorious series of disasters on K2 in 1986, when thirteen people died from storms and avalanches over the course of the summer, and again in 1995, when another seven climbers were killed on K2 in a single storm.

The webmaster back in Utrecht, Maarten van Eck, had been posting regular updates about the team's progress on the Dutch team's website. The site had become the main source for news about what was happening on K2 this year and was being watched by the families of many of the climbers around the world, especially today, the summit day.

Now, from the Traverse, the Dutch team radioed down to Base Camp, and news of their progress was communicated back to the Netherlands. Within a few minutes, the latest update went live on Van Eck's website.

"Gooooooood Morning Netherlands!" Van Eck wrote. "Wilco, Cas, Gerard and Pemba are way above the Bottleneck and in the Traverse."

CHAPTER SIX

3 p.m.

From where they were standing, the climbers still could not spy the summit. At the end of the Traverse, the great ice face curved up to the right beneath the western edge of the serac, and then the route cut back on itself in a diagonal onto the top of the final summit snowfields.

From this position, they could hear a voice calling out from above around the edge of the glacier, urging them to hurry. They realized it was Alberto Zerain, the lone Basque climber, who had earlier climbed ahead of everyone up the Bottleneck. He had fixed the rope across most of the Traverse but had then gone on. He had rounded the curve after the Traverse and was now waiting out of sight.

"Come on!" he cried. They heard the frustration in his voice. "Come quickly! Watch for those ice screws. No good."

After a while, Zerain's voice fell quiet. The South Koreans at the front now fixed the remainder of the rope up the ice slope. They took a long time, forcing the climbers behind them to wait again patiently. The route was less steep and covered with deeper snow than farther down the Traverse—and some of the climbers eyed it warily. A massive slab of snow had unloosed from this section of K2 just two years earlier, crushing four Russians.

As they waited, the climbers drank deep drafts of water from bottles they were carrying up. Some had brought flasks of warm tea, which was even better. Keeping their bodies well hydrated was essential in the mountains—they lost a lot of water through exertion and stress—not least because it helped combat the symptoms of high altitude. The Sherpa in the American team, Chhiring Dorje, shared a sausage—warm from an inside pocket next to his chest—with Pemba Gyalje.

As they waited, a few felt disquiet at the time that was passing but no one was concerned enough to turn around—even though their bodies were deteriorating with each minute from the effects of altitude, dehydration, and exhaustion, the day was moving on, and the oxygen tanks were running low

Gerard McDonnell used the downtime to tell Rolf Bae and a couple of the others about his accident on the mountain in 2006, when the rockfall punched a gash in his skull and he was flown by helicopter to the military hospital in Skardu. He had undergone emergency treatment in a dirty operating room without anesthetic, he said. A cruel hospital official had taunted him, asking, "Where are your friends now?"

McDonnell, Bae, and the others talked about the chances of the good weather holding and whether they still had time to make the summit.

McDonnell spoke of the delight they would feel when they finally climbed up onto the summit snowfields. "Just wait until you're up there and you can see the top," he said, speaking with some relish. "Then it'll look like it's reachable. No problem." He added: "You will want to go for it."

The ropes were gradually fixed and the line of climbers moved higher, but a final vertical ice wall proved too much for some of the Koreans up at the front. Two of the Korean climbers pawed at the ice, thrashing ice flakes into the air, unable to find any purchase with their crampons.

The Koreans' two Sherpas did their best to lift the climbers up, issuing frantic instructions. They were two of the four less experienced Sherpas on the mountain. These four Sherpas were all drawn from the same poor region in northern Nepal. In contrast to Pemba Gyalje and Chhiring Dorje, they had only started out in the guiding business in the last few years and were trying to establish themselves.

One of them, Jumik Bhote, a tall, smooth-faced man, had recently been promoted to the position of lead Sherpa for the South Korean team, a big achievement, though it had put him on a busy schedule. He had climbed with the Flying Jump team on Lhotse, the fourth-highest mountain on earth, that spring, then returned to Kathmandu for only a few days before he had flown back out to K2, leaving his partner at home, even though she was expecting their first baby any day. His younger brother, Chhiring Bhote, was also on the expedition to K2. Chhiring was somewhere down the mountain with his clients in the Flying Jump B team, which was due to set off for the summit from Camp Four later that night.

The climbers behind could have passed but the two Sherpas were working so diligently that they waited politely, and anyway it was easier to wait for the Sherpas to fix the ropes. One of the Koreans was trying to scale the bank with only one ice axe and he kept slipping back, so Wilco van Rooijen loaned him his axe.

Some of the climbers were again raising doubts about continuing. Marco Confortola assured them that if everyone worked together, and shared the task of breaking the trail, they would reach the summit. "Compagnoni and Lacedelli got to the top in 1954 at six p.m.!" he said in his halting English, as he pointed up toward the summit. "And they came down okay. If they could do it then, so can we."

At last, Bhote hung a rope down from the ice wall, and the two climbers dragged themselves up with a shout. Finally everyone on the line could see a way forward. Forgetting their frustrations, they surged over the top of the serac and into the summit snowfields. From here, for the remaining three or four hours to the top, there was no need for any more fixed lines. They passed the last anchor and unclipped from the rope, feeling free.

For the first time, they could see the final summit ridge, although the actual summit was still not visible. It was what they had waited for and it was a wonderful sight.

Sometimes the jet stream blasted the top of K2, creating a furious white summit plume, but today the top was clear. At the end of the long summit snowfield, it rose up in a hump against the blue sky. The climbers began to move up toward it in a line. Soon the first climbers appeared to those following behind as dots on the plane of white.

Breaths of snow swept across the snowfields, on this, the upper mountain. On this section, the climbing was less steep, the slope about 30 degrees. The snow was deep, however, and some of the climbers were worried about avalanches, or crevasses. They were on top of the hanging glacier and as it inched forward it left yawning gaps behind it. A few of the climbers were carrying ski poles, just like snow sticks, and they reached forward with them and prodded the snow. The area was deadly—a French couple, Liliane and Maurice Barrard, had disappeared somewhere between here and the bottom of the Bottleneck after reaching the summit in 1986.

At this point, they discovered that Alberto Zerain's patience had run out and he had gone on ahead. The sight of the summit, however, gave many of them fresh encouragement. Despite his exhaustion and empty oxygen cylinder, Hugues d'Aubarède decided to continue. He slogged away toward the distant peak beside Karim Meherban.

Wilco van Rooijen climbed onto the snowfield and rested for a while to let his colleagues in the Dutch team catch up. He was tired but he urged them onward.

"Let's go!" he cried. "Let's not hesitate now!"

Rolf Bae, however, had emerged from the Traverse shaking his head. He felt no better.

Whenever he led an expedition, Bae had three iron rules the team had to follow. One: Get home. Two: Stay friends. Three: Reach your goal. In that order. Today, it just wasn't working for him. If he was going to get home, he had to stop there.

"I am not going to the top," he told Skog reluctantly.

"Are you sure?" Skog was worried about him.

He nodded. Skog saw it was a brave decision. He had come a long way to get this far but he could not go on. Rather than descend immediately, though, he said he would wait for Skog and meet her when she came back down. He wasn't going to leave her. He intended to climb a little higher before stopping.

Having made up his mind, Bae bid farewell to Gerard McDonnell. The two men had become good friends a couple of years earlier on an expedition to South Georgia.

"It's been nice climbing with you today, mate!" Bae called. There was disappointment but also certainty in his voice as he watched the others go on.

Skog was already climbing ahead and he waved to her. His oxygen tank had nearly run out, so Skog dropped hers in the snow by the side of the route for him to collect as he climbed up. She could go on without oxygen. And then she waved to him one last time and was gone. For his part, Bae took a spare headlamp from inside his jacket and asked a Sherpa to give it to Skog at the summit. Just in case she needed it on the way down.

———

Alberto Zerain had pushed on ahead, and now he sat at the summit of K2 staring at his wristwatch. The watch was his father's, a gold-faced Zodiac. He had made perfect time, but the climbers below him were late.

Zerain was forty-six years old but he looked younger. He had short black hair and his suntanned skin showed off his fine cheekbones. He came from Subijano, a land of rocky hills, pine trees, and yellow stone houses on the southern edge of Basque country in northern Spain. He gazed down the length of the snowfields toward the distant lip of the diagonal that led down to the Traverse. Surely, he thought, the others would emerge soon. When they did, what would they see? A man in red crouched on the edge of a snowy ridge, sipping tea.

Back down the mountain, he had waited for two hours at the end of the Traverse. He had had to wait. When he began to climb across the ice face, he had handed his camera to one of the Sherpas—he wasn't sure of his name—so that the man could take a picture of Zerain opening the trail on the Traverse. He was the first person to cross it this year. But the Sherpa hadn't followed him across straightaway, and so Zerain had to wait. He felt he could not go to the summit without it; these days, sponsors wanted proof you had actually been to the top. He also didn't want to lose the camera. It was an Olympus, and he had bought it in Skardu on the journey in.

Eventually his patience ran out, and he had stood up and gone down a little way to look along the Traverse. The scene shocked him.

Earlier, Zerain had fixed the rope along the Traverse. On the way up, at the top of the Bottleneck, another one of the Sherpas had brought the length of rope to him, and though Zerain had thought it looked old, not fit to tie his shoes with, he had fixed it up along the ice face anyway.

He knew there had been meetings down in Base Camp but he had kept away from them so he knew nothing of what they had decided.

He also had three screws, though for a while he thought he had lost the third screw, and at one point he had had to dangle from his ice axe until he managed to find it in his backpack.

Now five people were bunched together on a single section of that old rope, edging slowly up and across in the bright sunshine, all their weight on the same screws he himself had rammed in. The Sherpa to whom Zerain had given his camera was back down in the line.

Fine, he thought. *No camera.*

By that time, it was 11 a.m., and Zerain had turned and climbed up onto the snowfields. At last he could see how far he had to go to the summit. Reaching it was possible, he told himself, nodding, psyching himself up. He was feeling good but he had to tell himself this. He felt a burning inside, the *gusanillo*, the passion to go on. It looked so close.

He was barrel-chested, with a confident, strutting gait. When he walked, his arms swung at his sides, and he gave the impression he could walk forever. He ran mountain marathons in the Basque hills. He had climbed in the Alps and in the Andes, where he met his wife, Patricia, a translator. He had been to the Himalayas. He had raised two sons; now that they were both nearly teenagers he could travel the world and climb again. But climbing was only part of his life, and not the most important thing.

He was attracted to K2 because of its shape, a beautiful pyramid. You could fit sixty Matterhorns in it. And he was attracted because of its dangers; only the most extraordinary climbers dared to challenge it.

He had arrived in the Himalayas in June with a team sponsored by, among others, Marqués de Riscal, the Basque wine company. He had intended to climb Broad Peak, a nearby mountain, first but two friends were airlifted out and Zerain also got headaches near the top. He knew when a mountain didn't want him—he had an inner voice that told him when to go up and when to go down—so he decided to switch to K2, an hour's walk along the glacier.

Alone among the other teams, he gravitated to the Pakistani HAPs in the Serbian expedition, who made him welcome. He helped to fix the ropes on the Abruzzi route and in return they let him share their tents.

The porters worked hard, each day shouldering heavy loads of oxygen tanks, ropes, and the Serbs' food up the mountain. They mostly had only wheat and dried apricots to eat so Zerain shared his cheese from his Tupperware container and sometimes made them a treat of strawberry-flavored milkshake. One night, he cooked risottos and pastas—though they gave these away to their Serbian clients.

Now, as Zerain waded through the thick snow on the summit snowfields, he discovered that despite his hope the summit wasn't close and the going was tough, intense, far harder than he had anticipated. His boots packed fresh snow at every step. He went from side to side, looking for ice or harder snow to walk on. His aching legs strained forward only to slip back. Sometimes he found nothing at all beneath him and was suddenly swallowed to his waist in cold snow. He scrambled quickly to his feet.

Only once had he witnessed death on a mountain. It was 2000, he was making a film for Spanish television, and he was on his way down from the top of Everest when he was told someone had fallen. He could see a body six hundred feet below, and when he rushed down, the climber was lying on the snow, unable to speak, and there was blood everywhere. Zerain did not know who he was. He tried to put some gloves over his hands but they were rigid. Then he tried to take his rucksack off because the straps were suffocating him, but the climber stood up and then fell and began to slide. The backpack came away in Zerain's hands and the climber fell nine hundred feet toward the Rongbuk glacier.

His name was Stolz, he later found out, and he was from Denmark.

Zerain crisscrossed the summit snowfield from left to right, prodding gingerly with his ice axe. He had wrapped its handle in silver tape to prevent the skin of his fingers from freezing onto the cold metal. He was tempted to escape the clinging deep snow by crossing far to the right, onto the ice of the serac. He strode across, his back bent under the sun. But then he left the serac behind him and was forced to plunge back into the soft snow.

As he had done since the base of the Bottleneck, he was opening the trail alone, and the snow was deep. The going was so slow that he had thought it would be only a matter of minutes before the pursuing group caught up with him. The ones who were using supplementary oxygen would be faster. Before long, they would be speeding along behind him and then they would share the work of opening the route.

But no one had appeared. He had gone on, feeling weary, keeping every unnecessary effort to a minimum, because even stopping to open his backpack cost energy. About three hundred feet before the summit, he had watched carefully for hidden crevasses. Then at last, he had climbed the final steep, diagonal ridge and had come out alone onto the summit of K2. The first climber to reach the top in 2008.

The afternoon was perfect. Not the slightest cloud. The summit was a 150-foot sloping snow ridge. He climbed up the ridge to get to the highest spot. About fifteen feet below the top on the other side was a comfortable flat area of about eighteen square yards where he could sit.

The surrounding mountains receded into the distance, lesser giants of the Karakoram compared to K2. On one side, they marched northeast into China, on the other into Pakistan. India, China, Pakistan—they all seemed close from up here. And Zerain could see the back of Broad Peak, the Gasherbrums, Nanga Parbat, and many more mountains, all of them wondrous sights. So too were the swirling patterns of the glaciers, like patterns on butterfly wings, 11,800 feet below on the valley floor.

Wait until he told his friends and family back home, Zerain thought. He wished he had his Olympus. He opened his eyes wide and scanned the horizon so that even without his camera he would remember every detail. He gloried in the view; he felt he could see every brushstroke.

The summit was broad, but he eyed it warily. He couldn't be sure of the safety of the snow. Maybe it was rock he was treading on or maybe it was an overhanging lip of snow waiting to collapse under him. He didn't trust it. Although his gaze wandered far, he drank some tea and stayed sitting and didn't move around much.

Down below, at the lip of the long snowfield, the other climbers were at last spitting up out from beneath the serac. Zerain checked his watch and frowned. He was surprised that they were still intending to shoot for the top.

He knew what they were feeling. Up here, on the summit slopes, you were close to the gods, or at least you felt you were. But you forgot there was work to be done to get up and down again.

Watching the climbers ascend the mountainside toward him, Zerain closed his eyes and felt sleepy. He lay back on the snow. The tea was warming him. The sun was on his face. He had had no sleep for more than twenty-four hours, since he had woken up at Camp Three.

To avoid the crowds going up the Abruzzi and Cesen routes, Zerain had climbed directly from Camp Three the previous night, arriving in Camp Four at midnight. He had waited under the quiet stars for people to leave for the summit. There had been no moon and, when he had gazed along the Shoulder, Zerain could barely make out the Bottleneck. He didn't want to be up there alone.

Soon he had noticed movement and a Sherpa approached from one of the tents.

"Namaste!"

It was Pemba Gyalje, the strong Sherpa in the Dutch team. Gyalje peered forward to see who was lurking near the tents, and Zerain explained who he was.

A few other climbers gathered with Gyalje at the edge of the camp and then headed out onto the Shoulder. Zerain joined them, third in line. Not far out of Camp Four—they had been walking for probably forty minutes—the two climbers ahead of Zerain stopped abruptly and started to pull rope from their backpacks.

Zerain was confused. At this point the Shoulder was as flat as a cow's meadow. Why were they doing this now? He couldn't see the other climbers' faces behind their balaclavas and hoods. Maybe, he thought, the Sherpas and HAPs were concerned their clients were not skilled enough for this terrain. Grasping the rope, he realized that if he helped them, they would be faster.

He went over the fresh snow up the Shoulder, the other climbers passing more rope to him from behind as he marched on. He went to the right, to the rocks, a little way out of the full glare of the serac above.

Finally, as the sun rose higher, Zerain had fixed two screws near the top of the Bottleneck and then waited for the others to bring more rope for the Traverse. He had 100 feet of rope in his backpack but they said they were bringing extra rope of their own, so he had waited, perched beneath the serac, so close then that he had been able to study it properly for the first time.

That was hours ago now. Abruptly, Zerain forced his eyes open again. He was still sitting on the summit. If he took a nap now, he might never wake up. He checked his father's watch: 3:40 p.m. Time to go down. Forcing himself upright, he climbed down from the summit.

When, about an hour later, he reached the other climbers and began to pass them, they greeted him warmly. Those who were using oxygen had made the quickest time. The Sherpa returned the Olympus. The South Koreans' leader, Kim, so far as he understood, thanked Zerain for placing the rope on the Bottleneck and for opening the Traverse.

In return, Zerain smiled and said thank you, but all the while he wanted to tell them to turn back. *It is late!* he wanted to shout. *Turn back with me. Is it worth the risk?*

One figure in the line was waving especially enthusiastically. He was wearing an oxygen mask and goggles and his face was partly covered by his hood. Hugues d'Aubarède took off his mask and wrapped his arms around Zerain.

"Alberto!"

"Bonjour, Hugues." But Zerain looked at d'Aubarède and thought that he would rather be seeing him in Base Camp already.

"How was it?" said d'Aubarède, speaking in French. He seemed tired, but excited.

"Be careful," Zerain said. "It is very bad."

He wanted to say more. Just a few words might have persuaded d'Aubarède to turn around. But the Frenchman's burly HAP hovered at his shoulder and Zerain did not want to interfere. The HAPs were being paid to get their climbers to the top.

He felt sorry for his friend because going down would be hard.

"Good luck, Hugues!" Zerain said.

"I will see you," said d'Aubarède, smiling.

Zerain passed Cecilie Skog, who asked him how far it was to the summit. The first time Zerain had met Skog was three weeks earlier at Camp

Two. It was soon after he had arrived on the mountain, while he had barely been able to speak because he was so tired after a day of climbing, Skog had marched into the camp, calling out greetings to her teammates. Her voice had seemed so happy. He had thought, *This is a strong woman.*

Skog still looked full of energy, even now. But Zerain knew he had to answer her carefully since he might give her false hope or wrongly discourage her.

"With a good rhythm, it should take you no more than two hours," he said.

She grinned, seeming to take heart. She looked so beautiful in the sunlight.

After saying good-bye, Zerain climbed down in the direction of the Traverse. Up above him, the line of climbers was spreading out, still meandering on toward the summit.

He wanted to shout, "It's okay if you turn around!" He hoped none of them would become the latest name on the Gilkey Memorial, the monument at Base Camp to the people who had lost their lives on K2.

On the Traverse, he found the old rope and the screws that he had punched in still fixed to the ice. No one had replaced them after all.

About two-thirds of the way across toward the Bottleneck, six orange oxygen bottles dangled from one of the screws and Zerain wondered who could have left them there.

At last he reached Camp Four. Outside one of the tents, a single climber was sitting and brewing some tea. One of the Americans, he thought.

Although the tea looked tempting to Zerain, he wanted to push on down. He nodded at the other climber and waited for a moment, still hoping perhaps for an invitation because the tea looked so good. But the climber said nothing, so Zerain left the tents behind. He climbed down the steep ridge to Camp Three, where he had spent the previous night and where he found two of the Pakistani HAPs from the Serbian team and was glad to share their tent.

CHAPTER SEVEN

5:30 p.m.

Ahead of Cecilie Skog, one of the South Koreans' Sherpas climbed up the final steep ridge and disappeared over the crest onto the summit.

A few minutes later, Skog's lanky Norwegian colleague, Lars Flato Nessa, overtook four members of the South Korean team and followed the Sherpa onto the top. Alberto Zerain had told Skog the last stretch up the snowfields would take two hours and they had done it in two and a half. She was relieved.

Fifteen minutes later, she joined Nessa on top of the world. She relaxed in the warm sunshine.

"Congratulations, Cecilie," Nessa said. The fair-haired Norwegian was grinning.

"We have done it." Rolf would be pleased.

The day was so hot that Skog had gone without gloves and jacket since the Bottleneck. She was wearing the purple down ski pants that were a gift from Stein Peter Aasheim, a friend who was on the first Norwegian expedition to Everest in 1985.

After the breathless exertions of the ascent, the conditions on the top were perfect. There was no wind. Skog took off her woolen hat and concentrated on the peaks around her. This was the first time she and Nessa had been able to see the Chinese side of the mountain. The ranges of perfectly formed peaks surprised them. They could have been standing in the Alps. Above them, the sky still shone a brilliant blue but the heat of the day was gone and the air was cooling.

The summit ridge was crisscrossed by footprints. Proudly, Skog and Nessa took out the Norwegian flag and posed in front of Nessa's Sony Cyber-shot. Skog also held up an orange banner from her hometown soccer team, Alesund. Skog was a soccer fan and a decent player; she had spent eight months as an au pair in Britain, in Bromley in Kent, and she had played for the Millwall Lionesses, one of the country's women's teams.

They followed a few more rituals planned for this special moment. The Norwegians had left their clunky satellite phone behind in one of the lower camps—they joked it was the size of a shoe box; it was like something out of the 1980s—so they had no way to call to tell anyone of their triumph even if they had wanted to. They took out three plastic red roses that they had kept around Base Camp to make the tent look pretty. They also unpacked a special hat that Bae had given them to carry to the summit—a pink rabbit hat with long, floppy ears. Bae had carried it with him on his expeditions to the North and South Poles, and when he stopped after the Traverse he had asked Skog to take it with her. Now, Nessa pulled it over his head with a big smile as Skog took a picture.

This one is for Rolf.

They shot some video. Skog said she was glad to reach the summit but she felt exhausted and was eager to start the descent. She was not celebrating yet.

By now, the other members of the South Korean team were arriving and spreading across the summit. Earlier, while he had been waiting for Skog, Nessa had spoken to the South Koreans' Sherpa. The Sherpa introduced himself as Pasang; he looked like he was in his early twenties. There was another Pasang in the South Korean expedition so he was called Little Pasang.

Even though they had been on the mountain together for weeks, Nessa had never spoken to him before. They talked about the peaks around them and Little Pasang described the countryside in Nepal, and his family. They took photographs and Nessa shared some water with him.

Now, Skog and Go Mi-sun posed for a few shots side by side, two women together on the peak of K2, a mountain that at times in its history had been unkind to women. Of the first five women who had climbed K2, three had died on the descent, and the remaining two had died on other mountains shortly afterward. This was a moment Skog and Go wanted to celebrate.

The Koreans took photographs of themselves with their sponsor flags. They called their sponsor, Kolon Sport, in Korea and a press release was sent out to announce that Flying Jump had successfully made it to the top. They were going to wait for the slower climbers in their team, who were still coming up the summit snowfield; Skog said good-bye. The heat of the day was ending and the air was cooling. She wanted to get down to her husband.

On the way up the long snowfield from the Traverse, Wilco van Rooijen hadn't been sure he was going to make it. He was not using supplementary oxygen like the Koreans or Norwegians, so it was hard going at twenty-eight thousand feet. He felt emptied. Everything he had was gone.

All he could do was focus on the tracks in the deep snow in front of him and on going forward. Somewhere nearby he heard the high-pitched voice of the Sherpa from the American expedition, Chhiring Dorje, shouting out that they should hurry. Unless they wanted to be buried in a sea of snow.

"There is avalanches here sometimes," Dorje shouted.

Van Rooijen tried to speed up but it was hard. The route seemed to take them up one hill of deep snow after another. It wound to the left up a steep ridge. *Almost there*, he thought.

He leaned forward to see if any of the specks up ahead had reached the summit yet. The top, still hours away, was rounded against the deep blue sky.

After the ridge, he arrived at a steep climb, so steep he could no longer see the top of the mountain. As he got closer, he heard a voice encouraging him from somewhere out of his range of vision. He recognized it: Cecilie Skog. "Keep going."

His Dutch team members were spread out up the slope. He summoned what strength he had and followed behind them, taking ten steps, then resting, leaning on the shaft of his ice axe or on his knee in the snow, then starting again. Finally he dropped to his hands and knees and crawled.

And then at last he came over the top onto the summit and he staggered to his feet.

It was wonderful. Gazing around him, he could hardly believe it. Years of frustration had come to an end. Seven-thirty p.m. After seventeen hours of climbing.

"K2!"

Letting go of his backpack, he raised his arms in victory. Then he started to cry.

The whole Dutch team was standing in front of him. They rushed together in a group hug, dancing, a jumble of snowsuits and ski poles, framed by the white churned-up ridge of the summit and the blue dome of the sky. Van Rooijen, Van de Gevel, Gerard McDonnell, Pemba Gyalje.

It was late, but the joy of reaching the summit was on everyone's face. They had joined an elite club, the nearly three hundred mountaineers in the world who had now scaled K2. He and Van de Gevel were only the third and fourth Dutchmen to reach the top. Gerard McDonnell was the first Irishman. Pemba Gyalje and Chhiring Dorje were among the first Sherpas to have done it without the help of extra oxygen.

Cas van de Gevel spoke on the radio to Base Camp to let the rest of the team know the good news. They heard whoops and handclapping.

On the way up, Van Rooijen had kept his satellite phone switched off in the folds of his jacket to keep it warm and to preserve its charge. He knelt down now and took it out, and he called Maarten van Eck at the Dutch team's home base in Utrecht.

"Maarten, we are standing on Kaay Tooo!" he shouted. The news would be immediately relayed to the world via the Dutch team's website.

Van de Gevel filmed his friend and they panned the scenery with their HD camera. Talking to Base Camp, they learned that Dren Mandic had died. It was sad but they didn't let his death dull the mood for long. They couldn't get over how beautiful it was up on the summit.

Gerard McDonnell was especially fired up. He had removed his helmet and was also crying. The air was colder now but he took off his big climbing gloves and pulled an Irish flag from the pocket of his coat. He arched his back and unfurled the flag with two hands above his head.

He tried to call his family in Kilcornan but for some reason the satellite phone wouldn't work and he couldn't get through. But he spoke to his girlfriend, Annie, in Alaska. They talked just for a few moments. "I'm feeling great," he said. He was elated.

While McDonnell was celebrating, Van de Gevel strode across to congratulate Hugues d'Aubarède. "Very good that you did this at your age!" the Dutchman said to d'Aubarède. Despite running out of oxygen, the Frenchman had made it to the top and was taking photographs of the spectacular scenery.

He looked tired but he was happy.

"Yes, but I was using oxygen," said d'Aubarède. "So not so good as you, Cas."

After talking to Van de Gevel, d'Aubarède walked across the little ridge to greet Pemba Gyalje from the Dutch team. The two men had met at Base Camp when Gyalje helped him arrange some prayer flags around his tent. They had talked about Buddhism, and the political situations in Nepal and Tibet.

The Sherpa was well-traveled and knew the world; he had spent time in France, the Netherlands, Britain.

Before they had set off from Base Camp for the main summit ascent, Gyalje had warned d'Aubarède to take four oxygen bottles with him. But d'Aubarède had insisted two would be enough. The Sherpa didn't say anything now about the oxygen though he could see that d'Aubarède's tanks were empty.

Instead, the Frenchman handed the Sherpa his video camera. "Will you take a picture of me talking to my family?" he said.

While Gyalje filmed him, d'Aubarède took out his satellite phone and called his partner, Mine Dumas, in Lyon.

D'Aubarède had come to climbing relatively late in life. His infatuation had begun in 1972 when he glimpsed the summit of beautiful Kilimanjaro from an airplane window as he returned from Madagascar on military service. He had never forgotten it. Back in Lyon, he had gotten on with his life, marriage, two lovely daughters, and his job at the Audiens insurance company. His wife didn't really approve of climbing, so he rarely went to the mountains, even though Mont Blanc loomed just over the horizon. But in 1993, they divorced; a year later, at the age of forty-seven, he had traveled with Mine back to Kilimanjaro.

"The summit is so beautiful," he said now, shaking his head at the beauty of it all. "The scenery. I am so happy."

D'Aubarède had discovered he had an exceptional ability for high-altitude climbing. On May 17, 2004, he became only the fifty-sixth Frenchman to climb Everest. But his family didn't climb with him in the really tall mountains of the world, and Mine and his daughters worried about him during the time he spent away. One day, he might not return.

With the satellite phone pressed to his lips, he promised Mine this would be his last climb. "Next time, I will be near the sea with the family!"

He said he kissed her over the phone but she told him to save his breath and to return home to France quickly. His daughter, Constance, was getting married in September in Chamonix.

"I will call you when I get down," he said.

The sun's light was fading and the temperature was dropping. They spoke for a couple more minutes and then d'Aubarède telephoned the director of Audiens in Lyon, Patrick Bezier. In recent years, d'Aubarède's work had become a sideline, compared to his climbing, but he was featured in the company newsletter and his adventures were a favorite talking point among the clients. The company gave him time off from work for his mountaineering and helped sponsor his expeditions.

He reached an answering machine. "This is Hugues d'Aubarède," he said, speaking quietly into his phone. "It's minus twenty. I am at eight thousand, six hundred and eleven meters. I am very cold. I am very happy. Thank you."

When he had finished talking, he offered the phone to Gyalje, who was still standing beside him.

"Did you contact your wife from up here?" d'Aubarède said. "You have to do this, Pemba. Please. You can use my satphone."

But the Sherpa was serious and said they were already late. "It's time we climb down," he said.

"Yes, I agree, but we have reached the summit!"

When Gyalje still refused, d'Aubarède took back the camera and spent a few more minutes snapping more photographs.

One of the Sherpas did call home, however. Jumik Bhote, the lead Sherpa in the South Korean team, had left his cell phone with his partner in Kathmandu. He borrowed the Koreans' satellite phone to call her. When he got through, Dawa Sangmu told him she had had the baby, a boy.

Bhote closed his eyes and thanked her. *I love you! Say hello to everyone. I will be back soon.*

He was so happy. He was going to name his son after his own late father, Jen Jen.

After the celebrations, the expeditions packed up their gear for the descent—cameras, telephones, water bottles, flags. The radios and the satellite phones each weighed about a pound. Gerard McDonnell handed his phone to Pemba Gyalje to lighten his load.

Some of the teams had arrived later than the rest and some chose to spend longer than the others on the summit. By now there was a haze in the air, and it was clear evening was coming on. The sky was a deeper blue. In the valleys, some of the distant craggy peaks stuck up through mist like sharks' fins. Cumulus clouds lined up like trains on the horizon.

The teams gazed down toward Camp Four. It was a distant, alluring pinpoint, beyond the summit plateau, beyond the serac and the Bottleneck.

The two Norwegian climbers were the first to descend. Skog knew that Bae was waiting for her somewhere on the snowfield. She was impatient to share the good news with him. He had insisted on setting a deadline of being back at the Traverse and clipped onto the fixed ropes before nightfall. Once they were on the ropes, they would be fine. It was easy—they could just follow the lines back to Camp Four.

Since leaving the Traverse, Skog had been climbing without the aid of extra oxygen but she felt she needed some now. Nessa was carrying their only remaining cylinder, and he pulled the two pipes from his nose and passed them back over his shoulder to her. In that fashion, one closely following behind the other, they climbed down over the eastern side of the summit ridge.

Directly in front of them, the late afternoon sun cast the shadow of the mountain over hundreds of miles of land. The shadow was stark and huge, a perfect triangle, and so long that it rose above the horizon.

The sight made them suddenly realize the size of the mountain. *The second-tallest mountain on earth.* And they were at its very pinnacle. They waited for a moment and Nessa took a picture.

―――――――――

At nearly 8 p.m., the Dutch team quit the summit. Everyone else had already left and it was empty.

They began what everyone knew would be one of the most dangerous parts of the climb—the descent. This was true on any mountain—the climbers were exhausted and the light was failing. On K2, this fact was illustrated by a telling statistic: of the sixty-six people killed on K2 in the past seven decades, twenty-four died on the way down after having successfully reached the summit.

Now, it was late and the sun was already sinking fast below the horizon. Just as the Dutch team was leaving, however, they met Marco Confortola, the Italian, who was still on his way up. Confortola said he needed someone to take a few photographs of him on the top and he asked Cas van de Gevel to wait.

"You take my camera?" he said.

Urging Confortola to be quick, the Dutchman agreed to stay behind. Confortola removed his hat and goggles and knelt in the twilight in his black and green suit. He held his ski pole aloft above his head with two flags tied to it, the Italian and Pakistani. The evening was so dark that Van de Gevel had to use a flash to take the picture.

They took five photographs, and then Confortola switched on his satellite phone to call his main sponsor, Miro Fiordi, the president of Credito Valtellinese, a local Italian bank.

"I am at the top," he said. He couldn't say much more. "I have to go," he said. "It's late."

Putting the phone away inside his jacket, he followed Van de Gevel down onto the dark summit snowfield.

Part II

DESCENT

Friday, August 1–Saturday, August 2

"There's no time for mourning."
—Lars Flato Nessa, K2, 2008

"No ropes! No rope left on the Bottleneck. Big problem.
Many danger."
—Chhiring Dorje, K2, 2008

CHAPTER EIGHT

8 p.m.

There are several types of major snow avalanches but two are probably the most common—the loose snow avalanche and the slab avalanche.

Both are caused by weaknesses in the layers of snow in the snowpack. Both are triggered by an energy disturbance such as heat, or movement.

In the loose snow avalanche, the fault point lies close below or at the surface. Loose, powdery snow sloughs away in an inverted V shape down the slope, like grains of salt cascading down a huge salt mound.

The slab avalanche is more dangerous for mountaineers. The weakness is deeper in the snowpack; a large, cohesive snow plate sometimes hundreds of yards wide and several yards deep fractures with a distinctive whumph and shears away.

If an avalanche accelerates over an abrupt change in slope, it becomes a powder snow avalanche. This type of avalanche has a small mass but can travel at 150 miles per hour, moving far along a valley bottom and even up the base of an opposite mountainside. Some of these avalanches are followed by an air blast that sucks up snow and has been known to blow people to their deaths.

Then there is another type of avalanche altogether, which can be more lethal still. Involving not snow but glacial ice, it can be caused when the leading edge of a glacier breaks off, and blocks shear away like children's bricks toppling from a tower. The technical term is "calving," a term that does not do justice to the violence of the event.

Some of the blocks can be as big as footballs, some as big as refrigerators or cars or houses. The blocks drop fast, bouncing, grinding, colliding down the cliff or slope like rocks in a rockfall. (Glacial ice is a type of metamorphic rock.)

The icefall is pursued by a turbulent dust cloud hundreds of feet high. The cloud can have a runout miles past where the icefall stops.

The most prominent hanging glacier on K2 is the one that sits brooding over the Bottleneck. It is a serac—defined, in the dictionary, as an irregular-shaped pinnacle of ice on a glacier, formed by the intersection of crevasses, or deep-running fissures. The name derives from the nineteenth-century French word for a compact, crumbly white cheese.

Through the years the serac above the Bottleneck had come to be called the Balcony Glacier or Balcony Serac. It was always an ominous sight. In 1993 a Canadian disappeared below the Bottleneck; his fellow climbers turned around and he was gone, and they believed he could have been hit by falling ice.

No one knows when a serac will collapse. It could depend on the heat, snowfall, or earthquakes but mostly on the speed of movement of the glacier, which can vary between many inches each year to yards.

In recent years, the Balcony Serac on K2 had been stable.

———

"Rolf! Rolf!"

As she had climbed down from the summit behind Lars Flato Nessa, Cecilie Skog had called out for her husband. *Where was he?* The snowfields were quiet and still. Her voice carried a long way over the waves of crusted snow.

After less than an hour, Skog saw him at last. He was sitting on one of the small hills of snow, and she sped up to reach him. They hugged and then she gazed into his face, feeling proud. His decision to stop after the Traverse proved he was more interested in the climbing, the teamwork, the *just being there* in this wilderness, than in reaching the summit. Not many mountaineers would have turned back after getting so close.

Some of the other climbers in Base Camp had felt slightly in awe of Bae before he had arrived on the mountain. He had an impressive track record. They knew about his reputation as a proficient rock climber, and they feared he would be aloof. But he had joined in and encouraged the others, which climbers like the Americans appreciated. He told them they just had to try their best. Be safe, but enjoy yourself.

Now, Bae congratulated his wife warmly. "Nice that it was a success," he said. His voice became more serious. "But now we have to get down safely."

Bae said he felt better than he had a couple of hours earlier. But his oxygen cylinder was nearly empty again. Skog had been breathing Lars Nessa's supply of oxygen since the summit, and she passed the tank to Bae. He was a cautious expedition leader; he did everything he could to reduce the risks his team faced, insisting they use oxygen even when the other teams criticized it as cheating.

Now, as always, the Norwegians marched in single file, watching for crevasses and drifts of snow.

Skog knew she was lucky in having the life she had always yearned for. On an expedition with Bae, she could be outside under the open sky with the simple goal of reaching camp and getting warm, and when she was warm, she was happy. That was all she wanted. All she needed. She and Bae had none of the tensions other climbers experienced with spouses who resented the months apart and the risks they took with their lives. When they were in the mountains or other wild places, they were home.

During the weeks on K2, when Bae had been away climbing Great

Trango Tower, Skog had missed her husband. She had worked the slopes beside the other teams, but despite the crowds the mountain still felt empty. After Trango, Bae had first returned to Norway for a guiding course in the north of the country, which meant they were apart for even longer.

Occasionally, around Base Camp, Marco Confortola blew her a kiss and greeted her across the rock fields. "Cecilie! The most beautiful woman in Base Camp!" Other times, the three Serbs called to her, though she didn't care to remember what they said to her.

She was lonely.

Then one evening in July, she had come down from one of the higher camps, sweaty and tired, and someone across Base Camp had called out, "Cecilie, there is someone here for you!" It was Rolf, and she had run to him.

They had gone into their big Bergen tent, amid the bags and mats on the floor, and he had told her about Trango. He and his friends had climbed a route called the Norwegian Pillar to the top, and had become the first people to return alive. It was an infamous route in Norway; two Norwegians died on it in 1984.

When they had spoken on the phone while he was in Norway, Skog had joked that he might want to bring some furniture from Stavanger to brighten the tent at Base Camp. Now, she saw, he had kept his promise. He had brought a plastic inflatable Ikea couch, sky blue with pink spots. She hugged him. It was a lovely gesture and so typical of Bae.

In the warmth from a fifteen-pound gas heater, they had sat on the couch and over the next weeks, when the rest of Base Camp turned in after nightfall they entertained friends from other expeditions. McDonnell came over. Eric Meyer, too. They sat watching cheap DVDs on Bae's Mac, movies like *Basic Instinct* and *Legally Blonde*, which Skog had bought in Kathmandu. The whole team was happier once Bae had arrived.

After walking for another hour down the summit snowfields, the three Norwegian climbers approached a stump of ice where on the way up Skog and Nessa had stashed a spare 120-foot coil of rope. Nessa had been given it by one of the Sherpas when they were cutting the lines at the base of the Bottleneck in the morning. After the Traverse, they had calculated they wouldn't need it on the summit snowfields.

Skog had to remind Nessa that it was behind the stump of ice. "Sure we'll need it?" he said, skeptically.

"Who knows if an ice screw will fail or something," Skog said, and they walked over to retrieve it.

Then they went on quickly, aware that Bae's oxygen was gradually running out and that the air around them was getting darker.

At 8 p.m., they came to the start of the fixed ropes that led down into the Traverse. They had made Bae's deadline of arriving at the ropes before dark, but only by a few minutes. The western sky over the Karakorum was blooming pink.

The three climbers had to clip on and rappel diagonally down about one 120-foot rope length to the first belay stance before they could duck along the Traverse under the serac. Soon, they thought, they would be back in Base Camp.

Nessa dropped down the rope first, followed by Skog and then Bae. Skog couldn't help thinking how well they were working together as a team.

They paused for a moment on a ledge where they could stand quite comfortably. The air around them was growing dark and shadowy. The two men switched on their lamps, which were secured around their helmets with elastic headbands and clips. Skog and Nessa waited for Bae to tell them what to do next.

Skog wanted to make sure her headlamp was functioning at full strength, so she unscrewed the back of the lamp to change its batteries.

Nessa asked Bae whether he wanted him to go first.

Bae's reply came from the dark. "No, I'll lead, and I want Cecilie to be between us," he said.

Skog watched her husband shift his clip across the rope and he shuffled quickly down into the darkening well of the Traverse, disappearing from sight.

Soon Skog had finished screwing on the back of her headlamp. She rappelled down another rope length but had to stop again when the rope became badly twisted by the force of her descent just before the next ice screw and she spent a minute getting past it. Then she continued her climb down, staring forward into the darkness with the cone of her lamp. It was another ten or fifteen minutes before she saw Bae's light. He was probably about eighty feet ahead of her.

They kept that distance between them for close to an hour. Lars Nessa followed somewhere behind Skog. Then Bae reached a spot, Skog calculated, that was somewhere in the middle of the Traverse.

Until that moment, there had been no movement or sound above them. But at that point, the mountain began to shake. There was a precise crack and roar. Cecilie lurched off balance against the ice wall. She felt the rope pull taut, then it snapped back again. In the convulsion, her headlamp went out and she blindly gripped the ice in terror until the shaking stopped.

She stared ahead of her along the Traverse but Bae's light had disappeared, too.

"Rolf?"

She called out, tentatively at first but more loudly as her alarm grew.

———————————

Lars Flato Nessa was climbing carefully down the Traverse, checking the rope as he pulled himself along, when he heard the rushing sound of ice falling.

He stopped, wondering what it could be. He had no sense for how far away the sound was. It could have been miles below him, lower down the mountain, or just a few feet away.

An instant later he heard Cecilie yelling for Rolf. Then he knew that whatever had happened was close by. From the sound in her voice it was serious.

He rappelled down and found Skog leaning in the darkness against the ice wall.

"Cecilie, are you all right?"

"Where is he?" Skog said. "Where is he, Lars? Where did he go? What just happened? I want to see him. Where is he?"

"Wait here," he said.

Nessa had no idea what he would find as he climbed out fearfully into the darkness. He followed the rope for ninety feet until he reached the ice screw where the South Koreans had abandoned their cluster of empty oxygen bottles on the way up. But there the rope ended abruptly, as if cut off by a knife.

"You there, Rolf?" he said, peering forward with his lamp.

He could see clearly that there had been a big ice fall on this part of the Traverse. The violence of it was obvious, as if there had been a battle. The snow had been packed down afresh; ice had battered down from above, obliterating any trace of bootprints from earlier in the day.

Nessa knew that his friend Bae was dead. He looked over the precipice and knew that his body was down there somewhere. They could try to find him but they would probably die trying.

When he got back to Skog, she looked at him imploringly.

"Tror du det er haap?" she said. *Do you think there's hope?*

No, Cecile, no hope, he thought. They were on the side of a mountain at more than 26,000 feet, surrounded by a cone of unforgiving darkness. Bae had been their leader, but he wasn't there for them now. Nessa wanted to make sure Skog realized there was no chance they would get her husband back.

"Nei," he said. *No hope.*

"We have to find him, Lars."

Nessa was not a full-time climber like Skog and Bae. The twenty-eight-year-old nurse was the junior member of the expedition. The two stars, Skog and Bae, had offered him a place on the team at the last minute. He had agreed to come to Pakistan almost on a whim to see how high he could climb, to see what this great marvel, K2, was like. He had never thought he would get so far. But he had done better than he had anticipated and now he surprised himself again. He expected to feel overwhelmed and instead he felt calm and rational. He looked at Skog, who was still clinging to the side of ice, and knew she needed his help if she was going to get down alive.

He told her they couldn't afford to mourn for Bae. "Something terrible has happened," he said. "We have to stay focused. There's no time for mourning."

But what were they going to do? They could wait for daylight. But in the Death Zone? On the other hand, they had no rope. Any fumble or misstep meant death.

Nessa reminded himself that it was not unusual to be on an expedition in Norway and discover they had forgotten some of the ropes or belays or screws. They just had to be creative and find some other way out of this problem. And then he remembered the coil of rope that they had stashed and collected again on the summit snowfield and which was in his backpack.

He brought it out and ran it through his hands. In fact, it was two lengths knotted together, one white length and one colored. He also realized he had a reliable ice screw to attach it to—the one that was still screwed into the ice of the Traverse. It had been tested by an avalanche and had held.

He climbed down again and tied the rope and when he came back he told Skog he was going to rappel down to look for a way out. She was in shock, but she nodded and seemed to understand what he told her.

Skog's headlamp was still not working. After she had changed the batteries, she had not fitted it together again properly and the batteries had fallen out when the avalanche hit. Letting himself down on the rope, Nessa watched as Skog was swallowed by the darkness.

He rappelled down diagonally to the right over broken rocks, bracing his legs to avoid swinging back vertically like a pendulum, and watching carefully for the end of the rope. In the darkness, he was unsure where he was heading but after about forty yards he recognized the rocks around him and realized he had reached the Bottleneck.

He yelled back up to Skog and soon he felt her weight moving down the line. He held the end of the rope tightly. Five minutes later, Skog's legs appeared out of the darkness and within a moment she stood beside him, only slightly out of breath.

The first thing she said to Nessa was "Have you found him?"

He shook his head.

"When will we find him?" she said.

"Cecilie, he is gone."

"How can you be sure?"

"Look, we can search tomorrow when it's light. You won't see anything now anyway."

Nessa remembered Bae's three iron rules. He knew he had to get Skog and himself home. They could not take the risk of looking for Bae. Now they saw that in addition to cutting the rope in the Traverse, the avalanche had also swept away or buried the lines fixed in the Bottleneck. The gully was littered with large chunks of ice. There was nothing to do but to turn their faces to the slope and descend without rope.

"We must go," Nessa said.

Skog nodded.

Nessa went first, punching grips with his ice axe and the teeth of his crampons. Every few feet he stopped and pointed his headlamp upward, trying to give Skog as much light as he could. He waited until she made it down to him, and then he climbed another few feet lower.

It was a slow, laborious way of descending the mountain; they were tired and their nerves were raw from Bae's death. Nessa called out encouragement to Skog and tried to guide her and she tried to concentrate and be patient, though the broken chunks of ice around them made the way perilous.

Skog doubted whether she could make it to the bottom. She climbed automatically, moving one axe down and then her boot. Axe and boot.

Half an hour later, the ice gully flattened out a little, and Skog and Nessa were able to turn and stand up straighter and walk down slowly in single file. They bent forward tentatively because the ice was still slippery, and held the blades of their ice axes in their hands and thrust the handles before them into the crust of the snow.

They were still walking amid the blocks of ice that had crumbled from the serac when Skog's boot caught on a brick of ice and she fell.

The surface was hard and slick and Skog slid fast, tumbling and rolling over and crying out for Nessa to help her. She was on a slope and she couldn't see where she was going. After sixty feet, she flung out her axe and slammed the point into the ice, which brought her to a jolting stop.

She gasped for breath. Her ski pants were ripped down her leg. But she was alive.

Nessa scrambled down to her.

"I thought I was gone," she said, still breathing heavily, as he helped her up.

"So did I," he said.

She was bruised and shaken and feeling more weak and exhausted than ever, but they continued making their way down. The wind was picking up.

After another hour, the line of fixed rope appeared suddenly and they clipped on to it. Ahead, a small, strong light was flashing on and off from the direction of Camp Four. Someone had put out a beacon. They fixed their compass to it.

As they approached the camp, Skog grew convinced that Bae would be in the tent waiting for her. Of course he was in Camp Four, she thought. Her husband was the one who constantly worried about safety. He never took risks. *Safe and sure. Get back home.* Nothing could have happened to him. She was late and he would be worried about her by now, she thought. *Cecilie, where have you been?* Skog told herself she must hurry. She had to get back.

At Camp Four, Skog and Nessa went straight to the tent of Oystein Stangeland, the fourth member of the Norwegian team. Stangeland had turned back after the Traverse. As Skog opened the tent flap, she looked immediately to see if anyone was sitting with him, but he was alone.

Inside, Stangeland asked where Bae was and Nessa shook his head.

"Rolf got lost," Nessa said.

That was all he had to say. It was short and brutal and all three climbers knew what it meant.

The night before, Skog and Bae had slept together in one of the tents at Camp Four, while Nessa and Stangeland had shared the second tent. Now Skog walked to her tent and went inside. Bae was not there either.

Nessa brought in a bottle of water that Oystein had melted for them. Skog felt thirsty but she was not hungry. She was cold and tired and sad. Nessa helped her remove her crampons. She left her boots, her thick climbing suit, and everything else on.

The two climbers lay down on the mat under the sleeping bag and Nessa held her.

CHAPTER NINE

The violent, shape-shifting nature of K2 was dramatically revealed during an expedition to the mountain in 1953.

A year before Desio, Lacedelli, Bonatti, and Compagnoni made their pilgrimage from Italy, a team of seven Americans and one Briton arrived on the slopes. They were led by a thirty-nine-year-old doctor from New York named Charles Houston, a Harvard graduate and a legendary figure of American mountaineering, although this would be his last climb. His team included a twenty-seven-year-old climber, Art Gilkey, who was a graduate student in geology at Columbia University in New York, and twenty-six-year-old Pete Schoening from Seattle.

For six weeks the team climbed steadily, defeating the most difficult landmarks of K2, including House's Chimney and the Black Pyramid, and discovering the empty tents of Wiessner's expedition. K2's notorious weather had already begun to blow in: In a violent storm, Houston's team was trapped in the tents at the expedition's Camp Eight at 25,500 feet, three thousand feet from the summit. They could not light the stoves easily, so the climbers struggled to melt water to drink, and to cook. They passed the time reading aloud to each other, painting, or writing diaries. Four days later, after one of their three tents had been pummeled by the storm, the wind dropped slightly and they staggered outside. Art Gilkey, however, had developed swelling in his left leg. He collapsed and passed out.

When Gilkey came around, he insisted he was only suffering from a cramp. "I'm all right, fellows; it's just my leg, that's all," he said. "I've had this Charley horse for a couple of days."

But he had developed thrombophlebitis, or blood clots, in the veins of his left calf. He could certainly climb no higher and was unable to descend alone.

Another storm swept in, confining the team once again to their tents, and the clots spread to Gilkey's right leg and eventually his lungs. Gilkey apologized for being a burden but his six teammates gave him a shot of morphine and then quickly composed a makeshift stretcher from his sleeping bag, a tent, a rucksack, and a cradle of rope.

The route they had followed on the ascent had become a major avalanche risk, so in the howling wind they tacked to the west, down a steep rock rib, dragging a now blue-faced Gilkey through deep snow. When the slope steepened, they lowered him down it with a rope tied to the stretcher and anchored from above by Pete Schoening. This involved Schoening's securing his ice axe in the snow behind a boulder, using the rock to support the axe, and looping the end of the rope once around the axe handle and around his waist.

Delicately, they lowered Gilkey until they reached a place where they began to cross the rocks to Camp Seven. But at this point, one of them lost his footing and slipped. He was roped to a teammate who in the force of the fall was also wrenched off his feet. The pair then crashed into the rope between Houston and another climber. Within a moment all four were hurtling down the slope toward the precipice. They snagged a fifth climber, who was attached by a rope to Gilkey's stretcher, and he too began to slide. Entangled, they were going to fall thousands of feet, it seemed, and they were going to die.

But Schoening was still supporting Gilkey from above and the incredible happened. Even as the weight of six mountaineers jolted onto his rope, Schoening's strength held the falls.

As he strained, the train of falling men stopped, hanging above the drop. Slowly, one by one, the mountaineers righted themselves. One had lost his gloves and his hands were frozen; another had a cracked rib and a large gash in his leg; a third had a nosebleed. Houston was unconscious and had to be revived by the reminder that if he didn't climb up now he would never see his wife and daughter again.

The climbers anchored Gilkey on the slope with two ice axes and explained that they would return to fetch him soon.

"Yes, I'll be fine," Gilkey said. "I'm okay."

The mountaineers crawled across to the small ledge where one member of the group was already erecting two tents. As they did so, they heard Gilkey calling out to them from his stretcher 150 feet away. Ten minutes later they returned to collect him, but he was gone.

At first they assumed an avalanche had taken him, but in the following years some wondered whether Gilkey had cut himself free so that his teammates would not have to carry him down. Had he sacrificed himself so that they could live? As they continued the descent over the next few days, they found no sign of Gilkey except for a tangle of ropes, a torn sleeping bag, the shaft of an ice axe, and blood-streaked rocks. They all studied the remains but none admitted until later that they had seen them.

K2 had its close Italian connection, thanks to the Duke of Abruzzi and the triumph of Compagnoni and Lacedelli. But down the years, after an American expedition in 1938, Wiessner's ill-fated attempt in 1939, and Houston and his colleagues' expedition in 1953, it also became known as "America's Mountain."

In 1953, the day after the Americans' safe return to Base Camp, their Hunza porters erected a ten-foot-high memorial cairn to Art Gilkey, a pile of boulders thrown aloft on a spur of rock at the confluence of the Savoia and Godwin-Austen glaciers looking across the southern face of K2 and down the glacier to Concordia.

It was a monument to teamwork and brotherhood. It was also a monument to mortality, and to the deadliness of the mountain. Over the years, names were added to the memorial, names punched into simple tin mess plates, or lives paid tribute to in pictures, elaborate stone carvings, or metalwork. If the remains of fallen climbers were discovered on the glacier, they were often carried up and interred in the crevices between the rocks.

Over the decades, it became a matter of duty for mountaineers coming to K2 to scale the cliff outside Base Camp and visit Gilkey's memorial. The glacier receded and each year the promontory reached higher into the sky.

There were plaques placed there to commemorate later disasters. The 1995 accidents that claimed seven lives, including Alison Hargreaves, a British mother of two young children who was blown off the mountain just below the summit by sudden, hurricane-force winds. And the 1986 deaths, when thirteen climbers perished over the course of the climbing season. One of them, an Italian, Renato Casarotto, climbed on the Magic Line, an especially difficult and renowned route also known as the Southwest Pillar, although he turned back before the summit. Near Base Camp, he fell into a crevasse. He telephoned his wife, who was waiting for him in a tent at Base Camp, to tell her that he was dying and needed urgent help. When rescuers reached him that night, they managed to lift him out, but he died soon afterward and at dawn Casarotto was lowered back into the crevasse.

During the summer, Gerard McDonnell and the Dutch team had climbed up to pay their respects. Marco Confortola visited and so did Alberto Zerain. Eric Meyer and three others from the American team made the pilgrimage, and in the silence linked arms and bowed their heads in prayer, ignoring the stench of rotting flesh on the breeze. Hugues d'Aubarède climbed up and studied the nameplates carefully.

They all brooded on heroism and eternity, accepting that death was a possibility, a risk—yet not fully believing that the Gilkey Memorial and what it stood for could lie in their own futures.

CHAPTER TEN

11 p.m.

In their tent on the Shoulder, where they lay in sleeping bags, waiting for people to climb down from the summit, Eric Meyer and Fredrik Strang didn't hear Cecilie Skog and Lars Flato Nessa return to Camp Four.

They monitored the radio for any transmissions, drank as much water as they could, and tried to stay warm and alert in case their help was needed. They had boiled noodles but it was hard to force any food down.

Earlier, as people had summited, the voices on the radio had been ecstatic. Chhiring Dorje was the only member of their own expedition who had continued to the top.

"Big Namaste," he had said when he called in. "Very happy to be on the summit, brother!" He and Meyer called each other brother.

"Congratulations," said Meyer.

Meyer was a Christian, Dorje a Buddhist. Spiritually, they found they had a lot in common. Dorje and his wife had visited Meyer in Colorado and Meyer had taught him to ski. On K2, Dorje had built a seven-foot rock chorten a few yards from the tents in Base Camp and encouraged the American team members to toss offerings of rice to the mountain; every evening he chanted his prayers.

Meyer and Strang were proud that one of their team had made it to the top. It was also a relief to hear good news in the wake of the deaths of Dren Mandic and Jahan Baig. They punched the air and gave each other high-fives. *Way to go!*

But then the radio had fallen quiet.

Toward 10 p.m., Meyer had noticed headlamps coming down from the summit. He walked outside to study them, the sight making him feel queasy. The climbers were already having to use lights even though they had far to go to reach Camp Four.

"Fuck, they are late!" Strang said, when Meyer returned to the tent. "Where is Chhiring?"

Camp Four was quiet. The Serbs had already gone down to one of the lower camps. About ten yards from the tents, the American team had planted a strobe light in the snow, taping it to the top of three bamboo wands. One of the other members of the American team, Chris Klinke, a climber from Michigan, had bought it at an outdoor adventure show in Salt Lake City. It was round and only about four inches long but it sent out a powerful flashing white beam that split the night and would help guide people down safely; Camp Four was surrounded by couloirs, or gullies, and you could easily stray into them if you didn't know the way back to camp.

Meyer and Strang waited for news on the radio. The American team had Icom five-watt radios. Some of the sets, which were about six inches high, had remote handheld microphones so the team members could keep the radio inside a coat pocket and the batteries would stay warm. Good communication was essential, the teams had agreed, and so they had established a common frequency for all of the radios that were being used by the expeditions on the climb, which the Americans had nicknamed the United Nations frequency. But the Dutch group's radios didn't always work on that part of the dial for some reason, and the South Koreans had gradually taken it over anyway, and no one in the other teams could understand what they were saying. As a result, the Americans tended to use their own frequency and so did the Italians. Meyer now checked the U.N. channel, but he also continued to turn the knob listening for anyone else who might be trying to call in.

Not everyone had taken a radio up anyway. Some had left them behind because they didn't want the weight. Others had simply forgotten them in their tents, and other teams had divided up, one person carrying the team's radio and another taking the satellite phone for the obligatory call to the family and friends from the summit. It all made perfect sense in the bright light of day but it seemed to Meyer and Strang a little stupid now that everyone was late and it was getting toward midnight. Why wasn't anyone talking?

The two climbers lay back on their sleeping bags and waited. At 10:30 p.m. the radio finally crackled. It was Chhiring Dorje. He said he had reached the Traverse but he had bad news.

"No ropes!" he said. His voice was anxious and excited. "No rope left on the Bottleneck. Big problem. Many danger."

Meyer held the radio and let the news sink in.

"That is a very difficult spot to be in, Chhiring," he said. He knew he didn't have to tell Dorje what he should do but he said it anyway. "I think you have to keep moving. Keep descending, no matter the danger. But be careful."

Dorje said he was alone, although he had been following two other Sherpas, who were somewhere ahead of him. He made Meyer understand that everyone else was still behind him and so they were also before the break in the ropes. Their umbilical cord down had been cut. Were they good enough to get down without it in the dark—or had they left their descent too late? Meyer and Strang began to realize they could have a full-blown catastrophe on their hands.

Chhiring Dorje was a stocky, wide-shouldered man with red cheeks and jet-black hair cut in a bowl shape. His friend Eric Meyer said he looked like Oddjob, the James Bond villain.

Dorje had descended from the summit with a large group of climbers. All knew they had left their descent late and were running out of time. They were also worried about falling on these slopes in the poor light, so the South Korean team fixed a rope down a steep section of the snowfields, beginning about one hundred yards below the top. This slowed the teams once again.

Dorje had helped the Koreans' chief Sherpa, Jumik Bhote, carry the rope lower and fix it. The time was past 9 p.m. and in the dusk the mountaineers clipped onto the line and backed down carefully and slowly in single file, the snow in places reaching up to their thighs.

The rope helped. Descending would have been faster if the climbers had divided into two lines. Then the speedier mountaineers could have forged ahead. But there was only one rope, and anyway creating two tracks would have doubled the avalanche risk.

Dorje believed this was the correct course of action. Everyone was staying together as a group. But after about four rope lengths, the climbers suddenly began unclipping and they wandered off independently into the darkness.

Dorje was a strong climber and he went on first with the two Sherpas, Pemba Gyalje and Little Pasang Lama. Up behind him, the slow procession of mountaineers backed down the slopes, seeming hardly to be moving. He could see the vague figures of the Koreans—Kim Jae-soo and Go Mi-sun—and Wilco van Rooijen and Hugues d'Aubarède. They were struggling, and Dorje felt that if he did not wait to help them they might lose their way. Securing his ice axe, he sat in the snow.

When Dorje turned around, Gyalje and Lama had disappeared from sight. There was no trace of their headlamps and he was seized by a fear that they had been taken by an avalanche. The snowfields were a terrifying blank. Suddenly, the Sherpa was worried about whether any of the expeditions were going to survive. He was concerned about himself, too; he was cold, and he wondered whether this time he was really going to be able to return home to Nepal.

"Oy!" he shouted up to the people behind him. There were a few shouts in response. "Come on quickly!" he called.

Dorje set off alone, but he had climbed only a few yards when he slipped and fell fast, bumping and sliding. Shoving his axe handle in behind him, he came to a stop after about seventy feet. He stood up, thinking how lucky he was, and still wondering where the two Sherpas were and whether they really were dead. Then he climbed down alone onto the Traverse, eventually arriving at the section where the rope dangled limply from the ice screw. This was different from the way up.

Testing the rope, he found it tight, probably from the weight of climbers below. His hope rose. Was it the two Sherpas? He climbed down backward, and staring over his shoulder into the darkness, he realized there was a point of light below him. It was a headlamp.

"Pemba, wait for me!" he called out. Someone called up to him and he recognized Pemba Gyalje's voice.

"Here is an avalanche!" Gyalje shouted. "Here is no rope!"

"Still, wait for me," Dorje called back in Nepalese, his high-pitched voice ringing across the slope. He said he was climbing down. "Ma tala jhardai chu!" he added. "I am coming!"

He clutched the rope and rappelled down over the rocks, making for the light, which was about 150 feet below him. He looked up at the looming shadow of the serac, which he thought looked like a god's brow. Dorje considered the mountain to be divine, one of the holiest of mountains; too many western climbers in Base Camp had showed disrespect. As Dorje got closer to the light, Gyalje shouted out that he was not alone. "Little Pasang is also here," he said.

The two men, Gyalje and Little Pasang, were clinging to a shelf of rock and ice. Little Pasang looked awkward. Both stared at Dorje questioningly. What were they waiting for? Dorje scowled. "We must go," he said. "We climb down. There is no other choice."

Gyalje gestured to Little Pasang to explain why they had not gone down. "Little Pasang has lost his ice axe," he said.

Dorje looked more closely at the young Sherpa. He could see he was afraid. His eyes were red from crying.

Dorje stared down with the help of his headlamp at the hard slope, littered now with blocks of ice. You might *just* be able to descend without an ice axe. But it was dark and they had been climbing non-stop for twenty hours and were tired. At least he and Pemba had their axes. The odds on falling without one were pretty high.

Gyalje said he was climbing down to look for the rope, but after he had gone about a hundred yards Dorje could see his headlamp was still dropping lower.

"What are you doing?" Dorje called. "Have you found the rope?"

"No! But I am going down."

"Pasang has no ice axe," Dorje shouted back.

Gyalje said the Koreans were following. They would help Pasang.

Dorje felt sorry for Little Pasang. He didn't know him well. They had called out greetings to each other occasionally when they passed on the route and from time to time they shared tea in Base Camp at the end of a working day, when he, Pemba, Pasang, and Jumik Bhote played cards and gambled for small change. He had met him first in the South Koreans' camp when Dorje walked over to sweet-talk the Koreans' Nepalese cook into giving him a jar of spicy kimchi, or Korean pickled cabbage, for Eric Meyer.

Dorje thought that if Pasang waited where he was he would freeze to death within an hour.

"Okay, Little Pasang," he said. "You clip on to my harness. I have an ice axe. We will go together."

Little Pasang looked shocked. "No!" he said. "Dangerous. Maybe we will die."

Could he hold the two of them? Dorje wondered to himself. If he slipped, they would both plunge to their deaths. If Little Pasang caught a boot or mistimed his step, he would drag Dorje down with him. The Sherpa pictured himself toppling from the Bottleneck.

His wife, Dawa Futi, had told him over and over back in Kathmandu not to go to K2 because it was too dangerous. She had cried, and she had never cried when he had left on expeditions before. He thought of his two daughters, Tshering Namdu and Tenzing Futi. They attended the expensive English-language school just outside Kathmandu, Little Angels' School. What would they do without him? And his brother, Ngawang, and his sister who had moved in to live with his family and depended on Dorje? How would they survive?

Dorje also had his own dreams. Not that long ago, it seemed, although it was ten or more years now, when he was about Little Pasang's age, he had started in the business as a mere porter, fresh from the Rolwaling valley. Gradually he had built a reputation and started his own company; he had climbed Everest ten times; his life had changed. He didn't want to throw everything away. One day, maybe, he and his family might move, to be near Meyer in the United States. His girls might go to an American school.

Now on the Traverse, Dorje felt his voice shake as he spoke to the young Sherpa who was looking at him so expectantly.

"We will go together," Dorje said again to Pasang. "We have two choices. Maybe we arrive together, or we die together. Don't worry. I will not leave you."

Each had a six-foot-long rope connected to his harness and they clipped the two ropes together. Dorje turned to face the slope, and Little Pasang climbed down a few feet below him, balancing with his hands and kicking into the ice with the crampons on his boots. Dorje felt the extra weight and then followed the other man down. He attempted to keep a short space between them and coordinated the placement of his ice axe and his crampons with Pasang's own steps just below. He concentrated hard, snapping out short commands and listening for Little Pasang's answer. He could hear Pasang's heavy breathing.

"Comfortable?"

"Fine! You?" said Pasang.

"You keep balanced, otherwise if you slip, we go!"

"You just hold on to that axe!"

There were further loud icefalls as they descended, and small pieces of ice from the serac pattered around them. Each time, the two men froze and gazed up nervously to see which way they should go to avoid the ice, until the air was quiet before going on.

"I am all right," Little Pasang said.

After one icefall, Little Pasang slipped and pulled Dorje down.

Dorje held the tip of his axe in the ice with both hands, trying desperately to control their fall.

"We are going!" he cried through gritted teeth. "Now we are finished!"

Pasang screamed. They slipped for ninety feet. But the axe blade struck a crack and held them.

"Little Pasang, I thought that was it!" Dorje said.

When the slope eased, they found Pemba Gyalje waiting for them. The relief of surviving made Dorje feel lightheaded. For the past hour he had forced himself to block out thoughts of his family, and only now did he allow himself to think of them again. He felt hot from the climb, and happy and lucky that the mountain had allowed him to survive.

Little Pasang stood quietly beside Dorje. "Thank you," the younger man said.

Dorje nodded and called on the radio to Eric Meyer and Fred Strang. He told them where he was.

"We are down through the Bottleneck," he said. "Everyone is okay. We are in a safe place."

He and little Pasang remained clipped together by their harnesses. As they approached Camp Four, Dorje saw the strobe light flashing from near the Americans' tent. He turned back to look at the summit.

The mountain was big and dark. He saw little groups of head-lamps sparkling high up and still descending from the summit. Some were in the Traverse, others in the diagonal on the western edge of the serac, and others were still up on the summit snowfield. He thought about the exhausted climbers who had been making their way down laboriously behind him. By now those in the Traverse were probably reaching the place where the ropes were cut.

Dorje hoped they too would have good fortune in finding a way down.

Then he saw Fredrik Strang come out of the tent and Strang rushed to embrace him. "Chhiring, you are back safely!"

———

When Dorje stepped into the light of Meyer and Strang's tent at 1:30 a.m., Meyer was talking on his satellite phone to his mother, Joyce, in Billings, Montana. He was telling her that she would probably be hearing some bad stuff on the news about the ropes being cut and people still stuck above 26,000 feet. But just so she was reassured, he said, he and his team were all safe now.

He cut short the call to greet Dorje. The Sherpa's face was almost hidden inside the hood of his red jacket. Meyer and Strang helped him unzip his suit and gave him some of the hot tea they had brewed for him. The tea would help rehydrate and warm him. Meyer examined him for injuries. After a few moments to collect himself, he told them what had happened. They were surprised by how coherent he sounded and the fact that he had no frostbite. They helped him into Meyer's sleeping bag beside Meyer. He told them how glad he was to be alive and said that in the morning he would call his brother in Nepal. A few minutes later, he took out his video camera and began to study the images of his successful summit of K2.

———

Chhiring Bhote and Big Pasang Bhote left their tent in Camp Four at midnight. They were carrying food, water, sleeping bags, and six oxygen cylinders.

The Sherpas for the Flying Jump team had planned to set off for a summit bid with the second group of South Korean climbers that night. But after 9 p.m., when the seven climbers from the first group still hadn't come in, the second summit attempt was postponed.

The Koreans' tents were just a few dozen feet away from the Americans' on the Shoulder. The alarm among the eight mountaineers waiting inside the tents had grown steadily until the two Sherpas were sent out to search for the missing Koreans and Chhiring's brother, and Pasang's cousin, Jumik.

Chhiring was anxious about his brother. Before Jumik had left Kathmandu, he had admitted he was nervous about coming to K2. They had grown up in a family of ten children in a poor village called Hatiya, in Sankhuwasabha district, which was east of Everest, just under Makalu. Their father was a farmer who had grown mostly potatoes and millet. Jumik had more experience as a climber. Chhiring had won his school leaving certificate at Pashupati Multiple Campus, and then studied education for a year before joining Jumik, who was already climbing regularly with the South Koreans. He remembered how Jumik had reassured and helped him on his first big climb on Lhotse.

As the two Sherpas walked out onto the Shoulder, three figures emerged from the darkness. It was Chhiring Dorje, Little Pasang, and Pemba Gyalje.

Greetings!

Why are you late? What went wrong?

"We pushed for the summit too late," said Dorje.

The three climbers were shaken and tired and they told the two Sherpas about the missing ropes and their difficult experience climbing down the Bottleneck.

The two Sherpas were pleased to see them. They handed the three men flasks of water, and waited for them to get their breath back before asking about the location of the other expeditions. Pointing, the three men said they were somewhere behind them but it was unclear where. There were a number of climbers following them down. Chhiring Dorje looked concerned and said it was going to be hard for some of the others to make their way in the darkness.

Where is Jumik?

Jumik had stayed with the slower Koreans. They were somewhere behind.

There were no ropes. Will you go up to rescue them?

We will search for them.

The other three were not strong enough to go back up with Chhiring and Big Pasang. They said they had to climb down to Camp Four as quickly as possible to get some rest.

The figures of the three climbers disappeared into the darkness. Chhiring Bhote and Big Pasang Bhote turned back toward the Bottleneck.

Chhiring Bhote and his brother had first started out in the Sherpa business in Hatiya when their older brother had gone out to trade for cooking oil and kerosene and instead had gotten caught up in the portering trade at Namche, a town near Everest. He had fallen into a crevasse and promised the gods he would never disturb them again if he got out. When he returned, he took Jumik with him to Kathmandu, bringing along their sister Bhutik to cook, swearing he was done with the mountains. A few years later, however, Jumik had joined the Korean team.

Half an hour after leaving the other Sherpas, the two men were still on the Shoulder when they saw another headlamp. They called out and Kim Jae-soo, the Korean leader, limped down toward them. He was alone.

Greeting him, they told him he was not far from the camp. Kim was tired and he knelt down in the snow. He asked for water and juice.

What happened? Big Pasang was polite. *Why are you so late?*

Kim wiped the frozen ice from around his eyes. *Everybody went crazy.*

Kim climbed because he loved the potential for danger in nature and possessing the ability to thwart it. The exhilaration of forcing himself to the limit and surviving. When people complained that mountaineering was dangerous, he waved them away. *You could have an accident driving a car, couldn't you?*

For a year he had prepared and trained his team for K2. When the Americans first met him at Base Camp, he was sitting outside the South Koreans' tents, his legs crossed, and he refused to meet their eyes or discuss strategy, claiming he spoke no English. A few weeks later, however, he had opened up, especially after Eric Meyer treated a Korean climber who was suffering from heartburn, and he joined in the cooperation meetings. It turned out Kim spoke English pretty well after all.

Everyone was so tired, Kim told the two Sherpas, as he drank deeply. The other teams had taken much time descending from the summit.

In addition, on the way up to the summit, the ropes fixed in the Bottleneck had swerved too far to the right, Kim thought—someone in the lead group had tried to lay them out of the direct line of the serac, which had added extra distance, delaying everyone. Yet still, despite everything, his team had beaten the Dutch expedition to the top. Then, on the way down, some climbers from the other teams had used the rope that Kim had told Jumik Bhote to lay at the top of the summit snowfields, again delaying his own climbers.

When they had reached the Traverse, he and Go Mi-sun had left the three slower Korean climbers behind with Jumik Bhote. Afraid his feet were getting frostbitten, Kim had climbed down more quickly and had lost Go somewhere along the way.

"Didi is not here," he said, meaning "sister," which was what the Sherpas called Go.

Mr. Kim, we look for her? The two Sherpas watched him restlessly.

Kim looked back up the great swerving track of the Shoulder. She couldn't be far behind, he said.

"She is following," he said, turning back to them. "You must meet her."

Chhiring Bhote and Big Pasang left Kim and climbed for a few more minutes, peering into the gloom of the rocks and snow around them with the light of their headlamps and up at the steep chute of the Bottleneck, when at last they caught a glimpse of something. It wasn't what they had expected. They saw an object plunging down in the darkness on the left-hand side of the route.

The two men scrambled forward.

You see?

Then they saw a second object dropping down the same area and heard the rustling scratching of a body falling.

Was it Jumik?

Bhote's stomach turned at the sight of the falling bodies.

The objects had disappeared so quickly. Maybe they were mistaken. Was it only ice falling from the serac?

But he knew inside that they were climbers, for sure.

They climbed up toward the Bottleneck until they saw a light, and slowly a climber approached them, a tall, thin man in an orange suit.

CHAPTER ELEVEN

Saturday, August 2, 1 a.m.

One moment everyone had been together in a line coming down from the summit, Cas van de Gevel remembered; then darkness had fallen like a blanket on the snowfields. Each climber was focused inwardly on his or her own breathing and exhaustion and aches. Then there were the difficult thoughts of just how many miles remained in the cold. They had drifted apart.

When he had arrived at the descent into the Traverse, Cas van de Gevel felt relief when his boots hit the ledge before the serac.

He was surprised to see the glare of a headlamp not far ahead of him. When he climbed along the ice face, he recognized a hunched figure in a dark yellow suit clipped onto the rope.

"Hugues!"

Van de Gevel wondered how d'Aubarède was feeling. The old guy had made good time since the summit. From the way he was resting against the slope, he looked tired. He was no longer with his HAP, Karim Meherban.

The two men put their faces close together so they could talk. D'Aubarède spoke first and motioned with his hand. "You go first, Cas," he said.

"Aren't you coming?" said Van de Gevel.

"Yes, yes," said d'Aubarède. "But you are faster than me. I will follow."

The rope stretched away down the rocky ice wall. Van de Gevel thought it was a good idea not to have too much weight on the rope. There had been too much of that today already.

Below the Traverse, several hundred yards away, down past the Bottleneck on the Shoulder, he could see a signal light flashing from Camp Four.

"No more talking," said d'Aubarède, prompting him.

Van de Gevel nodded and climbed out along the Traverse, leaving the Frenchman behind.

When he reached the point where the rope was severed, he saw that a new length of rope was dangling down loosely across the rocks. The Dutch climber had no clue of what had happened to Rolf Bae and Cecilie Skog and Lars Nessa, or to Chhiring Dorje or any of the Flying Jump team. He could only imagine that the other end of the rope had worked loose from the screw at the far side of the Traverse and the rope had simply fallen down. Or that it was some climber's idea for a new route. That had to be it.

The prospect of a new route didn't worry Van de Gevel. He had climbed many times in the dark in the Alps, though a person had to be ultra-careful. Sometimes you came upon frayed ropes left over from earlier expeditions, and they led only into the void.

Seeing no alternative, Van de Gevel grabbed the line, jumped over onto the rocks, and dropped backward, rappelling. He glanced below him as far as a turn of the head would allow, and concentrated on the grip of his strong fingers on the rope. When he felt a knot and the second length of line played through his gloves, he noticed that it was thinner than normal rope, and white. It was the rope that Gerard McDonnell had bought in Alaska for the Dutch team. The rush of familiarity buoyed him.

The Bottleneck fell away somewhere below him toward the Shoulder. After a few more feet, he saw the end of the line was approaching. *Steady!* He slowed and then let the rope fall back. It would be picked up by d'Aubarède behind him. The Frenchman had to be following by now.

He felt good to have reached the Bottleneck but felt trepidation to be without the protection of the fixed rope. The slope was still steep. Van de Gevel turned back to face the ice. He stuck his axe in and began the tough climb down.

A few feet to the right of the narrow channel something caught his eye. When he reached it, he discovered Wilco van Rooijen's backpack, which his colleague had dropped on the way up in the heat and crowds of the morning, a time that now seemed an age ago. It was about at this point that the American Chris Klinke had turned back.

The backpack offered Van de Gevel an indication of where he was on the Bottleneck. It was also a sign that Van Rooijen had not come this way yet. Cas left it for his friend to collect on his way down.

As he turned back toward the lower part of the Bottleneck, Van de Gevel's legs felt heavy. He told himself it was not far back to Camp Four.

Just then he heard a noise above him in the darkness, a scratching sound of something sliding down fast over the ice. Van de Gevel looked up and saw, twenty to thirty feet to his left, a body plunging headfirst down the Bottleneck.

There was no scream or shout. The climber still had his headlamp switched on. The body fell too fast for Cas to see his face in the light from his own headlamp, but Van de Gevel saw clearly that the climber was dressed in a dark yellow suit. The body disappeared into the night.

Lack of oxygen may trigger a complex physiological reaction inside the human body, one whose severity varies considerably from person to person. As oxygen levels decrease, the tiny arteries that feed the brain dilate. High-pressure blood floods the network of fragile cerebral capillaries, which begin to leak fluid.

The fluid causes swelling in the surrounding tissue. The brain swells, displacing the cushion of cerebrospinal fluid inside the head until the brain starts to squash up against the inside of the skull. When the compression begins to affect the area of the brain responsible for balance and coordination—the cerebellum—it causes ataxia, or stumbling and severe lack of coordination. As the compression progresses, the optic disk swells, causing blurring of vision.

As well as affecting the brain, lack of oxygen can lead to a surge in blood pressure in the arteries in the lungs, and cause more leakage. Fluid floods into the alveoli, the tiny thin-walled air sacs deep within the lungs where oxygen diffuses into the blood. An X ray of a climber suffering from this sort of high-altitude condition reveals a patchy image of fluid in areas of the lung normally filled with air. Among the first ominous signs are shortness of breath and fatigue, a persistent cough, then a gurgle and a coughing up of pink-tinged fluid. Eventually the climber drowns.

The effects of these fluid shifts can set in rapidly before a climber realizes anything is seriously wrong. Much like a drunk, judgment is impaired well before it is apparent to the climber. To help acclimatization or relieve the symptoms, some high-altitude mountaineers use drugs. For example, Viagra is sometimes used to drain fluid from the lungs. Many climbers circumvent the risk by carrying oxygen with them in tanks, but the effects can be disastrous if the supplementary oxygen runs out. When that happens, the climber abruptly enters a new, colder, and suffocating world of oxygen deprivation. There is no time to adjust. It is a massive, startling shock to the system.

Hugues d'Aubarède's oxygen had run out before the summit. When Cas van de Gevel had passed him on the Traverse, d'Aubarède wasn't sure he could go on. He was exhausted and his mind was filled with questions. Could he climb down? Should he stay where he was until daylight?

He remembered how he had almost missed the summit attempt. The bad weather had swept across K2 in the middle of July, forcing every expedition to push back their expected summit dates. But the contract of d'Aubarède's chief high-altitude porter, Qudrat Ali, expired at the end of the month. Qudrat had worked with d'Aubarède since they climbed Nanga Parbat together in 2005. He had been the Frenchman's guide on K2 in 2006, although he hadn't come to the mountain with him in 2007. Ali was tough and experienced. The second guide, Karim Meherban, twenty-nine, was Qudrat's cousin and a student from the same small town. They were both indispensable to d'Aubarède.

D'Aubarède's flight from Islamabad back to France left on August 8 and the journey to the Pakistani capital could take eight days. Eventually he concluded there was going to be no weather window opening up. He telephoned and brought the date of his flight forward and ordered up five porters from Concordia to fetch his belongings from Base Camp.

Gerard McDonnell and Wilco van Rooijen tried to persuade him to stay. They said their forecast showed the storms relenting around July 29. D'Aubarède called his friend Yan Giezendanner, who worked for the French government's meteorological service in Chamonix, who confirmed the better forecast.

"Is it possible for me, Qudrat?" he said when he found his HAP. "I want to get to the summit with Karim."

"You must try," Ali said. The guide knew how much getting to the top of K2 meant to d'Aubarède. "I hope you reach the top."

D'Aubarède called Mine in Lyon. "I have good news," he said.

"Do what you want," Mine said.

D'Aubarède called the airline to change his ticket back. Qudrat insisted he still had to leave—he had other clients waiting on another peak—so d'Aubarède hired a new high-altitude guide to replace Ali—Jahan Baig—whom Ali knew from Shimshal.

But once d'Aubarède believed he was going for the top, a creeping doubt had set in. He feared the lack of sleep that would come at the higher altitudes, the difficulty in breathing, the cold.

His friend Philippe Vernay in Lyon had tried to make d'Aubarède believe in God: If K2 was so beautiful it was because of God. But that was not the reason he was crazy about climbing. Yes, d'Aubarède fully appreciated the wonders of nature. But he didn't believe in God. Sorry, Philippe. He did, however, believe in something absolute, and that was probably what he was searching for.

But this year the climbing had been more difficult than ever. It was hard for a sixty-one-year-old. How his back hurt on the slopes, especially the steep slopes below Camp Two. At the end of the day it was hard just to bend to get inside the tent. He found sleeping increasingly tough, even at Base Camp, where he had an inch-thick mattress between his body and the glacier, but especially at the higher camps. He gulped aspirin to ease the blaring altitude headaches that squeezed at his temples.

He knew about the dangers. He knew all about death. In July 2005, he had shared a tent with his friend Bernard Constantine on Nanga Parbat. Three months later, on the slopes of Nepal's Kang Guru, Constantine had disappeared under an avalanche with six other Frenchmen and five Sherpas. Last year on K2, his friend Stefano Zavka, exhausted and alone, walked off the side of the Shoulder on the way down and was never seen again. This year, when d'Aubarède made the pilgrimage to the Gilkey Memorial, he studied the plaques stamped with the names of the dead. He said out loud that he hoped he would not be there one day.

He missed his family. He kept in touch with them almost every day. He had a friend back in Lyon, Raphaele Vernay, Philippe's wife, who kept a blog for him. And he took comfort reading in his sleeping bag the text messages his friends and family sent him on his satellite phone.

Back in July, his younger daughter, Constance, had sent him a

The two main approaches to the summit of K2, the Abruzzi and Cesen routes, converge at the Shoulder. From there, climbers must navigate the Bottleneck and the Balcony Serac, an overhanging glacier, before reaching the top. *(The New York Times/Michael Farris/Bruce Normand)*

On the morning of August 1, 2008, two mountaineers, Marco Confortola and Gerard McDonnell, climb up the Shoulder toward the Bottleneck. In the background is Camp Four, the last camp before the summit. Within a few hours, the crush of climbers at the top of the Bottleneck would lead to the first death. *(Lars Flato Nessa)*

Climbers grip fixed ropes to ascend the Bottleneck, a steep and dangerous gully, and then rest before crossing over toward the Traverse. At over 26,000 feet, the expeditions enter the so-called Death Zone, where balance, concentration, vision, and other human body functions break down rapidly under the searing effects of altitude. *(Lars Flato Nessa)*

The Bottleneck and the steep ice face of the Traverse lead the climbers beneath the overhanging serac, which glistens ominously in the midday sun. In past years, serac collapses sent huge chunks of ice hurtling onto the Traverse and down the Bottleneck. Climbers did not like to imagine what would happen if they got in the way. *(Lars Flato Nessa)*

The Serbian climber Dren Mandic, shown in foreground at right in one of the mess tents at K2 Base Camp in 2008. Mandic fell to his death among the crowds at the top of the Bottleneck on the morning of August 1. *(Predrag Zagorak)*

Jahan Baig, a Pakistani high-altitude porter. The HAPs, drawn from northern villages in Pakistan, were employed by foreign expeditions as guides and carriers on the mountain. They were often cheaper alternatives to Nepalese Sherpas. *(Hasil Shah)*

After the first two deaths, the line of climbers continues on the diagonal ascent beneath the serac toward the summit snowfields. The Basque mountaineer Alberto Zerain, the first to summit and the only climber to descend in daylight, is visible at top left. *(Chris Klinke)*

Two South Korean climbers struggle to climb the last ice lip from the route beneath the serac onto the summit snowfield. Three members of the South Korean expedition and one of their Nepalese Sherpas would die on the descent; another Sherpa would lose his life trying to rescue them. *(Lars Flato Nessa)*

Climbers arrive at the summit of K2 in the late afternoon of August 1. After fifteen hours or more of continuous climbing, the descent is one of the most dangerous parts of any attempt on K2—of the nearly 70 men and women killed on K2 over the course of its history before 2008, more than a third died on the way down after having successfully reached the summit. *(Lars Flato Nessa)*

Frenchman Hugues d'Aubarède pictured at K2 Base Camp with Qudrat Ali (left), the American climber Nick Rice (right), and Karim Meherban. Most climbers work as members of a larger expedition. D'Aubarède traveled to K2 as an independent climber, though he employed three Pakistani high-altitude porters and joined forces with Rice at Base Camp. *(Raphaele Vernay)*

Cecilie Skog and her teammate Lars Flato Nessa stand together on the summit of K2. Skog was the first woman to summit the tallest peaks on all seven continents, and reach both the North and South Poles. *(Lars Flato Nessa)*

The Basque climber Alberto Zerain gazes up toward the serac. On his way down from the summit, Zerain passed the line of climbers still ascending. He warned them the ascent was going to be difficult. *(Alberto Zerain)*

Representatives from different expeditions pose for a team photograph after one of the cooperation meetings at Base Camp. Wilco van Rooijen, the Dutch leader, kneels in the front row, fourth from right. The American Eric Meyer is middle row third from left; Chhiring Dorje stands to his left. Go Mi-sun kneels front row, third from left. Rolf Bae of Norway stands on the back row at far right. After the meeting, Bae commented to Lars Nessa that he had a feeling something was bound to go wrong. *(Lars Flato Nessa)*

ABOVE: Early evening, August 1: from left to right, Hugues d'Aubarède, Karim Meherban, Gerard McDonnell, and Wilco van Rooijen celebrate at the summit. Only one of the four would survive. *(Wilco van Rooijen)*

ABOVE: At 61, Hugues d'Aubarède was the second oldest person to summit K2. From the top of the mountain, he called home to Lyon: "It's minus 20. I am at 8,611 meters. I am very cold. I am very happy." *(Raphaele Vernay)*

LEFT: The Italian climber Marco Confortola. Italy had a long association with K2: in 1954, two Italian climbers were the first to reach the summit. *(Marco Confortola)*

TOP: Gerard McDonnell holds an Irish flag aloft on the summit. In 2006, during an earlier attempt on K2, he was caught in a rock fall and had to be airlifted from the mountain. (*The family of Gerard McDonnell*)

ABOVE: Cecilie Skog and Rolf Bae had been married for little more than a year when they came to K2. Unlike other mountaineers who left spouses or partners behind for months on end during expeditions, the couple saw exploring and traveling as a way to be together. (*Cecilie Skog / cecilieskog.com*)

RIGHT: Norwegian climber Lars Nessa came to the Karakoram curious to see K2, but with no fixed plan of making it to the summit. In the end, he made it to the top of the second tallest mountain on earth. (*Lars Flato Nessa*)

Kim Jae-soo, the leader of the South Korean Flying Jump expedition. The Korean team, the largest on the mountain, included fifteen members. *(Karrar Haidri/saltorosummits.com)*

BELOW: Kim Jae-soo and the star climber from the South Korean team, Go Mi-sun. Go would die a year later on Nanga Parbat, another mountain in northern Pakistan. *(Karrar Haidri/saltorosummits.com)*

ABOVE: Jumik Bhote, pictured here in Kathmandu, had recently been promoted to chief Sherpa of the South Korean Flying Jump team. His son would be born while Jumik was climbing on K2. *(Virginia O'Leary)*

Jumik with his brother, Chhiring. Chhiring and other family members from their village in Nepal also worked as Sherpas for the South Korean team. *(Virginia O'Leary)*

TOP: Members of different expeditions at Base Camp carry Wilco van Rooijen on a stretcher to the helicopter emergency landing pad on August 4. *(Chris Klinke)*

LEFT PAGE, BOTTOM LEFT: Dutch mountaineer Cas van de Gevel waits for helicopter evacuation from K2 Base Camp. Helping rescue his friend Wilco van Rooijen, he spent the night bivouacking at 24,000 feet. *(Chris Klinke)*

LEFT PAGE, BOTTOM RIGHT: Marco Confortola is helped by military officials from a helicopter in Skardu, northern Pakistan. Badly frostbitten, all his toes would later be amputated. *(The Associated Press)*

RIGHT PAGE, BOTTOM LEFT: The leader of the Dutch Norit K2 team, Wilco van Rooijen, survived two nights without shelter on the mountain and called his wife in the Netherlands to help him find his way down. He lost nearly all his toes from frostbite. *(Wilco van Rooijen)*

RIGHT PAGE, BOTTOM RIGHT: Sherpa Pemba Gyalje. A commercial mountain guide from Nepal, he joined the Dutch team as an independent climber in his own right. He wanted to become one of the first Nepalese Sherpas to reach the summit of K2 without the aid of supplementary oxygen. *(Wilco van Rooijen)*

The gregarious Gerard McDonnell called his girlfriend in Alaska from the summit. He was the first Irishman to reach the top of K2. *(Wilco van Rooijen)*

Fredrik Strang at Concordia on the trek toward K2. The Swedish climber turned back from his own attempt on the summit when he saw the delay on the Bottleneck. Later, he helped bring down Dren Mandic's body. *(Chris Klinke)*

The American Eric Meyer poses with Chhiring Dorje, a Sherpa from Nepal who was a member of the American team. Meyer, an anesthesiologist from Colorado, almost died when his rope snapped on his descent. Dorje helped another Sherpa climb down the Bottleneck in darkness. *(Chris Klinke)*

Using binoculars and a telescope, the American climber Chris Klinke sighted Wilco Van Rooijen wandering on the southern face of K2 on the afternoon of August 2, leading eventually to van Rooijen's rescue. *(Chris Klinke)*

A close-up of metal plates at the Gilkey Memorial, located a few hundred yards above K2 Base Camp. The memorial is named for an American climber, Art Gilkey, who died on the mountain during an expedition in 1953. Most climbers visit it but few imagine they will end up immortalized there themselves. *(Graham Bowley)*

bottle of Chartreuse and a note. She told him the latest plans for her wedding. The wine and champagne were purchased, the church at Houches reserved.

She warned her father not to be late. She said she didn't want to walk to the altar alone.

Now, on the Traverse, as d'Aubarède watched Cas van de Gevel disappear into the distance, he reminded himself that he had to descend from the clouds to share his success with his friends and his family. He had to get back for Constance's wedding.

D'Aubarède turned on his Thuraya and tried his family in France but he could not get through. A moment later, he stood up and followed the Dutchman along the rope.

In the Bottleneck, Cas van de Gevel climbed several yards down the steep slope in the direction he had seen the body falling. He knew it was Hugues d'Aubarède.

He gazed ahead with his headlamp but he could see no trace of d'Aubarède.

When he looked back up, two lights were quivering among the rocks a few hundred yards above him. He thought they probably belonged to the Korean climbers who were following behind. He braced himself with his ice axe and cupped his hand to his mouth.

"Someone fell!" he shouted, hoping they would help. "Hugues has fallen!"

Whoever it was that was following him down, there was no answer. They were too far away to hear him.

He couldn't waste any more time searching. A few minutes later, the slope lessened and he could turn around to face down the mountain as he climbed.

Near the bottom of the Bottleneck, he saw two headlamps approaching slowly up the gully. They turned out to belong to two

Sherpas or HAPs, who had come out from Camp Four; they were so bundled up behind balaclavas and goggles that he couldn't tell who they were for sure.

He told them what he had seen and pointed to where the body had fallen.

"You look over there," he said. "Can you help?"

The two men walked away in the direction he had pointed but they seemed to be in no rush.

As he approached Camp Four, Van de Gevel radioed Base Camp and spoke to Roeland van Oss. He told Van Oss he was okay.

Van Oss had been waiting all night for the climbers from the Dutch team to call in. He was pleased to hear from Van de Gevel.

"I am below the Bottleneck," Van de Gevel said. "I am safe."

"Okay, Cas," he said. "Good to hear from you."

Van de Gevel said he had no idea where the others in his team were. Van Rooijen. McDonnell. "We got dispersed," he said. He had seen something troubling, he added. "I think I saw someone falling down," he said. "You need to send someone up to find out what happened."

"You should get down to Camp Four as quickly as you can," Van Oss told him.

As Van de Gevel descended the Shoulder, the big light from Camp Four grew brighter.

He thought about Hugues d'Aubarède. He didn't know why d'Aubarède had fallen. Perhaps he had been concentrating so hard on climbing down the rope that he didn't notice when the line had ended. Or he had come off the rope successfully but then tripped on one of the ice blocks littering the slope.

When Van de Gevel reached Camp Four, it was some time around 2 a.m. He was so exhausted that he went straight to his tent. Van Rooijen had not come in yet, he saw.

He drank water thirstily and sank onto his sleeping bag.

Go Mi-sun's oxygen had finished just after the summit. Then she had had to start breathing the empty frigid air of the high mountain, which provided no energy or warmth at all.

When she reached the end of the Traverse, the line was cut, but she managed to turn down into the Bottleneck. She was surprised at the unusually thin rope playing through her hands but she followed it into the gully. Then, using her two axes, she navigated her way between the icefalls onto the Shoulder.

She was following Kim Jae-soo but by then she could no longer see his light. He was in front somewhere but his headlamp was facing forward.

The forty-one-year-old was a small, stocky, pretty woman, who had grown up in a small town about four hours outside of Seoul. She was single, and she lived in Seoul close to her sister and brother. Bouldering and ice and rock climbing were her main sports—she had been an Asian climbing champion for several years and had competed in the extreme sports championships, the X Games, in San Diego—but when she got older and put on weight (she had gained twenty-two pounds since 2003, she complained) she switched from sport climbing to mountaineering.

Now the night was especially dark and the wind started to pick up, so she decided to search for shelter from the wind, a large rock or something else that would protect her. Gradually, the realization dawned that she had made a huge mistake. She had lost the route across the spine of the Shoulder and had wandered instead down its side—probably the eastern side.

Luckily she hadn't gone too far down, probably a hundred feet or so. She was tough; she knew how to get out of tight situations. Once, on another mountain in the Himalayas, she had fallen 180 feet, shattering a bone in her back; she had been alone but she told herself she was not going to allow herself to die, and over several hours she had managed to crawl down to safety.

Now, laboriously, Go retraced her steps in the dark. But when she got back onto what she thought had to be the main part of the Shoulder, the night was still pitch black and featureless and Go had no idea where she was.

She called out Kim's name in frustration and shouted for help. She walked several yards forward, slowly dropping down the slope. But she was lost again. Rocks reached up on every side of her, black and ugly spikes. She remembered how when she was young and had first gone to the mountains, the leaves were so beautiful. But there was no beauty here, only rocks. The hard stone clunked against her axe. She swung her headlamp around, realizing she had no idea where to go.

———————

After two hours, Chhiring Bhote and Big Pasang Bhote saw a distant light and heard a voice calling for help, and it was then that the two Sherpas saw Go Mi-sun.

She was stuck in rocks some distance from the main route. They shouted to make her understand they had seen her. "Didi!" they called.

"Didi is coming!" she called back.

As they got nearer, however, she pleaded with them to get her down, and they reassured her they were on their way.

When they reached her, one of the Sherpas lifted her shoulders while the other held her legs, and together they carried her out. They tied her safety harness to theirs with a rope and led her down.

When they arrived back at Camp Four after about 4:30 a.m., Kim was lying in his tent, dozing. He woke when the two Sherpas helped Go under the nylon flap. At first, when Kim saw Go's familiar face and realized how late it was, he was angry with his star climber. He cared for her, and she had risked her life. He wanted to know why she had taken so long to climb down. Go, who was still shaken by her experience, bowed her head and apologized, until with relief he comforted her.

Go was surprised when she saw that most of the other tents in the camp were still empty. She was not the last climber from the Flying Jump "A" team to return. Four other climbers were still missing. The battery on the Koreans' radio was not working, so she and Kim could not contact them. The two Sherpas waiting outside might have to continue the search.

Chhiring Bhote and Big Pasang went to their tent to try to rest. They were glad they had found Go, who was a good friend to them. They couldn't sleep, however. They drank water and then stood outside, staring at the mountain.

The night was clear. Headlamps were burning above the Traverse. The serac that had so violently severed the ropes was still active and could yet toss more ice down the Traverse and Bottleneck.

The two Sherpas started packing supplies again. Jumik—their brother and cousin—was out there somewhere.

Part III

SERAC

Saturday, August 2

Tiocfaidh Ar La. Our day will come.
—Gerard McDonnell, K2, 2008

CHAPTER TWELVE

2 a.m.

Jumik Bhote had led the seven-man South Korean Flying Jump "A" team victoriously from the summit at around 7:10 p.m., carrying 230 feet of rope in his backpack.

Where there was a clear track and the snow was compact and safe, he anchored one end of the rope into the ground with a snow stake and the team members and other climbers plunged down it. The fit Sherpa brought up the rear and then climbed lower with the rope and fixed it in the snow again.

Bhote repeated the maneuver with the rope four or five times, bending and fixing and scurrying down, helped in his labors by Chhiring Dorje, the Sherpa from the American expedition. Eventually, the teams unclipped from the rope and climbed on independently, spreading out in the darkness. On the long snowfield, the two South Korean leaders, Kim Jae-soo and Go Mi-sun, rushed on ahead. As they disappeared into the shadows, Bhote was left alone with the last climbers in the Flying Jump team.

The three men had been so joyful on the summit, Bhote remembered. Before they had left for Pakistan, one of them, Park Kyeong-hyo, a twenty-nine-year-old from a mountaineering club in Gimhae, South Gyeongsang province, had written on the online bulletin board of his mountaineering club: "Now, it's not just a dream anymore. In some 150 days, we'll be climbing this mountain. Just imagine that. Isn't it fabulous?"

He had been good enough to climb Everest a year earlier, but now Park and the other two climbers—Kim Hyo-gyeong and Hwang Dong-jin—looked like they were dying. None of them said a word. Hwang had been part of the lead group that had left early from Camp Four to fix the rope up the Bottleneck. They just stared at one another dumbly from behind their climbing masks.

Bhote coaxed them onward. He was cold, too, and tired. *Keep going! We must be quick! Please.*

At the end of the snowfield, after searching for the way lower for a while, Bhote and the three Koreans dropped down toward the fixed rope that they hoped would lead them into the diagonal around the edge of the serac.

Slowly, they backed down on the ropes toward the Traverse. But after a few yards they stopped.

You have to go! Jumik shouted.

Finally, dangling on the rope, the three men underneath Bhote seemed unable to climb down another inch, no matter how much he urged them on.

He was worried about how long the rope would hold their weight, or whether there was danger of snow or ice crashing down from above.

Please!

Bhote's voice rang out in the cold darkness on the side of the mountain. He tried to focus—on the rope, the ice face, the lamps of the climbers below him—until he felt his own mind drifting away.

In Kathmandu, Jumik Bhote failed his school exit exam and started working on his older brother's fourth-hand family bus on the traffic-clogged streets of the capital, collecting five rupees each from the Nepalese passengers and the tourists traveling to the hotels around the Kathmandu ring road. After a year or two the bus was so broken down that his brother sold it. Later Bhote signed up as a porter with the South Koreans.

Nawang, the expedition cook, was from the same village as Bhote. He had introduced him to the Flying Jump team, warning him under his breath, "If you work for the Koreans, you have no future." But the unemployment rate in Nepal was more than 40 percent. This was good work for a poor man from the mountains.

In the spring of 2007, Bhote climbed Everest twice, once with the South Koreans, and became a favorite of Go Mi-sun, who gave him a digital camera. He was proud of that camera.

In the fall, the South Koreans asked him to climb with them on Shishapangma. He was worried about avalanches and he hesitated. No matter what blessings he called down, the gods would be unhappy. Yet by now his father back in Hatiya was dead from a gastric ulcer, his younger brother Chhiring Bhote was living with him in Kathmandu, and three more sisters had already left the countryside for the capital during the Maoist insurgency, in which the rebels had been rounding up anyone from the villages to fight the government. Jumik needed the money.

By now, he also had a partner, Dawa Sangmu, to support. He and Chhiring and their sisters all lived in their older brother's small apartment in the Boudhanath district near the stupa. The apartment had only four rooms, a kitchen, a dining room, a storeroom, and a small bathroom with a squat toilet. There were no beds, only mats, which during the day they packed away in the storeroom. He knew of no other route to success for a young man such as himself in Nepal. He didn't want to be like another brother of his, who had stayed behind in the village and was drinking himself to death on cheap rice wine, and died shortly before Jumik came to K2.

Bhote went to Shishapangma with Kim and the Koreans and it was a triumph. When he returned to Kathmandhu he had been promoted to lead Sherpa. To celebrate, Bhote spent $2,000 on a big, black secondhand Yamaha motorbike. Dawa got pregnant. She and Jumik moved into a new apartment, only a single room with a shared kitchen, but it was their own.

He still did not relish climbing in the mountains, but he realized they had been good to him. He took other jobs, guiding a banker from New York on a rapid ascent up Mera Peak in the Hinku valley. He learned a bit of Korean from language cassettes bought from Pilgrim's bookstore in Kathmandu. He took a $250 course in high-altitude climbing at the Khumbu Climbing School outside Namche Bazaar near Everest.

In the spring of 2008, he climbed on Lhotse with his brother Chhiring, and in June, despite last-minute misgivings, they left for K2 with the Flying Jump team.

Now, that all seemed such a long time ago. As he waited in the dark above the three Koreans, Bhote wished he had listened to his instinct. His mind was so distracted by the cold that he wasn't sure what happened next. He didn't know whether there was an avalanche or an icefall or whether the top screw had simply come away from where it was fixed.

The rope dropped suddenly and in a dark, roaring, confusing rush Bhote catapulted past the South Koreans.

He crashed painfully into the ice a little way below them and stopped. He was sprawled against a tiny horizontal ledge, held on the mountain by the rope and his harness.

If it had been an icefall that had caused the rope collapse, it had moved on and the lower screws holding the lines in place had held. Two other climbers were dangling above him.

Bhote was able to sit upright but it was a painful struggle to move: his legs and arms ached from the fall and he was tangled in a welter of rope.

Of the two South Korean climbers hanging above him, the one at the top was suspended headfirst against the ice face. His arms reached out toward Bhote. Bhote wasn't sure who it was, though he could see his bloody face.

The second one also lay head-down against the ice but at a less steep angle. Both of the climbers, he saw, were still clipped onto the rope and hanging in their harnesses, which were supporting them.

Bhote felt that if he struggled he could perhaps have gone on. But he wasn't sure if he could stand, and these men were his clients; he had a duty to stay with them. He was, however, confused. He could not see the third Korean climber. Perhaps he had escaped the rope collapse and had gone on; or perhaps the fall had knocked him completely off the mountain; or perhaps Bhote was mistaken and he was never on the rope and was now somewhere up behind above the serac.

Bhote knew he and the other two men couldn't stay where they were for long. He shouted out, calling for help at first, and then out of sheer panic, but he grew tired. The two trapped Koreans also occasionally shouted for help and moaned. Bhote wanted to reassure them, but the cold crept over him and soon he found he had no strength to speak.

He started to cry. He couldn't feel his hands, and that scared him most, since they were his livelihood. He thought of Dawa Sangmu and Jen Jen in Kathmandu. If he died, he thought, there would be insurance money, wouldn't there? More than $5,000.

But Bhote didn't want to die. He didn't want his family to be mourners, walking to the puja at the Boudha stupa, carrying corn nuts for the monkeys and birds as offerings in his honor.

He imagined them stopping on the way to give one-rupee notes to the beggars at Pashupatinath, most of them grateful but some complaining when the notes were old and wrinkled. He imagined his family bringing fruit for the monks in the stupa circle, jingling money into the monks' pockets and lighting candles, before his brother fell prostrate, wailing Jumik's name. His mother screaming in anguish because she believed his death could have been avoided if only she had been a better mother.

Bhote's mind was wandering. His only hope was that rescuers would climb up from Camp Four—or that other teams were still making their way down from the summit and would find them.

CHAPTER THIRTEEN

3 a.m.

Marco Confortola had waded alone along the sloping snowfield from the top of K2. After more than an hour, he had seen headlamps in a line a few dozen yards below him and had followed behind them. He thought they belonged to the Korean team but their faces were obscured by the bright spotlights of their headlamps, which cast hazy penumbrae in the dark twilight.

Near the steep slope before the lip of the glacier, Confortola drew closer to the other mountaineers. He saw they were from the Korean team, though there was another climber with them who turned out to be the Irishman Gerard McDonnell.

Where are the ropes?

McDonnell shrugged.

The group of climbers searched for the route that would lead them around the crusted edge of the giant serac onto the Traverse but to their mounting frustration they could not find any sign of the ropes.

The end of the snowfield curved down abruptly in front of them, a slope of 30 or 40 degrees. Confortola dragged his tired body to the left and then back to the right on the top of the steep slope, willing himself to find the ropes. The fixed lines had to be down there somewhere, though neither he nor McDonnell felt sure that they were on the same path they had followed on the way up onto the snowfield.

And then, when the Flying Jump team lurched ahead toward the lip of the glacier and one after the other went over the top, Confortola held McDonnell back. There was something about the look of the snow that made him uneasy.

Both men knew the risks of staying out overnight. It was ten o'clock. They were exhausted. The night was big and black around them. There was no moon and it was fiercely cold, minus 20, easy. Confortola's altimeter wristwatch said they were at 27,500 feet. They had no tent or sleeping bags, no extra food or oxygen. They knew their lives probably depended on descending quickly through the cold to Camp Four.

But they were on a steep slope and they had no idea where they were or where they were going. The lamp at Camp Four winked about half a mile below them, clearly but beyond their reach. Confortola's instinct told him it was no use looking for a way down anymore. They were better off waiting for daylight, when they could see where they were climbing.

"Let's stay here," he said.

He wanted to be certain that what lay beneath their boots was firm snow and not a crevasse. In addition, there were constant avalanches from these heavy snowfields, big, powerful falls that would crush them if they got caught up in one. Sure enough, minutes later Confortola heard a roll of thunder coming from the serac in front of them, then distant cries and shouts from beneath it. Then silence.

What was that?

I don't know.

Confortola wasn't entirely sure that what he had heard was an avalanche or ice collapsing from the serac but now he felt convinced they were right to stay where they were. They were going to have to bivouac, the term for staying outside without proper shelter under the night sky.

The two climbers sprawled on the steep balcony of snow. McDonnell was wearing his red climbing suit, gray balaclava, and climbing goggles. He was tired, Confortola could see. Confortola wanted to make sure he was making the right decision for them both. He wanted a second opinion, so he took out his satellite phone and called Agostino da Polenza, the president of the Italian Everest-K2 committee, and a friend and mentor. Da Polenza was in Courmayeur, Italy. Confortola explained that he felt uncomfortable about the direction they were taking and that they could not find the ropes. He said he had heard what was probably part of the serac falling.

Confortola didn't expect anyone to climb up to rescue them. He knew what he was doing. Back in Italy he had trained in high-mountain safety and rescue and earned extra euros helping stranded climbers stupid enough to venture onto the steep slopes above his house. He brought them in with curses, sometimes snapping their poles over his knee for good measure.

Da Polenza agreed with him. *Be patient.* "Stay there. Wait for the morning."

Confortola switched off his phone and slid it back into his jacket. "Jesus, let's wait," he said to McDonnell, using the nickname—Jesus—he had given the Irishman, and McDonnell agreed.

Da Polenza had warned him to keep warm; there was a danger of frostbite, which was feared by all mountaineers but common in these cold regions of high altitude. As a person's body cools, it directs blood away from the extremities to preserve its inner heat; even when skin temperature falls to 10 degrees, tissues numb, cells rupture. Hands, feet, nose, cheeks are most vulnerable. In 1996, Beck Weathers, an Everest mountaineer, lost his nose and most of his hands to frostbite.

Confortola felt better after talking to da Polenza. To keep themselves warm and to have a perch on the side of the mountain, the two climbers scooped seats out of the snow with a pole and the picks of their ice axes. Confortola made McDonnell's seat slightly larger so he could lie back down. They also made room for their boots.

Even though McDonnell looked exhausted, Confortola knew that on such a steep slope they couldn't allow themselves to fall asleep. The slope was 30 to 40 degrees and it would be easy to roll down.

"If you want to rest, I'll take care of the situation," he said.

McDonnell lay back, his blue water bottle hanging from his belt and his black and yellow boots planted in the hole they had cut in the snow.

Confortola turned off his headlamp. It was strange to be up there alone. It was dark and cold. The entire world was stretched out below in shadow. He watched the distant lights of Camp Four, and the single powerful light flashing near the tents. The camp seemed so close. They just could not get down to it. He was convinced they would be able to find the ropes easily in the morning.

At Base Camp, Confortola had gotten to know McDonnell during the final weeks of bad weather. When the storms roared in, the Italian was usually doing nothing much but sitting around in the two-man tent, listening to disco music on his iPod, chewing gum to help with the altitude, or taking long walks across the glacier to keep fit. He started calling in at the Dutch tent to discuss strategy, sometimes bringing bresaola to share, while Wilco van Rooijen or Cas van de Gevel prepared the basic cappuccinos.

He liked them all but he got along best with McDonnell, the handsome Irishman with the wonderful smile. McDonnell had let his hair grow long and had grown a beard, so Confortola had given him the nickname Jesus. McDonnell invited Confortola into his tent and showed him some of his photographs on his laptop—of the waxing moon over K2 or of his girlfriend, Annie, in Alaska or of Ireland. McDonnell took his photography seriously. Neither spoke much of the other's language but they understood climbing.

Outside his tent, above a string of Tibetan prayer flags, McDonnell hung a big Irish flag. He had had it hand-stitched by a tailor in Skardu. Confortola liked to joke with him: "It's just the Italian flag, all mixed up," he said, poking his friend in the ribs.

Now, as the night deepened on the mountain, Confortola forced himself to shiver to stay warm, gently shaking his arms and legs and clapping. Confortola's body bore the history of his mountaineering life. Tattooed around his right wrist was a Tibetan prayer from his 2004 Everest ascent. Another tattoo across the back of his neck spelled out *Salvadek*, or wild animal, which was how he liked to think of himself. He always wore a ring in his left ear. A self-styled "pirate of the mountains," at home he was known as a risk taker and headstrong. He liked fast bikes and speed skiing. In the mountaineering community, he was known as a wily survivor, a man with a big heart and good intentions, if also a little vain. Back in Italy, some other climbers called him, half in mocking jest, "Santa Caterina Iron Man." Around his right bicep he had a ring of six star tattoos celebrating the six peaks above 26,000 feet he had climbed so far in his life—soon now, there would be a seventh for K2.

Away to his left stretched the undulating top of the Great Serac. To his right the slope curved around to a huge gray buttress of rocks and the northern side of K2. In front of him hung the great emptiness beyond the serac.

Somewhere below was the way down into the Traverse. He could still see the light flashing at Camp Four. Everyone else who had made it to the summit must have climbed down onto the ropes and were probably back at their tents by now, he thought. The climbers down there had no idea where they were and if they were alive or dead. He and McDonnell were alone. He didn't know if anyone was still behind them on the summit snowfield.

Confortola was not worried. They were not going to die. They would escape their aerie in the morning. It was uncomfortable, that was all. Cold. To keep his blood circulating, Confortola stood up a few times and walked around the two holes he and McDonnell had dug in the snow.

Then the time passed slowly. The two men were both so cold and exhausted that Confortola was afraid they were in danger of falling asleep. To keep them awake, Confortola began to hum one of his favorite songs, a song from Italy, from the mountains. "La Montanara."

Lassu' per le montagne (Up there in the mountains)
fra boschi e valli d'or (among woods and valleys of gold)
fra l'aspre rupi echeggia (among the rugged cliffs there echoes)
un cantico d'amor (a canticle of love).

Beside him, McDonnell seemed to respond to the singing and moved his body.

"Don't give up, Jesus," Confortola said, and he was saying it to himself as well.

McDonnell was a singer, too. During the bad weather in Base Camp, when many of the climbers feared they would have to cancel their climbs, the Dutch team's camp manager, Sajjad Shan, an impish twenty-nine-year-old Islamabad taxi driver, organized a party to lift the depressed mood. He pushed together three large mess tents and paid an assistant cook to sing, although the cook knew only two songs, one in Urdu and one in Balti. The porters started drumming on the food barrels. Some of the climbers began to dance. An expedition had arrived in camp with seven cases of beer and whisky. The Serbs paid a runner to fetch twenty-four half-liter cans of beer from Askole. Stepping forward into the silence, McDonnell sang a Gaelic ballad that moved some of the fifty climbers packed into the warm tent to tears.

They said the song had to be about the love of a boy for his lass. But McDonnell said, "No, it's about the yearning of a shepherd for his goat."

McDonnell liked Confortola but then he liked most people at Base Camp. He loved the beauty and isolation of the mountain, but the camaraderie of expedition life also appealed to him. The Dutch team's bulbous tents were perched on the rocks close to the camps of Hugues d'Aubarède and Cecilie Skog. Around Base Camp, McDonnell often carried his video camera, with its small microphone boom, and he filmed the teams' strategy meetings.

On free afternoons, he regularly walked over for a chat with Rolf Bae or with Deedar, the cook for the American expedition. Deedar had cared for McDonnell when he suffered the devastating rock blow to his head on K2 in 2006. Among the Dutch team, he was especially close to Pemba Gyalje and had helped the Sherpa to build a small rock altar for a puja ceremony when they arrived on K2; they played chants from an MP3 player.

On a small computer, he tapped out text messages to his family in Ireland and to Annie, who for a few weeks during this time was climbing Mount McKinley, North America's highest peak. He posted thoughts to his blog. Alone at night, he lay in his tent, listening to the cracks and groans of the Godwin-Austen glacier—shifting more than usual this year, he thought.

"Night now," he wrote in one dispatch, "and one hears the glacier ache beneath and settle with sound of distant gun shots at times. Stars galore and silhouettes surround. Best of luck on Denali, Annie."

Annie sent piles of letters to him in Base Camp, which were carried up from Islamabad by the company that had arranged their expedition, Jasmine Tours. He called hi mother every Sunday. She sent him holy water.

McDonnell was feeling hungry and thirsty and tired now. Under stress, at these altitudes the body did not function normally in a number of ways, and he hadn't been able to eat properly for days. When he had tried, he had not been able to keep anything down.

For Wilco van Rooijen, the joy of the summit had soon evaporated in the pain of the heavy summit snowfield. He was so tired he had fallen behind the other climbers and lost sight of their headlamps.

He laid his exhausted body down and fell asleep in the snow. When he woke up, he climbed lower for several long minutes, but he couldn't shake the vague sense that he had taken a wrong turn. The snows looked unfamiliar and he wasn't coming to the abrupt drop down to the fixed ropes. So he veered back to the right for several hundred yards across the top of the serac. It was then that he heard the sound of someone whistling shrilly.

About one hundred yards away he noticed a headlamp. When he got closer he saw in the light of his own headlamp Marco Confortola, who was standing up and shouting at the top of his voice. Beside him sat the hunched figure of Gerard McDonnell.

He realized they were trying to attract the attention of people down at Camp Four. He wondered where everyone else was and why Confortola and McDonnell were just sitting there. Why weren't they searching for the ropes down? But then Van Rooijen saw that they were in trouble. Confortola was massaging McDonnell's knees.

"Gerard is cold," the Italian said in his halting English. "We can't find the way down." Confortola had hoped Van Rooijen was someone who could show them the way down and he was disappointed that the Dutchman was lost, too. "Not safe out there," he added.

Confortola said that he thought they were in the wrong area. He described the crashing sound he had heard. Looking back toward the part of the snowfield where Van Rooijen had come from, he asked whether they should try in that direction. Van Rooijen shook his head and said it wasn't the right way, either.

"I am lost," he said above the wind, which was picking up. "We must be able to see something we recognize."

The three men began to explore the snows again. The balcony of ice thrust out and down for a few hundred yards before dropping away. Feeling their way out a little distance, Van Rooijen went to the right, Confortola to the left, both men zig-zagging down the snow. McDonnell stayed where he was in the center.

With the help of his headlamp, Van Rooijen looked over the edge of a steep drop. Seeing the thick black air above a chasm, he realized that Confortola was talking sense after all. There was no way down here. Where were the fixed lines?

Far below, headlamps bobbed lower toward Camp Four. They tempted him. He turned and started to climb down but he had gone only a few feet when he heard Confortola behind him calling out loudly that he thought the snow was unsafe. Van Rooijen stopped himself and climbed back up. Confortola was right; it wasn't worth it.

When he reached the other two climbers, his headlamp lighting up the reflectors on their suits, he said, "Let's stay." But now it was Gerard McDonnell's turn to be seized by panic, warning that they couldn't stay there overnight. They had to try one last time to attract the attention of the people at Camp Four, he said. They would signal the way they had to go to get down. After a minute or two of yelling, however, they realized it was no use. There was no alternative but to bivouac for the night.

It was risky—some would say stupid—to stay on a mountain like K2 above 26,000 feet. Since they were proficient mountaineers, they should have been able to climb down the Traverse and the Bottleneck even without fixed ropes. They should never have been in this position in the first place. But having made up their minds, they settled back in the snow.

McDonnell sat in the middle; Confortola sat on his left-hand side; and Van Rooijen perched on the right. They turned their backs to the wind. It was not snowing. But as they hunched over, their coats were soon plastered with snow blown by the gusts.

Van Rooijen had bivouacked countless times before in the Alps, and often on the more perilous north face of high peaks, when the interminably falling snow filled the space behind your back until you felt you were going to be pushed off the edge. In comparison, he felt, this was easy. He was also in good company. He looked at the other two men. The emergency mountain rescue expert. And McDonnell, whom he could trust with his life.

Van Rooijen didn't even bother to take his satellite phone out of his jacket to call anyone. When the sun rose, they would act fast, descend quickly. In a few hours he would be down in Camp Four. Then they could tell everyone about their adventure in person.

———

Marco Confortola watched as the sky started to brighten at about 4 or 5 a.m.

"Let's go," he said, shaking himself.

Wilco van Rooijen was already on his feet, wading through the snow to the left-hand side of the ridge. McDonnell crossed to the right-hand edge while Confortola walked ahead to look directly over the head of the serac.

They were impatient. They wanted to lose altitude and relieve their bodies, which had existed above 26,000 feet for thirty-six hours. They wanted to get warm again.

They spent about half an hour looking for the ropes or a way down over the tip of the serac, until one by one they gave up and returned to the middle.

When he came back to the other two men, Van Rooijen muttered something but Confortola and McDonnell couldn't understand what he was saying.

Then to their surprise Van Rooijen turned away, strode forward, and began to back over the edge of the ridge.

CHAPTER FOURTEEN

6 a.m.

Wilco van Rooijen took a direct line down from the top of the glacier, backing slowly lower, securing his ice axe and feeling for each step with the points of his crampons.

While he had been searching for the fixed ropes to the left of the bivouac, Van Rooijen had realized something was wrong with his eyes. The eye is especially vulnerable at high altitude, where ultraviolet light is more intense than at sea level. Without protection, the ultraviolet radiation inflames the outer covering of the eyeball, resulting in excruciatingly painful snow blindness.

Van Rooijen recognized the symptoms because he had suffered the same problem at the North and South Poles. Dehydration, he was convinced, made it worse, and he was desperately thirsty. It had been a hot summit day and, foolishly, he had dropped his flask in the Traverse on the way up, so he hadn't had a drink since then.

Now he knew he had to get down immediately. If he didn't, and his eyes got slowly worse, he would be trapped.

Van Rooijen struggled to keep himself from panicking. On K2, the altitude was going to kill anyone in the end. And it was finally killing him. *Shit.* It only took a small mistake to slip and fall. He couldn't expect Confortola and McDonnell to carry him down, and no helicopter could get up to this height to rescue him. It was imperative that he descend quickly. He wasn't going to wait for Confortola and McDonnell. They hadn't reacted when he told them. They were too tired and too absorbed in searching for the ropes. He had to save himself.

Now he climbed down, not knowing where he was or where he was going. The slope was so steep that the other two climbers disappeared from view within a few yards.

Van Rooijen knew that somewhere behind him were K2's vast lower gullies and the distant glaciers at the valley floor, all opening out beneath the dark morning sky. He had a suspicion that by getting lost on the snowfield he, Confortola, and McDonnell had wandered onto a completely different side of K2. He didn't think he was near the Traverse and the lines that the teams had fixed on the way up.

However, three hundred feet into the climb down, he saw a rope a few yards away. He didn't recognize it; some other expedition must have fixed it on an alternative route, he thought. Nevertheless, he clipped on to it and it gave him some encouragement.

Then, facing the mountain, he glanced to his right and saw, only two yards away across the ice face, a dreadful scene.

Three climbers were hanging from ropes against the smooth ice wall leading down from the glacier. They were tangled in two ropes, one of which was still attached to their harnesses. It was keeping them from falling to their deaths.

At first Van Rooijen thought he must have simply lost his mind. It took him a few moments to accept they were real. *Who were they? How did they get here?* He didn't know which part of the upper mountain he was on, so as far as he knew, these strangers belonged to a completely different expedition than the ones he had climbed up with the day before. They could have climbed onto K2 from the Chinese side.

He focused on the trapped climbers. They were beaten up and bloody and unrecognizable.

The first one was dangling upside down, his harness wrapped around his feet. He was moaning from the pain and cold. His face was so badly smashed that Van Rooijen couldn't tell who he was. A large camera swung from his chest.

About thirty feet below him, the second climber was also hanging upside down but at a less steep angle. He seemed to be supporting himself with one hand on a ledge, and was almost lying down, but he was staring ahead listlessly, as if he had given up. Just a few feet below him, the third climber sat upright, awake and looking terrified.

It was a horrific sight. The three men had suffered a brutal fall and then must have been hanging there for hours in the subzero temperatures. They had been slowly freezing to death. Van Rooijen especially pitied the man at the top, the blood running to his head, barely able to breathe.

But even though they looked desperate, Van Rooijen, who himself was clinging to the side of the mountain, wondered what he could do. If he tried to untangle the ropes or cut them, the climbers would fall. Even if he were successful in freeing them from the ropes, the climbers could not walk for themselves, he thought. He had no strength left to lift them. And every extra minute he stayed with them, his eyesight was getting worse and he was becoming ever more befuddled by the altitude.

When the Dutchman climbed down to the third climber, the man asked him for help. He had lost his gloves. Van Rooijen handed him a spare pair.

"I have to go," Van Rooijen said. "Okay? I am going snow blind."

"I radio already," the climber said. Van Rooijen didn't recognize the accent. The climber added that people were coming up to rescue him.

His words made Van Rooijen feel better about going on. Still, he hesitated. It was against every instinct in his body to leave the climbers. If he left them, and the rescuers didn't come, he would be abandoning them to die. But Van Rooijen had to save himself. He had his own struggle for survival ahead of him. He couldn't help these men.

Still he hesitated. He stayed with the climbers for just a few minutes. Then he left them and continued to drop down the side of the mountain.

Van Rooijen's thirst was so desperate and he was so concerned about his eyesight that he had no time to worry about whether following an untested route down the side of K2 was a wise idea and whether it would lead him to safer ground or to a dead end.

The ice and rocks were steep and he held on with his wet gloves. He felt for each next step with the teeth of his right crampon.

On a stretch of icy rocks, he couldn't find a place to put his boot. Switching the way he was standing, he reached down with his left boot, but he fumbled, his boot slipping out from under him, scratching against the rock, and he managed to save himself only by gripping on to the mountain face with his fingers.

A few hundred feet later, the rope ended, and he climbed down without its support. The climbing became steeper, until finally, a few more yards on, he stood at the top of a stretch of sheer brown rocks and realized there was no way past them. He tried desperately to keep his balance as the world swirled thousands of feet below him. He laid his forehead against the rock. Every instinct told him to get lower in order to breathe oxygen and, when he reached camp, to drink water. The idea of climbing back up again was hateful but there was no other choice. He realized he had to do it.

Ascending through the ice and snow was far tougher than climbing down because he was so exhausted, and for every three painful steps up, Van Rooijen slid two back. He counted the steps and then stopped to refill his lungs.

The sun was higher now and he was hot. He forced himself to breathe through his nose, not his mouth, to keep the moisture in.

Once when he stopped, he slumped forward on his ice axe and, without meaning to, fell asleep. When he woke up, he blinked into the sun.

He saw he was getting closer to the place where the three trapped climbers had been hanging. Squinting, he thought he could make out two other figures with them now. Marco Confortola and Gerard McDonnell must have descended and were trying to help them, he thought. They were still a few hundred yards away from him.

Above him to the left were huge fists of black rocks, and to the right was a possible route beneath a serac. The serac looked as frightening and dangerous as the one he had passed under on the way up to the summit. He wasn't going to be able to make it all the way back to where he had started, so he could either follow the rocks around the western edge of the mountain, though he had no idea where that path would take him, or he could go under the serac.

He called out to McDonnell and Confortola, hoping they could see which direction he should take.

"Marco! Gerard!" His voice was hoarse. "Which way? Can you see? Left or right?"

He gripped the rocks and repeated the question but his voice was weak and they couldn't hear him. Then he went right, moving out under the serac.

Below him was a drop of thousands of feet and he still didn't know where he was heading. Yet, after about a hundred feet, he saw another rope fixed to a screw. That was good news. Traversing toward it, he clipped on to the rope and followed it.

It was taking him on some sort of route, although it looked unfamiliar. When he saw four oxygen bottles hanging from the next screw, he began to recognize where he was. He thought it had to be the Traverse. This was the same route he had followed on the way up. But it looked completely different. The snow was blasted away in sections on the slopes and there had been icefalls.

He reached a place where the rope hung diagonally over a huge rump of rocks. He rappelled down and after a few minutes he recognized Gerard McDonnell's 5mm Spectra line. Then Van Rooijen saw the Bottleneck and was elated.

He let go of the end of the rope and descended carefully until the ground started to level out. By now, however, clouds had started to blow around him.

At the lower altitude, Van Rooijen's eyesight was improving, at least temporarily. His next goal was to reach Camp Four. He was soon disappointed. The clouds had grown thicker around him and he couldn't make out the way along the Shoulder.

He climbed down several yards farther but the whiteout forced him to stop. He could see nothing. Below him somewhere was the Shoulder and the safety of Camp Four, but there also lurked crevasses and the steep drops on both sides of the long ridge. It was too much of a risk. He couldn't go on.

Faced by a cold wall of fog, Van Rooijen sat down. He fumed with frustration and with disappointment in himself. He had studied the history of K2. He knew how tough it was to find the high camp on the descent; that's why he had brought a lightweight GPS and a strobe light to the mountain. But when he had set out the day before, the weather had seemed so perfect, and the other teams had promised to put up flags and bamboo sticks and fish lines to guide climbers on the Shoulder. That was all part of the cooperation agreement. So he had left his GPS and the light behind in the tent. He thought now how reassuring it would be to hold the GPS or to have the fish line leading him down.

What a mess! Despite Van Rooijen's pains to assemble a team worthy of taking on K2, he thought, the Dutch expedition had become entangled with lesser climbers. They had forgotten equipment they had promised; they had underestimated the sheer difficulties of this climb. He was not saying the other climbers were incompetent. Most of them were good enough. But there was the beginning of the trend on K2 that had afflicted Everest decades ago. Unqualified climbers paying big money to come to a mountain they had no business attempting. With just a click on the Internet you got a place on a trip.

Van Rooijen remembered his satellite telephone tucked away inside his coat, and a new hope began to form in his mind. He pulled the phone out, nearly dropping it, then cradled it carefully. But when he held the Thuraya's glowing screen a few inches from his face to read the numbers stored in the electronic address book, he could not see them.

His thumb flicked desperately through the list. He wanted to call the Dutch team's main point man in the Netherlands, Maarten van Eck. Van Eck, he thought, would know what to do.

Van Rooijen tried to type in his friend's number but he couldn't remember it and the call failed to connect. Eventually he realized that the only number he knew by heart was his own in Utrecht, where his wife would be waiting. Though she might be out at the day-care center where she worked.

Van Rooijen dialed the number, and Heleen picked up. She was sitting on the sofa with their son, Teun. Heleen had not heard anything from her husband in three days and she had begun to give up hope that he was alive.

"Where are you?" she asked.

Relieved to hear her voice, Van Rooijen spoke quickly, telling Heleen about the bivouac and about leaving Confortola and McDonnell.

"I am alive," he told her. "But I can't see and I am lost. I don't know where I am."

Van Rooijen described his thirst but he tried to reassure her and said he thought he could see Base Camp so he knew he would get a drink soon. Even as he spoke, though, he realized in another part of his mind that he was babbling and making no sense. Base Camp was in reality still nearly 10,000 feet below him.

Then, as he was talking to Heleen, he saw shadows moving in the distance, which he thought were climbers in the fog. He told Heleen, and she shouted into the phone that he had to go toward them. But within a moment the shadows were gone. Van Rooijen realized he couldn't trust his own senses.

"Listen, write this down," he said, trying to stay as matter-of-fact as he could. He estimated his altitude as being about 600 feet above Camp Four. "I am at seventy-eight hundred meters on the south side. Below the Bottleneck. Call Maarten and ask him to call Base Camp."

He told Heleen he would call her back within the next twenty-four hours. "Don't worry," he assured her. "I am safe."

After she had hung up, Van Rooijen realized how alone he was. She had seemed so close, and now she was gone.

————————

Maarten van Eck, a fifty-one-year-old businessman with silver-tinged black hair and square platinum-colored glasses, was sitting in the kitchen of his two-story houseboat, the *Archimedes*, on the Merwede Canal in Utrecht when Heleen called to tell him about Van Rooijen.

It was here on the boat that Van Eck had set up what he liked to call K2 Base Camp Netherlands—essentially a kitchen table with three computers and a bank of phones. He had spent the previous few nights sleeping on his couch to be ready to take calls and updates from Wilco and the gang on K2. They had an agreement that on the descent Van Rooijen would call in at specified points—the start of the fixed lines, the Bottleneck, Camp Four—but he had heard nothing from him since the summit.

After reassuring Heleen, Van Eck called the Dutch climbers in the tents at the real K2 Base Camp in Pakistan and they radioed up the mountain to Pemba Gyalje, who was waiting at Camp Four.

In the whiteout above the high camp, Van Rooijen's Thuraya rang and he greeted Gyalje.

The Sherpa asked him to describe his location.

"I really don't know where I am exactly," Van Rooijen said. He squinted into the mist. There was snow and great hulks of rocks but nothing that struck him as familiar.

"I think I am near Camp Four."

Gyalje said he and Cas van de Gevel were coming up to find him. He told Van Rooijen to climb down toward them.

"Come down but keep left," Gyalje said. "Don't go right because that's the south face. We are coming up. We will shout."

Van Rooijen climbed down through the snow, excited now. Surely they couldn't miss each other. He didn't know what he would do if this plan failed. He called their names.

"Cas! Cas! Pemba! Pemba!"

He could already imagine their reunion.

A dark figure appeared in the distance in the swirling fog but it turned out to be a rock. Van Rooijen saw another shape and climbed down toward it. "Cas!" Again it was the mountain playing tricks on him.

After descending a few more feet, he abruptly stopped, feeling uneasy.

As the fog shifted, he saw he was standing above a steep drop. He turned slowly, then retreated quickly back up the slope. He had been close to falling. He saw a way to the right and climbed down in that direction, though it took him among huge rocks.

He began to get the disturbing feeling that he had missed Van de Gevel and Gyalje. He stopped and realized it was true. The world around him was cold and empty; he was lost and alone again.

The feeling was devastating. And now Van Rooijen was afraid that in trying to reach his rescuers he had strayed onto the big southern face, far down the wrong side of the Shoulder. Continuing in this direction meant getting even more lost, or at some point slipping unnoticed into the thousand-foot gullies beneath him. But it would take too much effort to climb back the way he had come. He couldn't face it. So he went on.

As he climbed down, he called Heleen again. He was worried the call wouldn't go through on the satellite because there was often a difficult connection, but she picked up on the first ring.

"Where are you?" he heard her say. "Can you see any other mountains? Can you see Broad Peak?"

"I am sure I am at Camp Four," he said abruptly. "Just tell Maarten. I am at Camp Four," he insisted. Hanging up, he regretted his blunt tone.

He continued down. He wanted to breathe the air of the lower altitudes and he wanted water. He looked longingly at the snow. He knew the snow had no calories; you lost energy melting it inside your body, and once he started eating it, it would taste so good he wouldn't be able to stop. Still, he hacked out a chunk with his ice axe, rubbed it against his lips, and swallowed a few flakes. They burned his mouth, yet for a few glorious moments they quenched his thirst. To avoid blisters and numb his throat, the next time he dropped the snow directly down into his throat.

Wherever he saw a safe stretch of ice or rock in front of him, Van Rooijen put his boot there and stepped another few inches lower. *Down, down,* he told himself, despite the exhaustion he was feeling. He fell asleep, then woke up angrily and forced himself on. Then he came to a point where the mountain face sank beneath him in the fog and there was no place to put his boot. Not to the right or to the left or straight ahead.

Folding his legs, he sat down. He grabbed his knees closer, trying to keep in the warmth. He had, he thought, reached the end.

Sitting on the precipice, he rested his head on the stone behind him and he reflected that K2 was such a beautiful peak, but that now amid the dark rocks and clouds it had turned ugly. He was trapped in a nightmarish otherworld of shifting fogs and bottomless voids. This was a place no man or woman was ever meant to be.

He tried to call again on the Thuraya but the batteries were either too cold or dead. He saw a group of climbers nearby and called out to them for help, but they disappeared.

CHAPTER FIFTEEN

7 a.m.

Up at the end of the summit snowfield, Marco Confortola and Gerard McDonnell followed the route Van Rooijen had taken lower around the edge of the serac. As they lowered themselves down, the two men could barely believe that the Dutchman had abandoned them. The altitude, the lack of oxygen, and the exhaustion must have finally driven Van Rooijen out of his mind.

Backing down several yards, Confortola saw three climbers off to the right. They were trapped in ropes and hanging several yards apart from one another against the rough ice on the side of the mountain. Some other lengths of old rope also hung down between the rocks. Confortola remembered the cries he had heard in the darkness the night before.

McDonnell was about eighteen feet above him, and Confortola called up to tell him to come and look at what he had discovered.

"Come here, Gerard!" he cried, his voice growing louder. "Come here!"

He couldn't tell who the climber at the top was. He was dangling headfirst down the slope. But Confortola recognized the big camera hanging around his neck. It was a German Rollei; one of the South Koreans in the Flying Jump team had owned a similar camera.

Confortola could recognize the climber at the bottom—he was a Sherpa. He had lost a boot; the man's left foot, exposed to the air, was covered only by a sock.

All three climbers seemed to be alive, though it looked to Confortola as if they were barely hanging on. He wondered why Van Rooijen had not stopped to help them. Maybe the Dutchman hadn't even noticed the climbers, although he must have passed close by. Van Rooijen had perhaps concluded that he couldn't do anything.

When Confortola looked down, he could see Van Rooijen about four hundred feet below them. He had descended rapidly but had now stopped and appeared to be peering tentatively over a stretch of steep rocks. McDonnell had come down closer to Confortola, and the two men whistled to Van Rooijen to tell him to change route, but it seemed he couldn't hear them.

Confortola, too, was doubtful about what he could do to help the trapped men. These guys had been hanging all night. Confortola and McDonnell had to think of themselves. But at the same time, Confortola thought, if the three men were going to die, it was better they died respectably, and not hanging upside down like carcasses.

McDonnell was already lifting up the head of the climber at the top, trying to make him more comfortable. He had a history of aiding mountaineers in distress—he had been awarded a Denali pin in 1998 for bravery on Mount McKinley and in 2003 he had helped an older Irish climber descend from near the top of Everest after his oxygen failed.

It took only a moment for Confortola to decide to help his friend. He knew that he could never have left these men.

Their first task had to be to relieve the suffering of the top Korean with the camera by turning him the right way up. They also had to untangle his harness, which was wrapped around his legs. Then they could lower him down to the other two climbers, where the slope was less steep.

The three climbers were hanging on a steep face of ice and snow. Confortola and McDonnell were a few yards away on a marginally less steep incline, about 30 to 40 degrees. If they could untangle or cut the rope, they could lift the climbers across and make them more secure.

"Give me a hand so I can help these people," said Confortola. "If you hold the head of the first guy up, I can try to get his harness off."

They had to be careful because the climbers were dangerously intertwined. When they tried to pull one of the men closer, another swung out, threatening to take all three down with them. They also had to think of themselves because they were not protected by ropes. It was going to be a terrifying balancing act.

McDonnell braced himself and held up the head of the first climber. Confortola descended a few yards to test the state of the ropes and to see whether he could untangle them or whether it was safe to try to cut them. He realized, though, that the ropes were too tight to untangle, and they were supporting the climbers; severing them would cause the men to tumble down the mountain. He searched for an extra loose bit of rope he might use, and for some spare oxygen cylinders.

He saw that the two climbers at the bottom had oxygen cylinders. They were next to their backpacks among the ropes. But the men were missing oxygen masks, which must have been lost in the fall.

The second climber was unconscious, he discovered. When Confortola reached him, he initially thought it was a Sherpa. But he realized later that it was Park Kyeong-hyo, one of the South Korean climbers. From his harness, Confortola retrieved a yellow and gray knife. A few yards away a yellow Grivel axe lay on the ice. Confortola thought he might be able to use the knife and axe to do something with the ropes. Holding both like weapons, he climbed back up to a position a few yards above McDonnell and the uppermost Korean. There he cut ten yards of old rope from one of the spare lengths.

Dropping a few yards, he rammed the Grivel axe into a crack in the ice and secured the rope around it. He tied the other end of the rope around the Korean's waist, and then he opened the man's harness. He took the weight of the Korean from McDonnell and began to lower him down.

All this took a long time, more than an hour, it seemed, although Confortola wasn't sure how long. He and McDonnell had been exchanging only a few words as they worked, and Confortola now realized that McDonnell had gone quiet.

When he looked up, he saw that McDonnell was climbing back up the ice face toward the top of the glacier.

"Where are you going?" he called.

At first he thought his friend was climbing higher to take a photograph for evidence. But when the Irishman continued to climb past the ropes, Confortola became alarmed. He didn't know where his friend was going.

"Jesus! Come back! Jesuuus!"

There was no answer. Without turning around, McDonnell scaled the slope and disappeared around the edge of the serac.

Confortola was mortified. The altitude must finally have gotten to McDonnell's brain. No wonder, after everything he had been through. The bivouac. No oxygen. No water. The horror of the trapped climbers. His mind had been plunged into delirium and perhaps he thought he still had to reach the summit.

Confortola paused to consider what he could do now that he was left alone. He stared up at the top of the serac but McDonnell had really gone. He couldn't climb up after his friend. Should he descend now? Was he going to lose his mind like McDonnell?

The sun was bright but he was freezing, hungry, and so tired. Anger, however, gave him new energy. He climbed down to the first climber. He was on a less steep slope and Confortola secured him and propped him upright with a ski pole so that he could breathe more easily. He also lifted the second climber to a sitting position. He hadn't freed them from the ropes entirely because it was the ropes that were keeping them on the mountain.

He climbed down the final few yards to the Sherpa, who was awake. Confortola didn't know his name. The man was confused but of the three he was the least injured. His foot had been exposed for the entire night, and in a weak voice he begged the Italian to help him.

Confortola urged him to stay calm. The Italian took his own outer high-altitude glove from his right hand and pulled it over the man's left sock.

"I call for rescue with the radio," he said to the Sherpa.

He had seen a radio microphone coiling from one of the climbers' jackets and he thought he could see the radio set down the slope, where it must have fallen on the ice. Confortola climbed down slowly, careful not to slip, and retrieved it.

When he held it in his hand, he shouted into the mouthpiece, and heard the voices of two Sherpas answering him. *Emergency!* he shouted. Confortola explained where he was and what had happened. *But I'm exhausted. It's impossible for me to help anymore. Come quickly.*

About this time, a strong avalanche roar sounded somewhere across the mountain, and Confortola realized he had to be quick. The serac was unstable.

He had spent three hours with the trapped climbers. It was going to take another four to get down to Camp Four. Now he climbed above the three men and shoved his own axe in the ice to give further support for the ropes. Then he left them and crossed down toward the Traverse, which yawned without fixed lines. He thought of the roar he had heard earlier and guessed that ice may have fallen from the serac and swept the lines away.

Confortola went vertical, scrambling out onto the slope beneath the serac on his crampon tips. He only had one outer glove. His feet felt heavy and numb. Because he had left his axe in the ropes with the three trapped climbers, he had to use the point of his ski pole as an axe to support him, thrusting it like a dagger into the ice. In that way, he pulled himself across, staring straight at the face, feeling the frightening overhang of ice above him and not daring to look at the drop below.

He was relieved when the end of the Traverse came close. He wanted to get out from under the serac.

Here he found a length of what seemed like old rope that he followed down into the Bottleneck. It was still hard climbing, and he was exhausted, but it was easier than it had been in the Traverse. He felt some relief.

When he came off the rope, he paused, hot and thirsty. He wished he could rip off his heavy suit to get some air. Several yards down in the gully he noticed an ice axe lying in the snow. It had probably been dropped by another climber. It would be invaluable to him, but to get to it he would have to climb down and across the ice for twenty yards. As he climbed out to reach it, his boot caught on a piece of ice and he tripped.

Confortola rolled fast straight down the gully, bumping hard against the ice, screaming and thrusting his arms out and kicking his legs, desperate to stop himself. This was it. He knew he was going to die.

He rolled for about ten yards before he stopped himself. He lay back on the snow, breathing hard. He was alive.

Standing up slowly, he found his legs and arms were stiff but he was uninjured. He had lost his other glove, however.

He climbed down several more feet, though he wasn't sure exactly how far he went. He was not sure of distances anymore. He was close to the Shoulder, but still within range of any avalanche from the serac, when he heard an explosion.

Several hundred yards away, up at the top of the big glacier, a huge avalanche cloud burst from the head of the serac. The ice and snow poured down across the Traverse and pummeled into the rocks at the side of the Bottleneck.

There were big chunks of ice, tumbling and bouncing down over the rocks, followed by hovering clouds of snow, rolling in a channel beside the Bottleneck but also beginning to spread out across the gully.

Confortola watched, transfixed, his ears filled with the great rushing groan of the avalanche. The ice river bounced and poured toward him: within a few seconds, surely, he would be engulfed. But the avalanche's momentum slowed, the snow cloud died away, and only a few tributaries passed close by, stopping about thirty feet away from him.

As the avalanche had poured down from the Traverse, he had noticed something yellow caught up in the ice. He thought he had recognized something. Gerard McDonnell had been wearing yellow and black climbing boots.

Now, a few yards away, there was a dark spot in the snow. When Confortola crossed down to it he saw blood streaked across the ice and human remains. He saw bits of brain and a human eye, a blue eye. He picked the eye up and held it for a moment in his hand, staring at it, and then he placed it back down again.

Confortola knelt in the snow. He felt hopeless. He thought about McDonnell, about the good times they had had in Base Camp. *Gerard. Jesus.* He couldn't be sure, and his mind was struggling to function properly in the altitude. But he thought that McDonnell had probably climbed up onto the top of the glacier after he had left the three trapped climbers and he had been hit by the avalanche.

After a few minutes, Confortola forced himself to stand and he climbed down.

He hated the mountain now and wanted to go home. But he was so tired that several minutes later, he stopped and lay down on his back in the snow.

He told himself he could not fall asleep. He had to fight the feeling that the mountain had finally gotten him. But it felt good to rest at last, to lay his head against the slope and close his eyes, forgetting what he had witnessed.

His hands burned with the cold, and he put them behind his head, tucking them inside his hood.

Clouds crept over the slope and slowly snow started to fall. Confortola didn't move.

What must have been minutes later, he shook himself awake.

"Marco! Marco!"

Someone was standing over him, calling his name, and trying to thrust an oxygen mask over his face.

CHAPTER SIXTEEN

8 a.m.

Eric Meyer and Fred Strang were surprised by Pemba Gyalje's appearance when he came to the door of their tent. The usually stoic man was nearly hysterical.

They unzipped the nylon tent door and helped him inside and onto the mats.

"Come on in," Meyer said in a soft voice, seeing that the Sherpa needed comforting. "What's wrong? Sit down."

The two men were resting on their sleeping bags. They helped Gyalje sit against some gear, made him tea, and told him he had to calm down. The tea would help him rehydrate.

Gyalje looked exhausted and was barely able to lift his head.

He had been up for most of the night since he had come down from the Bottleneck. He was zipped up in his dark blue Feathered Friends climbing suit. His breath billowed out in the cold air.

He started to cry as he told Meyer his account of how he had found the ropes cut in the Traverse and how he had made it down. Gyalje was a survivor, Meyer could see, but he had had to draw on deep reserves to descend and it had cost him.

It seemed to Meyer and Strang that Gyalje was also feeling guilty because though he was safe, his friends Wilco van Rooijen and Gerard McDonnell had still not made it down. Yet he was terrified about returning to the Bottleneck.

"What can I do?" he said, rubbing his eyes with the heels of his hands. "I am feeling bad."

Earlier, before dawn, he had confronted Big Pasang Bhote and Chhiring Bhote before they left Camp Four, urging them not to go back up into the Bottleneck to search for survivors. It was too dangerous. He suspected that Kim, the South Korean leader, was pushing them to go up there because the three Koreans were missing—Park Kyeong-hyo, Kim Hyo-gyeong, and Hwang Dong-jin. But the two Sherpas had told him they were going of their own free will. They wanted to go because Jumik Bhote had still failed to return.

Talking now to Meyer and Strang, Gyalje was adamant that they all should descend from Camp Four soon. None of them should stay at that altitude for many more hours, he said.

"We must go down," Gyalje said. "Before we lose more energy. The weather is also getting worse."

Meyer realized Gyalje could use some of his doctor's help. He shook some pills into Gyalje's hand, dexamethasone, dextroamphetamine, and 200 milligrams of Provigil. The capsules seemed to help; Gyalje soon seemed more alert. He said he was going back to his tent to rest.

The sun rose and Meyer and Strang went outside. At this altitude, the dawn was quick and already the sun's rays shone on the Bottleneck and the hanging glacier. The air temperature, which had dropped sharply during the night, had risen again and was a few degrees above freezing. They could see the slopes. A dozen or so climbers were standing around the tents—including Go and Kim and the six or seven members of the Korean B team, and the group of the other mountaineers who had been expecting to make a summit attempt today but had now called it off.

Everyone was staring up at the mountain. Meyer could see the day was going to be stunning again; the air was so clear. The sky arched over the summit. Crystals of snow seemed to jump across the waves of the Shoulder, where the wands and red flags Marco Confortola had set the day before fluttered in the breeze.

At about 7 a.m., Cecilie Skog and Lars Nessa walked over to the Americans' tent. Skog borrowed Strang's satellite phone to call their manager in Norway who was going to let Rolf Bae's parents know about his death.

She spoke of walking out a short way onto the Shoulder for a small ceremony to say good-bye to her husband properly. But at around 8 a.m., she, Nessa, and Stangeland set out for Base Camp, leaving their two tents standing.

Those who remained behind looked to see whether they could locate anyone beyond the Shoulder. The Bottleneck and the serac were a beautiful blue-gray. Up to the left of the serac, on its western edge, where the climbers had seen headlamps the previous night, the onlookers at Camp Four could now see black specks in the snow. They pointed, able to make out the specks with the naked eye but also staring through binoculars. The specks, they realized, could be bodies but they were not moving, except one. A single figure was standing alone in the snowfields above the serac. As they watched, the figure moved slowly through the snows to the right, zig-zagging higher and then descending again toward the lip of the serac. His mind must have gone, or he was panicking, for he was heading in the wrong direction if he was going to descend to the Traverse and come down the Bottleneck. After a short while, when clouds started to drift in, the mountaineers at Camp Four lost sight of the figure.

A few of the climbers took photographs. Strang shot some film. It had been so dark and cold during the night that forming a clear picture of what happened had been impossible. But now they counted who was missing: Van Rooijen, McDonnell, Confortola, Jumik Bhote, Hwang, Kim, Park. There was still some uncertainty about Hugues d'Aubarède. His HAP, Karim Meherban, was also not accounted for.

Standing outside his tent, Meyer took out one of the Americans' radios and tried to make contact with anyone who was still up on the mountain and alive. He went up and down the frequencies, turning the knob on top of the radio, even though he still did not know for sure who among those missing possessed a radio and who didn't. They believed that Gerard McDonnell wasn't carrying a radio or a satellite phone because they thought he had given his satphone to Pemba Gyalje at the summit. Wilco van Rooijen had only his Thuraya.

"This is Camp Four," Meyer said. "Do you hear us?"

He spun the dial around and listened to the static. Some of the others still had binoculars trained on the specks.

What if someone was alive but couldn't talk? What if they were frozen or in such a state of hypoxia that they couldn't speak?

"Press the talk button if you hear us," Meyer said, hoping.

Still, nothing.

Strang had lit three burners and was melting snow just outside the tent to prepare water for anyone who came in. Survivors would need liquids quickly.

They were ready to go up to rescue people if there were signs of life, but so far they had none. They could not bring down a person unable to move on his own.

Among the climbers gathered around the tents, the sense grew that they were in the middle of something serious, an escalating tragedy beyond their power to cope. Cas van de Gevel stalked out of his tent. He looked exhausted. His eyes were bloodshot. He said he was going to search for Wilco van Rooijen and Gerard McDonnell, but Strang pointed out that he couldn't just run up into the Bottleneck without any idea of where they were likely to be.

"This is not a guided tour," added Meyer. "If there were one person, we could go get him. But there are nine missing."

Down in Base Camp, the Dutchman Roeland van Oss and the American Chris Klinke, who together were now leading the information gathering and setting up the emergency operations, made plans for people still in Camp Four to organize and send a rescue party into the Bottleneck. At the high camp, however, there was an overwhelming reluctance to go up. As far as Meyer and Strang could tell, they had no ropes, save those that were pinning down the tents. And they had only a single bottle of oxygen, which was the six-kilo bottle Chhiring Dorje had taken all the way to the summit and back again without using.

By 10 a.m., the serac and the Bottleneck were cut off from view as the weather turned. Gray clouds rolled over the summit and billowed around the great face of K2, closing around it like a curtain. The temperature plummeted again to minus twenty degrees or lower.

By noon, most of the climbers decided they had had enough and they couldn't wait any longer. Who knew what was going to happen to the weather next? Not to mention the fact that they had been above 26,000 feet for nearly forty-eight hours.

"We're going down," said Meyer. He knew it would be dark before they reached the base of the mountain.

The American team packed up their belongings but left their tent. A second American expedition had arrived at Base Camp and they had an agreement they would use Meyer's tent for their summit push.

Van de Gevel was still lying inside his tent. He was going to wait at Camp Four. Pemba Gyalje said that he would stay awhile as well, in case there were any survivors, but he wasn't going to wait for long.

"I stay for a few more hours but I come down today," he said.

The Koreans were also staying.

A group of five climbers led by Meyer and Strang came together on the slope outside Camp Four to begin their descent. Some of those who had come up a day late to try for a second night's summit attempt were disappointed that they had never gotten the chance because people had not turned back when they should have. They were not going to go for the summit while climbers were still missing.

The mountaineers had a big descent ahead and Meyer handed out a few more drugs—Provigil, dextroamphetamine—to give a kick to their systems. They left Chhiring Dorje's oxygen bottle with Gyalje along with a bag of resuscitation pills. One by one, they climbed down the last hundred yards of the Shoulder and over the brow onto the Abruzzi ridge.

Up on the great hump of the Shoulder, the two Sherpas Chhiring Bhote and Pasang Bhote scoured the area below the Bottleneck for the missing Korean climbers.

Just after noon, through the mist, they noticed something in the distance. Thirty or forty yards away, a climber was crawling on his hands and knees.

When they reached him, he wasn't making much sense. Pasang, who was carrying the radio, called Pemba Gyalje farther down the mountain. *We have found someone! He is collapsed.*

They said the climber was wearing a green and black suit, and hearing this description, Gyalje realized the climber had to be the Italian, Marco Confortola.

He told the two Sherpas to get out of the Bottleneck area quickly and bring him down. But Pasang said the climber was out of the most dangerous area and they still planned to go higher to search for Jumik Bhote and the Koreans.

You climb up to bring this one down?

Gyalje thought about the Bottleneck, and the hell he had survived the previous night.

Pemba?

Big Pasang and Chhiring said they were setting off.

Pemba relented. His teammates in the Dutch expedition were still missing. He wanted to find them. *Okay. I come. I will bring the oxygen.*

Pemba Gyalje and Cas van de Gevel packed up and climbed out tentatively onto the wasteland of the Shoulder. They were following the same route over the snow they had climbed a day earlier. This time, Van de Gevel thought, he was without Wilco van Rooijen and Gerard McDonnell. He looked from side to side but he could not see his colleagues anywhere in the snows.

Occasionally, the mists above them parted, revealing the great summit slopes. At one point they saw two black figures moving several hundred feet above them. It was the two Sherpas from the South Korean expedition who had gone out to search the slopes.

Then the clouds came down again and Gyalje and Van de Gevel could see nothing.

Van de Gevel felt his body giving in. It had been a long few days. He stopped and said to Gyalje, "If I go onto the Bottleneck, I will never come back." Even for Wilco, he couldn't go on.

"We should not split up," said Gyalje.

"It will be safer," said Van de Gevel. "I am sorry."

The clouds were thick now, and the two men agreed that Van de Gevel would sit where he was and mark the way back to Camp Four for Gyalje. They each had a radio and could communicate if they got into any trouble. The Sherpa turned and climbed up into the mist.

The man in the black and luminous green climbing suit lay unconscious in the snow. His hands were folded behind his head. He wasn't wearing any big climbing gloves and his harness was half off. Pemba Gyalje saw that the snow was cut and churned up around him.

Gyalje took a photograph to record the state of the climber and then he took out the oxygen tank he had carried up and tried to rouse Confortola. As the gas began to flow into his body, Confortola struggled and pushed the mask away. Confortola had reached the summit of K2 without using supplementary oxygen, and even now he didn't want to diminish his accomplishment.

Gyalje forced the mask back over Confortola's mouth. Confortola stopped struggling. After a few minutes, taking gasps of air, he was able to stand.

Gyalje's top priority was to get the exhausted man down to Camp Four as quickly as possible. It was hard going—Confortola's feet were frozen, and Gyalje had to watch every step he took. Gyalje knew they had to keep him moving at a steady pace to be really sure they were out of the reach of the serac; he urged Confortola on.

As the two climbers struggled down the top of the Shoulder in the mist, Gyalje received another crackling radio call from Big Pasang Bhote, who was still about six hundred feet above them. Pasang had more news.

He had climbed to the top of the Bottleneck, Pasang told Gyalje, and there he had met up with the Sherpa Jumik Bhote and the two South Korean mountaineers who had been trapped on the ropes. They were injured but they had been able to make their way slowly across the Traverse. Incredibly, they were still alive. Big Pasang was now helping them to descend.

"We met at the top section of the couloir and we come down now together," Pasang told him. "There are three. Two Koreans. One Sherpa."

Gyalje listened to the report and could hardly believe it. It was the best news in the world. Jumik and the Koreans had survived!

"We come down, though we have no ropes," Bhote said on the radio.

Gyalje looked up in the direction of the mountain but the mist was so dense that he could see nothing beyond ten yards away. Somewhere up there Big Pasang was now helping the injured climbers down the Bottleneck.

The radio continued to crackle. Awkwardly, Gyalje paused with Confortola on the Shoulder and held the set close against his ear. Big Pasang had something else to tell his friend.

Bhote said he had seen, on the lower sections of the Traverse, a fourth climber following about ten yards behind the two Koreans and Jumik Bhote. But he said another part of the serac had collapsed and had killed him.

"Okay, Pemba, there is one member falling down from the Traverse, the lower section of the Traverse, because hit by serac," Pasang said on the radio.

Pasang said he had watched as the climber had fallen to his death.

Gyalje wanted to know who it was.

"Can you identify him?" said Gyalje.

"He had a red and black down suit."

Gyalje heard this description and his heart fell. He knew immediately who it was.

It could have been Karim Meherban, Hugues d'Aubarède's HAP, but in Gyalje's memory Meherban was wearing a pure red suit, like many of the other climbers on the mountain. Alberto Zerain had a red suit, but he had already descended. So did the Koreans but he didn't think the description fit them. Only one person had a red suit with black patches, and that was Gerard McDonnell.

"A red and black down suit. Definitely Gerard."

Gyalje's friend was dead. Gyalje was devastated. It was too much. The mountain was taking a heavy toll.

Holding Confortola securely on the slope, Gyalje put the radio up to his mouth and told Big Pasang to get out of the Bottleneck and bring Jumik Bhote and the two Koreans down as quickly as he could. It was too dangerous for anyone to be up there any longer.

We are below you. Come down.

It was going to be a hard task for the Sherpa to get them down safely with minimal equipment and he hoped they were going to be okay.

Five minutes after the radio call from Pasang, Marco Confortola was concentrating hard on climbing down the slope below the bottom of the Bottleneck when he felt Pemba Gyalje's hand on his arm pushing him harder.

Up close beside him, Gyalje shouted that something terrible was about to happen.

"Run, run!" Gyalje screamed. "Go fast!"

Confortola moved his clumsy legs more quickly. He was exhausted but he tried to hurry. Gyalje, he realized, knew something that he did not.

Then, the world exploded. The serac was collapsing again.

Because the slopes were hidden in cloud, the two men could see nothing at first. But the roar grew louder and they realized an avalanche was spilling onto the Bottleneck. There was a second blast and another and they understood there were repeated icefalls. The avalanches punched down through the fog toward the two climbers, spitting out a great shower of ice and snow that was funneled and multiplied by the Bottleneck.

Struggling down the steep slope Confortola felt something slap hard into the back of his head and throw him forward. An oxygen bottle had been caught up in the avalanche and had been tossed down with the rest of the mess of ice and snow. Reeling from the blow, Confortola was convinced he was going to fall to his death, but as he toppled forward, Gyalje, who was still beside him, pulled Confortola back and pinned him against the snow, covering him with his own body until the rumbling stopped and the avalanche had passed. It had missed them by just a couple of yards.

They had survived. Confortola owed his life to Gyalje's quick and brave action. But several yards below them, visible through the cold fog, four bodies were lying scattered on the top of the ice that had been swept down the mountain.

It was another scene of death. Gyalje and Confortola climbed lower toward the bodies, Gyalje helping Confortola navigate the big chunks of ice that littered the slope. When they came within a few yards, Confortola sat in the snow while Gyalje stepped across the slope to the bodies.

Watching him walk closer, Confortola could see that it was the climbers who had been trapped up at the other end of the Traverse. The climbers he and Gerard McDonnell had tried to save. They were tangled in ropes and lying on the ice, lifeless bundles in big jackets and climbing gear, the crampons on their boots sticking up in the air.

Big Pasang was also among them. He was dead. Gyalje had spoken to the Sherpa just a few minutes before the serac collapsed and now he was gone.

Gyalje took out his camera and shot some photographs of the dead. Then he returned to Confortola and helped him up and the two men started to climb down the Shoulder through the fog.

They had gone several yards when Confortola heard a voice calling from up above them on the Bottleneck. A person climbed down toward them, waving his arms to attract their attention.

They waited until Chhiring Bhote climbed down. He had accompanied Big Pasang on the rescue bid but he and the other Sherpa had become separated; while Big Pasang had climbed ahead up the Bottleneck, Chhiring had stopped to pick up some of the fixed lines off the lower slopes in case they needed them later. He was about eighty feet below Big Pasang when the avalanche occurred. When he heard the roar, he had screamed and unclipped his safety harness from the rope as the ice swept by. In that way, he had saved himself. He was close to a rump of large rocks, which had protected him.

The young Sherpa was crying as he stepped gingerly past the avalanche debris and joined Gyalje and Confortola.

They went down together, and farther down the slope two Korean climbers and Little Pasang came out to meet them. Near Camp Four, they met Cas van de Gevel.

"Come with me," the Dutchman said to Confortola, taking his arm.

Van de Gevel was disappointed that his friend Wilco van Rooijen, had not been located, but he was glad nevertheless to see Confortola.

As he was helped down, Confortola couldn't shake the sense that the mountain could have killed him three or four times by this point. It could still claim him, he knew, and he just wanted to get off its slopes.

The snow was falling more heavily, the clouds wrapping even more tightly around the peak. K2 seemed to be closing in on itself.

At Camp Four, he went directly to the Flying Jump tents to talk to the Korean leaders. Confortola told Go Mi-sun and Kim Jae-soo about his attempts to free the Korean climbers and Jumik Bhote from the ropes. He related what they knew about the deaths of the Korean climbers at the base of the Bottleneck. But Confortola couldn't speak much. He was in tears, and as they heard the news Kim and Go cried, too.

Chhiring Bhote had calmed down, but he still seemed in shock about losing his brother. He would return now to Kathmandu without him. He feared the moment when he would have to tell his mother and his older brother about Jumik's death. He wondered how they would support Dawa Sangmu and Jen Jen. Big Pasang also was dead. He had children, too, back in Kathmandu.

Van de Gevel then led Confortola to his tent but the Italian refused to go inside. He was in a terrible condition after thirty-six hours on the upper mountain, and he was badly shaken by all the suffering and violence he had witnessed. He was talking fast, incoherently, wanting to tell his story about what he had seen.

Van de Gevel, however, insisted that Confortola should sleep. He was forced to push Confortola into his tent and help him into a sleeping bag. Then Confortola wanted to call his brother Luigi. He had to tell Luigi he was alive. He searched desperately among his gear for a battery for his satellite phone, but he couldn't find one. At last he gave in and asked to be left alone to sleep.

Part IV

RESCUE

Saturday, August 2–Monday, August 4

"Yes, yes," she whispered.
You can do it, Cecile. Just keep going.
"Yes, I can."
—Cecilie Skog, K2, 2008

"There! I see something. I see someone moving
on the south face."
—Chris Klinke, K2, 2008

CHAPTER SEVENTEEN

In the huddle of tents on the Godwin-Austen glacier at 16,400 feet, Chris Klinke and Roeland van Oss were busy coordinating information-gathering and emergency operations. The night before, after the early reports came in of the delays and the first serac collapse, Van Oss had worked from the South Koreans' communications tent. But this morning they moved to the Dutch mess tent, which was closer to the middle of the camp and had a better sight line of the routes.

They tried to work out who knew what, who was still missing, and where climbers had last been spotted. They set up a table with a row of four radios, one for each of the frequencies being used on the mountain. They also had a satellite phone, spare batteries, and paper and pen for emergency note taking. There were photographs of the routes pinned to the tent wall. The solar panels for the satellite phone were set up outside on the stones, though Van Oss was anxious about what they would do for power when night fell.

Van Oss was a lanky twenty-nine-year-old with curly brown hair. Through June and July, he had worked hard to get used to life so high up, climbing steadily to the higher camps, but one day he was traversing slowly at altitude when something snapped inside and he realized he would never be able to reach a summit as high as K2. He was relieved to be free of the pressure and expectations, and instead had become the main point man at Base Camp for the final summit attempt.

Whenever he got any news, he called it through to Maarten van Eck in the Netherlands, who posted updates on the website. Some of the other climbers were keeping blogs—Nick Rice was also posting updates to his site—but it was mainly through the Dutch team's website that information about the escalating tragedy was spreading to the families of the climbers and the rest of the outside world.

Chris Klinke had climbed up to the Bottleneck with everyone else the previous morning but he had gotten a furious headache, a result of being hit in the head by a baseball-sized chunk of ice a couple of days before, and had turned back. As he had climbed down, he had become dehydrated and then he had started to pee blood, like tomato juice, and that worried him. Now he was maintaining a list of the people who were confirmed killed. It was a balled-up sheet of paper he kept in his pocket. Rolf Bae was on it, and Dren Mandic and Jahan Baig. Klinke called it the "death list," even though it also included the names of everyone who had so far come down safely.

Alberto Zerain had walked into Base Camp. The Spaniard had slept at Camp Three on Friday night, and then descended the Abruzzi, collecting litter at the camps he passed through—an empty gas tank, cans of ham and tuna.

He was oblivious to the problems unfolding above him. When he got down to Base Camp, however, he witnessed a grim scene on the Godwin-Austen glacier. Crowds of people stood about on the gray rocks speaking into their telephones. The place looked like a cemetery. He headed for the little clump of tents sheltering beneath the slopes of Broad Peak a mile away, where he could rest.

Farther up the mountain, Cecilie Skog and her two Norwegian teammates were still climbing down the Abruzzi ridge. They were met on the way by the Singaporean expedition and a climber from the American team, Mike Farris, who had interrupted his ascent because of ear trouble. They were offered consoling cups of hot tea and coffee.

When they prepared to move on, Skog said she didn't want to go down.

"I want to stay with Rolf," she said. She was tired and her hips ached from her fall and she couldn't stop thinking of Bae up there on the mountain.

Lars Nessa was beside her. He said she had to go on.

Skog emptied her mind and tried to avoid thinking about her husband. It was then that she heard a voice speaking inside her head. Quiet at first, and then more insistent. *Cecilie.* She realized it had been there all along. It was Bae talking to her. He was with her, she was convinced.

Come on, he said. *Get down.*

"Yes, yes," she whispered.

You can do it, Cecilie. Just keep going.

"Yes, I can."

At Camp Two, where they had left tents to sleep in on the way down, including one for Rolf Bae, and where they had stashed their satellite phone, Skog summoned up the courage to call Bae's parents in Norway. Bae's father was a retired pilot and his mother was a nurse. Rolf was their only child, and now they would have no grandchildren.

"Jacob," Skog said. "I am sorry."

"It's okay," Bae's father reassured her. "We only have you now. You must get down safely."

They rolled up their tents and tossed them down a long slope below House's Chimney. They collected them when they got down to Advance Base Camp at about 17,500 feet, where they planned to spend the night before they walked the three miles farther to Base Camp on Sunday.

Another climber, Nick Rice, the young American who had been a close friend of Hugues d'Aubarède, came into Base Camp. Like

Zerain, Rice had gone to sleep at Camp Three on Friday evening unaware of the troubles up above him. He woke on Saturday morning to a 6:43 a.m. text message from his mother in Hermosa Beach, California: The disaster on K2 was all over the news, she said.

"A big chunk of ice has fallen below the summit, taking a large part of the fixed lines with it," she reported. "Twelve members are stranded high on the route. Sta—"

The last sentence was cut off but Rice was sure she had signed off, "Stay safe."

When Rice finally climbed down onto the rocks at Base Camp, another mountaineer from a different expedition rushed at him and declared excitedly that everyone who was still up on the mountain was dead, but Rice refused to believe it.

He felt the world was going crazy. Later, in one of the tents he passed, someone was speaking on a telephone, negotiating to sell a photograph of an icefall on the serac. *Let's make some money,* he heard the climber say. *This is a money shot!* Rice was overcome with exhaustion and emotion.

In the early afternoon, Eric Meyer radioed in from Camp Four to inform Klinke and Van Oss that he was starting his descent.

A few hours later, Klinke got an update that Cas van de Gevel had probably seen Hugues d'Aubarède falling the night before. Klinke sadly moved the Frenchman's name from the "presumed missing" column on his list to "presumed dead." Pemba Gyalje radioed in from Camp Four to relate what he had witnessed in the Bottleneck. Klinke learned that the three missing Koreans and two of their Sherpas were probably dead but Marco Confortola was back safe.

He had nine climbers who were presumed dead—d'Aubarède, Dren Mandic, Jahan Baig, Rolf Bae, Jumik Bhote, Kim Hyo-gyeong, Park Kyeong-hyo, Hwang Dong-jin, Big Pasang Bhote.

There were still three people missing—Gerard McDonnell, Wilco van Rooijen, and d'Aubarède's HAP, Karim Meherban. Klinke did not yet know of Pemba Gyalje's conviction that McDonnell was the climber in red and black who had fallen from the Traverse; or Confortola's belief that McDonnell's were the remains he had discovered in the icefall.

At Base Camp, they had received the reports that Wilco van Rooijen had telephoned his wife in Utrecht to tell her he was lost. When Klinke heard that news, he thought, *Shit*, since he knew the story of climber Rob Hall on the South Summit of Everest in 1996 who had made a final call to his pregnant wife in New Zealand just before he died of hypothermia. Van Rooijen had a baby son at home.

Things also looked bad for Gerard McDonnell, in truth. It was getting late and the chance of anyone else coming off the mountain was slim. But no one knew absolutely for certain what had happened to him, and his family in Ireland still held out the hope that he had survived. In Kilcornan, when his mother and sisters had gone to bed on Friday night, they had known that he had reached the summit. But on Saturday morning they heard nothing from him and there was no fresh sighting. The local newspaper, the *Limerick Leader*, reported McDonnell's triumph on its website, but telephone calls to his satellite phone were not going through. McDonnell's brothers-in-law sent text messages to friends around Kilcornan to announce that he had reached the top. They cautioned that descending was the hard part. Then the news had come through of the icefall and Rolf Bae's death; they had heard that the fixed ropes had been swept away.

As Saturday wore on, his family gathered in his mother Gertie's farmhouse in Kilcornan. They swapped reminiscences of McDonnell to keep up their spirits and reinforce their belief that somewhere, four thousand miles away, he was alive. They laughed and made cups of tea.

Behind them on the sideboard, McDonnell's hurling stick had

pride of place in a case beside a picture of him on Everest. McDonnell had sold it at a charity auction but his family had bought it for him. Ger's older brother J.J. was on vacation in Lanzarote and was due to return to Ireland the next morning.

After a while, they moved to Gerard's sister's house and waited. They had their laptops open and constantly checked for email updates and refreshed the Dutch team's website for news.

⸻

At about 4 p.m. on K2, Eric Meyer and the four climbers who were descending together to Base Camp from Camp Four arrived at the top of a steep, 60-degree ice slope above Camp One.

Two ropes had already been fixed in parallel down the slope. The Australian climber, Mark Sheen, rappelled down first and waited at the anchor 150 feet below. Then it was Meyer's turn.

The two ropes appeared somewhat worn to him. There were other ropes partially buried in the snow but these two were probably as good as any the climbers would find; they looked as though they had probably been fixed by one of this year's expeditions. He selected what appeared to be the newest, and clipped it into the special descending carabiner on his safety harness. As he descended, he watched the rope spool quickly through the carabiner near his waist.

He was about one hundred and twenty feet down when he saw the three distinct strands of the rope passing through the mouth of the carabiner unravel, and a second later, disintegrate as the rope split. Meyer fell backward from the mountain.

He swiveled head over heels; the world suddenly turned in fantastic slow motion around him. He could see Broad Peak and some of the other beautiful Karakoram mountains hanging weirdly upside down.

Meyer thought, *I guess this is how it is going to go down. I am going to die.*

Before he had started to rappel, he had attached a two-foot-long tubular nylon safety sling from his belt to the second fixed rope.

Now, he somersaulted and crashed down onto the ice but stopped ten feet below Mark Sheen as the sling snapped tight. He had fallen forty feet but he could have gone airborne over the 4,000-foot drop if it weren't for the sling.

"I can't believe you didn't keep going!" Sheen called down to him.

Meyer's adrenaline was pumping. "I can't believe I am alive," he said.

His weight—and he wasn't a heavy guy—must have found a weakness in the rope that had caused it to snap; it had probably already been weakened by someone else's ice axe or crampon. In the air, as he fell, he had reached over with his right arm and caught the safety line in the crook of his elbow in an attempt to stop himself. That had left a sharp rope burn on his skin, but otherwise he was okay.

He remembered thinking, as he tumbled, how beautiful a way it would have been to die. The other three climbers still up at the top of the slope—Chhiring Dorje, Paul Walters, and Fredrik Strang—climbed down cautiously after him.

Klinke and Van Oss stood outside the tents at Base Camp peering up thousands of feet at the gullies and ridges on the enormous southern face of K2. To watch the slopes, they had three pairs of binoculars and a telescope. The telescope, which the Serbs had donated to the rescue effort, was mounted on a tripod on the rocks.

Earlier, it had been warm in the sunshine but the temperature was dropping again. Clouds drifted across the sky. The two men were surrounded by other hopeful mountaineers. Wilco van Rooijen was still unaccounted for and everyone prayed that he and the other climbers who were missing would put in an appearance before night fell. They were unlikely to survive another night out in the open.

The climbers gathered at Base Camp had divided up the mountain into grids in their heads, and each had taken a grid to watch. Gazing carefully through the binoculars, Klinke's eyes roamed up and down his grid, which was to the left of the Cesen route. After a while, he switched to the Serbs' telescope.

At about three o'clock, the clouds parted and Klinke thought he saw an object moving on the southern face but no one else could make anything out—only the mist and black shapes of rocks amid the dull fields of snow. Then the clouds closed together again. The slopes were getting darker. The sun would set in three or four hours.

Back in the Netherlands, in Utrecht, Maarten van Eck had an idea about how to locate Wilco van Rooijen. By now Van Rooijen had called in a handful of times on his Thuraya. So perhaps they could track the GPS coordinates of his satellite calls?

He contacted the company in Colorado that had rented Van Rooijen his phone, and asked for the position of his last five calls. At first the people at Thuraya said the data was personal and refused to give it up. But when the circumstances were explained to them by a furious Van Eck, they relented and Van Eck plotted the coordinates on a 3-D model of K2 on Google Maps he had on his desktop.

The first three calls were all over the place. But Van Rooijen's last two calls showed the same position. Van Eck called Base Camp.

"Where is he?" said Van Oss.

"Seventy-five hundred meters near the Black Pyramid!" Van Eck declared, confident they had found him.

On K2, Klinke was still watching the mountain, and at around 5:30 p.m. the clouds cleared and he saw a small orange dot scaling down the southern face.

He grabbed a pair of binoculars, which had a wider field of view.

"There!" he shouted. "I see something. I see someone moving on the south face."

Everyone stared where Klinke was pointing. Was he sure? No climber was supposed to be in that area of the mountain.

Klinke was also confused. The Black Pyramid and the coordinates from Van Eck were nowhere near that part of the southern face where he had glimpsed the orange figure. Eventually he realized that Van Eck was mistaken and he had confused the real Black Pyramid with another area of black rock where the climber in orange had been seen.

"It's a climber." Klinke was adamant. "I am not sure but I think it's Wilco."

By now, the others had picked out the figure, too. They cheered when they saw him. They thought it was a climber in an orange suit, although it could have been a different color. Whoever he was, he was about 1,500 feet to the left of the Cesen route and 1,800 feet below the Shoulder. And he was on the move.

A dozen mountaineers stood in the middle of Base Camp near the Serbian tent staring up at the south face of the mountain.

Van Oss called through to Van Eck in the Netherlands, who posted a report on the website:

K2 Base Camp (Roeland) can see a person in Orange suit between C3 and C4. That person is slowly moving down.

Who was it?

The Dutch team hoped it was Van Rooijen. As the news spread to Kilcornan, Gerard McDonnell's family prayed it was him.

Soon, however, the clouds closed in again, concealing the climber from view.

To try to make sure of the identity of the climber in orange, Van Eck called the clothing company North Face. It had supplied the gear for many of the climbers on K2. Of the list the company gave him of mountaineers wearing orange suits, only Van Rooijen was unaccounted for.

Klinke was not ruling out McDonnell or Karim Meherban or even Hugues d'Aubarède but gradually a consensus grew. It had to be Wilco.

At around 6:30 p.m., the clouds drifted apart, and in an opening they saw the figure in orange again. He was still there, and this time he seemed to be sitting down. Whoever it was, it was a survivor. The mood at Base Camp was jubilant. Van Oss and Klinke jumped up and down on the rocks.

They still had to bring the climber down alive, they realized. They had to act quickly if they were going to get him to safety before nightfall. If it was Van Rooijen, they had no idea what sort of condition he was in. Clouds filled the gullies again and the sky was growing even darker. Daylight was failing.

Ten thousand feet above Base Camp, Cas van de Gevel and Pemba Gyalje had stayed in their tent at Camp Four, resting and still not willing to go down while Van Rooijen was missing. Klinke and Van Oss decided they had to call them on the radio to tell them the news and ask them to attempt a rescue.

They knew they had to be quick before night came in but it took a while to raise them. Eventually Klinke and Van Oss got through and told them a climber had been spotted somewhere below them between Camp Three and Camp Four. It was probably Wilco van Rooijen.

"Go down the Cesen and signal over," Van Oss said.

It was not going to be easy for the two exhausted climbers to climb down the Cesen. The rocky slope was steep at any time of day; in the dark, it was deadly.

"We go down," said Pemba.

It took the two men about an hour to hastily grab some food, zip on their suits, and gather Chhiring Dorje's extra oxygen bottle. Then Klinke watched two headlamps set out from the tents up on the Shoulder and begin to move lower.

"Cas and Pemba will descend from C4 toward C3 to try to locate the lone climber," Van Eck reported on the website. "More news to follow as soon as we hear something."

CHAPTER EIGHTEEN

7 p.m.

When Wilco van Rooijen woke up on the ledge of rock, he was alive but he was trapped at 25,300 feet.

Although it was still light, he realized some hours had passed. He felt stiff and cold.

He called his wife again, and the battery worked. He left the phone on so that Maarten van Eck could get through to him. This was the first time that Van Eck had managed to speak directly to his friend. Van Rooijen told Van Eck he was stuck at the top of a large ravine. His eyes were in such a bad state that he could see almost nothing now. He was so thirsty he could hardly speak. All he wanted to do, he said, was fall asleep again.

"You must not sleep," said Van Eck. Van Rooijen heard the words leach into his brain over the satellite phone and he knew his friend was right.

By now, since he had the phone coordinates, Van Eck believed he knew where Van Rooijen was. He told him he had to continue climbing to his left.

"That's the only way back to the Cesen." It was imperative, he said.

Once Van Rooijen had gotten off the phone, he sat for a few minutes. Then, when the clouds thinned, he spotted a narrow snow gully a few hundred yards to his left as he faced out from the mountain. If he could reach that gully, he could drop down six hundred feet.

He stood up and climbed around the ledge. Then he slid lower, letting himself go, taking a chance, and he made it. After that, the going was easier.

Soon, however, he saw that there were huge crevasses that split the snow along the bottom of the gully. They were like toothless mouths, and he was terrified he was going to fall into one.

The only other way down was to turn to the east onto a big ridge of brown rocks. But the rocks were steep and Van Rooijen had no idea where they would lead him.

By now, the sun had set. A bright line cut across the horizon. He was desperate to continue but he discovered that his headlamp had slipped from his pocket. He searched his coat but it was gone, as was his camera.

He raised his eyes to the sky and cursed. He couldn't go on. If he stumbled in the dark, he risked falling forever into one of the crevasses.

There was nothing to do, he soon realized, but to stop and bivouac for a second night.

The prospect appalled him. At least on the first night's bivouac, he had Marco Confortola and Gerard McDonnell for company. And that bivouac had started past midnight and lasted for only a few hours. Now it was 7:30 p.m.; he had hours ahead of him alone in the freezing dark.

The bivouac was a terrible thing, he felt, but necessary. Before he stopped, he climbed a few more feet toward the rocks. There in the twilight he made another grim discovery. A few yards away, a dead climber dressed in a yellow jacket lay on a shallow incline. He was tied by rope to a second dead climber, who was sprawled a little farther up. Van Rooijen didn't know who it was, though he thought it was somebody from this year's groups.

He sat down beside the corpse in the yellow jacket. By now Van Rooijen was desensitized to the terrible things he had seen on the mountain and the corpse didn't register with him. There was also the fact that his mind was no longer functioning properly after the days at high altitude. He didn't focus on the body. Kneeling down beside the corpse, he reached up with his ice axe and climbed onto a higher part of the slope. He climbed on and found a place to spend the night. Sitting down, he crossed his long legs. He stabbed his ice axe into the steep slope behind him so he could attach a rope.

Wind gusted across the face. Now it was really cold. Van Rooijen tried to keep his back to it and, now and then, he stood up and turned around to stretch his limbs and keep the blood circulating, especially in his feet, which were feeling numb. That was how he was going to survive. The numbness of his feet was a bad sign, but Van Rooijen had no energy to rip off his boots and massage his toes.

He closed his eyes, but after a while he opened them again and concentrated on the line of the horizon, the dark shadows of the tops of mountains and the huge blankness of the sky. What with the wind and the cold and the cramps, sleep was impossible. He waited. He took out a tube of energy gel he remembered he had in a pocket and ate it with some snow. That he had only remembered it now was another sign of his deteriorating faculties. He avoided looking at his watch. He didn't want to be disappointed by how slowly the minutes passed.

Once during the dark night, Van Rooijen thought he saw a bright light flash less than nine hundred feet away. He followed its progress with his eyes for a while but it abruptly shut off. He remembered his Thuraya and pulled it out. He tried it twice but either the battery was too cold to work or the charge had seeped away. Hoping his body warmth would revive it, he slipped the phone back in his coat, closer to his skin.

He may have slept after all. He wasn't sure. He wasn't certain of anything anymore. Finally, the sky over K2 grew light. It was Sunday morning, August 3, 2008. He was still alive.

At last, he allowed himself to check his watch. Five a.m. More than two days since he had set out from the tents at Camp Four leading the Dutch expedition gloriously toward the Bottleneck. And it was more than thirty-six hours since his lips had touched any water.

I am going down, he told himself.

He decided he could cut a path down the side of the rocks, thus avoiding both the hump of the ridge and the crevasses that frightened him. He stood up from the bivouac and climbed uncertainly downward.

On Saturday night, when they received the joyful radio call from Klinke and Van Oss at Base Camp, Cas van de Gevel and Pemba Gyalje had set out as quickly as they could from Camp Four.

The idea was to descend rapidly to Camp Three on the Cesen route. Van Oss and Klinke had given them directions about where they should be able to see the climber in orange. They knew they were risking their own lives and they wanted to get off the Cesen route before dark, although it was already nearly black outside.

The Sherpa climbed ahead down the rocky fissures. Van de Gevel was moving more slowly and he watched his friend gradually moving away from him down the steep route.

Snowflakes blew across the Cesen but from time to time Van de Gevel could see a little distance ahead. He hollered out Van Rooijen's name, but his voice was sucked away by the gray emptiness of the snow and rocks. All he could see in the sweep of his headlamp were dark empty slopes freckled with rocks and silent stone ledges.

"Wilco! Wilco!"

Van de Gevel had only climbed down a few hundred yards when his headlamp lost power and flickered out. The batteries were dead. He was carrying a radio, which also had batteries. Crouching on the slope, he radioed down to Gyalje to say that he was switching his radio batteries to the headlamp and would be off air for a while. He opened the back of the radio, but when he lifted out the batteries they were encased in plastic and he couldn't pull them apart. He picked at them with his axe but fumbled and dropped the batteries. They slid away down the mountain. It was a bad mistake. Alone without communication or light, Van de Gevel realized that he was stuck.

He wasn't going to give in, however. He grabbed one of the ropes that led down the slope, following it for several yards, but it came to a dead end and he stopped himself abruptly. *Not that way.*

The rock and snow beneath him were cold as he slumped down in the snow to wait until dawn. Taking off his gloves, he unfolded a lightweight sleeping bag. He lay back on the snow and spread the sleeping bag over his head like a cover. There was a little warmth at least for his body.

An hour or so later he blinked open his eyes and realized he had fallen asleep without putting his gloves back on. A sharp pain ate into his hands and he realized it was frostbite. Hastily, he grabbed for his gloves, pulling them over his stiff fingers, but it felt like he was too late. It was still dark, and all he could do was sit tight and wait.

He had set out to rescue his friend but he himself was lost in the night. Below him, Pemba had probably made it down to Camp Three by this time. Van de Gevel wondered how many hours were left until the sun came up, what had happened to Wilco van Rooijen, and what now would become of him. He pondered his fate. *No one knows where I am.* It was a terrifying thought.

When night enveloped the mountain, like a hand closing its grip, the climbers in front of the cluster of tents at Base Camp watched the lone figure in the orange suit being swallowed up by the darkness.

Van de Gevel and Gyalje had not reached him before nightfall.

Then one of the two headlamps shimmering down the Cesen

route from the Shoulder suddenly blinked off. The remaining lamp moved lower for an hour or so before it disappeared into a tent at Camp Three. Shortly afterward, Chris Klinke received an alarmed radio call from Pemba Gyalje, who said Cas van de Gevel had not come in.

"I have lost him," Gyalje said, sounding both frightened and exhausted. "Cas is not here!"

Gyalje hadn't been able to see the climber in the orange suit, either, he said, although he had shouted for more than an hour.

The Sherpa said that while he had been outside, he had heard a satellite phone ringing. He thought it had to be Van Rooijen's. But it had stopped. The ringing was coming from an area that was prone to avalanches and Gyalje was wary of searching further, though he offered to go.

"I don't want you to go out," said Klinke, who was getting worried about the latest turn of events. "We don't know where Wilco is. Cas's light has disappeared. This is getting scary!"

He told Gyalje to stay where he was and sleep.

As the night closed in, the failure to locate the climber in orange depressed the spirits of the climbers in Base Camp. Roeland van Oss, who had only had about three hours of sleep during the last two days, ducked into his tent to get some rest. Wilco van Rooijen was spending a third night on K2 above or close to 26,000 feet. Van Rooijen was tough, Van Oss thought, but few people could survive that.

After Van Oss had gone, Chris Klinke stayed outside to keep vigil, sitting on a big rock and gazing up at the darkened south face. The rock was the size of a dinner table and flat on top. The thirty-eight-year-old Klinke had given up his job as a vice president at the financial advisory firm Ameriprise to follow the mountaineering life. Now he had the sheet of paper, the "death list," folded in his pocket. He looked for the distant dots of headlamps but he saw none. He listened for any voices on the radio but there was an eerie silence. He shivered.

Damn, it was cold. He was wearing a down coat, down booties, and insulated pants. But the rock and the stones beneath his feet seemed to rip the warmth out of him.

Now and then, the American expedition's cook, Deedar Ali, or his assistant brought him warm tea or biscuits and stopped to watch with him. Just after 9 p.m., Klinke received the news on the radio that the remainder of his own American expedition, including Eric Meyer, Fredrik Strang, and Chhiring Dorje, were descending the last few hundred feet of the Abruzzi and were at Advance Base Camp.

At about 1 a.m., Deedar walked up to them with hot tea and more biscuits. They would be glad to get them. Klinke walked out a few hundred yards from Base Camp to meet them and was relieved when at last he saw headlamps, and Meyer and the team walked wearily across the boulders toward the tents. The descent had been a tough one. Meyer's fall down the 60-degree ice slope had been a reminder of how close anyone was to losing their life on this mountain.

Other members of the team, Paul Walters and Mike Farris, joined them and the whole team went inside the mess tent to sit and decompress. They drank whisky from tin cups. The mood was grim because people were still missing. Klinke told them the news that Van Rooijen was alive. If the Dutchman survived to the morning, he was going to need medical treatment.

Klinke went back out onto the rocks. It was past 2 a.m. Now and then he touched the list of the missing and the dead in his pocket. He had made contact with the Pakistani military to arrange for a plane to fly over K2 to locate any survivors. But the plane that would conduct the "low-and-slow" was being kept on the runway at Skardu by the bad weather. The conditions had to be perfect for a low-and-slow.

CHAPTER NINETEEN

Sunday, August 3, 5 a.m.

As the morning light started to brighten the vast white and gray snows above Chris Klinke, clouds were still gusting across K2's massive promontories but most of the mountain was visible. And that is when he saw the orange figure again.

At 5:15 a.m., he woke Roeland van Oss, who was in his warm sleeping bag in his tent.

"Roeland, he is moving!" he shouted urgently. "Wake up! He is moving!"

The climber in orange was now about nine hundred feet to the left of the Cesen route and about three hundred feet above Camp Three, which itself was at about 24,000 feet, and he was traversing to the right.

Several more climbers joined them on the rocks and one of them, an independent Serbian climber, could also see another figure above Camp Three struggling down the fixed lines of the Cesen, and they realized that this had to be Cas van de Gevel. They were relieved he had survived though they didn't know what injuries he had sustained after being outside all night.

They called up on the radio to Pemba Gyalje, who was in one of the tents at Camp Three, but there was no answer. Perhaps he was sleeping or his radio was off. A few minutes later, however, the Sherpa's voice abruptly broke the silence. He sounded flustered.

Here is Pemba, over.

A rock had been dislodged from above, probably by Van de Gevel as he descended, and it had smashed into Gyalje's tent, waking him with a fright. But he had stuck his head outside and he could see his Dutch colleague making his way toward him.

"I see Cas!" he told them. "He is twenty to thirty meters above me."

Within a few minutes, Van de Gevel arrived at the tent and both men spoke on the radio again to Base Camp. Klinke and Van Oss suggested that the two men step outside their tent and begin shouting to attract the attention of the climber in orange.

"He must be two hundred and fifty to three hundred feet away from where you are," Van Oss said.

They wouldn't be able to see him yet because of the large ice fins and promontories that crossed the southern face. Van Rooijen was on the western side of one of these. No one looking from Camp Three could spot him yet, and they were invisible to him.

"You will see him soon," said Van Oss. "He has to cross around the ice corner."

Gyalje put on his down suit and boots. He melted water on the burner. Then he and Van de Gevel went out. As soon as they started calling, the climbers at Base Camp, gazing through the Serbs' telescope and the binoculars, saw the orange figure respond. He stood up and began moving faster.

Klinke and Van Oss saw that Van de Gevel and Gyalje were so close to reaching the climber in orange. They prayed that they weren't going to miss this chance to save him.

———

Cecilie Skog, Lars Nessa, and Oystein Stangeland were met at Advance Base Camp by their cook, who helped them carry their equipment the final three miles back to the tents at Base Camp, where three or four mountaineers from other expeditions greeted them. Just outside the camp one of the other climbers tried to take

Skog's backpack but she insisted on holding on to it because it was Bae's.

After wanting to stay up on the mountain, Skog was now intent on leaving K2 as soon as possible. It was a place of so much pain and death.

Then at Base Camp she climbed inside her tent, the tent she had shared with Rolf.

Inside, Skog looked around at their belongings, lay down on her sleeping bag, and felt again suddenly that she couldn't leave him behind. It was too hard to think that he was still up there, his body left alone in the snow.

Over the next few days, she would appear outside the tents on the glacial moraine for a few hours but would become inconsolable. At night, the others in the expedition heard her crying.

Skog felt paralyzed. She couldn't go back to Norway, to the little apartment she and Bae had shared in Stavanger, back to their life, back to their friends and their families, back to Fram Expeditions, back to all the questions—not without Rolf.

She sat alone inside the tent, but soon she realized Bae was in truth no longer on K2. He had gone. She had known it all along. Then she wanted to pack up and leave before the Norwegian media descended on her.

Nessa and Stangeland said they would stay for a few more days to get the team's gear together, call porters, and help with the rescue, but Skog started to prepare to leave quickly.

High on the southern face, Wilco van Rooijen picked his way down the rocks at the bottom of the gully. The world stretched out before him in the morning light—hundreds of miles of beautiful, startling peaks, though he cared nothing for that now, only his survival.

Amazingly, he felt better after his rest and it seemed the energy gel had worked.

He passed some of the big crevasses, cutting between them and some of the huge rumps of brown rock that lay farther over to the left.

The sun must have warmed up Van Rooijen's phone in his jacket because it started to ring. He realized he had left it on after trying it during the night. It was Heleen. She had waited for his call but had finally given up waiting and in the darkness in Utrecht at 2:30 a.m. had tried the number. She hadn't expected him to answer.

She screamed, "Wilco!"

He said he was feeling confident. The terrain was easing off. He was nearly down.

"I think I can see Camp One," he said.

"Keep on going!" Heleen was overjoyed by how positive he sounded. "I am here on the couch with Teun," his wife said. "Do it for us," she said, speaking so loudly that she woke her son. "You have to keep on going. Keep on going!"

He told her he would call her again when he reached the camp.

He rounded the corner, and he saw some fixed ropes snaking lower. He had stumbled onto a route, though he didn't know whether it was the Cesen route. A long way below were what looked like two yellow North Face tents.

Van Rooijen realized now that two figures were climbing across toward him, between him and the tents. They appeared to speed up. When he saw them, he was overjoyed. Climbers meant a stove, and that meant melting snow for water. It would be an end to his thirst. Van Rooijen walked on slowly, pausing every few steps and bending down on one knee to lean on his ice axe, catching his breath.

The two men were still about three hundred feet away from Van Rooijen when they came into focus. The one at the rear was wearing a dark blue suit. The one leading was dressed like Van Rooijen in orange. *Shit! It's Cas!*

When Van Rooijen reached Cas van de Gevel, he embraced his friend and Van de Gevel hugged him back. Chest to chest, they screamed their joy into the other's face. Both men cried, so desperately happy to have found each other and cheated death.

"I didn't think we were ever going to meet again!" Van de Gevel said.

He looked into Van Rooijen's gaunt, sunburned face. Van Rooijen's lips were sore and blistered, and his eyes were bloodshot. The wind and the cold had marked his cheeks with red blood vessels.

Van de Gevel helped Van Rooijen down the Cesen and they crammed into one of the Dutch tents. He was in shock and they helped him get himself together. Gyalje had already melted two liters of water from snow in a pan and Van Rooijen gulped it down. He also breathed some oxygen from the tank Gyalje had carried lower, and forced a Sultana biscuit into his mouth.

Van de Gevel took out his video camera and filmed Van Rooijen speaking into the lens under the low roof of the tent, his silver hair sticking up crazily. Even after his adventure he was well enough to give an interview for posterity. But when they explained he was only at Camp Three, he was disbelieving and then angry.

"What do you mean?" he said. He was convinced he had been climbing so long that he must have bypassed the top three camps. "Not funny."

After all his hard work there was still about 7,000 feet between him and Base Camp.

"It's true!"

Van de Gevel told him about the deaths on the mountain. They had rescued Marco Confortola. But Hugues d'Aubarède was dead. They also thought that Gerard McDonnell was gone. Van de Gevel and Gyalje didn't go into greater detail because they didn't know more. Chris Klinke had the list at Base Camp.

Van Rooijen was devastated and shook his head ruefully, only half comprehending. He said he thought he had been the only one caught in this nightmare.

He said he could not feel his feet and asked Van de Gevel and

Gyalje to take a look. They peeled off the outer part of his boots, then his inner boots. It looked bad. His toes, swollen and hard, had turned gray and light blue. They had severe frostbite.

They radioed Base Camp to report the news that the lost climber had been found. It was a terrific, joyful moment. After all the bad news, there was immense relief. The voices on the radio were full of congratulation.

Van Rooijen thanked them all. "Now you have to focus on finding Gerard and getting Marco down," he said. The Italian, still above them at Camp Four at 26,000 feet, was in a bad way.

They discussed the state of Van Rooijen's injuries. Eric Meyer's gravelly voice came on the line, and he told them they had to lose height as rapidly as possible if they were going to save Van Rooijen's toes. Some of the teams at Base Camp had made a rescue plan and offered to climb up carrying ropes and oxygen tanks to help lift Van Rooijen down. But Gyalje demurred, saying they would manage on their own; the mountain was dangerous and there had been too many deaths already.

Van Rooijen insisted he could walk, and with the oxygen tank on his back the three men descended toward Camp Two. If anything, Cas van de Gevel was more exhausted than Van Rooijen. As they climbed, his colleague passed him the bottle of oxygen, and breathing the extra gas gave him some new energy, though the bottle was empty after a few minutes.

At Camp Two, Gyalje melted more snow for water and Van de Gevel was so tired that he crashed into a deep sleep outside the tent. When he woke up, he told the others he wanted to stay at the camp for the night. It looked like he had some frostbite on his hands; his fingers were turning rigid and painful. "You must get up," said Gyalje, insisting. The other two men forced him to his feet and they began climbing down the route again.

Van de Gevel fell behind. Walking down alone, he forced himself onward. Later, he would think about what K2 had done to him and to his friend; Van Rooijen had lost twenty-two pounds. Van de Gevel had lost thirty. They had both nearly died. He would think how dreadful it would be to face Gerard McDonnell's family. He had met the Irishman for the first time on this expedition. They had gotten to know each other on the trek in from Askole. Now McDonnell was gone. Ger's mother, his sisters, his brother would hate them all for having allowed this to happen.

The tragedy would no doubt stop some people from coming back. But it would not keep Van de Gevel from returning to the mountains. If he gave up climbing, he knew, he wouldn't be the same person. When he was climbing, he felt at ease, the most comfortable he ever was.

He couldn't stop thinking about the moment on the summit when the guys—d'Aubarède, McDonnell, and Van Rooijen—had embraced under the dome of the perfect blue evening sky.

That is what it was all about. Even this disaster could not rob him of that.

Ahead of Cas, Van Rooijen, for his part, reflected that he had finished with K2. After three attempts, he had conquered its summit. K2 was a mountain you climbed only once in your lifetime. To try again would be stupid. As he hobbled lower, he knew he was not coming back.

Marco Confortola had woken up alone on Sunday morning at Camp Four with only his two Balti HAPs for help. The last of the large South Korean contingent had cleared out without waiting to assist him down.

The sun was high in the sky. Confortola felt dizzy. After his hours outside unprotected on the mountain, and his fall down the Bottleneck, he ached, and pains burned in his left hand and in his feet, but he climbed over the misty ridge onto the rocks of the Abruzzi. He was familiar with it, whereas the Cesen was strange to him.

The two HAPs followed him down, but they stayed a few hundred feet behind him, as though Confortola were bad luck or too much work. He cursed them. He knew he couldn't rely on them.

The Abruzzi was deserted. He followed the ropes alone. When he climbed down onto the cut-up snows at Camp Three, he found nobody. No one to wave or run to him or bring him in.

The climbers who had waited to help the Norwegians had abandoned the camp, but he found a Sprite in one of the tents and drank it, and found two energy bars in another tent and ate them. He found a battery for his phone and called Luigi at his bank in Valfurva.

"This is Marco!" he said, pressing the phone eagerly to his mouth.

But Confortola's luck wasn't getting any better. Luigi wasn't there. His brother was out.

Confortola nodded. "Okay."

He hung up, and then slept.

━━━━━━

As Wilco van Rooijen, Cas van de Gevel, and Pemba Gyalje dropped onto the steep paths near the bottom of the mountain, they were met by climbers from Base Camp. There had been no ropes on the lower thousand feet of the Cesen so the rescue party had fixed new lines to help the injured climbers get down.

Roeland van Oss and others from the Dutch team, including the Base Camp manager, Sajjad Shah, gathered around the men. They had brought water, Pepsi, Coca-Cola and Snickers and Kit Kat bars.

One of Sajjad's jobs in Base Camp had been to keep Van Rooijen in supplies of cookies and peanut butter. It was one of his favorite foods, so much so that halfway through the season Shah had had to send down for another dozen jars from Skardu. Now, when Van Rooijen saw the Pakistani, he bellowed out: "Sajjad!" Then added with a smile: "Where are my peanut butter and cookies!" Shah could see that the ebullient Dutch leader had emerged from his trials with his spirits undiminished.

As they gathered around, Van Rooijen, Van de Gevel, and Pemba

Gyalje asked the climbers from Base Camp whether there had been a sighting of Gerard McDonnell. It became clear as they talked that if there had been any chance that the Irishman was alive, it was now finally gone.

Roeland van Oss got on the radio and satellite phone to report that the rescue party had reached the stricken climbers. "Wilco, Cas, and Pemba are safe," he said somberly. "But we are now fairly sure that Gerard died in the Bottleneck."

In Utrecht, Maarten van Eck had called Heleen as soon as Van Rooijen reached Camp Three. He posted the news of the successful rescue on the Dutch team's website:

WILCO IS ALIVE EXHAUSTED BUT HE SOUNDS GOOD. ONLY PROBLEMS WITH FEET. WE HOPE TO UPDATE SOON!

In Ireland, the hopes of Gerard's family that he was the lone surviving climber were finally extinguished. On Sunday morning, the McDonnells called a news conference at the local school, just a few hundred yards from the farmhouse. It was a gray day. His brother-in-law stood in the parking lot to announce that they accepted he was dead. A few days later the family issued a statement to the press:

We are extremely proud of the many heroic and brave achievements of Gerard, whose death has left a major void in our lives. He brought honour not only to us his family, but the whole country when he became the first Irish man to summit K2.

On K2, the decisive realization that McDonnell was dead seemed to have the most powerful effect on Pemba Gyalje. From that moment, he hung his head and fell silent, the other climbers noticed.

He was convinced now that the climber in the red and black suit that Big Pasang had reported seeing being hit by ice and falling from the Traverse was indeed McDonnell. That meant the Irishman had not abandoned Jumik Bhote and the two injured Korean climbers on the slopes at the end of the Traverse. He had stayed behind after Marco Confortola had left and had helped them to descend, before he had been swept off the Traverse to his death.

Another Sherpa, Little Pasang Lama, had received a radio call in Camp Four from Big Pasang Bhote before the final avalanche; Big Pasang said again that he had reached the Koreans and Jumik Bhote near the Traverse. Jumik had even come on the radio to say his limbs were frozen and the injured Koreans were suffering from snow blindness but he could walk, and when he reached Base Camp he hoped he could be flown by helicopter to Islamabad and home.

Then Big Pasang and Jumik and the Koreans had died when the serac collapsed.

But it was already becoming complicated. Another Sherpa, Chhiring Dorje in the American team, believed that Gerard McDonnell had probably been the lone figure witnessed at 10 a.m. on Saturday, trapped above the serac and walking up and down on the snowfields. He had either fallen over the serac, Dorje felt, or climbed down onto the Traverse where he was hit by the avalanche and had little to do with the rescue of Jumik and the Koreans.

On the Cesen, it took the three injured climbers and their retinue another few hours to reach Base Camp. It was dark, approaching 9 p.m., when Pemba Gyalje walked in first, assisted by one member of the rescue team. It was a while before the other two men followed across the dark rocks of the Godwin-Austen glacier, hobbling away from the maw of K2 and into the blessed safety of Base Camp.

A lot of effort was now directed toward saving the men's frostbitten toes and fingers. The Americans had converted the big Dutch mess tent into a medical emergency room to receive the injured climbers.

It soon became a busy crowded scene inside. The cooks boiled water and put down blue basins for the men's feet. The Norwegians' heater blasted some warmth from the corner. Eric Meyer and Chris Klinke had their headlamps strapped on their foreheads. Their lights illuminated the prone figures of the two stricken Dutch climbers who were laid on bed mats, their backs propped up against the inflatable Ikea sofa that Rolf Bae had originally carried from Norway for Cecilie and that the Norwegians had also donated to the rescue effort.

In their orange North Face fleeces, both Dutch climbers looked years older. Cas van de Gevel, in particular, seemed shrunken and gray, his skin lined and hanging from his cheeks. Klinke and Chhiring Dorje handed out Pepsi in tin cups and with Lars Nessa they scrubbed and warmed Van Rooijen's and Van de Gevel's hands and feet, while Meyer prepared to apply what medicines he had. Roeland van Oss was relieved to let Meyer take charge, to see now whether the descent had been rapid enough to save the climbers' fingers and toes.

Meyer inserted plastic tubes into veins on the back of their hands and injected a cocktail of medicines. First, morphine and Valium to ease the painful thawing of their flesh. He also possessed two bottles of a new drug, tPA, or tissue plasminogen activator. Normally used to treat heart attacks, it had shown in university trials that it could help frostbite, though it had never before been tested at altitude and it had side effects such as internal bleeding. Meyer was worried about what dosage to try, so he called a specialist at the medical school in Denver, who advised against using it. The drug also had to be injected within twenty-four hours of the initial exposure. This applied only to Van de Gevel, but Meyer was growing so concerned about their condition that he injected it into both men. He followed it with another drug, heparin, to stop the blood clotting in the tiny vessels of their fingers and toes.

Fredrik Strang came into the tent and turned on his camera. Wilco van Rooijen looked disoriented as the Americans filled him in on the full extent of the disaster.

"How many victims are there?" he said.

"Eleven," said Meyer. "Eleven people."

"Missing?"

"No, dead. Rolf, Gerard."

Blowing out his cheeks, Van Rooijen gazed emptily around the tent.

They told him Marco Confortola had left Camp Four and that another rescue party was climbing up to meet him on the Abruzzi. Down at Base Camp, Roberto Manni, Confortola's Italian colleague, had been desperate for volunteers to help Confortola and had offered money to any Sherpa who was willing to go up to find him and bring him down. Eventually, after a day's delay caused by the need to get equipment together, another American climber, George Dijmarescu, had set off up the Abruzzi with the two Sherpas in his expedition.

Lying beside Van Rooijen, Van de Gevel sank lower against the mattress. Initially Meyer was most concerned about Van Rooijen's frostbite. He had slept two nights in the open, the first night at about 27,000 feet, the second at somewhere around 25,000 feet. But Van de Gevel's hands looked bad, too. He told Meyer about waking up with his gloves off. The Dutchman was a carpenter, Meyer knew, and his fingers were important to him. But the fingers on his left hand were limp blocks of gray, with purple streaks across the mid portions. Meyer could see hemorrhagic blisters, which meant serious frostbite damage.

They dunked his hands in a tin basin of warm water and soaked his feet in a bowl but repeatedly he dozed off, trying to stretch out, and pulling his hands and feet out of the water. Chris Klinke had to keep lifting them back in.

Looking in a concerned fashion at both men, Meyer said, "I hope they will keep their digits."

After a few hours, the only thing left that Meyer could do was bandage the two men up and prepare them for their departure. It was about 3:30 a.m. There was talk of helicopters flying up from Skardu to airlift them out.

CHAPTER TWENTY

Monday, August 4, 8 a.m.

Helicopter transportation for injured climbers is being organized for tomorrow morning," Maarten van Eck wrote in an update on his website late on Sunday night.

At K2 on Monday morning, Roeland van Oss thought the helicopters would not arrive until late, but at eight o'clock one of the military liaison officers at Base Camp rushed to his tent with the news that they were only forty minutes away. The Pakistani military had established a private company precisely with the aim of plucking injured mountaineers out of the Karakoram, and it had choppers stationed at the military airport at Skardu. Van Oss had spoken by satellite phone with the owner of Jasmine Tours, the Dutch expedition's organizer, and he had made the arrangements.

Suddenly Van Oss had much to do. He scurried to collect Van Rooijen's and Van de Gevel's bags. The Dutch climbing leader sat upright in the mess tent shooting instructions at Van Oss about all the jobs he had to do after Van Rooijen was gone, such as paying the porters and dealing with the remaining food barrels.

Away from the tents, about three-quarters of a mile down the glacier toward the southeastern shanks of the mountain, the Serbian team's liaison officer and a team of helpers shifted rocks to build a landing pad for the helicopters. They marked it with flags and a windsock.

At nine o'clock, two former Pakistani military Eurocopter Ecureuils, or Squirrel helicopters, flew in from the south, casting shadows against the mountainside. They came noiselessly at first but then thudded above the glacier near the tents.

Almost everyone left in Base Camp took turns in the scrum helping to lug Wilco van Rooijen over the rocks on a red stretcher. After they set him down, Chris Klinke shielded the Dutchman's head with his arms as the chopper blades billowed gusts of wind over the rocks. Then they lifted Van Rooijen through the helicopter door and the chopper hovered into the air and flew away.

Roberto Manni persuaded the pilot of the second Squirrel to take a detour up the Abruzzi ridge to attempt a long-line cable and harness rescue of Marco Confortola. The arrangement was that Confortola would climb down onto a flat space below House's Chimney, but when the helicopter got up to 19,000 feet the pilot could not see him. Confortola hadn't managed to descend to that point yet. The weather forced the chopper to wheel away without waiting.

The Squirrel flew back down to the Godwin-Austen glacier for Cas van de Gevel. His hands bandaged, the Dutchman walked from the tent to the landing strip.

The trip was a stunning hour back down the Baltoro glacier, past Masherbrum and Trango Towers, to Skardu. There, Van de Gevel was reunited with Van Rooijen, and the two men were hooked up to monitors in the military hospital, a one-story complex of run-down cream-colored buildings beneath the hot, sandy hills on the outskirts of the town, where military officials strode the grounds and loudspeakers repeatedly called people to prayer.

Back at K2, more porters were arriving to carry away the teams' gear. Mules waited around on the rocks. The big South Korean team climbed down to Base Camp, and Nawang, the cook from Nepal, prepared a special meal in the mess tent. His *bibimbap*—warm rice mixed with vegetables, chili, and meat, when they had some—had become a favorite of the Flying Jump team. Now he cooked the meal even though he had lost two friends from his own region, Jumik Bhote and Big Pasang. From outside, people heard him crying.

Chhiring Bhote was preparing to return to his village near Makalu to observe two months of mourning for Jumik.

The Korean climbers drank suji, which they had brought to K2 intending to celebrate Go Mi-sun's birthday. Instead they were marking the deaths of their two Sherpas and three of their own climbers. The Koreans were not going to wait around. They were crushed by the deaths. They rolled up their flags and their gear. Then the survivors walked out of Base Camp and left the tents standing for the porters to dismantle. They walked for two hours down to Broad Peak Base Camp, which was at a lower altitude for the bigger helicopters they had ordered up. Then the sky was full of helicopters, which flew them out of the Karakoram toward Islamabad.

Before they left, Lars Nessa spoke to Go Mi-sun. She was distraught at the deaths in the Korean team and she offered her commiserations for Rolf Bae. But she was not going to give up climbing; she was leaving to move on to the next peak in her quest to reach the top of all fourteen 26,000-foot mountains. She would die a year later on Nanga Parbat, another tough mountain in northern Pakistan.

Nessa thought about what he had learned from K2. The human costs of mountaineering. Not just those costs inflicted on a climber caught up in a tragedy like this, but the pain for the families left behind.

The Serbs from Vojvodina were leaving. Without Dren Mandic. Predrag Zagorac and Iso Planic intended to sell the team's spare oxygen cylinders and give the money to Jahan Baig's family.

Cecilie Skog had left earlier on Monday, trekking out alone with a single porter to reach Askole as quickly as possible, planning to barely stop to eat. Sixteen months later she would trek across Antarctica, her love for the wilderness undimmed. Nevertheless, her burden was heavy. And, Nessa thought, was it fair on his own family, his parents, who were farmers near Stavanger, or his girlfriend? Nessa had decided he would climb again but never on a killer mountain like K2.

After Van Rooijen and Van de Gevel had gone, Roeland van Oss left a lot of what he couldn't take with him for the porters to burn. Wastepaper, his Alistair MacLean and Tom Clancy novels, all the other garbage. He would never return to K2, never again face those weeks of climbing, all that danger, just to stand on a summit. What did it mean? Most of the people who died had been victims of bad luck, he thought. They were in the wrong place at the wrong time.

As the remaining Dutch climbers were packing up the equipment in Gerard McDonnell's tent, they discovered a bottle of beer among his belongings. That night, a group gathered in the Americans' mess tent and toasted the Irishman. They went around the table reminiscing about him.

"He was a gift to the world," said Eric Meyer in his toast. "He was a gentle, kind spirit."

A Serbian climber borrowed two tin plates from the kitchen tent and punched out the names of the dead. It took him five hours. He made a mistake with one plate and had to go back for a third.

Lars Nessa also made a plate for Rolf Bae, using a hammer and chisel.

Before they left K2, the climbers scaled the brown cliffs at the western edge of Base Camp to hang the plates on the Gilkey Memorial.

One of the oval plates was for Dren Mandic. It read:

DREN MANDIC

13.XII.1976–01.VIII. 2008

SUBOTICA

SERBIA

The Serbs sprinkled whisky on the plate and knocked some of it back themselves in honor of Mandic.

Another plaque was for Gerard McDonnell.

GERARD McDONNELL
20.01.1971–02.08.2008
LIMERICK
IRISH

Rolf Bae's plate had a cross hammered above his name:

ROLF BAE
19.01.1975–01.08.2008
NORWAY

On Monday morning, Marco Confortola had woken up alone at Camp Three, anxious because he had to navigate the Black Pyramid on his own. His feet throbbed as if they had nails in them, he feared he had frostbite in his left hand, and his penis was frozen.

He heard the sound of a helicopter and saw it rising from below, but then it went away and its buzzing faded. As he got down the Black Pyramid, clouds and snow blew in, and out of the mist he saw the three figures of the rescue party from Base Camp approaching. It was George Dijmarescu and two Sherpas from the Makalu Valley, Rinjing Sherpa and Mingma Sherpa. They gave him extra oxygen. They helped Confortola down to Camp Two, where he borrowed Dijmarescu's satellite phone so that at last he could call Luigi. He told his brother he was alive.

Confortola limped down to an area below House's Chimney where Dijmarescu and the two Sherpas had cleared a landing space for the helicopter. Confortola was excited that he was finally going to be delivered from his torment. But then Dijmarescu's radio blurted out the dispiriting news from Base Camp that the helicopter was canceled because of poor weather. Confortola's suffering was not going to end quickly and he realized he had to find yet more energy from he knew not where to keep going down.

The four men climbed down to Camp One, where they spent the night.

The next morning, Tuesday, they climbed down to Advance Base Camp, where a welcoming party hiked out from Base Camp to meet them, Red Bull, Coca-Cola, and salami in hand. The group included Eric Meyer, Chris Klinke, Chhiring Dorje, and the members of another newly arrived American expedition. They were carrying a stretcher but it was too difficult to walk with it on the rocks. They had heard he had been hit by an oxygen bottle, and Dijmarescu had radioed down that Confortola had also been caught in a rockfall. But Confortola was not in as terrible shape as they had feared, and his mood was improving now that he was convinced he was going to survive.

The weather was turning again. It was cold and damp, and a mix of snow and rain was coming down. Confortola sat on the rocks. The others gathered around while Meyer tried to diagnose his frostbite and they attempted to work out how they were going to carry him back to Base Camp. But Confortola soon lost patience and after ten minutes he stood up and started walking, and the others scrambled to catch up.

They walked slowly on the path between the mangled walls of the icefall. Despite his eagerness, he was unsteady on his feet and they coaxed him on for the three miles to Base Camp.

Halfway to Base Camp, he met another Italian climber, Mario Panzeri, who had hiked across from Broad Peak after news of the K2 disaster spread. Seeing someone he knew burst something inside Confortola, it seemed to the others, and he broke down. Sipping Red Bull, he sat for half an hour with Panzeri.

When the group reached Base Camp later on Tuesday, Confortola was surprised by how many of the tents had been taken down. The long strip of rocks was much barer. He learned about the number of people who had died. He hadn't known.

The Americans helped him inside the large, comfortable domed tent he shared with Roberto Manni, and Meyer treated him there, filling him with pain-relief drugs. He took off his boots and there was a purple line across his toes as if they had been burned. His worst fears were borne out. It was the damage wreaked by frostbite.

Confortola looked up at the doctor. "What a disaster," he said in astonishment.

Meyer shook his head. "I don't know," Meyer said uncertainly.

Confortola was angry at his HAPs, and at the whole country of Pakistan. One of his HAPs came to the tent and spoke to the other climbers. The Americans' Sherpa, Chhiring Dorje, chided him for not doing enough to help Confortola, for showing no respect to the people who employed him. The HAP went away looking embarrassed.

Meyer had no tPA left over since he had used both doses on Wilco van Rooijen and Cas van de Gevel. He would not have given it to Confortola anyway because of the blow the Italian had received to his head at the bottom of the Bottleneck, which increased the risk of internal bleeding. Instead, the only thing he could do was scrub Confortola's skin clean and try to kill the pain as much as possible.

Klinke thawed Confortola's feet in warm water, careful with the ribbons of frozen flesh that were peeling away. The feet didn't look as bad as Van Rooijen's or Van de Gevel's had but if the frostbite worsened, Meyer said, it could lay bare tendons and bones. They wrapped iodine-impregnated gauze around his toes.

As they worked on him, Confortola tried to talk about some of the things that had happened up above Camp Four. The story of his terrible experience was boiling inside him, they could see. Starting to cry, he talked about stopping to help the Koreans and he mentioned Jesus. But he was so emotional and exhausted that Meyer and Klinke could not understand much. They felt sorry for him.

"What do you know about Gerard?" Meyer said.

"I am grateful for you helping me," Confortola said.

The next day, Wednesday, August 6, a helicopter came up the valley and took Confortola away. He spent a night at the military hospital in Skardu, where he related the story of his rescue of the Koreans to the Italian embassy staff. Then he caught the Pakistani Airways flight back to Islamabad. From there he flew via London to Milan.

In the next few weeks, he became increasingly upset, and on some days he drove around the roads near his hometown and he didn't know where he was going, sometimes in tears, unable to come to terms with the deaths on the mountain, until he went to a friend for help. His feet were in a bad way by then but he was given emergency medical treatment. About six weeks after he left the mountain, he was treated in a hyperbaric chamber at a hospital in Padua. It was one of the best hospitals in Italy for frostbite and burns. The people around him assured him he was going to be all right but he knew his condition was bad, and in the end all of his toes were amputated.

After packing up at Base Camp, what was left of the Dutch team trekked out in a line down the Baltoro glacier, passing quickly through the camps at Concordia, Goro II, and Paiju, and skirting the big rock at Korophone, until in a few days they reached the muddy campsites at Askole.

From there they sped in dirty blue jeeps on the mountain road, packed tightly, swaying through the dust clouds thrown up by the Toyotas' wheels. Sajjad Shah, the team's bearded Base Camp manager, had traveled to K2 with the team on this same road two and a half months earlier. Now he gazed at the seat left empty by Gerard McDonnell.

The once polite, talkative Pemba Gyalje watched the ravines sullenly. When a fall of rocks blocked the road, Sajjad stayed with the equipment while the climbers switched to jeeps sent up from the western side. They drove four hours to the hotel in Skardu, to its cold showers and hard beds, delights after the mountain, and to the attentions of the international media. Wilco van Rooijen was already freely airing to the press his conclusions about what had gone wrong. When he returned to Europe, he would lose all the toes on his left foot and almost all the toes on the other. But a year later he would tell people he was considering another return to K2.

To the climbers left behind at Base Camp, the spine of rocks where the tents had stood seemed eerie and silent. The rocks were spotted with muck from the donkeys. Since the emergency helicopter evacuations, the crowds of fifty or more had fallen to less than a dozen people in a few days. Porters were taking down the Koreans' tents and burning the garbage. Eric Meyer and Chris Klinke's team was one of the last to leave, and before he walked out, Klinke left Meyer and Fredrik Strang and climbed a few hundred feet up to the Gilkey Memorial.

From high on the lonely promontory, he gazed down at the foot of K2, the spits of black and brown rock stretching onto the rubble of the bare glacier. The air was cold, still, and loud with the cawing of ravens. On the memorial, the metal plaques to the dead lined the wall, tied together with wire and tinkling slightly in the breeze.

Klinke was preparing to return to America and the real world. Before he came to Pakistan, he had split with his girlfriend, and he wasn't sure where he was going to live when he got back. He would find a job or join another expedition to somewhere else in the world.

Now that he was leaving K2, he thought of the people who were staying behind.

Before he had traveled to Pakistan and to K2 this season, the names on these plaques had been just that, names. But now there were new plates. Some of the names belonged to friends he had come to know. They had chosen to venture toward the ultimate prize, the summit of K2, and they had paid a terrible price. They had become a part of its history.

As he turned away, he saw their faces, heard their voices, remembered their kindnesses.

THE DEAD

Dren Mandic

Jahan Baig

Rolf Bae

Hugues d'Aubarède

Karim Meherban

Gerard McDonnell

Jumik Bhote

Pasang Bhote

Park Kyeong-hyo

Kim Hyo-gyeong

Hwang Dong-jin

EPILOGUE

My own journey to K2 began in Kilcornan in western Ireland. I flew from New York to Limerick and, in a jet-lagged haze, drove one hundred miles to the southern mountains to meet McDonnell's climbing mentor, Pat Falvey, a fast-talking Irishman in his fifties who organized climbing expeditions and had taken Gerard on his first climb of Everest. We sat in front of his computer and he pointed out the Bottleneck and the serac on photographs of K2. Scraps of climbing gear cluttered his house. A helmet. Boots. In the kitchen he tied a rope between two wooden chairs and clung on, demonstrating how the climbers on K2 had progressed up the Bottleneck and how Dren Mandic had unclipped from the fixed line. Falvey's own life had been hurt by his passion for climbing, he explained. His wife had left him; his sons called him names for risking his life. Behind him on the wall he had hung a painting of McDonnell beside one of Ernest Shackleton—"another Irish hero," he said.

Among the burble of drinkers in Kate Kearneys, a nearby pub, Falvey balanced a wallet on top of a beer glass and tipped it, flopping the wallet onto the table to demonstrate the effect of the serac falling. As we drove back in his Land Rover, I asked whether Gerard McDonnell had ever thought he was going to die. I expected Falvey to say, *Of course not*. But he shrugged and with an air of resignation said, "Everyone who ventures into the Death Zone knows they are dicing with death."

The following morning I drove back north to McDonnell's hometown for McDonnell's wake. A big white tent covered a rainy parking lot behind the Kilcornan school. Inside the tent, more than a thousand people dressed in their Sunday best stood at the edges or sat in rows in front of a long, white table. It was the first time many of them had heard the name K2. Behind the table hung a framed picture of McDonnell—a blue shirt, blue tie, a lick of brown hair, his enigmatic smile.

I was struck by how bewildered the people of McDonnell's village seemed to be. What exactly had motivated their son and brother to travel four thousand miles across the earth to risk his life on a mountain? they wondered. Was it worth such a cost?

The priest, Father Joe Noonan, uttered a few words through the microphone.

"We know we are here to honor Gerard, to praise him, and welcome Gerard to his heavenly home. Gerard, who died on the K2. That is his burial place, and in a sense where he wished to die."

McDonnell's mother, Margaret, a small woman dressed in black, was helped from the front row to the table to light a single candle that stood for her son's absent body. As she turned back, her uncomprehending loss seemed to ripple across the faces of the whole community.

"It was on a mountain that Moses communicated with God," Father Noonan went on. "It was on a mountain where Jesus was transfigured. It was on a mountain that Gerard achieved one of his life's ambitions. It was such a spiritual experience that he even referred to it as being an honor to die on a mountain."

A friend of McDonnell's read William Butler Yeats's poem "Aedh Wishes for the Cloths of Heaven."

Had I the heaven's embroidered cloths,
Enwrought with golden and silver light,
The blue and the dim and the dark cloths

Of night and light and the half light,
I would spread the cloths under your feet:
But I, being poor, have only my dreams;
I have spread my dreams under your feet;
Tread softly because you tread on my dreams.

Then, one by one, people who had known McDonnell carried gifts to the table. A drum, a picture of his home in Kilcornan, a Kilcornan flag to illustrate Ger's love of his parish, a passport. An Irish flag, a book for his love of literature, his late father's wristwatch. Annie Starkey, his girlfriend from Alaska, a trim young woman with dark curly hair, carried Tibetan prayer flags.

"Ger was a brave one," said his older brother, J.J., who also stood up to speak. "Ger, we miss you and we will love you. The future will be hard to face without you. Ger, God bless you, and may God have mercy on your brave soul."

Clearly, or at least it seemed to me, few of the people present could comprehend what drove McDonnell to K2. I encountered the same yearning for understanding, the void at the center of things, when I visited Hugues d'Aubarède's family in Lyon, France. In the elegant dining rooms of his friends, I listened to the stories of his love for the mountains and came to grasp the fascinating alter ego he had carefully constructed through his pursuit of distant peaks. But as well as the love, I witnessed the anger—in his partner, Mine, a wondrously robust woman who at first refused to talk to me before spending hours describing Hugues, and in his thirty-one-year-old daughter, Julia. Julia, who remained silent, carefully listening to my questions to others about her father's death only five months earlier, while Hugues's grandchild played at her knees.

I visited the dead, but I also had to confront the living. One morning in late November, I landed in Milan with an agreement to meet Marco Confortola. That evening he was to travel to Rome to receive a medal from the Association of Olympic Athletes of Italy. I was two hours late flying into Malpensa and by the time I was sprinting across the station platform at Milan's grand main station, the train was leaving with him on it. My phone beeped with a text message from his agent, Barbara Baraldi, explaining that he could not wait around any longer because his feet hurt so much. It had been only a month since his toes had been amputated.

In Rome, later that evening, at the Hotel Torre Rossa, I finally got my chance to meet Confortola. A young man emerged from the crowd, hopping awkwardly on crutches, broad-shouldered, wearing a white top and jeans, with a shaved head and a long sunburned face. An earring shone in his left ear.

"I am Marco," he said.

He immediately swung around and moved awkwardly back into the crowd, greeting well-wishers and pulling off his socks to show off his bandaged feet. Over dinner, he was treated like a rock star. Women flocked to the table. When I finally asked him what it was like on the summit of K2, he glanced up at me with sullen brown eyes as if he had been waiting for my question.

"Did it fill you with joy?"

"No. People died," he replied in his poor English. The conversation was over before it even began.

The next morning at Rome's Olympic stadium he gave a speech in front of five hundred people. He praised Gerard McDonnell. "It is important to say that Gerard, because he stayed too long above eight thousand meters, he went out of his mind. He is no longer with us. He gave his life. I was lucky not to go out of my mind. A part of this medal is also his."

Just as it was getting interesting, he cut the talk short. There was loud applause and then to my surprise I was called to the front to give my own assessment of the 2008 climb and of Confortola's heroics. Even as I spoke, staring at the rows of intent faces eager for further praise of their national hero, it struck me as implausible that I was speaking at all. Confortola stood at my side, listening, too, as if he were waiting for some sort of judgment about himself and the mountain.

On the journey back to Milan, he was less than keen to talk. Grimacing, he placed his feet on the table and massaged them through his socks. He hid behind his iPod earphones, insisting he wanted to sleep. Barbara looked embarrassed. She said he had been bombarded with media interviews. I felt both that he was wasting my time and that I was intruding on a terrible memory. But just when I felt like giving in, Confortola removed his earphones. He stretched out his legs and for the rest of the way to Milan sketched detailed scenes from the mountain on a napkin and gave me a blow-by-blow account of his fight to save the two Korean climbers and Jumik Bhote. His mood improved. We ended our journey standing in Milan Stazione, eating grilled cheese and ham sandwiches, while he pointed out the tallest stilettos on the women striding by and grinned at me.

He talked for hours, but even then there were questions he would not answer, and parts of his account already felt rehearsed, as if he were not telling the whole story. Two days later, we traveled north to the Alpine village where he grew up, and I saw another side of Confortola. By now it was clear to me he was a wily survivor, a full-time mountaineer who climbed to make money. I met his father, a plain, pleasant man. Marco was liked in his village, even if he was regarded as something of a hothead. We sat on the lawn in front of his house in Via Uzzi. He did not invite me inside. Tibetan prayer flags fluttered from the roof in the breeze. His nephew, who had Down syndrome, played with a dog, Bobby, and Confortola occasionally showed off his strength by tussling with them. He grew taciturn again and shook his head when I asked questions, such as whether his Pakistani high-altitude porters were responsible for forgetting essential equipment at Camp Four, just before the main summit push. Baraldi said he would not be able to climb for a long while and he needed to find other ways to make money. When we said good-bye, he joked about the amazing strength of his arms. I expected a crushing handshake but his hold was surprisingly weak. He dropped my hand quickly.

I was relieved when I returned to New York to receive an email from a friend of Cecilie Skog, who said that she would talk to me. She had granted no other interviews. I expected to be flying to Norway but instead I was told to meet her in Denver, Colorado. There, two weeks later, a small, beautiful woman dressed in a white blouse with lace cuffs stepped into the Holiday Inn Crowne Plaza.

Only sixteen weeks after the death of her husband on K2, she had traveled to the Rockies to return to the mountains. She had brought her ice axe with her and was planning on going ice climbing near Boulder.

"I will see how I feel," she said, shrugging as she sat opposite me in the booth in the hotel restaurant, explaining that she had just wanted to get away from Norway.

Skog began to cry as she poured forth her memories of how the mountain shook that night in the dark beneath the serac, how she called for Rolf Bae until Lars Nessa finally urged her to go down, and she talked of her guilt about leaving Bae behind.

"We did look for him," she said, wiping her eyes on her red napkin. "For so long, I regretted going on. I still do sometimes. I ask myself sometimes. I don't know how I got down."

Despite her grief, Skog communicated something that I found infectious. It was a powerful joy for the outdoors—she called it a "devotion to the outdoors"—a love of life in the open. I saw this same physical joy in the Spanish climber Alberto Zerain when I visited him at his home in a small village about forty miles outside Bilbao. We talked for hours on the sofa in his living room, watching the homemade film of his K2 trip—bizarrely set to the soundtrack of the Who's "Baba O'Riley."

Afterward we drove to a nearby highway restaurant for a late lunch. He was a gentle, polite man who had bonded most strongly on the mountain with the Pakistani high-altitude porters and said he wanted to write a book about the region from their perspective. I told him I would send him Greg Mortenson's *Three Cups of Tea*.

Like all of the climbers I met, Zerain was extremely fit, and when I asked him how long it would take him to prepare if he wanted to go back to K2, he pushed back his chair and clenched his fist demonstratively. "I would go back now!" he said, in a surprisingly loud voice, gazing through the window as if the mountain were already calling him.

But while Zerain exuded the same physical passion as Skog, there was something Skog and Bae shared in their love for the outdoors that the others lacked. The mountains were the place where Skog and Bae could be together. It was where and how they expressed their love for one another. In contrast, Zerain's wife, Patricia, a teacher, glanced over uneasily when he talked about his plans to spend months away again on Kanchenjunga; and in the case of Hugues d'Aubarède, frictions with the loved ones he left behind ran through his life. When Skog discussed their life at Base Camp—the conversations with friends, the days side by side on the slope—it made me think how the couple had brought their relationship to the wilderness and imposed it there, a very human urge. Cruel then that K2 had cared nothing for that and wiped it blithely away.

One January morning, I flew to the Netherlands for what I considered would be my most difficult interview, with Wilco van Rooijen. I had talked to him at the wake in Kilcornan, where he had sat erect in a wheelchair, his bandaged feet pushed out in front of him. His wife, Heleen, sat beside him looking weary of the attention, and a bit resentful. At that time, Van Rooijen had told me he had no time for involved explanations of what went wrong on K2.

"Bullshit," he said. "It's K2. You know it is going to happen," he said, referring to the collapse of the serac. "Some people had bad luck."

His subsequent emails were abrupt, though eventually he offered a time and a date for another meeting. One evening I found myself in the east of the Netherlands near the German border, walking across a plowed field in the dark on the outskirts of a village called Voorst. Even now, I was worried that Van Rooijen would slam the door in my face. How could I presume to pry into the inner experiences of his profession? A white Land Rover, splashed with mud and sponsors' logos, was parked outside the old straw-roofed farmhouse into which he had recently moved.

When he opened the door, wearing slippers and holding back a golden retriever, he looked me up and down and seemed both surprised and impressed that I had managed to find him at all. He switched on the kettle for tea but it went unpoured for four hours as he stood before me and gave a fevered, nonstop recounting of his horrific experiences on K2. He sat on the stone floor, legs crossed, to demonstrate how he had bivouacked, and paced across the room as he waded through the deep snow and the whiteout below the Shoulder. I listened in wonder and gratitude for the time he was giving me.

At 1 a.m., my tea cold, Van Rooijen stopped. My notebook was full as he called a taxi for me.

I heard a faint crying, and when we opened the door to the hallway his young son was screaming.

By now my taxi driver, a young man from Afghanistan, had arrived.

I asked Van Rooijen if his wife was with his son but he said no, it was her night off. He was in charge.

"But she must be in the house."

"No, in Utrecht."

I wondered how long the boy, about a year old, had been crying.

Van Rooijen sold me a book about his expedition to K2 in 2006 and I left.

The taxi driver, a doctor, had been watching all of this. "He is a focused man, if I may say so, egocentric," he said as we drove away toward the highway in the dark. I had to agree.

Still, Van Rooijen had given me insight into mountaineering psychology. Before I left, he had said something unsettling. Leaning back in his chair, he shook his head. "Shame about Marco, though, that he got it all wrong. He was exhausted. His mind was obviously gone. He may have . . . exaggerated."

He was referring to the story that Confortola had recounted on the train from Rome to Milan: the struggle beside Gerard McDonnell to free the two trapped South Koreans and Jumik Bhote; McDonnell subsequently wandering away in a hypoxic haze; his subsequent death in the avalanche. It was one of the most devastating chapters of the entire tragedy. But recently, McDonnell's family had begun to dispute it.

Confortola stuck tenaciously to his story, but McDonnell's family put forth a rival account, the rewriting led by Annie Starkey, McDonnell's partner in Alaska. She could not believe that McDonnell would walk away from the trapped climbers, no matter what pressure his mind and body were under. In fact, she insisted it was McDonnell who had stayed and Marco Confortola who had climbed down. It was not McDonnell whom Confortola saw killed in the avalanche but instead another climber entirely, Karim Meherban, Hugues d'Aubarède's high-altitude porter. She had photographs she believed showed Karim on the top of the serac before he fell. McDonnell had freed the trapped mountaineers and was descending behind them when he was thrown to his death by a separate avalanche.

For evidence, Starkey relied, among other things, on a radio call that Pemba Gyalje said he had received from Pasang Bhote. In the call, according to Gyalje, the Sherpa reported having reached the trapped climbers and that he was guiding them back down toward Camp Four, just minutes before they were swept away in the serac collapse. Pasang also said he had seen a climber in a red and black suit following behind. In Gyalje and Starkey's view, this was Gerard McDonnell, who had just freed the Koreans and Jumik Bhote.

When I sought out the opinion of Chris Klinke, the American climber who had been closely involved in coordinating the rescue attempt from Base Camp, he said, "I don't believe Gerard freed the Koreans; they had been hanging there for twenty-four hours, and you don't just get up and walk down after that, though he may have rescued Jumik Bhote. I believe however it was Gerard that Marco saw killed."

I also called Michael Kodas, a climber and author who writes about mountaineering and who knew some of the people involved in the tragedy. He said he had studied the photographs of the serac and Bottleneck on the morning of August 2, purportedly taken by Pemba Gyalje and published on the website ExplorersWeb, which Starkey claimed showed Gerard working to free the climbers. But Kodas was unconvinced. The narrative Starkey and ExplorersWeb had imposed on them was just "too perfect," he said. In a follow-up email, he said that the "evidence—Pemba's supposition that the man described in a radio call from a now-dead colleague was Gerard, tiny dots in photos that can't be identified for certain as climbers, much less as specific climbers engaged in a rescue, and a faint line in the top of the glacier—one of scores of such marks—was inadequate "to contradict the description of the only living eyewitness to the events," Marco Confortola.

It is possible that McDonnell stayed or returned after Marco Confortola descended and helped the two Korean climbers and Jumik

Bhote begin their journey down. If it is true, it could be one of the most selfless rescue attempts in the history of high-altitude mountaineering. Confortola would be right in his speech in Rome to say McDonnell deserved at least part of his medal. Even the fact that, in Confortola's account, McDonnell stayed for one and a half hours alongside the Italian to try to free the climbers is unimaginably brave. It sits alongside other acts of heroism over those three days, such as Chhiring Dorje's descent tied to Little Pasang, Fredrik Strang and Eric Meyer's ascent to try to resuscitate Dren Mandic, the decision by Pemba Gyalje to retrieve Marco Confortola. And, perhaps most of all, the willing climb by Big Pasang Bhote, and behind him by Chhiring Bhote, into the terrifying dangers of the Bottleneck to reach their cousin and brother Jumik, only for Big Pasang to lose his life.

It is a terrible sadness that McDonnell died. It is made worse that we will never know for sure about those last minutes of his life, just as we will never know for certain what Big Pasang found at the top of the Bottleneck.

This was the point in the story about which there was sharpest disagreement, but it was not the only one. In piecing together the tragedy, I had expected a clear narrative but I found myself in some postmodern fractured tale. For example, I put it to the Serbs that in the final ascent to the summit, their HAP had turned around and that important equipment he was carrying was left behind below Camp Four. They retorted that this was ridiculous. The lack of equipment for the summit bid was someone else's fault. Chhiring Dorje, the Sherpa in the American expedition, told me how he caught Wilco van Rooijen when the Dutchman slipped on his way up in the Bottleneck, and several others corroborated this version of events; but Van Rooijen reacted with surprise when I asked him about the incident. Many people I have interviewed claimed that it was under the Korean team's influence that the ropes were set low before the Bottleneck and that their climbers were responsible for the extremely slow progress across the Traverse. But when I caught up with Go Mi-sun and Kim Jae-soo in a guesthouse in Islamabad, they claimed that the ropes on the Bottleneck had been set too far to the right—this had nothing to do with the Korean team and it was this that had caused the delay. And the real reason for the late descent was that exhausted climbers from other expeditions were using their ropes on the way down and holding everybody else up.

There were several more points of disagreement—not surprising given the fact that there were so many strong characters on the mountain with different points of view, and then there is the trick that lack of oxygen can play on memory at 20,000 feet above sea level.

Fortunately, in most cases the differences were a matter of shading. Most people agreed on the significant points, and a clear story emerged.

Ten months after the accidents I flew to Pakistan, intending to travel to K2, still unclear after all my conversations as to why people would risk their lives on such a mountain. The Taliban was intensifying its insurgency and the country seemed in uproar; climbing K2 at this time meant traveling through a nation at war.

One hot night, I crept out of Islamabad in a white Toyota minivan, sitting beside six climbers who were also heading north to the mountains—in their case, to Gasherbrum I and II, two peaks near K2. We followed the Karakoram Highway, skirting the Swat Valley where the Pakistani Army was launching its latest bloody offensive. From Askole, we trekked six days east surrounded by the cold solitude of the Baltoro glacier to K2 Base Camp.

In the frigid morning, my heart beating wildly from the altitude and exhaustion, I gazed up two miles in the sky, trying to make out the serac's cruel, jagged outline. My seven porters, fearful of avalanches, and superstitious about this place, clattered impatiently around me, eager to leave these altitudes. Finally, in the presence of this awesome mountain, I considered its reputation for death, the group of people who had challenged it, and the questions that had filled my mind ever since I wrote the first story in the *New York Times* about the disaster.

K2 was terrifically beautiful—its beauty exceeding anything I had expected. Yet, still the questions remained. Why had they come? Why had I come? For me, their story possessed an archetypal force, specific to their time and location and the personalities involved, but also basic and timeless.

They had broken out of comfortable lives to venture to a place few of us dare go in our lives. They had confronted their mortality, immediately and up close. Some had even come back to K2 after serious injury in earlier years, attracted like flies to the light to some deeper meaning about themselves, human experience, and human achievement.

In return, K2 had required from them heroism and selflessness and responsibility. It had also laid bare fatal flaws and staggering errors.

I thought about Rolf Bae waiting below the summit for his wife—forever waiting now.

I thought of Pasang Bhote, doing his duty by his clients and climbing back along the Traverse to reach Jumik Bhote and the other trapped men.

Some had emerged from the ordeal; others had perished. All had burned brightly in their lives.

ACKNOWLEDGMENTS

I owe a debt of gratitude to the many people who graciously gave me many hours to tell me their story or the stories of their loved ones who died.

In particular, I thank Cecilie Skog, Annie Starkey, Mine Dumas, and Raphaele Vernay.

For historical discussions of the Himalayas and technical climbing descriptions I am grateful to Phil Powers, Kurt Diemberger, Agostino da Polenza, Maurice Isserman, and Qudrat Ali as well as to the following books: *Fallen Giants*, by Maurice Isserman and Stuart Weaver; *K2: The Story of the Savage Mountain*, by Jim Curran; *Going Higher*, by Charles S. Houston; *The Avalanche Handbook*, by David McClung and Peter Schaerer; and *Wilderness Mountaineering*, by Phil Powers. These books are all good introductions to the mountains and their dangers.

I would also like to thank the following people: Halyna Freeland; Andrea Kannapell, who worked side by side with me on the foreign desk at the *New York Times* on the day I wrote the first story and is such a wise adviser; and Andrew Ensslen, who risked his life by venturing with me north past Concordia and was flown out by helicopter from the mountains. I am also indebted to my excellent editors Jennifer Barth and Joel Rickett, and to my wonderful agent Andrew Wylie.

Thanks as well to: John Makinson, Mary Boies, David Boies, Bruce Nichols, Gillian Blake, Rick Gladstone, Greg Winter (for the better intro), Susan Chira, David Gillen, Jim Roberts, Chris Conway, Mike Nizza, David Smith, Marc Charney, Dexter Filkins, Alberto Zerain,

Patricia Prevost Zarate, John Elsen, Mick Sussman, Mark van de Walle, George Semler, Hannah Semler, Santiago Lyon, Rob Lerner, Kim Jaesoo, Go Mi-sun, David Hamilton, Peter Truell, Jerry del Missier, Rosa Shipley, Alan Cowell, Su-jin Chu, the families and friends of Philippe Vernay and Hugues d'Aubarède, Hervé Perouse, Nick Rice, Roeland van Oss, Jelle Staleman, Lars Flato Nessa, Bjorn Sekkesaeter, Tom Sjogren, Alisa Dogramadzieva, Predrag Zagorac, Milivoj Erdeljan, George Martin, Chuck Boyd, Andy Selter, Virginia O'Leary, Judy Aull, Natalka Chomiak, Chrystia Chomiak, Anne Freeland, Justine Simon, Eric Meyer (for many things, especially the many hours he gave me and his good-natured patience), Fredrik Strang, Chris Klinke, Chhiring Dorje, Marco Confortola, John Fisher Burns, Wilco van Rooijen, Cas van de Gevel, Tilak Pokharel, Donatella Fioravanti, Enrico Dalla Rosa, Barbara Baraldi, Asghar Ali Porik, Sajjad Shah, Erika Koning, Alan Terry, Douglas Bowley, Audrey Hintzy, Nicolas Mugnier, Yan Giezendanner, Nazir Sabir, Dirk Grunert, Jacek Teler, Paulo Roxo, Daniela Teixeira, Michael Kodas, Maarten van Eck, Jon Yellen, Jack Reilly, Elisabeth Rosenthal, David Roberts, Mike Farris, Pat Falvey, and Gary Landeck.

Also, Chris Warner of Earth Treks (who helped me care), Bruce Normand, Len Kannapell, Liz Alderman, Miguel Helft, Carol Bowley, Matt Ericson, Alexis Gelber, Bill Brink, Stuart Emmrich, Jawaid Iqbal, Anup Kaphle, Jerome O'Connell, Eelco Jansen, Paul Golob, Mike Oreskes, Paul Walters, Julian Curnuck, Karrar Haidri of Saltoro Summits, Chhiring Bhote, Tim O'Brien, Christian Trommsdorff, Yannick Graziani, Captain Shan-ul-Haq, Katarzyna Sklodowska, Pavel Wojas, Serge Civera, Alex Friedman, Salman Masood, Jane Perlez, Katherine Ensslen, Elettra Fiumi, Peter Chang, Choe Sang-hun, Joe Bowley, Jane Bowley, Anya Stiglitz, Tilak Pokharel, Jason Sack, Alan Arnette, Au Bon Pain at the Port Authority Bus Station in New York (for the table in the corner), Natalka Freeland, David Goodhart, John Lloyd. Finally, I would like to thank with all my heart my children, Natalka, Halyna and Ivan, and my wife Chrystia Freeland.

NOTES

In researching *No Way Down*, I relied heavily on interviews with the climbers and their families, friends, and colleagues. Unless indicated otherwise, all of the following interviews were conducted in person:

Qudrat Ali, Skardu, Pakistan, June 2009, also by email, April, June 2009; Judy Aull, by telephone, February 2009; Alan Arnette, July 2009; Barbara Baraldi, Rome, Milan, Valfurva, November 2008, and by telephone, January, March, June 2009; Chhiring Bhote, interview by local stringer, Tilak Pokharel, Kathmandu, January 2009; Chuck Boyd, by telephone, December 2009; Serge Civera, by phone, April 2009; Marco Confortola, Rome, Milan, Valfurva, December 2008, also by telephone, August 2008, and by fact-checker Elettra Fiumi in New York via telephone, December 2009; Agostino da Polenza, by email, December 2009; Kurt Diemberger, by telephone December 2009; Chhiring Dorje, New York, January 2010, and Kathmandu, January 2009, with local stringer Tilak Pokharel, and by telephone, December 2008; Mine Dumas, Lyon, France, January 2009; Milivoj Erdeljan, interview by email, December 2008, and in Belgrade, Serbia, by local reporter Alisa Dogramadzieva; Mike Farris, January 2010; Pat Falvey, Ireland, August 2008, and by telephone, July 2009; Donatella Fioravanti, by email, May 2009; Yan Giezendanner, Chamonix, France, January 2009; Go Mi-sun, and in Seoul, January 2009, by local reporter Peter Chang (Islamabad, June 2009) Yannick Graziani, by telephone, December 2009; Maurice Isserman, by telephone, April 2009; Kim Jae-soo, Seoul, 2008, by local reporter Peter Chang, and Islamabad, June 2009; Chris Klinke, interviews by phone, November 2008, August, September, October, November, December 2009; Michael Kodas, by telephone and email, October 2009; Eric Meyer, Denver, Colorado, December 2008, and by phone and email, December 2008, and April, October, and December 2009, January 2010; Nicolas Mugnier, Chamonix, France, January 2009; Lars Flato Nessa, Stavanger, Norway, January 2009, and by telephone and email, October, November, December 2009 and January 2010; Bruce Normand, by email, January 2010;

Jerome O'Connell, Kilcornan, Ireland, August 2008; Virginia O'Leary, New York, April 2009, and by telephone and email January, July, and December 2009; Asghar Ali Porik, Islamabad, Pakistan, June 2009; Phil Powers, Denver, Company, December 2008 and by telephone and email, May 2009; Nick Rice, interviews by phone, from K2 Base Camp, August 5, 2009, and by phone November 2008 and January 2009; Nazir Sabir, interview by email, December 2009; Bjorn Sekkesæter, interview by email, December 2008, December 2009; Andy Selter, by phone, December 2009; Sajjad Shah, Islamabad, June 2009; Cecilie Skog, Denver, Colorado, December 2008; Jelle Staleman, by telephone, December 2008; Annie Starkey, by email, October and November 2009; Fredrik Strang, interviews by phone, December 2008, April 2009, June 2009; Christian Trommsdorff, by phone, December 2009; Cas van de Gevel, Utrecht, the Netherlands, January 2009 and by email and phone, December 2009; Maarten van Eck, Kilcornan, Ireland, August 2008, and by phone, December 2008; Roeland van Oss, Lyon, France, January 2009; Wilco van Rooijen, Voorst, the Netherlands, January 2009, and by email, December 2009; Philippe Vernay, Lyon, France, January 2009; Raphaele Vernay, Lyon, France, January 2009; Paul Walters, by email, December 2009; Chris Warner, by telephone, February 2010; Predrag Zagorac, by telephone, December 2008, and in person with local stringer/reporter Alisa Dogramadzieva, Belgrade, Serbia; Alberto Zerain, Subillana-Gasteiz, near Bilbao, Spain, January 2009, and by email, December 2009.

For perhaps understandable reasons, two of the climbers, Pemba Gyalje and Pasang Lama, did not agree to an interview. Pemba's friend Gerard McDonnell had died and Little Pasang had lost friends. As a result, some parts of the story are weighted away from them more than I would have liked, especially in the case of Gyalje, who was a pivotal figure. However, I managed to see filmed video evidence Gyalje gave in Islamabad in August 2008, and which was provided for me by Annie Starkey.

PROLOGUE

The confused departure from Camp Four in the early hours of August 1 was described to me by many people, including Eric Meyer, Nick Rice, Alberto Zerain, and Chhiring Dorje. These moments, and other parts of the story, were captured to differing degrees by some early and excellent magazine treatments of the 2008 accidents. These early accounts include: Michael Kodas's "A Few False Moves," *Outside Magazine* (September 2008); Freddie Wilkinson's "Perfect Chaos," *Rock and Ice* (December 2008); and Matthew Power's "K2: The Killing Peak," *Men's Journal* (November 2008).

Meyer's Talus cold-weather mask warmed and added moisture to the air he was breathing—important because at altitude the air is especially cold and dry.

The volume of air breathed per minute increases with altitude, and this also adds to the dryness of a climber's airways—causing mountaineers' well-known "Khumbu cough."

The description of the ropes situation is drawn from interviews with Wilco van Rooijen, Chris Klinke, Cecilie Skog, and Lars Nessa, among others.

Meyer and Fredrik Strang provided details on their climb up the Shoulder, and their deliberations about whether to turn back, which are also captured on Fred Strang's film, *A Cry from the Top of the World* (Mastiff AB, Stockholm, Sweden, 2010).

The description of their return to Camp Four is based on interviews with Strang, Meyer, and Rice.

The documentary film *Disaster on K2*, shown on the Discovery Channel in March 2009, provides a good setup for the climb, and includes footage from the weeks surrounding the final ascent, as well as interviews with the climbers.

For climbing statistics, I relied on data from adventurestats.com or www .alpine-club.org.uk; explorersweb.com; 8000er.com, and the Himalayan Index.

CHAPTER ONE

Details of the journey into the Karakoram from the Pakistan side come from my own trip to K2 in June 2009. For historical treatments of K2, I relied on: Jim Curran, *K2: The Story of the Savage Mountain* (Seattle: Mountaineers, 1995); and Maurice Isserman and Stewart Weaver, *Fallen Giants: A History of Himalayan Mountaineering from the Age of Empire to the Age of Extremes* (New Haven, Conn.: Yale University Press, 2008). Another overview is provided by Kenneth Mason's *Abode of Snow* (New York: Dutton, 1955).

For further details on the Duke of Abruzzi's early expedition, see Mirella Tenderini and Michael Shandrick, *The Duke of the Abruzzi: An Explorer's Life* (Seattle: Mountaineers, 1997).

For insights into the 1954 successful summit attempt, Lino Lacedelli and Giovanni Cenacchi's *K2, The Price of Conquest* (Seattle: Mountaineers, 2006), provides Lacedelli's account. David Roberts also provides a considered assessment of that expedition in "K2: The Bitter Legacy," *National Geographic Adventure* (September 2004); Ardito Desio provides an account of his climb in *Victory Over K2* (New York: McGraw Hill, 1956); as does Walter Bonatti in *The Mountains of My Life* (New York: The Modern Library, 2001).

Kurt Diemberger supplies a great overview of the attraction and challenges of K2 in *The Endless Knot* (Seattle: Mountaineers, 1991).

Sivalaya, Explorations of the 8000-meter Peaks of the Himalayas, by Louis C. Baume (Seattle: Mountaineers, 1979), is a good handbook of the world's biggest mountains.

CHAPTER TWO

The details of Dren Mandic's climb in the Bottleneck are from Predrag Zago-rac. His life and weeks on the mountain are based on interviews with Zagorac, Milivoj Erdeljan, and on the team's blog reports. Zagorac's thoughts and comments inform my description of Dren's point of view. The account of the team's ascent from Base Camp is drawn from interviews with Zagorac and Qudrat Ali, and from the Serbian expedition report:

http://www.vojvodineanexpedition.net/index.php/K2-2008./REPORT-OF-THE-EXPEDITION-SERBIA-K2-2008.php4

Details of conditions and events in the Bottleneck were provided by Lars Nessa, Cecilie Skog, Zagorac, Wilco van Rooijen, Marco Confortola, and Chhiring Dorje.

There is some dispute about whether Mandic stood up or not before falling a second time.

CHAPTER THREE

Eric Meyer, Nick Rice, and Fred Strang described the scene at Camp Four after Mandic's death. Some of these moments are also shown in *A Cry from the Top of the World.*

Strang's ascent, his meeting with the Serbs, and confrontation with Jahan Baig were related to me by Strang and Predrag Zagorac. Along with Eric Meyer, Strang and Zegorac also provided an account of Baig's death. Again, there was some divergence in accounts: Strang insisted Baig had an ice axe, but Meyer reported that Baig had no axe to arrest his fall. Nick Rice provided insight into Baig's possibly hypoxic state at Camp Four, as well as background on Baig's behavior around Base Camp. Baig's background is from Qudrat Ali, both an interview in Skardu and several email exchanges. Details of the return to Camp Four are based on interviews with Strang, Meyer, Zagorac, and Paul Walters.

Charles S. Houston, David E. Harris, and Ellen J. Zeman's *Going Higher: Oxygen, Man and Mountains* offers an excellent overview of the effects of high altitude on the body.

CHAPTER FOUR

The story of Fritz Wiessner's attempt on K2 is told brilliantly in the afore-mentioned books *K2: The Story of the Savage Mountain* and *Fallen Giants.* See also Andrew J. Kauffman and William L. Putnam's *K2: The 1939 Tragedy* (Seattle: Mountaineers, 1992).

CHAPTER FIVE

The conditions in the Bottleneck and the Traverse on K2 appear to have changed somewhat over time. A few decades before the teams arrived in 2008, snow was so heavy on the Traverse that in some years expeditions required no fixed rope at all, only their ice axes, and ascended to the summit and descended without fixed lines, according to Chris Warner, an experienced American climber who summitted in 2007.

The definition of what constitutes the Traverse and the Bottleneck has also shifted. Earlier in the mountain's history, "Bottleneck" may only have referred to the very narrow passage at the top of the couloir, but by 2008 most people understood it as the entire part of the route rising from the Shoulder to the Traverse. The Traverse proper is the short but steep horizontal crossing beneath the serac. The name, however, is also often extended to include the rising but less steep diagonal that climbers follow around the edge of the serac up to the top of the hanging glacier.

There are differing accounts about the amount of time spent considering whether to continue to the summit. Marco Confortola, Lars Nessa, and Wilco van Rooijen described the frustration experienced by the climbers who had to wait in the Traverse. Confortola's book, *Giorni di Ghiaccio* (Milan: Baldini Castoldi Dalai editore, 2008) conveys this, and also provides an overview of his climb. As Michael Kodas pointed out to me, the groupthink that leads expeditions onward often happens and is regularly cited as a cause of accidents in the mountains. For insight into the South Korean team, I relied on interviews with Go Mi-sun and Kim Jae-soo. It is a feature of many mountaineering seasons that some expeditions arrive late to take advantage of the resources put in place by the bigger expeditions. The wait for the Koreans was related by, among others, Lars Nessa, Van Rooijen, and Alberto Zerain. The dynamics of the Norwegian team, and details of Rolf's life, were drawn from interviews with Cecilie Skog, Bjorn Sekkesaeter, and Lars Nessa. Jelle Staleman, Chhiring Dorje, and Lars Nessa contributed the story of the yak. Lars Nessa and Marco Confortola provided details about Hugues d'Aubarède's condition; d'Aubarède's blog, maintained by Raphaele Vernay, also served as a terrific resource on Hugues's time on the mountain. Other information about Hugues came from Yan Giezendanner, Serge Civera, and Nicolas Mugnier. For physical descriptions of the Traverse, I am grateful to Nessa, Van Rooijen, Confortola, Phil Powers, and to Chris Warner. Details on the Dutch team were provided by Cas van de Gevel, Roeland van Oss, Jelle Staleman, Maarten van Eck, Nick Rice, and Van Rooijen. Insights into its dynamics were also drawn from the Norit blog and from Nick Rice's blog, http://www.nickrice.us/index_files/k2dispatch.htm, which provided good exposition on the weeks at Base Camp. Additional information on Marco's life was provided by Donatella Fioravanti and Enrico Dalla Rosa.

Information about Gerard McDonnell at this point on the climb was supplied by Lars Nessa and by Van Rooijen. Details on McDonnell's early life and preparation for K2 were drawn from interviews with Van Rooijen, Annie Starkey, Pat Falvey, Jacek Teler, Alan Arnette, Chris Warner, and Jerome O'Connell.

CHAPTER SIX

Details on Alberto Zerain's ascent and his background are drawn from an interview at his home, and from his wife, Patricia Prevost Zarate. The order of the climbers he passed on his descent varies in other accounts.

CHAPTER SEVEN

Information on the Norwegians' ascent to the summit was provided by Cecilie Skog and Lars Nessa. The account of the South Koreans' summit was drawn from an interview with Go Mi-sun in Islamabad. For the Dutch team's arrival, I drew on interviews with Wilco van Rooijen, Cas van de Gevel, Maarten van Eck, and the Norit blog, and from Van Rooijen's book, *Overleven op de K2* (Netherlands/Belgium: National Geographic/Carrera, 2009). Gerard McDonnell's call from the summit was confirmed by Annie Starkey. Hugues d'Aubarède's conversations at the summit were related by Raphaele Vernay, Mine Dumas, Chhiring Dorje, and Agence France Presse. Virginia O'Leary and Go Mi-sun provided background on Jumik Bhote's call from the summit. Marco Confortola and Cas van de Gevel described their last-minute picture-taking.

CHAPTER EIGHT

Good detailed descriptions of avalanches are provided by David McClung and Peter Schaerer's *The Avalanche Handbook* (Seattle: Mountaineers, 2006); Phil Powers's *Wilderness Mountaineering* (Mechaniscsburg, PA.: Stackpole Books, 1993), is a great account of the dangers of the mountains. Details of the Norwegians' descent are drawn from interviews with Cecilie Skog and Lars Nessa.

CHAPTER NINE

The 1953 expedition is recounted in Curran's *K2: The Story of the Savage Mountain*, Isserman and Weaver's *Fallen Giants*, as well as in Bernadette McDonald's *Brotherhood of the Rope: The Biography of Charles Houston* (Seattle: Mountaineers, 2007).

See Jim Curran's *K2: Triumph and Tragedy* (New York: Mariner Books, 1987) for the full story of the 1986 tragedy.

CHAPTER TEN

Eric Meyer and Fredrik Strang provided the account of their time spent in the tent at Camp Four; Chris Klinke provided details of his strobe light. Chhiring Dorje and Meyer supplied information on Dorje's descent, and on his background. Chhiring Bhote offered an account of his climb up the Shoulder with Pasang Bhote; details of Chhiring Bhote's life were drawn from interviews with him, as well as with Virginia O'Leary and Judy Aull. Details of Kim Jae-soo's climb came from interviews with Kim and Chhiring Dorje and from reports in the South Korean press.

CHAPTER ELEVEN

Cas van de Gevel's descent from the summit and his encounter with Hugues d'Aubarède on the Traverse was described to me by Van de Gevel. I am indebted to Raphaele Vernay for the use of the blog as a source. Nick Rice, who was with d'Aubarède for many days at Base Camp, and Serge Civera, who visited him at Base Camp, gave insights into his character and state of mind, as did Mine Dumas. Qudrat Ali also offered background and insights. Chris Warner described the death of Stefano Zavka. Van de Gevel described his sighting of Hugues's fall. His description of the encounter with the two Sherpas or HAPs matches Chhiring Bhote's account of his ascent toward the Shoulder with Pasang Bhote. The phone conversation between Cas and Roeland van Oss was related by both men. For details on the effects of high altitude, I consulted Charles Houston's *Climbing Higher* and Mike Farris's *The Altitude Experience: Successful Trekking and Climbing Above 8,000 Feet* (Guilford, Conn.: Globe Pequot Press, 2008) as well as other medical experts.

Details of Pasang Bhote and Chhiring Bhote's rescue of Go Mi-sun were related by Go and Chhiring Bhote.

CHAPTER TWELVE

The description of Jumik Bhote's leading the Korean team from the summit was drawn from interviews with Go Mi-sun and Chhiring Dorje. Marco Confortola described what is likely the collapse of the serac or an avalanche that caught Bhote and the remaining Korean climbers. Both Wilco van Rooijen and Confortola offered descriptions of the Korean climbers and the likely series of events that led to their being trapped in the ropes. Virginia O'Leary and Judy Aull provided insight into Jumik's life and his character and his relationship with the Korean team. O'Leary's blog was another wonderful resource: http://ginnynepal.blogspot.com On the blog, she described the actual puja ceremony for Jumik in Kathmandu, on which my own description was based.

CHAPTER THIRTEEN

Details of Marco Confortola and Gerard McDonnell's bivouac were related by Confortola and Agostino da Polenza. Wilco van Rooijen provided the account of his meeting the other two men and their decision to stay overnight above the serac. Annie Starkey, Sajjad Shah (the Norit team's Base Camp manager in 2008), Eric Meyer, Cecilie Skog, Wilco van Rooijen, Cas van de Gevel, Roeland van Oss, and Jelle Staleman all offered insight into McDonnell's time on K2, as did his brief blog.

CHAPTER FOURTEEN

The details of Wilco van Rooijen's descent were drawn from my interview with him in Voorst, his conversations with my own fact-checker, Mark van de Walle, as well as from interviews he gave to wire services and magazines in the wake of the disaster. He also outlines his long climb down in his own book. Maarten van Eck, Roeland van Oss, and Chris Klinke provided descriptions of his telephone calls from the mountain.

CHAPTER FIFTEEN

The description of Gerard McDonnell and Marco Confortola's struggle to save the trapped Korean climbers and Jumik Bhote was provided by Confortola's official post-accident statement, his book, and several interviews I conducted with him. For the controversy surrounding Confortola's account, please see the Epilogue.

CHAPTER SIXTEEN

The scene at Camp Four on the morning of Saturday, August 2, was drawn from interviews with Eric Meyer, Fredrik Strang, Paul Walters, Lars Nessa, Cas van de Gevel, Chhiring Dorje, Chris Klinke, and Roeland van Oss. Meyer also provided insight into Pemba Gyalje's condition and conversation. Various climbers, including Walters and Dorje, recalled seeing the figure above the serac. The decision by the five climbers to go down to Base Camp was recounted by Meyer.

Cas van de Gevel provided the account of the return up the Shoulder with Pemba Gyalje. Chhiring Bhote and Pasang Bhote's progress up the Shoulder and Bottleneck was described by Chhiring Bhote and Chhiring Dorje, Pemba Gyalje offered an account of his discovery of Marco Confortola, which Annie Starkey backed up with records of the radio calls; she also offered insight into Pemba's thinking at the bottom of the Bottleneck. For the descriptions of the avalanches, I relied on testimony by Gyalje, and interviews with Chhiring Bhote and Marco Confortola. Confortola detailed the return to Camp Four.

CHAPTER SEVENTEEN

The scene at Base Camp, and the location of the climber in orange on the south face of the mountain, was drawn from interviews with Chris Klinke, Roeland van Oss, Jelle Staleman, and Maarten van Eck. The various climbers' descents came from Alberto Zerain, Nick Rice, Cecilie Skog, Lars Nessa, Mike Farris, Chuck Boyd, and Andy Selter. Jerome O'Connell and Pat Falvey provided information on the McDonnell family's vigil in Ireland. Eric Meyer described his fall above Camp One.

CHAPTER EIGHTEEN

The description of Wilco van Rooijen's further attempt to descend, and the effort by Cas van de Gevel and Pemba Gyalje to locate him, was based on interviews with Van Rooijen, Van de Gevel, Roeland van Oss, Chris Klinke, Jelle Staleman, and Maarten van Eck. Chuck Boyd and Andy Selter also provided information on the rescue effort at Base Camp.

CHAPTER NINETEEN

The account of Wilco van Rooijen's rescue was related by Van Rooijen, Cas van de Gevel, Chris Klinke, Roeland van Oss, and Maarten van Eck. Marco Confortola provided details of his descent. The description of Cecilie Skog in Base Camp was based on interviews with Skog, Lars Nessa, Chuck Boyd, and Andy Selter. The descent of Van Rooijen, Van de Gevel, and Pemba Gyalje was described by Roeland van Oss, Jelle Staleman, Van Rooijen, Van de Gevel, and Sajjad Shah.

Details of the scene in the medical tent were drawn from Eric Meyer, Chris Klinke, Lars Nessa, Wilco van Rooijen, Sajjad Shah, Fredrik Strang, and Strang's film, *A Cry from the Top of the World*.

CHAPTER TWENTY

For the account of the climbers' departures from the mountain, I relied on the Norit team's blog, and on interviews with Roeland van Oss, Wilco van Rooijen, Cas van de Gevel, Chris Klinke, Eric Meyer, Chuck Boyd, and Andy Selter. Lars Nessa, Sajjad Shah, and Chris Klinke described the visits to the Gilkey Memorial. For the account of the Koreans' departure, I drew from various Korean press reports, as well as on my interviews with Eric Meyer, Lars Nessa, Chuck Boyd, and Andy Selter. The description of the helicopter journey and the military hospital in Skardu (where Gerard McDonnell recovered in 2006, and Wilco van Rooijen, Cas van de Gevel, and Marco Confortola were treated in 2008) was based on my experiences in the Karakoram in 2009.

INDEX

He just wanted a decent book to read ...

Not too much to ask, is it? It was in 1935 when Allen Lane, Managing
Director of Bodley Head Publishers, stood on a platform at Exeter railway
station looking for something good to read on his journey back to London.
His choice was limited to popular magazines and poor-quality paperbacks –
the same choice faced every day by the vast majority of readers, few of
whom could afford hardbacks. Lane's disappointment and subsequent anger
at the range of books generally available led him to found a company – and
change the world.

*'We believed in the existence in this country of a vast reading public for intelligent
books at a low price, and staked everything on it'*
Sir Allen Lane, 1902–1970, founder of Penguin Books

The quality paperback had arrived – and not just in bookshops. Lane was
adamant that his Penguins should appear in chain stores and tobacconists,
and should cost no more than a packet of cigarettes.

Reading habits (and cigarette prices) have changed since 1935, but
Penguin still believes in publishing the best books for everybody to
enjoy. We still believe that good design costs no more than bad design,
and we still believe that quality books published passionately and responsibly
make the world a better place.

So wherever you see the little bird – whether it's on a piece of
prize-winning literary fiction or a celebrity autobiography, political tour
de force or historical masterpiece, a serial-killer thriller, reference book,
world classic or a piece of pure escapism – you can bet that it represents
the very best that the genre has to offer.

Whatever you like to read – trust Penguin.

read more
www.penguin.co.uk